"GOING TO CO... WRITING A BO... YOU ARE 'GIVIN... BUT IF YOU LOV... ...NT TO GIVE YOURSELF."—Dorothy Day

Dorothy Day has been giving of herself in many ways for many years. To art. To social protest. To union organizing. To love. To religion. And above all, to people—the neediest and most desperate among us.

In her books, Dorothy Day gives of herself in a very special way. Her books do not preach. They do not argue. They simply *are*, just as Dorothy Day *is*. And what they are, and what she is, is something very important to every reader.

In 1972, Dorothy Day celebrates her 75th birthday. To commemorate this occasion, Curtis Books is making her three major works available in paperback editions, both as a tribute to this remarkable woman, and as a recognition that her message is perhaps more vital today than ever before.

Also by Dorothy Day

THE LONG LONELINESS
LOAVES AND FISHES

All available in paperback from
Curtis Books

ON PILGRIMAGE:
THE SIXTIES

BY DOROTHY DAY

CURTIS
BOOKS

NEW YORK, N.Y.

A FOOL'S CALLING

(January 1, 1972)

I put to myself a fool's calling;
    to take seriously a few things
that for inattention (the irresolute eyes
    of the rich and drugged) go by the century's board.

At center eye
    lost among money sacks, staining them red
I saw, as though eyes were for seeing (a fallacy)
    and cried aloud (a crime)
murder murder murder for sale for hire for lending for free—
    apples and lemons and chestnuts and murder
products and services, murder and goods and welfare
    and for that, reverend collars of mink
I sojourn here

Having at your hands perished
    (bones fused, case closed)
and you walk like geese on my grave
    where in spite of all
I am served
    manna by ravens
am taught to pavan
    by the peacock incised on my stone
and the locks and bars
    flower like a bridegroom's trellis
and the phoenix
    treads my ashes to fire
and the worm
    eats death to the bone

(and you walk like geese on my grave)
    and the mink at your throat fastens
teeth at your throat and whispers
    certain directions
and you walk like geese to your grave.

This was written in prison and
hereby in dedication to Dorothy Day
for her 75th birthday
comes to a second birth of meaning.
Daniel Berrigan, S.J.

INTRODUCTION
by Stanley Vishnewski

☐ St. Teresa of Avila once said that "Life is a night spent in an uncomfortable inn," inspired, no doubt, by her ceaseless pilgrimages throughout Spain founding, inspiring and reforming the houses of the Carmelite Order.

Her life was one of great pain and suffering. Traveling then was extremely uncomfortable and many nights were spent in dirty inns where she was kept awake by the shouts and screams of drunken louts, the night air hideous from the stench of unwashed bodies.

But despite all this, St. Teresa managed to keep her sense of humor. Once as she was crossing a stream her mule balked, throwing her into the water. She heard a voice saying that this is how God treats those whom He loves, whereupon St. Teresa replied "That is why He has so few lovers."

Dorothy Day has been on a ceaseless pilgrimage ever since she started *The Catholic Worker* movement in 1933. Every month in the pages of *The Catholic Worker* she has related to her readers her experiences, her observations, and the events of the day. Here we see the events of the turbulent Sixties through her eyes. This was the decade that saw the assassination of President Kennedy and Martin Luther King, the escalation of the Vietnam War into a major conflict, the Selma-Peace March, the rise of the civil rights movement, and the burning of slums as the race war in the country deepened.

It was the decade of Pope John XXIII and the Vatican Council. It was the period when theologians openly began to question the authority of the teaching Church and heretofore sacred doctrines. It was a sad era, marked by the wholesale desertions of many priests and nuns as well as laymen. But it was also a time of great expectations as the laity began to assume a more responsible position in the activities of the Church.

In the midst of all these catastrophes, changes and spiritual travels, Dorothy writes with hope and reassurance. She recognizes that it is sometimes easier for a woman than a man to accept the tragedies of life "because no matter what catastrophe has occurred or hangs overhead, she has to go on with the business of living. She does the physical things and so keeps a balance."

Dorothy begins her journal by quoting with pride founder Peter Maurin's remark that *The Catholic Worker* "was not just a journal of opinion, but a revolution, a movement, a way of life."

The purpose of *The Catholic Worker* is not just to print news but to create it, and that is exactly what the *CW* has done in its nearly 40 years of precarious existence. It has inspired articles, news items, feature stories, documentary films, and novels; that a group of dedicated Christians tries to live the Sermon on the Mount and practice the Folly of the Cross seems to make good newspaper copy.

When *The Catholic Worker* was launched during the Great Depression, it was much alone in its advocacy for social reform. It was condemned as a Communist front because it supported the right of workers to organize.

It was denounced to the Chancery for saying Compline—"Theatrical prayers" one critic said. *The Catholic Worker* adopted the unpopular position of pacifism from the beginning and won for sincere Catholics the right to be classified as conscientious objectors. *The Catholic Worker*, long before the Vatican Council, pleaded for the right of the laity to assume its obligations in working for the Church. The *CW* has had the satisfaction of seeing many of its policies, often pioneered in loneliness and disgrace, become an accepted part of Catholic life. But most important of all, the *CW* has never lost its faith in the hierarchy as teachers of the Faith.

Dorothy writes with hope of the great stirrings within the Church—the powerful use of spiritual weapons: prayer, fasting, penance, non-violence. When she deals with wars and strikes, unemployment and hunger, racial strife, jails and the utter misery of the destitute she writes with hope and with faith in the ultimate victory. She has never lost sight of the cardinal virtues of faith, hope and charity—faith that truth and goodness will prevail, hope that the good will triumph

8

over the evil in our midst, charity, the love of God, that will transform the world and penetrate into eternity.

This is nothing Pollyanna-ish about Dorothy. She is only too aware of the evil and ingratitude of people. When she writes about fear and anxiety, she is not writing theoretically. She has been shot at, she has been pelted with rotten eggs. But as always, such experiences inform her: "It was fear in the flesh, the fear of the flesh, and I am glad I have it because it helps me to understand the fear that is eating at the hearts of people in the world today. No one is safe."

Dorothy is not only a first class journalist and observer, she has also been an actual participant in the events she describes. When she writes of jails and the horrors of imprisonment she writes from first hand knowledge. She has served several jail sentences because of her activities against the air raid drills being held in New York City. She is able to write of the sufferings of the women addicts in the Women's House of Detention and the utter callousness of those placed over them.

". . . I told of what I had seen, of the hideous suffering, the pale and ghastly faces of the victims, the spasmodic contortions of the body, the lack of any medical help unless they were taken dying to Bellevue prison ward."

Dorothy has lived and shared the life of the poor. She writes of the life in the slums, ". . . the problems of lice and dirt . . . with neither bath nor shower. Such is our life in the city . . ." She has also shared the insults and contempt of the poor. She writes about violence always around her at *The Catholic Worker*: "We may have murderers around us, among the hundreds who come in from the Skid Rows of our country to eat with us, but we ask no questions—a man has to eat."

But in the midst of all this suffering and anguish there is hope, because as St. Teresa, the Little Flower, says: "All is Grace." "We are happy because today the sun shines, there is a symphony on the radio, children are playing on the streets, there is a park across the way and a church around the corner where we receive our daily Bread."

Dorothy often gets discouraged over the vastness of the work to be done and of how few there are to do it. She groans when she says ". . . the vast majority of Catholics have not begun to think on these things yet." But she finds faith and comfort in the realization that "A thousand years are as one day in the sight of the Lord and Christianity is only two days old."

Dorothy travels light. She carries a shoulder bag with the essentials, ". . . powdered coffee, toilet articles, a kimona, diary, short breviary, New Testament and a missal." She says that she does not know how she can do without them, ". . . coffee included . . ."

The cars that she uses for her journey are often old and often fall apart, the price one must pay for the gift of poverty. She writes, "I have had clutch rods come out in my hands, gas pedals go down through the floor, batteries fall out into the roadside, windshield wipers fail in cloudbursts, lights go out, fan-belts break, etc., etc. Some of these things happened after inspection!" But she looks upon these occasions with equanimity. It is a good time to rest and to relax. "With a good book in the car one could only regard these halts as little unexpected gifts of time to oneself, time to relax and rest for a while."

There are constant demands on Dorothy and she feels she must respond. Her travels take her across the country several times in the Sixties. She goes to California to give support to Cesar Chavez who is organizing the Farm Workers Union. She goes to Cuba to report on the revolution that is taking place. She goes to Rome to attend the International Congress of the Laity as an official delegate. But everywhere she goes she keeps her diary in which she jots down names, impressions and notes while everything is still fresh in her memory, the account of her On Pilgrimage.

Dorothy does not escape the criticism and envy from those who share her hospitality. "Only this morning," she writes, "one of the poor women staying with us said bitterly, 'It costs a lot of money to travel around the way you do.'"

Dorothy felt that she had to explain to the poor tortured soul the reason for her many trips. She was paid to lecture. The money was needed to keep the work going. Her bus fare and expenses were paid by the people who invited her. But the accusation pained her: "What resentment between those who have no money in their pockets and those who have—between the worker and the scholar, in other words."

When Dorothy writes about the many twisted and tortured souls, "the wounded in spirit" who have come to share the hospitality of her "Inn", she does not write to exploit them as literary characters. Both Dickens and Dostoyevsky would have found rich material for their books had they shared the life in *The Catholic Worker*. But Dorothy writes with love and compassion for she sees Christ in every person who comes to her door—the very rich as well as the very poor. She lives by the awesome truth that we love Christ as much as we love the least of our brothers. If we despise or hate anyone, it is Christ whom we are hating. Dostoyevsky gets to the heart of *The Catholic Worker* when he has Father Zossina, in *The Brothers Karamazov* say: "*Love in action is a harsh and dreadful thing compared with love in dreams.* Love in dreams is greedy for immediate action, rapidly performed and in the sight of all. Men will even give their lives if only the ordeal does not last long but is soon over, with all looking on and applauding as though on the stage. But active love is labour and fortitude, and for some people too, perhaps, a complete science. But I predict that just when you see with horror that in spite of all your efforts you are getting further from your goal instead of nearer to it —at that very moment I predict that you will reach it and behold clearly the miraculous power of the Lord who has been all the time loving and mysteriously guiding you."

Stanley Vishnewski
Catholic Worker Farm
Box 33—Tivoli, New York
12583

A NOTE ON
THE CATHOLIC WORKER

☐ The Catholic Worker is an eight-page tabloid which appears nine times a year. It was first issued and sold in Union Square on May 1, 1933.

From a first printing of 3,000, the circulation rose to over one hundred thousand. At the time of the Spanish Civil War it was reduced to 40,000, when the churches and Catholic associations began to realize what the Sermon on the Mount meant to the editors in time of class war, race war, civil war and international war. The Catholic Worker professed itself pacifist and anarchist in principle, and those who did not like those terms used "personalist and communitarian."

Its editors are mostly Catholic, and if they are not, they agree that without brotherly love there can be no love of God. They profess voluntary poverty and sharing—living together in city and country with the poor and the wounded in spirit in what are now called communes, but which Peter Maurin who was the theoretician of what has now come to be called the Catholic Worker Movement, termed "Houses of Hospitality."

Dorothy Day is editor and publisher of the paper. She spends some months of every year travelling and visiting readers of the paper, which now has subscribers and followers around the world.

The editors who live in C.W. houses receive no salaries, but room, board and clothing. The subscription price of the paper is twenty-five cents a year. However, many of the subscribers send more, so that the Catholic Workers have been able to buy some farms and houses. Many have been in prison for participating in demonstrations, for their conscientious objection to war and conscription, and for their refusal to pay taxes for war. The number of houses of hospitality and farming communes around the country vary in size and character from year to year, according to the age and vocational status of the young people who run them. In general, though, every house has a resemblance to a large and disorderly, but loving family.

Committed as they are to non-violence in thought, word and deed, they accept the hard saying "Love your enemies," many of whom are of their own household.

Paradoxically, the Catholic Worker has brought not only peace to many, but also the sword of division. Yet as the late anarchist Ammon Hennacy, one of the paper's most extraordinary editors, once said:

"There is room in the Church for Democrats, Republicans, Socialists, Marxists and Anarchists . . . contrary to public opinion, it is not the anarchists who throw bombs but the governments."

D.D.

1960

January 1960

☐ Dear Ammon: This is the last month of your six month sentence and it is good to hear that you are being released for sure on January 20 and will set out on your journey around the country. Since this is an open letter, and there may be many new readers this month to add to the usual 62 or 63,000 or whatever it is whose names are on our mailing list, let me explain here that an editor of the Catholic Worker is in jail this time not for making a demonstration in City Hall park against the war game of a civil defense drill but for trespassing on the Omaha missile base and giving out copies of *The Catholic Worker*.

Peter Maurin used to say proudly that the Catholic Worker was not just a journal of opinion but a revolution, a movement, a way of life. To say the least it is an unusual paper, with one or another of its editors in jail. This last year for instance, there were three of its editors in jail in April for fifteen days, and another editor arrested for providing shelter for a deserter and letting him escape (leaving him free to make up his own mind as to the when and how of his return to the army). The head of the Chicago Catholic Worker Karl Meyer also served a six month sentence and came out on Thanksgiving Day to go back to his work of running a Catholic Worker house of hospitality in Chicago, with the help of two or three other young men. Karl was the youngest to go to jail and it is a happy thing to know that there are constantly young ones coming into the movement to join the old ones who persist in their "starry-eyed idealism" as the Nation once termed our state.

The Catholic Worker began in 1933, and is in its 28th year and since its beginning there have been wars—the Japanese-Chinese war, the Ethiopian war, the Spanish Civil War, the Second World War, the Korean war, not to speak of the little wars in one or another part of the world, like the Indo-China War and the present French-Algerian war. Peter Maurin kept reminding us that the way to reach the unemployed, the poor, the workers, was through the works of mercy and starting in the midst of a depression as we did, there was plenty of work to do.

Our salvation depends on whether or not we perform these works. "Inasmuch as you did not do it unto the least of these you did not do it to me." But war is the opposite of the works of mercy. Instead of feeding the hungry, it forces more to go hungry. Instead of sheltering the homeless it destroys homes. If we are "peacemakers," and Jesus said blessed are the peace makers, we must fight war.

And is it not a wonderful thing that the government considers us dangerous enough to their war preparations and so imprisons us? The newspapers may pay little attention to these demonstrations but the voices of men in jail carry farther than those at liberty. And besides how many more of the works of mercy are we practicing when we visit the prisoner, become one with these poor, the most impoverished of all, since they are deprived of man's most precious possession, his freedom . . .

Cuba

I had been writing Ammon about the talks by Wm. Horvath, and his study groups on co-operative housing, and the project he is trying to start in Harlem. Next summer we hope to have a folk school at the Peter Maurin Farm for some weeks in July so that people can get together and put in some serious sessions on these ideas of mutual aid and self help.

On one Friday evening during the month of December we had had speakers on the co-operative movement and the emphasis was all on enlightened self interest. "How to get people interested in cooperatives and credit unions?" "Teach them how to save a dollar." Having listened to this approach for a few other meetings, I could not resist talking about other motives that move men, that inspire their actions. So I

16

began quoting Claudel, "Youth demands the heroic." The series about Castro's Cuba had just come out written by Tad Szulc, summing up what had happened in this first year since the Castro revolution, and I could not forbear reading aloud some of the paragraphs from the article. "The revolution had given the Cubans an honest government and a feeling that their rulers cared about them. The promise of social justice, erroneous as the regime's road toward it may be in the opinion of critics, brought about a foretaste of human dignity for the millions who had little knowledge of it under the old order of near feudal economy. Socially and economically, the revolution's supreme aim is to provide reasonably full employment all year."

There are 6,500,000 inhabitants of Cuba and the agricultural workers have had only three months work a year on the sugar plantations. Now they are working for diversification of crops through government cooperatives which are taking the place of the vast estates. There has been a great deal of expropriation of land, and most of the newspaper accounts have neglected to say that there is going to be compensation for the land taken over for the people. Most of them are emphasizing the fact that the "frantic and disorganized practices of land reform are said to have already caused serious injury to agriculture." Certainly it must have caused serious injury to capital invested in Cuba.

The Rev. Doctor Arthur Miller, moderator of the General Assembly of the United Presbyterian Church in the U.S.A. asks the United States to be patient with Cuba and the Castro revolution. At least 95 per cent of the people he met fully supported Castro and said he was honest, not a communist and is working for his own people. "I cannot become excited by the loss of land by companies like the United Fruit. These companies came to Latin America knowing the risks and have made huge profits for many years."

You see, Ammon, you are not the only one criticizing the United Fruit company.

There has not only been land reform, which I am especially interested in, after visiting so many of the migrant labor camps throughout the United States but there has been attention paid to the educational system long neglected, which is being rebuilt from scratch; new schools are rising, teaching techniques are being modernized; children are being given free text books and materials. Under the Castro regime, according to the story in the New York Times, the city work-

17

ers received a 50 per cent decrease in rent and a 30 per cent decrease in power costs. Their salaries have been raised 30 per cent on the average.

"Their living standards were thus suddenly raised and in the first flush of gratitude they have not yet looked beyond tomorrow to notice the pitfalls of an artificially stimulated economy. They saw the ambitious public works programs, the construction of new schools, housing units, aqueducts, hospitals and playgrounds. But few seem to have fully realized that an economy that in the view of most experts is bound to contract soon may eventually offer the dilemma of deficit financing or sacrifices of an austerity economy to keep these programs going."

This is the economics that is hard for me to understand. Of course it is necessary in times of crisis to have an austerity regime. "Let your abundance supply their want," St. Paul said. "If everyone tried to be poorer," Peter Maurin used to say, "there would soon be no more poor." The old I.W.W.'s used to refuse to work overtime when there were other men out of work, and one of the things they fought for was shorter hours so that all men could have jobs. Now the word automation is in the headlines, and the strikes in the steel plants, among the longshoremen, and in the transit system are partly caused by automation.

Fr. Gustave Weigel writing about the Catholic Church in America stated recently that the three things most demanded of Christians today were austerity, preached and lived; a deeper awareness of the reality of God; and a truer and more effective love for all men, including those who are our enemies. . . .

And it is these same things that are needed in a non-violent revolution, and in Castro's violent one.

Another writer quoting Fr. Weigel in the Times of London sums up his three points as austerity, God awareness and brotherly love. These are the motives which should urge us on to a greater effort to reform the social order.

In the life of the CW we have had the privilege of meeting such priests as Fr. Marion Ganey, who started credit unions and rescued the poor from loan sharks in British Honduras and in the Fiji Islands and Fr. McCarthy in our own South West, with Santa Fe for his center. There is Fr. Donald Hessler of Yucatan, the Maryknoll priest who has been the forerunner of much of this work in the mission field. These are priests who have come to talk to us, and now we have

18

our friend William Horvath, who is a bricklayer by trade, a union man, a worker, who is a dedicated enthusiast for cooperatives and who has been having articles in each issue of the Catholic Worker. If we do not use this way, the workers will have recourse always to bloody revolution.

"Thou art neither cold nor hot . . . because thou art lukewarm . . . I am about to vomit thee out of my mouth," our Lord says. Far better to revolt violently than to do nothing about the poor destitute.

Our own particular gifts are those of editors and pilgrims, speakers and writers, with a love of poverty and hospitality which go together. I don't think there will be any cooperatives started around *The Catholic Worker* office on Spring street, but we can certainly patronize the small grocer and baker, if there is no cooperative in our district. You, Ammon, will be the pacifist anarchist who more nearly exemplifies the life of austerity than any we know, not to speak of manual labor and availability to all . . .

February 1960

Last night I stayed awake until four a.m. after reading too stimulating an article by Thomas Merton, a reprint from the Winter issue of *Thought*, the Fordham University Quarterly. The name of the article is THE PASTERNAK AFFAIR IN PERSPECTIVE, and it is a long analysis, a thirty-two page article in fact. In it Merton not only analyzes the Communist concept of man, but goes on to talk of the attitudes of the West. The concluding paragraphs of the article are what caused my happy sleeplessness. Merton had written on the cover of the reprint, "To Dorothy Day and the Catholic Workers with all blessings and affection in Christ and in union of prayers." Signed Fr. Louis. The concluding paragraph was:

Pasternak . . . "is just as likely to be regarded as a dangerous writer in the West as he is in the East. He is saying that political and social structures as we understand them are things of the past, and that the crisis through which we are now passing is nothing but the full and inescapable manifestation of their falsity. For twenty centuries we have called ourselves Christians, without even beginning to understand one-tenth of the Gospel. We have been taking Caesar for

God and God for Caesar. Now that "charity is growing cold" and we stand facing the smoky dawn of an apocalyptic era, Pasternak reminds us that there is only one source of truth, but that it is not sufficient to know the source is there— we must go and drink from it, as he has done.

"Do we have the courage to do so? For obviously, if we consider what Pasternak is saying, doing and undergoing, to read the Gospel with eyes wide open may be a perilous thing!"

It was not only Merton's article but also Anne Fremantle's DESERT CALLING, her biography about Charles de Foucauld that kept me awake. It is a wonderful book, and the more I read it the more I get from it. I was repelled at first by it, because of the picture she painted of de Foucauld as a young man, harsh, repulsive, a fat, self-indulgent youth, and my reaction was that since I had read the magnificent biography of Rene Bazin, why read a further account, why dwell on an aspect of his life that he put far behind him so soon, so early? But Anne Fremantle not only had access to all his letters to his family and to his spiritual adviser, and their letters to him, but she knew the country, many of the people there who helped her, and she had the intuition of a woman throughout, to get to the heart of the matter. Her insights, her understanding are marvellous. It is wonderful that we have such a biography in English, the first to be written in English, and I am only afraid that it is out of print, as *Seeds of the Desert* by Pere Rene Voillaume is out of print. These two books surely deserve to be put in pocket editions, by one of the big publishers and made available to students throughout the country. But they are dangerous material and might start a revolution!

Anne Fremantle points out that the spirituality of Charles de Foucauld was nearer to the east than to the west, in his love of poverty and abjection. I could not help but remember another fascinating book, "The Humiliated Christ in Russian Thought" by Gorodetsky, published in England by the Philosophical Press, as I read.

How utterly and completely Brother Charles tried to follow in the footsteps of Jesus, and how little we ourselves do to rejoice in mockery and contempt and misunderstanding. As a matter of fact, how fearful most of us are! Just a few Sundays ago Judith Gregory and I were coming from eleven o'clock Mass at our parish church, St. Patrick's old cathedral on Mott street, and as we walked down Mulberry street to get to St. Joseph's Loft on Spring street (which is between Mott and Mulberry) we suddenly felt objects whizzing past our ears. I thought it was snow balls thrown by the small boys, because we had had snow the week before and there was still a little in the corners of buildings. But as I turned another missile flew past and Judith said, "Those are meant for us all right," and went to investigate the broken mass where it had struck against a garage door, and found it to be bits of hard-boiled egg. Two had been flung at us as we passed, and I was literally afraid to turn and look, for fear some would hit me in the face. I should have been delighted, as Charles de Foucauld was when he was pelted in the streets of Nazareth, but my feeling was one of fear, just as it was when I was shot at at Koinonia. It was fear in the flesh, the fear of the flesh, and I am glad I have it because it helps me to understand the fear that is eating at the hearts of people in the world today. No one is safe. We are no longer protected by oceans separating us from the rest of the warring world. Yesterday the Russians fired a rocket 7,760 miles into the central Pacific which fell less than one and a quarter miles from its calculated target. The U.S. Defense department confirmed the shot's accuracy.

Anywhere, at any time, we can be reached. Leaders of governments say that none but a madman would launch a war today. But there are many madmen, human senses are faulty, men may think they see and hear approaching planes, bombs, rockets and the button may be pushed to set off a counter offensive. Everything depends on the human element . . .

There are all kinds of fear, and I certainly pray to be delivered from the fear of my brother, I pray to grow in the love which casts out fear. To grow in love for God and man, and to live by this charity, that is the problem. We must love our enemy, not because we fear war but because God loves him.

Mike Wallace asked me that question—Does God love murderers, does He love a Hitler, a Stalin. I could only say, "God loves all men, and all men are brothers."

There is so little time on a broadcast, in an interview, little time to answer or to think. I could have said, "Christ loved those who crucified Him. St. Stephen loved those who stoned him to death. St. Paul was a murderer. We are all murderers."

Deane Mowrer and I knelt by the side of women who

were charged with murder and who were awaiting trial, the last time we were in prison in New York, put in the corridor with those awaiting trial, because we would not give bail. There were four homicide cases on that corridor, one a very young girl, one a somber very dark Negro who had hired someone to kill her husband, it was said, and just opposite us, a sad Puerto Rican woman nearly forty, mother of many children, who had been beaten by a drunken husband so many times that on the last occasion, as he held her choking over the kitchen table, she reached behind her for a knife and struck at him any place she could so that he would re-lease his strangle grip upon her throat. How many of us would not do the same. I remember seeing my own daughter as a child, and again one of my own grandchildren casting a heavy block at one of the others, and realized how any ges-ture of anger can kill. Thank God for our guardian angels, thank God for all the evil we are delivered from. And oh how close we need to be in pity and in love to such a woman, thrown into jail, separated from her children for many months. In spite of the promise of speedy trial, the right to which is guaranteed by the bill of rights, people stay long periods in jail, eight months, ten months, awaiting trial.

But of course Mike Wallace was not talking of such mur-derers, of whom we may feel no fear. He was speaking not only of the Hitlers and the Stalins, but of such men as those accused of putting bombs in aeroplanes to collect insurance.

What to do about them? I remember asking Fr. Roy how God could love a man who came home and beat up his wife and children in a drunken rage (there was one such in our midst) and Fr. Roy shook his head sadly and said, "God loves only Jesus, God sees only Jesus." A hard lesson to take, to see Jesus in another, in the prodigal son, or members of a lynch mob. Have we begun to be Christians? . . .

Today, Sunday, Fr. Edward Grzeskowiak (they call him Father Ed) came to breakfast. He had recently attended the meeting in Chicago to consider the plight of the migrant workers. He teaches sociology at the minor seminary, and has always been interested in agricultural problems and in the plight of the minority groups. We talked about the work on the Indian reservations throughout the state of Minnesota, and how little contact they had with the priest who could often go to them only in the summer. Fifty per cent of them are Catholic. On or near one reservation the Bulova watch people had set up a factory nearby and hired 120 workers, eighty per cent of whom were Indians. Contrary to expectation there had been no turnover in the years it existed, and the work was well done. Employing Indians on road work and lumbering operations had not been so successful though the wages were high, but the work was too heavy perhaps. Though they could get as much as a hundred and twenty a week, they left the job and the turnover was great. Probably they earned what they needed to live and then left the work; or perhaps drink had something to do with it. Or perhaps, one suggested, they were as averse to construct heavy labor as we ourselves are.

Fr. Ed talked about the reservation system and said the ward system under which the Indians now lived was doomed, but he saw no reason why Indians had to be moved to big cities as they had been, and forced to leave their lands. The system could be changed, but they could still operate under a communal or cooperative system. But all over the country Indians were being moved into cities. Here in Minneapolis there were entire apartment houses crowded with them, living under the poorest conditions, one family moving in on another and crowded families living in unspeakable squalor. Edmund Wilson had a wonderful series of articles on the Iroquois and their system of government, and their present status, running in the *New Yorker* and it has now come out as a book. I remember in one article he spoke of the poverty of the home he visited of one of the leaders. He brought out too, the world feeling of the colored races, the ferment that was going on, the desire to assert themselves and their rights, their feeling themselves part of the movement towards justice, the desire to right the wrongs perpetrated upon the Indian, the Negro, and all those of mixed color.

To become part of this, to share in their poverty and suffering, this is the strong desire on the part of many today, in the movement of lay apostles, who are trained to serve as teachers, nurses, engineers, doctors and must follow those vocations. But many who have no special talents can just go and live among the poor as the little brothers and sisters of Jesus do, finding the most abject, the most abandoned and living under these squalid conditions, and going out to work at factory jobs, or day labor.

I have visited the Little Sisters in Montreal, in Boston, in Washington and in Chicago and hard work has made them clean, some cheap linoleum on the floor has made them bright, and discarding all that is not essential, there is a sense of space and beauty, in spite of the destitution of the surroundings.

We talked of other things that could be done, the little ways of social change that could begin here and now. I told of Fr. McCarthy down in Santa Fe and his work among the Indians and Mexicans, starting credit unions, which rescued them from the toils of the loan sharks, or helped them to achieve ownership of their tools of work. And of Fr. Ganey in the Fiji Islands whom I first met at Pendle Hill, the Quaker house of studies in Wallingford, Pa. He had come to talk of his work in the British Honduras along these lines. When the governor general of Honduras was transferred to the Fiji Islands, he asked for Fr. Ganey to be sent there, and his provincial allowed his transfer.

"Those are the only ways which will be effective," Fr. Ed said. "Not Federal Grants, no unionization, but the small way of working through education, from the bottom up."

The problem is too large on the one hand so that wherever I speak, people say the Government, the State, has to step in. And on the other hand, the solution is too simple, too small, so people end with a sense of futility. What is the use?

How we need to pray for vocations, all kinds of vocations. . . .

Monsignor Shannon, president of St. Thomas College in St. Paul gave us the use of his car while I am in the St. Paul area. He was going to Conception, Missouri, to give a retreat and would not be back for a week. A little blizzard had started Sunday night as we came out of church after making our holy hour, and I thought I would have to take the bus, which would mean going back into St. Paul and starting out again from there. We were already on the way north, in Little Canada, and it was good to wake up yesterday to sunny skies and a clear road. Mary Hlabain and I set forth, with a lunch packed by Lucille Lynch, and by noon we were already in Sandstone, which is more than half way to Duluth.

It was an easy trip and we enjoyed first the level prairie, snow covered, completely flat at first, and bare of trees and then the increasing woodlots of birch and pine. The scenery became rolling as we reached Duluth, and when we tried to turn off to go to Superior without going through Duluth, we got lost. The two cities are rivals and always have been. Duluth is built on hills, and is a beautiful little city on the lake, and last time I passed through, Georgia Kernan, who was a school teacher in Proctor, on the outskirts, met me for a few hours between buses and we went down by the lake and watched the big ore boats coming in. Superior is an inferior city in beauty, but Sister Bernice, my friend who is the superior of the convent of Franciscan Sisters who teach in the high school told me that she loved the people here most especially. "They are very good and responsive" she said, "and the children are bright and lively. This brisk weather (it was ten below outside) fills them with high spirits. Tremendous vitality."

We finally found out the way over from route sixty one to route twenty three and came through great hills and past deep gullies and finally into the flatness of Superior. We came over the St. Louis River on a wooden bridge, with railroad tracks overhead. The bridge which leads into Duluth, the only way over, has been condemned for a long time, and the new bridge is slow in opening. There are traffic snarls every night. There is more work in Duluth and many Superior people commute. Both cities are picking up, however, on account of the St. Lawrence seaway and the city already feels the difference. The men who load and unload the boats however, complain that the foreign crews are now doing the work that they used to do, and at far lower wages. For a long time there has been unemployment due to the steel strike all through this area. The mines of the Mesabi range are about exhausted, they say, which will mean more unemployment. Now that natural gas has been brought in the gas companies assure the public that now industry, having cheap fuel, will follow. The question of unemployment is an ever present menace however.

When Ammon was here last week he visited the I.W.W. hall in Duluth, where he found Finnish comrades who welcomed him. The ideals of the I.W.W. are still alive, though industrial unionism and the giant unions of the CIO-AFL have taken over the workers and the leadership is far from the idealistic leadership of the Wobblies, who took little salary, refused overtime when other men were out of work, and had Wobbly halls where the pot of mulligan was always on the stove and brother was served not in charity in its modern sense, but in justice. It was the I.W.W. who organized the Mesabi range as well as the ships and lumber industry and their search for justice made many martyrs.

25

The Franciscans Sisters here are truly poor. They are called the School Sisters of St. Francis and they teach and care for the sick. Their mother house is in Lacrosse and there they have perpetual adoration of the Blessed Sacrament, day and night. Motherhouses always have the appearance of comfort of a well run college, but when the sisters go out on the mission they have crowded quarters, as crowded as the poor who live in our slums in New York. Here in Superior, they occupy, and have for the last thirty years, an old building which used to be a chancery office, and the rooms are divided up by sheets for curtains, and four beds are crowded in a bedroom which is a decent size for one person, if that one person was a student, a teacher who had much work to prepare for his classes and mark papers. There are a few rooms where the sisters have desks back-to-back all around the room and even in the center of the room where they do their home work. The chapel is on the attic floor and there too they are crowded together. This morning and every morning there is a sung Mass at a quarter after six (the sisters have been in the chapel since five-thirty) and since they specialize in music in all their schools, the Mass is a thing of beauty.

After Mass there was a quick breakfast, and then we went to the Cathedral which was about six blocks down the street. It was the mainstreet and during the Mass there was the sound of shifting gears, trucks starting and stopping, motorcycles roaring by just as in New York. The sisters went out in fifteen degree below zero weather with nothing but their mantles on, and a woolen shawl, scantily clad, one would say, for such rigorous weather. But the houses are all warm, almost too warm for me, used to as I have been to our beach and the east wind blowing through the summer houses we have there. Even winterizing them has not brought them up to normal warmth.

Mary Hlebain comes from a farm family near St. Stephen, which is on the way to Collegeville. St. Joseph is the name of the town where the great woman's college, St. Benedict's is situated; and at Collegeville, there is St. John's College and the seminary. St. John's has had a great influence on all the priests in this section of the country, indeed in all the country. But the priests here have gone thoroughly into the work of teaching the laity to participate in the Mass, and there are more sung Masses than in other parts of the country in which the congregation can participate. Another thing, when the priest distributes Holy Communion he says clearly each time he places the wafer on the tongue of the communicant, Corpus Domini nostri Jesu Christi custodiat animam tuam in vitam aeternam. Amen. Even when there is an entire school receiving as they do at Monsignor Durand's.

Mary, one of the Maryhouse women, says she doesn't know how she became interested in secular institutes. She met Fr. Egan while she was working in a wealthy home and he suggested she join the group which had already formed Maryhouse in Minneapolis. Some of the others had gone to him, saying like St. Paul, "Lord what wouldst thou have me to do?"

Ten women got together, pooling their savings, and bought the house in an old run down neighborhood, with the intention of helping the pastor work among the Negroes, catechizing and performing the corporal works of mercy. One of the girls died of leukemia and there were grave rumors around the section that the girls led too rigorous a life, denied themselves too much and so on. They were scornfully called the "detachers" because they tried to detach themselves from the world to follow Christ. But certainly they were women of good solid sense, with a background of hard work and a readiness for sacrifice. Two of the women left to work on their own, one went to the South to a group in Greenwood, Mississippi, to work with the poorest of the Negroes (Alma was a good musician and gave music lessons and tutored anyone who asked.) Seven remained, of whom Dorothy McMahon teaches, Jane Judge, Lucille Lynch and Rose McDonnell nurse, Marion Judge is a receptionist and Mary Hlebain is a housekeeper. They pool all their resources, take simple promises of Poverty, Chastity and Obedience from year to year and now live in this delightful rural spot, of Maryhouse, little Canada, living the contemplative life in the world, the beginnings of a secular institute.

March 1960

I arrived in Chicago at two in the afternoon, and it was good to see Nina Polcyn waiting for me at the train as I got off. I am carrying too much luggage, what with a briefcase, big suitcase and over-the-shoulder bag which is always full. The shoulder bag has lunch in it, powered coffee, toilet articles, a kimona, diary, short breviary, New Testament and a

27

missal. I do not see how I can do without any of them, coffee included and Ammon would laugh at that. He is always talking about these people who can't start the revolution without an aspirin and a cup of coffee. . . .

Nina and I went to the St. Benet Book Shop on South Wabash long enough to see if there was mail, and to pick up some of Nina's "home work" before we went to her apartment at Thirty-third street and South Park, a great block of buildings, with sixty five per cent Negro families. It is called Lake Meadows and was built by the New York Life. There is another project going up called Prairie Shores which is 35 per cent colored and seventy five per cent white, which is swankier, Nina said. Gordon Zahn lives in the same block as Nina and our old friend Don Klein who spent some time with us on Chrystie street, and wrote an article about us in Milwaukee, is part of the management in this project, where he lives with his wife and children. There are twelve buildings in the block and five thousand people in them and there are great spaces all around and a vast view of the lake and sky, and the buildings are so far apart that this expanse is not obscured. Right now however, a thick fall of fine snow is coming from the east, and whereas before I could sit and look out at the lake, slate-grey yet clear so that I could see the horizon and the water towers far out, now a dizzying whiteness fills the air, and sky, lake and buildings are all obscured. It is good to be inside, no engagements, and time to sit at the typewriter and catch up on this travelogue.

But I am glad it was so clear yesterday, because Nina drove me along Cottage Grove Avenue to 37th street where the Day family lived when we came east after the San Francisco earthquake. It is still there, that long block of flats, three stories high, and there is still the apartment with one window looking out to the lake, where my sister and I used to draw pictures, and write stories and dress our dolls. It is a solid colored neighborhood now but then it was all white, and our school was the Doolittle school where I had a fine teacher in fourth grade who made school stimulating for us all. There was a little Episcopalian Church where I learned to pray the Psalms and the minister's name was Wilson and he had a daughter by the name of Dorothy too.

It makes me realize what a hard thing, what a supernatural thing a devotion to voluntary poverty is, when I remember how snobbish I was at the age of eight. I was much ashamed of the house in which we lived, and used to walk down the

28

street with my little school friends who lived on Ellis Avenue and duck into the apartment house on 37th street, pretending to live in that more respectable building instead of in a flat over a saloon and a row of stores. One could go out the back way and up the back porches to one's own apartment that way and all the buildings were owned by the same man. The laundries in the apartment house were used by the tenants on Cottage Grove avenue as well as in the higher priced house.

What a suffering children go through over clothes and appearance! And yet how happy I was the year I lived there. There was a row of Stevenson and Dickens and Poe on the mantelpiece and my father would not allow any newspapers or magazines in the house. There was no radio or television then. We had to buy on the installment plan, having lost everything in the earthquake, and that was a shame to my mother. Our beautiful old things, which had followed us from Bath Beach, New York "around the Horn" we used to say, to California, had all been sold to get us east and to give my father a new start. He did not go to work right away, but wrote a novel and short stories and we had our first taste of poverty there. It was there too that I first began to pray, on my knees by the side of my bed at night, because I had seen Mrs. Barrett playing, and her little daughter Kathryn and Mary Harrington had introduced me to the Blessed Mother and the lives of the saints.

I am glad the house is still there and I should have liked to go up and see the back porches where we spent so many happy hours, and the kitchen which my sister and I used diligently to scour, after we had read the Polly Pepper books and got a little philosophy of poverty and of work.

If I lived now in Chicago, I would like to live there in that same place, which is a slum most certainly. Or one could take one of those little houses and do much with it to bring beauty and simplicity there, the beauty and simplicity which are part of the poverty exemplified by the Little Sisters of Jesus over on West Adams street, in their third floor tenement apartment.

Of course I am enjoying mightily the comfort of this great block of buildings on 33rd St. which is interracial and most successfully so, and I feel that all families should have the conveniences and comforts which modern living brings and which do simplify life, and give time to read, to study, to think and to pray. And to work in the apostolate too. But

29

poverty is my vocation, to live as simple and poorly as I can, and to never cease talking and writing of poverty and destitution. Here and everywhere. "While there are poor, I am of them. While men are in prison, I am not free." As Debs said and as we often quote.

Nina is doing a wonderful job of integrating cult, culture and cultivation, the synthesis which Peter Maurin was always talking about. Her shop is always my headquarters in Chicago, and it is there people come together, from there ideas are spread, people are brought together in all branches of the apostolate. She is as much a Catholic Worker as ever and her works of mercy reach out in all directions. She has an understanding of poverty and of destitution and always a readiness to share in the one and to alleviate the other.

When we got home from our little tour of the neighborhood and I had explored the view from the eleventh floor, Ammon came for supper and brought us up to date on his journeyings as well as on the news of our own workers in Chicago. He had no sooner arrived in town on Saturday when he was called on to picket in front of the courthouse for Eroseanna Robinson. They are keeping up a vigil night and day, people joining for a stint of three hours at a time. I certainly hope to join them sometime these next few days. Eroseanna is a young colored woman who has refused to pay any income tax 85 per cent of which goes for war, or to file any returns. She has been given an indeterminate sentence and she is now for two weeks on hunger strike. I suppose they will forcibly feed her. The newspapers are paying little heed to this, so it is necessary to have the picket line, and Karl Meyer has gotten out a leaflet which is signed by The Catholic Worker, 164 West Oak street and the War Resisters League which takes in all those who are not Catholic who wish to participate but might hesitate if it were only under Catholic leadership.

Already there have been complaints and the Chancellor of the diocese has telephoned the headquarters telling them to take the name Catholic off their headquarters and literature.

Fr. LaFarge, in his latest book said that one of the evils in the church (which our Lord compared to a net filled with good and bad fishes and a field filled with tares as well as wheat) was a bullying clergy and a fearful laity. Those are not the exact words but I hope I am not misrepresenting his idea. Certainly the Monsignor in this case was abusive and domineering in his telephone conversation, but Karl who is anything but fearful, submitted cheerfully and now the house is called St. Stephen's House, since St. Stephen was the first disciple to serve tables. As for the leaflet which was being distributed, the new edition was to be signed "friends of Eroseanna Robinson."

I had also been reading Evelyn Waugh's life of Ronald Knox as well as glancing through Fr. LaFarge's, and in the book on Fr. Knox, I began to get a glimpse of what was meant by various priests who felt that we should not use the name *Catholic Worker*.

According to Waugh, Knox was the fourth chaplain at Oxford, and whereas the others had called themselves Catholic chaplains of Oxford, he always was so exact as to term himself the chaplain of the Catholics at Oxford. When the Association of Catholic Trade Unionists started years ago, the chancery office in New York saw to it that they did not call themselves The Catholic Association of Trade Unionists.

The Catholic Association or The Catholic Worker sounds official, as though we were speaking for all Catholic trade unionists, or Catholic workers. Karl Meyer got this point right away, where as it took me years to understand the objection to our using the name. After all, we have the right to use it as well as the Catholic War Veterans, I used to say. Karl said, "After all, there are only two or three of us at Oak street doing this work, and even those who help feed and house the poor may not agree at all with us on pacifism or on the demonstrations, and jail going, and giving out leaflets. We are certainly not *the* Catholic worker in the broad sense."

Some few months ago we were accused before some Congressional Committee of usurping the name Catholic, and the statement was made that the Cardinal had threatened to take us to court to make us change it. And also it was implied that we were not good Catholics at all, otherwise we would not be pleading for such prisoners as Martin Sobell. We were pleased to see that James Carey, one of the vice presidents of the CIO came to our defense. Certainly Cardinal Spellman has never spoken to me on the subject, and in all 27 years of our existence, he has given us absolute freedom and shown us courtesy and kindness.

But I begin to get the point, and I am glad to see that Karl was so agreeable about it. We do not represent the Catholic worker. We are merely a group of Catholic Workers (and not manual workers at that) who are trying to express *a*

31

Catholic point of view, one of many Catholic opinions. We cite our authorities, for instance, in our stand on peace,— Archbishop Roberts, S.J.; Dom Bede Griffiths, O.S.B.; Canon F. H. Drinkwater; Fr. Franziskus Stratmann, O.P.; Mgr. Ottaviani, Cardinal Secretary of the Holy Office; Pere Regamy, O.P.; etc. etc. But the vast majority of Catholics have not begun to think on these things yet. A thousand years are as one day in the sight of the Lord, and Christianity is only two days old.

April 1960

Somewhere along the road, I will stop long enough to write more detailed stories of some aspects of this trip I am making, stories about the Sioux Indian Mission school I visited in South Dakota, about the work in the Franciscan Parish of St. Boniface in San Francisco, about Father McCullough's mission to the braceros, and the organizing of the agricultural workers going on in Stockton, Tracy and Modesto and other cities in California.

In this account, I can only synopsize my trip, to indicate the ground covered and to give a report to our readers. The purpose of the trip is of course to communicate ideas, to talk about the aims and purposes of the Catholic Worker movement in schools, colleges and parishes, wherever one is invited. It is also to learn, and I have learned many things on this trip, and have seen much that is happening in the Church which is encouraging: eleven students from Gonzaga pledging a year to the Indian missions of Alaska, 15,000 high school students in the San Francisco area pledging themselves to more work among the agricultural workers, and showing a film the students made of their living conditions, a growing social consciousness among the young and a desire to give themselves to the lay apostolate,—these are some of the good things I have encountered. I have met with many families, many groups of families, and groups of students. (One way a school disclaims any responsibility for inviting one is by having a student organization sponsor the talk. It avoids controversy.)

The theme of many of my talks was, "Christ came to make the rich poor and the poor holy." and "The works of mercy and their opposite in war." Pacifism was practically unknown to the students, who are expected, of course, to be pacifist in class war and race war.

There are some demonstrations and meetings going on among college youth, picketing of Woolworth's, giving out of leaflets to acquaint students with what is happening to their Negro brothers in the south, activity about ROTC and whether it should be compulsory in the colleges. . . .

Superior, Wis.

Monsignor Shannon, president of St. Thomas college in St. Paul loaned us a car and Mary Hlebain of Maryhouse and I set out for Duluth and Superior. We made it to Superior but snow interfered with our visiting Duluth. I spoke to the Franciscan Sisters one evening. They are teaching at the grade and high school, in a coeducational school, and they are housed in the old chancery office, in such crowded conditions that whoever is responsible might be convicted of being a slum landlord if he were in our stricter district of New York. They are truly Franciscan in their poverty and work very hard indeed.

Sister Bernice gave me a wonderful book to read, *Maria Montessori, her life and work*, by E. M. Standing, a convert to the Church who worked with her for many years. It is published by the Academy Guild Press Box 549 Fresno, California, a new publishing house on the west coast—the only Catholic publishing house that I know of in California . . .

In St. Paul I also visited a school for "exceptional" children which was started by Sister Annette Marie, a sister of St. Joseph who carries on her work in a motorized wheel chair. After a bad accident which permanently crippled her, she started to work with children who had speech difficulties and this work led to the building of a school. Students from St. Thomas drive the children to and from school. There are 105 in this school for children who have various mental and physical disabilities. It is a beautiful place and should be a model for many such schools in the country . . .

Wisconsin and North Dakota

I spoke at the Newman clubs at both Madison and Fargo, and it was good to see the work done by both. In Fargo Fr. William Durkin is not allowed to wear his clerical garb when he teaches religion at the State College so he has a mighty fine variety of colored shirts to wear! A cyclone hit his old Newman club house and that meant a new center, which has a beautiful chapel, and fine meeting halls and dining room and living quarters. The Newman clubs are active everywhere and well used by the students. There are great numbers of married students and Father had a number of baptisms the Sunday I was there. In Madison Fr. Brown met me with a Chinese student eighteen years old and homesick. We visited the Martin de Porres center with John McGrath of the Progressive staff, then to Ed and Kathy Burdulis for dinner. Bernard Arcanz called, who had been with us at Maryfarm at the time that Peter Maurin died. He is terribly crippled and is married to a crippled girl and they have two children and another coming. Mrs. Burdulis heard me speak at Grand Rapids when she was in high school. That night I stayed with Helen C. White who has written so many famous historical novels, besides heading the English department at the University. In her sisterly fashion she gave me a dress and three blouses to supplement my wardrobe on my trip.

South Dakota

After an all night trip I arrived at Rapid City, South Dakota and spent the day at the Mother Butler center for Indian girls who are working in town. The house is run by a group of women whom I had heard called Nardines, and who are really Servants of the Immaculate Heart of Mary. They are an order founded during the French revolution, of women in secular garb but in truth religious and it is only recently that the hidden congregation has been made known.

Father Edwards, S. J., called for me at dark and we drove the 115 miles to the Holy Rosary mission, passing the Black Hills which are really mountains. The highest of them is 8000 feet and the roads are impassible in winter. I slept the next two nights in a trailer while I visited the school and a trading post and Pine Ridge which is the nearest town. South Dakota is so big that all of New England could be tucked in with space left over. The east is farming land and the west grazing land and there are eleven reservations for the Sioux Indians. I will write about this further another time.

Rapid City

At Rapid City, prosperous because of all the military establishments, airfields, rocket bases, etc. round about, I stopped overnight at the St. John's McNamara Hospital, where Sister Edith and Monsignor Boyd are good friends of ours and where I met also Mother M. Romaine briefly.

Early the next morning I took the bus for Butte and Spokane, going right through and enjoying every minute of the trip. When you have been making many stops and visiting many people, a long ride through desert and mountain country on a bus, in the dead of winter, is a most delightful and restful trip. I arrived so late in Spokane that I could indulge in the luxury of a hotel, a block away from the Cathedral, and there I spent some hours in the quiet of Church to make up for the "hours" I had not been able to make on the trip. Guiton's *Genius of St. Therese*, paper back, 90c, was good spiritual reading on the bus. (I am delighted to say that as far as I know, God willing, my book on Therese will be published in the Fall by the Fides Press of Notre Dame, Ind.)

It was here in Spokane that I met Archbishop Roberts and had a good evening at the Osborne's home with him, and the next afternoon at Gonzaga University also.

I visited the House of Charity, which is an old hotel down by the railroad yards, still in the process of being torn apart and rebuilt. But the chapel and dining room are finished and in use now. Brother Martin needs help badly in his works of mercy here, where he works in carpentry, cooking, baking bread and many other things. A good place for manual labor, and a chapel right there where the Bishop himself says Mass, and a Bishop too who serves the poor himself, dressed in a long white apron! Monday morning I took the bus north for British Columbia.

The Doukhobors

Ammon had instructed me to take a bus from Spokane which would bring me into Thrums, British Columbia around four in the afternoon. We drove through the most magnificent scenery north, through the customs, and on into Trail, a city tucked down between the mountains, with a smelter which I understand employs 5000 men. Zinc and silver and I do not know what other metals are smelted there, but it is a huge vision of hell set down in the midst of the great scenery of the Canadian Rockies. The lover of the machine age and technological advances would rejoice of course, and see great beauties in the complicated machinery of the smelter but all I could see was the defacement of the landscape, and I was assailed as soon as I got off the bus by the fumes.

There was quite a little wait in Thurms, but still not long enough to take a walk. The bus to which I was transferred was a through bus coming from Vancouver and going on to Winnipeg, St. Paul, Chicago and ending finally at New York. It seemed strange to be sitting in another Greyhound and turning east for a bit again. But Thrums was not more than an hour away. Up again, high up over the mountains, and out of that particular pit of a valley, and then down again, along precipitous flanks, until we reached the shores of the Kootenay river where the heavy bus rolled on a flat raft of a ferry and was guided by cables to the farther shore.

There were a few stout, old women in the bus, clad in full skirts and kerchiefs or babushkas, and they got off on the other side of the ferry. And we rolled on for some miles until I passed a store which I noticed was marked Thrums.

Fortunately I saw the store, and fortunately I was near enough to the driver to call out, "Is this my stop," and without slowing up he cried back, "Where do you want to get off. This is all Thrums for the next five miles." I had no idea where to stop, Ammon had not mentioned this, so I begged him to put me down at the next gas station which happened to be a British American station, I think, and there with my one small bag I stopped to ask directions. Fortunately I had checked my other suitcase at Trail through which I would return. The girl at the gas station was helpful. Yes, Pete Maloff lived right down the road and she would call him. I was fortunate to have gotten off at just the right stop. In a moment Pete Maloff was there, a tall handsome man of perhaps sixty, strong and vigorous, who welcomed me and walked me back some hundred yards along the road to the farmhouse where he lived. Probably he has not more than five acres, but on this five acres he has stock and fruit, and there is milk, butter, cream and cheese products from his work, and plenty of fruit to sell in the nearby markets of Trail and Nelson. His wife too was a beautiful woman and they were at ease and happy with visitors. Pete Maloff, as I found later, is a man of the world, in the sense that he has travelled and worked in San Francisco and has been writing these last years a detailed history of the Doukhobors. He gave me half a dozen chapters to take with me and read along the way, and I am making notes from them now before I send them back. He says in his introduction:

"I have never held any position among the Doukhobors and have never appeared as an official spokesman of any kind.

36

Many have been indignant with me that I enjoyed the good will of the deceased leader of the Doukhobors, Peter Petrovich Verigin. This was true. Peter Petrovich appeared to like me for my straightforwardness, my simplicity and my alert responsive soul." And he goes on to talk of the different kinds of men, those whose egotism is fed by the social movements which they espouse and those who give themselves to an ideal. And he tells of his own struggles for the last twenty years, in which he "gave all, and spared no one, neither my wife, my children, nor myself."

He refused registration in 1943 and was arrested and jailed and it was at that time, after the most acute suffering which tempted him to leave the Doukhobor community and settle in South America, that he decided to remain among his own people and write of them. He has written one volume and there are two others in preparation. One has been printed in Russian and I found it later in the library of the Russian Center in San Francisco. One of his friends has translated the work in San Francisco, and Anna Brinton, famous Quaker leader, has helped him prepare the manuscript for publication. But he has not yet found a publisher. Perhaps some university press will bring it out.

It was not only Tolstoi who gave the royalties of his book, *Resurrection* to help the Doukhobors get to Canada from Russia to escape persecution, but also Almayer Maude, the translator, and the Quakers also, always interested in those who struggle for conscience' sake.

Pete Maloff's autobiography is very much a part of his history of the Doukhobors since he confessed that he never intended to write a complete history but he performs his work with the hope that by recalling the past and trying to understand their experience they will again reach the spiritual heights and the unity they occasionally had in the past. He appeals to the youth of his community which is settled all through the fertile lands of western Canada, but also to "the youth of other spiritual wrestlers, the Molokans, Quakers, Mennonites, Tolstoyans, Gandhians."

It is certainly not possible here to recount the long and complicated history of this Russian sect but their saga certainly deserves a place in an account of Russian spirituality. Pete Maloff states that they appeared for a long time in Russia under different names, calling themselves spiritual Christians. They appeared as a separate movement in Russian history at the end of the seventeenth century. There are accounts of their exiles and wanderings to Siberia, to Finland, to the Canary Islands. The emphasis was on preaching, as they had no books, and many could not read. The scriptures and tradition were handed down by word of mouth, and "whoever heard their words would at once give up all his evil deeds."

According to Pete Maloff, the Molokans were part of them back in history, and the difference between the Doukhobors and the "milk-drinkers" was that the latter kept the written scriptures which the former rejected as distorted and rewritten.

The chapters Pete Maloff gave me to read have an account of his work as a young man in California. He was influenced by his grandmother who remained a practicing Doukhobor, though his family, as many others, fell away from it. There are chapters on the life of Peter Vasilievich Verigin, called "God's own Verigin," or "Peter the Lordly Verigin," a chapter on The Sons of Freedom, the most extreme members of the sect who live in a separate colony of their own on a plateau, and the Independent Farmers. . . .

After my visit with the Maloffs their son and his beautiful young wife drove me down the road a few miles for my visit to Helen Demoskoff. We have corresponded with her for many years, Ammon and I, and I felt already as though we were old friends. To get to her place, we had to cross a field of deep snow where the path was marked only by a single file of footsteps, and then over a swaying wooden foot bridge, built by the Demoskoffs with cables and lumber and which made me dizzy indeed as we crossed over a turbulent river. On the other side there was a sign, "unsafe for crossing" and I was glad young Pete Maloff found another way back. We drove down a long lane, passed a number of wooden houses, sturdily built but small, and at the end of the lane, there was Helen Demoskoff, running down the icy path to meet us. Helen is a grandmother, in her forties, and she was younger and more beautiful than her pictures. She has such warmth and friendliness, and one felt too, such strength! She was baking bread and just bringing the first batch of half a dozen large loaves of whole wheat bread from the oven and putting a second batch in. And it made me homesick for our own farm kitchen on Staten Island.

The women of the Doukhobors wear full skirts, aprons, blouses which come out over the top of the skirt, and felt shoes. Their long hair is plain, drawn back behind and of course their faces are free of cosmetics. They sing a great deal and I imagine a great deal of their religious services are made up of song, and while I was there, not only the Maloff children and adults had sung for me, but also the Demoskoffs, singing not only their hymns but the songs they had composed in jail. They had been to prison for opposing the conscription, for demonstrations in Vancouver, and also for setting fire to the communal houses when they returned from jail to find that most of the Doukhobors had given up the communal life and had divided the common homes into apartments. They had burned some of these community houses, and then set fire to their own, or perhaps they burnt their own first; and when they were arrested for arson, they removed their clothes as though to say—"you have forcibly taken our children away from us for public school education, your ways have perverted our religion, and you may now have our clothes also." Perhaps a St. Francis gesture, since he too had removed his clothes in the presence of the bishop and his court and had handed them over to his father, telling him that from now on he had none but a heavenly Father.

But there are other meanings to their cult of stripping themselves and my repulsion from this aspect of their rebellion they would interpret as the result of man's fall, when he became ashamed of his nakedness and hid himself until he could be clothed. When they stand naked and unashamed, they feel they are doing this as a religious gesture, returning to the innocence of paradise.

Peter Maloff deals with this more completely in his book. Another aspect of the cult is the practice on the part of some of their members of a community of wives. Like the Mormons, they feel that there is nothing contrary to the natural law in this Old Testament institution. How they reconcile it with the words of Christ it is hard to see. But they say that when they repeat the Lord's prayer, and say "Thy Kingdom Come," they are helping on God's kingdom by doing away with the institution of marriage, since there is, in the kingdom of heaven, no marriage nor giving in marriage.

They use these texts, but at the same time they do not believe in reading scripture since they feel that many translations and tamperings over the years have mutilated it and they prefer to convey by word of mouth the sayings of Jesus. Even now there are so many groups, so many rifts among the Doukhobors that it reminds one of the many sects in the Protestant church, and the many divisions in the Communist party.

Ammon loves the Doukhobors as lovers of freedom, as freedom fighters, as wrestlers with the spirit, and admires them because they have been to jail so often in defense of their beliefs. Helen Demoskoff herself has spent eleven years of her life in prison. And I love them, not so much for their militant aspects but because they are a simple, hard working, devout people, trying to walk in the way of the early Christians, following Christ, despising earthly goods, loving the family, and praising God in psalms and hymns and spiritual canticles.

The next day I took my leave of them all, and Helen told me that from now on we were indeed sisters, and her husband and her brother who had sung so beautifully the night before, saw me off to the Maloffs. I said goodbye to them, being admonished by them that meat eating was not a part of the Christian life, since it involved the taking of life, no matter how humble. "One would not even eat a little piece of a Turk," Mrs. Maloff told me gravely (the Turks being the traditional enemies of these Russian people!)

The bus I took went right by the Maloff's door, and it brought me into Trail where I took the bus for Vancouver.

June 1960

During the month I spent four days with my daughter and her family in Vermont and had the usual joyful time. The boys spent all their time fishing after school and Saturday. Up to May 15 (the season opens May first) Eric caught thirty-one trout and Nickie thirty-three. Until they explained to me, I could not imagine what Tamar was talking about when she told them to go feed their worms. They dig a supply of night crawlers which sell for two cents apiece, and when they have a few hundred ahead, they have to feed them a hand full of grain and breadcrumbs.

"When I am not fishing," Eric says, "I clean out the barn, help my father with the cows and the bull and help carry water to the barn in winter, and to the fields when there is a drought in summer. I can help feed the stock, chop and carry wood, feed the chickens and so on. But we are all the time fishing now." There is no homework in the country school because the children have chores.

Six children are in school and at home there are Hilaire and Martha, three and five years old this summer. There will be a new baby in July.

Hilaire is a do-er, not a talker, but Martha enjoys conversation. "The reason the children" (the six older brothers and sisters) "have to go to catechism is because they swear," she told me gravely. "Me, I never swear . . . God sees everything," she added, "but I can't see Him because He's in back of me. I know my prayers and I tell them to Hilaire too." Hilaire, red curly hair, blue eyes, broad red face, was leaning against my other knee most seriously. "When mama says prayers with us at night, the children laugh. I don't like the way Daddy says prayers. He prays too loud and long."

Probably she does not like them because Daddy's prayers usually end in a roar for quiet. Tamar goes down stairs, leaving them to their usual riotous play before the great silence drops all at once over the house. Suddenly you realize there is quiet, blessed quiet.

How good it is to get away from the city, from radio and news every hour on the hour, and demonstrations and crises. I'm all in favor of communities of desert fathers, or desert families, "the building of a new society within the shell of the old." Not that any place is safe. Up in Vermont there are missile bases all around Lake Champlain, and Swanton, they say, is a booming town. We need to get to that state of mind where we reject prosperity and embrace poverty, to find the freedom St. Francis sang about. How far we all are from it! But we can keep talking about it, reminding people of it, and striving a little way to attain it. A lot of the college students I talked to on my trip had never thought in terms of voluntary poverty as a great and powerful means towards peace. My friend Alice Kathryn says she is going to be a cheer leader for the saints even though she cannot get very far in practicing what she so admires. One thinks of the psalms, "Draw me, and I will run to the odor of thine ointments!" "Enlarge thou my heart, that thou mayest enter in." It will have to be the Lord's doing, not mine.

West Coast Continued

Next winter when I return to the west coast, I shall arrange my trip in another way. For one thing, I will not accept so many speaking engagements and so become too tired to write. One or two a week will be enough. This three a day business, besides lunch and dinner and so on, takes it out of one. What I hope to do is rent a little hut in Starvation Flats, near Kay Brickey, on the outskirts of Tracy. She is the wife of a railroad man, mother of a family of boys and her little house is right next to Christo Rey center which is like the Guadalupe Center, the Holy Spirit Center, etc., with Chapel, Recreation Hall, kitchen, basketball, stations of the Cross, and a center for fiestas.

Fr. Duggan whom we first met when he was at St. Mary's as a nearly ordained priest, near our Maurin House of Hospitality in Oakland, (now no more) has been working with the poor Mexicans for the last eight years. He met me at Kay's and drove me around the section, pointing to a group of huts as his "cooperative housing" and a toolshed, barn, pig-pen and tiny garden as his "farming commune."

We visited homes where little girls were busily engaged in making the supper of tortillas, in this case made not of cornmeal but of white flour, and beans. It is their staple diet. The mothers and fathers were out in the asparagus fields and the packing sheds these days and often work begins for them at four in the morning.

But there are many unemployed. With the importation of "the bracero," the local farm laborers are not hired.

For the last year the CIO-AFL has started organizing farm labor in the area and we visited their headquarters in the Labor Temple, in Stockton.

Fr. McCullough and I visited Norman Smith and had lunch with him next day. He is an old autoworker organizer and has been on the job for the past year. Henry Anderson, their research worker was in Washington, but Norman Smith gave me a series of reports compiled by Anderson, which are comprehensive, brilliantly written and cover the situation better than any writing I have seen on the problems of farm labor on the west coast. Anyone who wishes to go into this study more thoroughly should write for the research papers which the Agricultural Workers Organizing Committee are putting out.

The growers have encouraged the immigration of Japanese, Hindus, Filipinos, Arabs, American dust bowl refugees, Mexican wetbacks and Mexican contract workers. "In each case the imported group has been poverty stricken, disadvantaged, inarticulate, and undefended," one report reads.

"In their cropping practices, California growers have never had to be concerned with normal problems of labor supply and utilization. They have chosen to plant those crops which tended to yield maximum profit, which have been, for the most part, those requiring a large amount of hand labor."

Mr. Anderson has compiled a great amount of data as to the kind of crops, the peaks and troughs of employment in the various counties, and has reached conclusions with a vision which is rare in such studies.

If agriculture were for the common good, and for the service of men and to supply their needs for work as well as for food there could be worked out more diversified farming practices so that there could be work for all the year around.

"The AWOC rejects categorically the rationalizations of growers who claim Mexican-Americans have wanderlust in their souls, and the like. A survey recently conducted among migrants by the Oregon Bureau of Labor revealed that the overwhelming majority were migrants because they could not survive any other way.

"The human costs of such an enforced state of impermanence are beyond calculation, and among other costs must be reckoned the damage this condition works upon the collective conscience of our civilization."

. . . "By and large, the abilities latent in this sizable population group are forever lost to the society at large . . . Everyone who has examined conditions as they actually are, agrees that the hardest working migrants are burdened by extended periods in which they are travelling, looking for work, or unable to work due to inclement weather, sickness, or some other reason."

Anderson goes on to point out that although migrants have received a great amount of attention from popular writers and religious groups, they still make up only a small portion of people who work on the land. On the average the largest number of migrants employed at the peak of the harvest in one year was 16.7 percent of the total labor force. Local workers accounted for 21 percent. The bulk of the farm labor is performed by braceros, imported Mexican workers.

Mr. Anderson makes a detailed analysis in this paper, "Human Resources and California Agriculture," to point out that "California has nearly enough residents to fill her season farm labor needs, if seasonal demand curves are smoothed out by staggered plantings, crop diversification and the like.

"In the absence of such developments, the reservoir of potential resident workers is unemployed much of the time. Or more accurately, under-employed. The peculiar labor practices of agriculture permit available work to be "spread around" almost without limit. It makes little difference to the farmer with 25 acres of apricots whether ten men or 50 men pick his fruit. Under the piece rate system his labor costs are exactly the same in both cases. In fact, there are at work within the farm labor market powerful influences toward the employment of more workers than are objectively needed. Most farmers turn over their harvesting operations to labor contractors. The temptation is very great for these contractors to use labor inefficiently. They customarily receive from the grower a fixed profit per box or crate, and in addition, they are permitted whatever they are able to pry from the workers for services rendered. The more workers in their crew, the more they are able to realize from the sale of sandwiches, cold drinks, cigarets and so forth."

Contractors who operate out of Oakland charge their workers $1.50 a day for transportation, 25 cents for the use of a sack, and a dollar a day for lunch. Soft drinks are 15 cents and charges for other incidentals are proportional. The minimum cost to the worker for the contractor's services is $2.75 a day."

According to government figures, the average cotton picker earns about fifty cents an hour and cannot pick more than 250 lbs. of cotton a day. They leave as early as 2:30 a.m. and return as late as 9:30 p.m.

The fact that such research is being done; that organizing has gotten under way for the first time by the CIO-AFL, and lastly the presence of a grower such as Frederick S. Van Dyke of the Van Dyke Ranch Stockton, California, who has gone over, one might say, to the cause of the poor and the worker—these are the things that give one hope. Not to speak of the presence of such priests as Fr. McDonnell, Fr. McCullough, Fr. Duggan and Fr. Garcia who are working with farm labor in this section of California.

When one remembers Gandhi and his association with industrialists, and his overcoming class hatreds; and of Vinoba Bhave and his land-gift movement, one has reason to hope that with prayer and work, changes will eventually come about in the savage picture which has not changed in California, nor any where else in the country since Steinbeck wrote *Grapes of Wrath* and *Of Dubious Battle*.

REFLECTIONS ON THE CONNECTION

Forgive us if we talk too much about prisons. The prison has become for us a symbol. We are imprisoned in the flesh in our pain and in our loneliness. Who will deliver me from the body of this death? To be delivered, to be released—these are common terms of speech.

Last month on the front page of the CW there were stories of the French being imprisoned for protest against the Algerian war, and there was Ammon's story of our *not* being imprisoned this year after the successful protest against the mock air raid drill, and there was the letter from Karl Meyer in Chicago, also from prison. He was jailed for distributing leaflets about the arrest of Rose Robinson, on federal property. He and Terry Sullivan both bore imprisonment to keep Rose company in her year sentence. But she was released after eighty days, and the others are free too.

It was in prison that I first saw drug addiction close at hand. Addicts are known there even by the special robe they wear. I would not have known this if I had not picked out one of these wrappers as being my size, and having it taken away from me as "only for addicts". It is made of seersucker, a coverall with big pockets and it is a more adequate garment, more all-embracing than the other sleazy affairs they hand out for our wear in jail. But I suppose they are given it *because* all other clothes are taken from them. The last time Deane Mowrer and I served a brief sentence of ten days, we were put in a dormitory and the young woman next to me, usually very taciturn, spoke one day.

"When I wake up you are reading that prayer book and when I go to sleep you are reading it." (It was a little Fr. Frey psalm book.) "As for me, the first thing I think of in the morning is how I'll get me a fix as soon as I get out, and it is the last thing I think of at night."

"And me too," another woman, an older white woman, called out from across the aisle.

There was a young Negro in the end bed, who had made a shrine by her bedside. She was reading Keye's life of the Little Flower, and she came over to me. She frankly admitted to being an addict. One had to, in the Woman's House of Detention, because the method of treating it there is the cold turkey cure. In other words nothing is given to enable the women to endure the breaking off pains, and their suffering is most obvious to all. A mild tranquilizer is the extent of their medication.

She was not talking of a "fix," but of the book she was reading. "If I had had a home like this," she cried, showing her book. She had become a Catholic the year before, and though she might fall again seventy times seven—still, there was something to go on, and who can tell how the grace of God would work in that soul.

Last summer, I was called upon to testify before the State legislative hearing on drug addiction about conditions in the women's prison. Commissioner Anna Kross had taken the stand before me and after a very good talk about the need to reach the higher ups instead of arresting the little fellows, the pushers, the addicts themselves, she went on to say that not only the profits were enormous, but the stuff was cut and diluted to such an extent that the girls were not suffering at all as they seemed to be suffering, and that their withdrawal pains were largely simulated. Her total lack of sympathy for the women in her charge, as one might say, was horrifying.

When I spoke I told of what I had seen, of the hideous suffering, the pale and ghastly faces of the victims, the spasmodic contortions of the body, the lack of any medical help unless they were taken dying to Bellevue prison ward. There were three or four stories which came out in the daily newspapers of girls setting fire to their mattresses—why such suicidal madness?—and the last time I was there, there was another flurry in the night, a mattress set afire again.

It is because of this that I had been interested for some time in visiting The Living Theatre, where Judith Malina, who had been my cell mate for twenty-five days in 1958 in this same House of Detention and for the same reason, together with her husband, Julian Beck, have been putting on plays that have aroused the drama critics to fury or enthusiasm.

Judith is an accomplished actress. She cannot help but respond to the situation in which she finds herself and her beauty and responsiveness made her a target for attention in jail which made me anxious for her safety. To save her from the attentions of a little drug addict, I demanded that she be put in my cell which meant that Deane was in a cell alone at the end of the corridor for a time until a young Protestant member of the Fellowship of Reconciliation came to join us on the same charge and she was put in Deane's cell.

We occupied ourselves, Judith and I, when we were not on our work assignments, me in laundry and sewing room, and she wielding a mop in the reception and administration section of the jail, reading as we lay on our two beds, one pulled out from beneath the other in that tiny cell built for one. We read missal and breviary, and she read a Jewish prayer book, and I read Kon Tiki, most refreshing, while she read Dr. Faustus, a play later put on by the Living Theater.

She was an amazing mimic and varied her acts from tragedy to comedy. With mop in hand, in the vestibule of the jail when visitors were entering, she could suddenly be cringing in a concentration camp, cowering before a hulking matron. She drew a sketch of herself thus which was the delight of the other prisoners. Or she was the busy housewife serving afternoon tea and slicing up a lemon meringue pie and serving it on the roof during the scant half hour of recreation in the evening.

From the same roof we could stand on benches and peer through the screens over the parapet down Sixth Avenue, the Avenue of Americas to Fourteenth Street where she pointed out a building that they hoped, she and Julian, would house the Living Theater the next year. It is the entire building on the northeast corner and there are three entire floors facing two streets, all windows brilliantly colored, housing an actor's school, a ballet school, a scene painting studio, offices, theater, lobby and so on. There is a most ingenious hanging in the lobby which turns out to be a wildly-twisted copper pipe, from which water comes as from a fountain from the spout of which one can drink copiously of the good cold water.

Last night, Ammon Hennacy and I went to the Living Theater to see The Connection, which had been so much talked about, before the closing which Ammon said was imminent. (He was wrong, it is still continuing.)

I remembered as I sat in the comfortable theater seats (it is a "little theater" and does not accommodate more than a few

47

hundred) the early Provincetown Playhouse on McDougal street in 1918 when Christine had a restaurant on the second floor, and the theater itself was bare as a barn, and had only benches for seats. But it was there that Eugene O'Neill's first one-act plays were produced. Jig Cook was the producer.

Thanks to out-of-town visitors, I had seen all the Chekhov plays at the Fourth Street theater a few years ago, in another small and intimate setting which is so good for such drama.

Actually, until these last few years, I had seen no plays at all for many many years, and I came to them, fresh and impressionable. It was one of the Chekhov plays which helped me understand a neurotic young poet who had been tormenting us around the Catholic Worker, rather than engage our sympathies as he should have done. And I thought suddenly that this is what the theater and the novel, is supposed to do —to take people and present them to you in perspective—disengaging you from their present suffering and turmoil because, after all, it is only a novel or a play, and so freeing you from the sense of irritated frustration at the knowledge that there is nothing really that you can do, liberating you from the kind of involvement which is an obstacle to love. It is hard to make this point clear. I mean that it is not we who can change people, and besides, who are we to change anyone, and why cannot we leave them to themselves and God.

What we can do is to understand, to love, to sympathize in the sense of trying to bear a little of the suffering and leave them—not to intrude on them with the corroding pity which is often self-centered and obtuse. People must live their own lives. They must bear their own crosses. We have enough to do to bear our own, and how we bear our own will achieve something for those around us.

And that, in a way, is what The Connection does for us—it helps us to realize, to understand. There is a recurring line in the play, "That's the way it is. That's the way it really is."

In jail I tried to tell one of the girls that what she wanted was God, that what we all wanted was God, a sense of well-being, the beatific vision. That vision was described as the marriage feast, as union with the bridegroom in the Bible. Nothing else was ever going to satisfy us.

In the play one of the characters, Solly, says, "You are fed up with everything for the moment. And like the rest of us you are a little hungry for a little hope. So you wait and worry. A fix of hope. A fix to forget. A fix to remember, to

48

be sad, to be happy, to be, to be. So we wait for the trust-worthy Cowboy to gallop in upon a white horse. Gallant white powder."

And one of the other characters replies, "There ain't nothin' gallant about heroin, baby."

There is a pecular construction to the play. Because junkies, as Kenneth Tynan in the introduction to the published play remarks, are as a class contemplatives rather than talkers, the author, Jack Gelber contrives this: "a nervous producer explains to the audience that he has hired a writer to bring together a group of addicts for the express purpose of improvising dialogue along lines that the author has previously laid down. The results are filmed before our eyes, by a two-man camera crew. There are thus, acting as a collective bridge between us and the junkies, four intruders from the world of getting and spending."

At the end of the play, the author, (not the actual author but the author's author), has been enticed into taking heroin himself in order to experience what he is writing about, and he feels the play falling apart and confesses his failure. "It was my fault," he says vaguely. "I thought maybe the doctors would take over. That's the message for tonight from me." And Cowboy, who is the connection, who has been the Godot they have been waiting for, who has brought them the drug says, "Hell, the doctors would be the *big* connection." And another character says, "I don't trust them. Those are the people who mildly electrocute thousands of people every year . . . Oh no, I do not trust them as a group any more than I trust the police as a group. Or junkies . . ."

So no solutions are offered either. The police do not trust the doctors, nor the politicians, hence the Sherman act. And the doctors do not trust the police, so they too can do nothing, and the habit grows, until North Brother Island is filled with teen-age addicts, and Lexington hospital is overcrowded with a waiting list, and other hospitals in the great city of New York offer a scant dozen beds for medical care of those afflicted in this way.

I came away from the play with the thought again of Peter Maurin's program of action.

One of the things the play might accomplish would be to make people realize that these men, Negro, Caucasian, as the play describes them, are even as you and I. Fear of them and their desperation is to be feared. Courage and love can do much. And the exercise of that faith that there is in each one of us, a power greater than we think, and a Power outside of us, a personal God, a Father, who loves us and hears our prayers.

Yes, we must each of us, and groups of us, try to make that kind of society where it is easier for man to be good, as Peter Maurin said, and counter the hopelessness of ever achieving that kind of society in our lifetime by hearty prayer. God help us, and help them, those so real people in The Connection, so attractive, so gifted—in one way but dust and in another, just a little less than angels, whom God so loved that He gave His only son to save us. But also He gave us our freedom, and respecting our free will, He leaves it to us to make the beginnings.

The play is dedicated to Thelma Gadsden, a drug addict whom Judith and I met in prison two years ago, who suffered so from her confinement that she could not bear to look out the bars at the end of the corridor. Every night as she called out her good-nights to her fellow prisoners she called the number of the days she had left to serve. When she was released she came to us for a visit, but later she died from an overdose of heroin.

October 1960

FALL APPEAL

October, 1960

St. Joseph's Loft
39 Spring Street
New York 12, New York
Dear fellow workers in Christ,

It is good to sit down to this letter right after Mass when you still feel God is so close, and prayer still in one, like a warmth and strength. Outside it is grey and cloudy and fog horns come up from the river and one must burn electricity in the day hours. In the damp a slum seems like a dung heap and age and decrepitude and human misery remind one of Job. Only the young, and our neighborhood is filled with the young, shine like bright cheerful birds in the grey morning. There are not only the children but all the young Puerto Ricans who work in the factories around on Lafayette Street and Broadway. Harry Golden says all those little factories are filled with debt collectors on paydays, getting their share first from the thin pay envelopes of the poor. (All this section of New York west of the Italian section, west of the East Side, is filled with small loft work shops and factories.) On the one hand we are a country of abundance, and on the other of destitution. The newcomers are tempted to buy on the instalment plan and pay interest to finance companies and this emphasizes always the evils of usury. That is why we refused interest from the city—to make our point strong and clear. Together with this witness, we run articles in the paper on credit unions and voluntary poverty and ways of doing away with it. People say, "who will answer your appeal, when you are so improvident?" But just the same we write with faith in our readers that they will be generous and help us as they have so often these last 28 years. As a matter of fact we only sent out one appeal these last two years, because we were living on the money that came in from the purchase by the city of our St. Joseph's House on Chrystie Street. We also added extra rooms to the beach houses and put in two new cesspools, two furnaces, a plumbing system for the C.W. community on the farm on Staten Island. In town we pay rents not only in St. Joseph's Loft but also on eight apartments and on furnished rooms and beds on the Bowery. We live more than ever from day to day in town renting as the poor do. The taxes on Staten Island (and we of course pay all real estate taxes) amount to several thousand a year. What with the Narrows Bridge going up, taxes were doubled this last year. All this by way of accounting. At St. Joseph's Loft alone, our food bill is at the least $1,140 a month, and rents are $676. The cost of printing is around $900. And of course there are no salaries and the expenses of the editors are included in such food and shelter and enough clothes come in for us all. In the city we are among the destitute but on the Island we are blessed with the beauty of the farm and beach, and over a weekend there will be as many as forty, like last Sunday, who came for a day of recollection and discussion. Fr. Conway from the Dominican House of Studies came last weekend and started us all studying more about the one thing needful, to know God and love Him and be happy in this life and the next. (That next life which seems so imminent during these discussions on disarmament at the United

51

Nations.) I often feel that the farm is an oasis of prayer and adoration and intercession for all, as well as a place to shelter the wounded of the class warfare all around us. Not to speak of the war against sin, most important battle of all.

Yes, we are broke again and are beggars, like St. Francis whose birthday is October 4. He too illustrated the paradox of Christianity by first advising his followers to give away whatever they had, and then telling them to beg some of it back again, not only for their own sustenance but to give to others. It is the foolishness of the Cross that St. Paul speaks of. It is the foolishness not of the childish but of the child, and it is the way of spiritual childhood that St. Therese of the Child Jesus whose birthday is Oct. 3 tells us about, I have a book coming out about Therese this month, published by Fides Press, Notre Dame, Ind., and it would be nice if there were enough royalties to pay some of the bills. But only best sellers do that so we have to depend on our readers to support us. This is also the month of the Guardian Angels so we are praying too, not only to St. Joseph the householder, and St. Francis the poor man and St. Therese, but also to your guardian angels, to prompt you to help us again. And may your help return to you a hundredfold.

November 1960

It is not easy, having acted upon principle, to explain it in ways acceptable and understood by others. An instance is our recent sending back the interest on the money given us for St. Joseph's House on Chrystie street.

During the course of the month we received a few letters, not very many, of criticism of our act. One letter from a generous benefactor who had given us a large sum when her father died, pointed out that if her parent had not invested his money wisely she and her mother would not have had anything left to live on; also that we probably received many donations which came from dividends, interest, etc.

I only try to answer as best I can. But sometimes one confuses others the more by trying to answer objections. When we wrote our letter to the city, and published it in the paper, we also printed some excerpts from the teaching of St. Thomas Aquinas on interest and money lending. We used some of Peter Maurin's easy essays on the subject, and an article by Arthur Sheehan on credit unions, which however, ask for a small interest on their loans. How can this be reconciled with the "gesture" we made of returning to the city the large check which represented the interest for a year and a half on the money paid us for our property on Chrystie street. First of all, we asked with Chesterton, whose money is this interest which the city was paying us? Where did it come from? Money does not breed money, it is sterile.

Answering our correspondent, of course we are involved, the same as everyone else, in living off interest. We are all caught up in this same money economy. Just as "God writes straight with crooked lines," so we too waver, struggle on our devious path—always aiming at God, even though we are conditioned by habits and ancestry, etc. We have free will, which is our greatest gift. We are free to choose and as we see more clearly, our choice is more direct and easier to make. But we all see through a glass darkly. It would be heaven to see Truth face to face.

We are publishing a paper in which ideas are discussed and clarified, and illustrated by act. So we are not just a newspaper. We are a revolution, a movement, Peter Maurin used to say. We are propagandists of the faith. We are the Church. We are members of the Mystical Body. We all must try to function healthily. We do not have the same function, but we all have a vocation, a calling. Ours is a "prophetic" one as many priests have said to us. Pope John recently, July 30, cited the courage of John the Baptist as an example for today. Prophets made great gestures, did things to call attention to what they were talking about. That was what we did, we made a gesture, when we sent back the money to the city. It was calling attention to a great unsolved problem which we are all involved in, Church, State, corporation, institution, individual.

There is no simple solution. Let the priests and the economists get to work on it. It is a moral and an ethical problem. We can work on the lowest level, the credit union in the parish, the union, on the missions, etc. Through the credit union families have been taught to resist the skilful seductions of the advertising men and by doing without many things, to attain to ownership, homes, workshops, tools, small factories and so on. These things have happened in Nova Scotia, in missions throughout the world and this is one way to combat what the bishops call the all-encroaching state. It is the beginnings of the decentralist society.

So primarily, our sending back the money was a gesture. It was the first time we had to do with so large a sum of money. We were being reimbursed by the city, and generously, as far as money went, for the house and our improvements on it. Twelve years ago we paid $30,000 for the house money which our many friends throughout the country sent to us. When I was sentenced as a slum land'ord (I am under suspended sentence now) and forced to make all kinds of changes in an old house which had no violations on it when we bought it six years before, we again with the aid of our friends and readers, put $24,000 into the house. (Such items as steel self-closing doors cost $150 apiece.) With wooden floors in the halls, wooden stair railings and wooden stairs, the place remained as much of a fire trap as before, in reality. Our two fire escapes were the real necessities and one of them they forced us to take down! But one cannot argue with bureaucrats.

When two years later they took over the property by the right of eminent domain because a subway extension was going through they reimbursed us of course. The lawyers who handled the deal for all the property owners on the block were very generous with us and only took 5 percent for their work. When after a year and a half we were paid, it was very generously. One can argue that the value of the property went up, that the city had the 18 months use of our money, that money purchases less now and so on. The fact remains the city was doing what it could to pay off each and every tenant in the two tenement houses from which they were being evicted, giving bonuses, trying to find other lodgings though these were usually unacceptable being in other neighborhoods or boroughs.

We agree that slums need to be eliminated but that an entire neighborhood which is like a village made up of many nationalities should be scattered, displaced,—this is wanton cruelty, and one of the causes of the juvenile delinquency of our cities. Also, it is terribly bad and ruthless management on the party of the city fathers.

Is Robert Moses responsible? He is the planner. But he deals recklessly with inanimate brick and cement at the expense of flesh and blood. He is walking ruthlessly over broken-hearted families to make a great outward show of a destroyed and rebuilt city. He has been doing what blockbusters and obliteration bombing did in European and British cities. Right now an entire neighborhood just south of Tompkins Square where some of our poor friends live is being demolished and the widows and fatherless are crying to heaven. The city fathers try to recompense them, try to give them bonuses to get out quickly. But what good does the money do them when there is no place to go? They do not want to go to another neighborhood or even to another block. Actually, as piled-up furniture on the streets testifies, many cling to their poor homes until the last moment, and probably forfeit the two or three hundred dollars they are offered, rather than be exiled. That money means as much them, as the two or three thousand did to us.

Of course the great problem is to build quickly and economically instead of finding a place for whole buildings of families while the work is going on. They talk about doing things economically, yet money is poured out like water in all directions and scandals are always being unearthed of cheating and graft in high places. This extends down to the smallest citizen too, who is trying to get in on the big deal and get his, from the building inspector who expects to be tipped to the little veteran around the corner who is speculating in real estate by buying and improving and renting and then selling back his property to the city at exorbitant prices. "It doesn't matter if it is going to be torn down in a year or so," he assured us. "Rent out all the apartments and stores and then you can ask more from the city." Big deal! Everyone is trying to get in on the Moses big deal.

So to put it on the natural but often most emotional plane of simple patriotism, love of country or city, this feeling too prompted us to send back the interest. We do not want to participate in this big deal. "Why are there wars and contentions among you? Because each one seeketh his own."

We considered this a gesture too towards peace, a spiritual weapon which is translated into action. We cannot talk about these ideas without trying to put them into practice though we do it clumsily and are often misunderstood.

We are not trying to be superior, holier than thou. Of course we are involved in paying taxes, in living on money which comes from our industrial capitalist way of life. But we can try, by voluntary poverty and labor, to earn our living, and not to be any more involved than we can help. We, all of us partake in a way in the sin of Sapphira and Ananias, by ho ding back our time, our love, our material resources even, after making great protestations of "absolutism." May God and you, our readers, forgive us. We are in spite of all we try to do, unprofitable servants.

1961

March 1961

☐ This is Balmorhea, Texas, within four hours of El Paso, and I am within two stops of California. I am writing from a little house called Bethany, which looks over miles of desert to the foothills of the Davis Mountains. Those foothills are five thousand feet high, and here it is three thousand feet up so that the first few days I suffered with a nagging little headache. I am resting here, to get the car fixed up, a valve job, and to wait for my 1961 plates to be sent on to me from New York. I do not know how I started out on December 28th without them. Everything else about the car was checked carefully, but we all overlooked a most important item, our plates, without which I would soon be stopped on the road.

Down the highway about half a mile from where I am, the old highway dips off over an irrigation ditch and leads through a grove of cottonwoods, to the Church of Christ the King, and to the Casa Maria Reina, formerly the rectory of the priest and now the center for one of the Combermere missions. Theresa Davis is in charge, and there is Marilyn and Joe, who make up the team, together with Fr. Paul and Anne, an associate who is teaching in the grade school of nearby Saragosa, and Eddie Doherty, who is visiting for a month here in this southwest desert. All are members of the secular institute founded by Catherine Doherty which is made up of men and women and priests, and numbers right now seventy-five with fifty in training, a preparation which lasts five years. There is also another visitor, Raejean, so the center is busy indeed.

The day begins at a quarter of six and continues until eleven at night, because some of their teaching must be at night. Their job is to teach catechism to all the children of the district and last night there was an evening of film strip, scenes from the Old Testament, with accompanying comments. I have been able to see some of the surrounding country since Joe and Anne and Marilyn all have to drive the children home who stay for catechism and the Mass which is at five each day.

It is amazing the number of visitors who drop by. I have been here just a week and during that time there were five nurses taking a winter vacation and they came from Belgium, England and Canada; there were two young hitchhikers fed; there was the family stranded on the road that Mary and I had met on our way here from San Antonio (Mary has gone back to New York by bus, a three-day trip, non-stop, and I am proceeding alone). There are visitors from the neighborhood, young Mexican girls, mothers who come in with delicious bowls of Mexican food, children who are waiting to go to Mass, who sit in the big living room and either listen to music or look at picture books; there are the young Mexican women being trained to teach catechism, too.

The house is made up of kitchen, dining room, small room where Eddie sits at his desk and divides his time between typewriter and his rock collection; living room and recreation room (television); two bedrooms and bath. It is small as rectories go, but makes a very good and homelike meeting place and all the mothers and young women and children seem to take much joy in visiting there.

The Pius XII Center a mile away has three classrooms and it is near the public school so catechism is taught there and Mass offered every other day. On the other week days, Mass is at the Church of Our Lady of Guadalupe in Saragosa, and it is there, too, in another little center which used to be another adobe brick church, that the children are taught. It is cold now and the children are all wearing shoes, but they still dress in thin cotton clothes and perhaps short-sleeved sweaters but show little indication of suffering from the cold. They are used to suffering and accept discomfort. But on cold, cloudy days one wonders how they keep warm in their little one-room huts which dot the landscape or cling to the banks of the irrigation ditches and creeks. But there are sometimes a dozen in such a hovel and just human warmth, I suppose, takes off the chill.

How hard it is ever to mention our voluntary poverty in such surroundings. No one is working now among the few thousands in the district. It is the tail end of the cotton picking, and I have seen only a dozen braceros still here, working in the fields, and only one cotton gin among the dozens hereabouts under operation. The people are living frugally on beans and tortillas, and occasionally on the delicious green chile which they peel and cook up with cheese and milk. One of the families brought us some tortilla dish last night and the girls stayed to show Marilyn how to make this side dish.

One of the reasons there is still cotton picking is that this last fall has been one of the rainiest seasons Texas has had for a long time, and the bolls did not open. So there has been a sporadic picking of cotton up till now. We got out of the car, Theresa and I, and went over to the truck to watch one of the men dumping his long sack into the great trailer by the side of the road. He carried it over his shoulder like a long bolster, weighed it (it was 76 pounds) and then clambered up on the truck and loosening either end, hung it over a beam and shook out the cotton which was being picked at this time of the year, husks and all. They are getting a cent and a half a pound now, and by working ten hours at high speed can make five dollars a day.

And they do work speedily. The sack is tied around their waists like an apron, and stretches out between their legs. They proceed down between two rows, and pick fast with both hands, stuffing the bag between their legs, which they have to shake back every now and then to push the cotton back. It is a long, heavy job, picking seventy-five pounds of cotton, dragging it along the field after one. The growers justify the contract with the Mexican government by saying they have not enough local labor to do the job in this long rich valley where the finest cotton in the world is grown, soft as silk, long fibered. But perhaps the people are not around because there is no work for them. One sees many a pickup truck on the road with moving families, looking for work. There are many abandoned huts along the roads and ditches.

When the season is at its height, some growers have more than 300 braceros and the taverns and general stores are full. On the one little road where Casa Maria Reina is there are ten taverns, some little more than a hut, with the word

BEER lettered in black across the front. In one larger tavern in Saragosa during picking season there are one hundred prostitutes brought in on Saturday nights for the entertainment of the braceros, and nothing is said or done about what might be really white slave traffic. Where do these women all come from? And are they are not forced, many of them, into prostitution because of the insufferable conditions under which they have lived? It is no use saying that people are used to hunger, cold and hovels and hard gruelling work under a sun that blazes down day after day, until the heat reaches 130 degrees.

The group at Casa Maria Reina are where the children need them most, and they realize keenly the difference between their condition and that of the people they are serving. Such contrasts make the need for the constant daily practice of little sacrifices, little mortifications, a constant denial of self which is certainly harder than the occasional large gesture, an outward show of sacrifice which gets acclaim. I so often think of this around *The Catholic Worker* with its outward show of poverty an appearance very often and not a reality with the self-indulgence which is so prevalent among each and every one of us Americans. (Reading a story like the one we presented from Korea two months ago, makes us realize this over and over again, and it is good to print such stories so that we may constantly repent and start over again, God help us.)

April 1961

Our destination was Ajo, which was 125 miles from Tucson, and is a company town of the Phelps Dodge people who mine the copper in southern Arizona. The two diocesan priests in the town are Fr. Reinweller and Fr. Stromberg. The latter had a belated vocation. He had formerly been an anthropologist in Mexico when his vocation suddenly descended upon him, as it were. He was much concerned this night with a "rumble" that was slated for the evening around the square of the little town, between the Anglos and the Mexicans from a neighboring town, and sat up rather late to forestall any trouble in a little coffee shop down the street from the church where the Anglos hung out. We saw some of the outposts of a gang of kids, armed with staves, hoping for something to start. As usual all over the country, the teen-agers have nothing to do, no work to absorb their energies, nothing of any importance, no philosophy of work, as Peter would say when he told people "to fire the bosses" as he used to say in the depression, advising young people to find some work that they wanted to do and study for it, train themselves for it—but where are those who have a philosophy of work and can convey the idea to others, and who have the gift of leadership? And what kind of work is there in a company town that is not just "made work."

The Phelps Dodge people dominate the towns of Douglas, Bisbee, Globe, Cliffton, Morency and many other places. I shall look up a history of the company which I can probably find in the files of *Fortune* magazine. A movie, "Salt of the Earth," was made in New Mexico, of a strike of the Mine, Mill and Smelter Workers' Union. An injunction was gotten out against picketing, so the women took up the job, leaving the men to stay home and do the chores, drawing the water, cooking over little wood fires and washing for the babies. The picture was taken with local people with only a few imported actors, and it was a true and valid picture, and with humor, until the "capitalist bosses from Wall Street" came on the scene, looking like big blond German Nazis, driving around in limousines that were more fitted for Wall Street than the desert. Since it was a Communist-inspired movie it did not get much of a showing through the country but we saw it in New York.

Ajo is a neat, orderly, well laid out town. For vast miles across the desert, as we approached it, there was the equivalent of the slag heaps of the coal mining towns of the north. At the top of this dead white palisade runs a little train with a few cars, cauldrons of burning molten waste which is dumped out to lengthen the long mountain which rises up over the desert. The mine itself looks like a great amphitheater, terraced in many-colored rock of pastel shades—turquoise blue, rose and pale pink, green, russet. Men and machines look like ants and toys in this vastness. How many men? A few thousand perhaps. There is segregation in housing in this company town—first an Indian village, for the many Papagos who work in the mine, and it is here we found Fr. Camillus, a warm Italian, very youthful, originally from Oregon where his family have a fruit farm. He loves the Indians and took me into the kindergarten, the only school, where doll-like children sang for me and prayed for me, and then during recess, played like other children with guns and cars, imitating police sirens and fire trucks and ambulances.

Fr. Camillus is proud of his church where the Papago sing the Mass in Papago chant set to the music of the *Green Rainbow Song*. Brother Robert had made fifteen rattles like the medicine men use, with metal disks which the altar boys, fifteen of them, shake during the singing of the Gloria and the Creed, as gourds are shaken to give rhythm. The candlesticks on the altar are carved of mesquite wood, and the holy water fonts and cruets are of lovely russet pottery made by the Indians. There are beautiful Navajo rugs under foot and on the benches sheepskins and goatskins and a buffalo hide. Papagos are highly skilled in leather work. They do no weaving and when I asked what the priests wore, he said when it was cold they used to wear skins and in hot weather they used to wear nothing at all. The pictures of the early missionaries, riding over the desert on their horses, show the Indians with nothing but a loin cloth.

Father Camillus preaches in Papago and his sermon is in three parts, he says, first the sermon, then the explanation of liturgy, then Scripture.

Everywhere there are the beautiful baskets of the Indians, made by the women from the materials collected by the men from the desert. Even the Monstrance is part basket woven, and the metal part is inlaid with semi-precious stones collected and polished from the desert. (Fr. Lambert polishes stones in tumblers which revolve for weeks, and one can get little motor-driven tumblers as big as coffee pots, for twenty dollars in the Woolworth stores.) Many of their baskets have plain round designs, surrounding, or basing the figure of the legendary hero, E-E-Toi. Stones, roots, branches, cactus, everything is used in the desert. A cactus syrup is made from the Suhuara fruit which tastes like a refined blackstrap molasses. The fine seed of the fruit is pounded and made into a paste-like candy, or the seed is sprinkled like poppy seed on bread. All the fruit of the cactus is eaten, and there is a wild spinach called evak and acorn nuts and wild onions and chile and so on. Fr. Camillus goes out with the Indian boys and they gather the fruit when it is in season and then there is a great boiling down rather like the sugaring in New England.

Further down the side of the mountain is the Mexican village and since I was with a teacher who had a specific job to do, I did not visit the houses but the school instead, where I talked to the seventh and eighth grades, some of them the very students who were looking for a "rumble" the night before. The Sisters of Charity of Mother Seton, from Seton Hill, Pennsylvania, teach here and they invited us to their convent on the top of a high hill for dinner, where they ate with us and the two priests and we had a very pleasant discussion.

Traveling in the desert is most fascinating, and I was amazed to hear Father Lambert talk of the actual farming some of the Indians were able to do. They raise corn, squash and wheat, and have both wheat and corn tortillas as their "bread." They cook and bake in big outside ovens as the Pennsylvania Dutch do. "But they do not buy and sell," he said. "They have no business sense. They give their surplus away."

I was interested to learn that one of those St. Benedict terms "wandering monks," Stanley Becker, who had spent a summer with us when he came up from New Orleans, and who when he departed left a painting on wood of St. Francis Xavier, had spent some time with Fr. Camillus a year before. St. Francis Xavier is a favorite saint of the Papago, and Fr. Kino, the Jesuit, was the one who brought Christ to the Indians centuries before and built up many missions in southern Arizona and northern Mexico.

Another wandering layman was Tom Carstairs who came as a volunteer and helped and I do not know whether it was he or some other who gave music lessons too, to the Mexican boys. There is much to be done in these small Indian schools throughout the country, and a peace army could be at work there right now, without waiting to be drafted. There would be no pay besides a living, and so no bother about income tax and so no contributing to war in this way. It would be a test of courage too, for city youth to go wandering through the land, learning more of their country, and the work to be done in it. And what a field for anthropologists, geologists, botanists! I can still hear Peter Maurin say, "Fire the bosses!"

At another mission church way off the highway in the desert, we saw a beautiful unfinished painting of our Lady of Guadalupe and Juan Diego gathering roses into his tilma, kneeling at her feet. It is the drawing of Juan Diego which remains unfinished and perhaps some wandering monk will drop by and finish it. It was started, the sisters said, by one who was obviously not in the "wandering monk" class, since when he started back to Chicago to report to a parole officer, so the story goes, he was shot and killed in a holdup in a liquor store in some town on the way.

Next month, more about Tucson and a housing project there, and a visit to El Centro, Calif., where the recent lettuce strike took place, and then to San Diego and Los Angeles where I am now. A few weeks more, and I will be starting home, with notebooks far fuller than the brief notes I have given here. What with letters and writing, my manual labor these days consists in pounding on the typewriter.

So now up and out to a special showing of *The Hoodlum Priest*, with Frances Langford, faithful friend of the CW almost since we began. It is the story of Fr. Dismas S.J., of St. Louis, and the showing tonight is sponsored by the Quakers and we have been invited to attend at Sam Goldwyn studios.

June 1961

It is true we have had a long cold rainy spring and most of the time the skies have been overclouded. It is hard not to be oppressed on such days so it is not to be surprised that everyone complains, every one is looking for comfort and reassurance. "God comforts us," St. Paul tells us, "that we may comfort others." The trouble is that in trying to comfort and reassure, we plunge into giving the advice asked for, and that always adds to the problems of those who have come for comfort. I hereby withdraw all advice I have given to members of our staff about cutting down on food bills, not paying so many rents,—not accepting so much furniture which has crowded our dining room this past month at 175 Chrystie Street. By advising I have only added to people's problems. I have been giving worldly advice and have been quenching the spirit!

The Sun Shines

Today is a beautiful day with a gentle wind, the fresh cut grass smells delightfully, the frogs have begun their strange music again down by the pond at Peter Maurin Farm and some sweet clover which is cropping up by every roadside can be cut and brought into town to hang in a window and give a reminder of open fields. This fact is an answer itself to the guilt one feels at having a farm and a beach place, houses of hospitality, extensions which are so near to the city (thirty-five cents carfare one way) that picnickers can come down and spend the day.

Bills Will Be Paid

It is true that the appeal was answered and bills were paid. Twenty-one thousand dollars came in, and went out again. And now there is no money ahead for the summer! No visible means of support, as the saying is. We pay a thousand dollars a month in rents, and rent must be paid on time. Evictions are very real things. We have a mother and child with us whose furniture was put out on the street. "It disappears quickly," she told us when we were complaining of being cluttered up with furniture. "Just put it out on the street, and it disappears in the night."

But having been served with summons before for not having the garbage can lids on, and being under suspended sentence (a $250 fine) for being a slum landlord, we are shy about such direct methods. We must return to the daring and fearlessness of former years. We have given away what we can to all our neighbors. "Can't you take a chair with those spring hats? And what about a sack of potatoes?" But mothers' arms are always filled with bundles and babies and moving furniture up flights of stairs is a heavy job.

Yes, we are rich in furniture and in potatoes this month, and such donations come in each day, but they do not pay for the rest of the staples which seem to be consumed in vast quantities. "We spend ten dollars a day just for sugar and margarine," Dianne says. We get day-old bread which Mike picks up at an East Side bakery and some of it is good pumpernickel and rye. Dianne and Stuart, two of our editors, have charge of the kitchen and they are both in their early twenties, generous and strong. They work like Trojans and try to feed everyone who comes along, and Charlie who pays the bills and has to worry over the finances wonders, "shall we feed everyone who comes along?" And then I start advising again. But I have to do it,—it is really talking to myself, reassuring myself when I do it.

I know that I have said in the past that we must not play God,—that we are always overcrowding, always biting off more than we can chew, always taking on more than we can accomplish. So we must try to limit ourselves. Baron von Hugel says that each morning we should think over what we have to do that day, and then cut our schedule in half. All very well for those in public life "who wish to be seen and

65

esteemed by men." But for the mother, the householder, the family, the man at work,—this advice is not possible. The "industrial engineer," the speed-up artist, the efficiency expert is going to pile it on as much as he can in factory and workshop. And there is no end to the destitute which we will always have with us.

The second principle to remember is that as anarchists or personalists, whatever we choose to call ourselves, "we must be what we want the other fellow to be," as Peter Maurin said. In other words, look to ourselves alone, do our own job as well as we can and not worry about the other fellow's job. But what if one is in charge of the finances and worrying about the bills?

The person who is willing to take charge of the kitchen should be given leeway, his judgment should be trusted. He will do the best he can. And who is paying the bills anyway but God alone? We admit we are beggars and we are not ashamed of it. We will work as hard as we can, with no salary and trust to the Lord to care for those He sends us. He will put it into the hearts of our readers, to keep us going, as He has for the last twenty-eight years. So let us pray too for the one who carries the heavy load of our debts on his shoulders.

Chrystie Street

No one has given a realistic description of our new headquarters, St. Joseph's House at 175 Chrystie Street, and everyone who comes there is shocked at how miserable our surroundings are. If the loft on Spring Street was inadequate and dingy, though spacious, the new site is dingier and smaller. There is a cellar, half of which the landlord uses. When the cellar door fell in, we paid for a new one, seventy-five dollars, so he allows us to use the back of the cellar. Our rent is $275 a month. The ground floor is cemented and impossible to keep clean with hundreds of people tramping in and out each day. We cannot seat more than twenty at a time and the others sit on benches towards the front of the store, or go up the one short flight to the "sitting room" floor where the clothes rooms are, for women and for men. On the third floor are offices, and the floors slant, and every time anyone walks across the room the boards shake. From the interstices of the metal ceiling, the rain pours in so that on rainy days we have had three large metal wastepaper baskets filling up with water over and over again. Tarring the roof around the skylight does not seem to have helped much.

Even with all this, given the money for materials a few skilled workers could affect a change, but the clutter and filth would remain the same. It is not just books and papers and overflow of desks all over the place. All Catholic Workers feel their desk is their home, and all have demanded one, save Peter Maurin alone, who made his knees his desk, and his pockets his bookcases.

The filth comes from a packrat we have with us, a most lovable guy whom we have known for many years and who is evicted over and over and always returns, with more and more clutter, boxes upon boxes of trash, garbage, old papers, books, bits of furniture, piled in every corner, hallway, toilet, cellar, and roof. He rooms in an apartment with two other men, and he has surrounded himself there also in the same way with this inconceivable quantity of trash which is impossible to get him to move, without all the moral and physical force one can command. And if one is anarchist-pacifist to the unreasonable degree that so many around *The Catholic Worker* are, an Augean stable is the result of this respect for man's freedom.

Authority and freedom, reason and faith, personalism and communitarianism—all these were the subjects of Peter Maurin's discussions, but if you asked him what to do about Kichi Harada or Roy Bug, he would give you a few essays on the Thomistic Doctrine of the Common Good to read and digest which would help you solve your problems and come to your own decision. Peter having died in 1949, such problems are left for me to solve when I return home from a trip.

So far Hercules has not arrived to solve this problem for us. The thing to do is hire a truck, find out if we can bring it down to the river to load on one of the garbage barges to be taken off to some far off dump to be used as fill, or burned, or both. They have lost some beautiful swamp land which was a game preserve, and where even wild orchids grew, by such city efficiency. But this line of thought would lead one to give up and to wander away and become a desert father, and we are a family, which includes Roy Bug and must stick together. The only thing is to be ruthless and energetic and start afresh. Is there anyone ruthless and energetic around the CW?

But this outward show of destitution is nothing compared

to the destitution suffered by those whose plumbing is out of repair, whose toilets overflow, who have no sixty dollars to call a Roto-Rooter to unstop the pipes and drains.

And of course there are always the problems of lice and dirt in slum tenements with neither bath nor shower. Such is our life in the city, and it is a gigantic effort for the destitute to try to live decently, a Herculean effort.

If we comfort ourselves that we are sharing in some small way with the misery of the migrant worker and the slum dweller by enduring these things, our places on the land, being loved, take on an aspect of true comfort. There is always work to do. Young and old, able and disabled contribute to the common good. And if some of those problems of personal dirt and disorder remain with us even there, they are more easily handled and fresh air, sky and green trees are all around us.

The Catholic Worker headquarters remains in the city because our work is here, and it is where people can find us. Visitors abound to the extent that it is hard to get work done. Mail piles up that needs to be answered, there are meetings to go to, and meetings each Friday night. There is a mysterious attraction in the great city for the young. So we remain in the cities, the gutter sweepers of the diocese, working yet beggars, destitute yet possessing all things; happy because today the sun shines, there is a symphony on the radio, children are playing on the streets, there is a park across the way and a church around the corner where we receive our daily Bread. "Lord, I believe, help Thou mine unbelief." So please "give us this day our daily bread," and the money we need to keep up with our rents.

July-August 1961

ABOUT CUBA

Each day there is some new word about Cuba and the revolution going on there, and we have had many letters from our readers asking us to clarify our position. This is extremely difficult to do, since we are religious in our attitude with a great love for Holy Mother Church; and we are also revolutionaries, in our own fashion.

No matter what we say, I am afraid we will not be able to make ourselves clear. I shall write from my own point of view, from my own experience, which is a long one, among the poor, the workers, organized labor, and throughout a long series of wars, "imperialist wars," class wars, civil wars, race wars. Shall I say that it is almost fifty years of struggle, since at 14 I began to read the class-conscious fiction of Upton Sinclair, who is called the Dickens of America, and Jack London, who is a best seller in Russia, not to speak of the Day book in Chicago which was a socialist, ad-less newspaper on which Carl Sandburg worked, and one of my brothers also.

A good part of this will probably be written in Church where I'll be groaning and sweating, trying to understand and clarify my ideas to present them so that our 70,000 copies of the paper will be read and understood. I won't say 70,000 readers, since libraries and schools get copies and many read them. Who knows who reads the paper or who will be so influenced by the paper that they too will try to see things in the light of the faith, in the light of the history of the Church, and the history of the poor, who are the first children of the Church.

In the pile of mail waiting for me when I returned from the west coast there was a clipping from The Sunday Visitor, read by millions of Catholics and found in practically every church in the land. It certainly influences the thinking of our Catholic people.

The first part of the clipping is about the counter revolutionary movement in Cuba and among the exiles in Miami, the move towards an invasion and the formation of a peoples' revolutionary front which had defected from Castro and "possibly deliberate Communist plants, designed to retrieve the revolution after the fall of Fidel Castro." "What is even more disturbing and frightening is the indication that the formation of this leftist dominated provisional group was facilitated by men within our own government."

Then the clipping goes on to discuss the Catholic Worker, calling Dave Dellinger's article "so blatantly filled with misstatements, out and out lies, that it does not seem to me possible it could have been written in good faith."

There is a great deal of name calling in the article as well as name dropping, so the article gives the impression that the writer is "in the know," is acquainted personally with every-one he mentions, as indeed he may be, having been a journalist and having lived in Cuba for some time. But I too come from a newspaper family and know well the widely divergent points of view that there can be in one family on men and events. One brother was a foreign correspondent for twenty years, another the editor of a Hearst paper in New York. We are, as a family, trained journalists, one might say. And we interpret the news quite differently.

I have not been in Cuba, except as a stopover coming home from Mexico, but I was in Mexico City during the persecution of the Church in the 20's, when the Churches had just reopened in 1929. The laws of the state against the Church are still on the books in 1961, though the church is functioning as normally as it can in our materialist civilization. While I was in Mexico, at the same time that the Church was being persecuted and Mexico was being denounced by the Catholic press as being communistic, my friend Tina Medotti was being arrested and other communists were going into hiding. When I interviewed General Sandino, the Nicaraguan leader, who was opposing United States troops in his own country, he stated clearly he was a communist for his own country not for Russia; that he was a communist because he was for the poor.

Aided by Communists

When the CIO was being organized in 1936 there was many a communist organizer whose skill and courage was made use of by non-Communist top brass, including Joseph Curran who even testified as to this position before the House UnAmerican Activities Committee. "Sure I accepted help from the Communists," he stated flatly. (I was present at the hearing in Washington D.C. with Mrs. John Brophy, whose husband was vice president of the CIO and worked closely with John L. Lewis.) "Who else gave us any help?" he asked boldly, ignoring the fact of the CW headquarters on Tenth Avenue where tons of coffee, peanut butter, cottage cheese, jam and bread had been consumed during the three months' strike of 1937. Though it cost us thousands, and many a ship's crew took up collections for repaying us this aid, it probably was but a drop in the bucket in building up the organization of the National Maritime Union, its headquarters, publications, officers, legal help, etc.

And since when have there been free elections in any of

the great unions of the United States? Once the workers get a leader who delivers the goods, they hold on to him. And when they want a change, it is a bitter struggle to bring about democratic elections. Joseph P. Ryan, of the East Coast Longshoremen for many years used to call meetings with a gun on the table in front of him. Strongarm tactics, the use of force and bribery, are well known in our unions.

But there is no use in the pot calling the kettle black. It is not the "clean hands" policy that I am speaking of. I know how complicated all these problems of justice are, how deep the roots of corruption in our human nature. "The just will be judged first," St. Peter said, and we must think of the power of example. "What you do speaks so loudly that I cannot hear what you say."

With the Poor

It is hard too to say that the place of The Catholic Worker is with the poor, and that being there, we are often finding ourselves on the side of the persecutors of the Church. This is a tragic fact. It is hard too to be writing from New York, where one is not in danger. It is hard to write this way, when I know that were I in Cuba and I heard a mob shouting outside a church for the blood of the priests and worshippers within, I would then be on the side of the "faithful." Of course persecution is deserved and undeserved. And also it is promised us. "The servant is not above his master and if they have persecuted me they will persecute you also." If we are not being persecuted there is something wrong with us. This is not having a persecution complex.

One could weep with the tragedy of denying Christ in the poor. The Church is the Cross on which Christ is crucified and one does not separate Christ from his cross, Guardini wrote. Christ has left Himself to us in the bread and wine on the altar; He has left Himself to those who gather together, two and three in His name; He has left Himself to us in the poor: "There I am in the midst of you." "If you do it unto the least of these my brethren you do it unto me." "I am Christ whom thou persecutest." Saul was imprisoning and putting to death those who walked in the Way, and Christ cried out on the road to Damascus, "Saul, Saul, why persecutest thou me?"

Fidel Castro says he is not persecuting Christ, but Churchmen who have betrayed him. He says that he differentiates between Christ and the clergy, the Church and the clergy. He reassures the people that they can administer the sacrament of baptism themselves. That a marriage is consummated by the act of marriage and is blessed by the priest. The fact that he has to make these things clear to his people shows how deeply religious they are, that they need reassuring. He asked the clergy to remain and to teach when he took over the schools and nationalized church property. God knows he needs teachers to send out all over the island to reach the furthermost corners of it. But the reply, according to our diocesan press, was that priests and nuns would not teach communism to their students. And Castro in his turn taunted them with the fact that all they thought of was money and property.

We are a spectacle to the world, we Catholics, fighting each other like this, flinging taunts back and forth. (After all Castro is a Catholic.)

California

A few months ago I came back from the west coast where I saw the hierarchy silent in the face of the slavery and exploitation of the bracero and the agricultural worker. There had been a lettuce strike in the Imperial Valley where thousands of braceros, imported from Mexico, were harvesting the crop. The Agricultural Workers Organizing Committee, and the Packinghouse Worker's Union held meetings at the entrance to the fields urging the workers to come out on strike and not to take the jobs of their brothers. There were many arrests and some of the organizers were put in prison. Some sympathetic priests came to speak at the meeting and were rebuked by the diocesan officials, some of whom even went so far as to say that some communists masquerading as priests had appeared at the union meetings.

The strike was over by the time I reached El Centro, and I talked with some of the townspeople, all of whom thought it had been a great loss of crop and manpower, a real defeat for worker, for grower and for "broker." I went to the large Catholic Church and found a notice on the door "Anyone asking for jobs or help, go to the police department."

Later I heard Billy Joe Shelby, one of the agricultural workers and himself an organizer, tell how the police were filling up the jails with workers. It was obvious that those in need were not going to go to the police department. And how strange it is that the very priests who complain of the State taking over and of what amounts to state ownership of

72

the indigent, should be the ones who shout communism when the principle of subsidiarity is being put into effect through efforts to organize into unions, and who send the poor to the police and to the State.

Stockton

Later I went with Andy Arellano to skid row in Stockton at five o'clock in the morning and saw the artificial labor shortages created to bolster up the importation of braceros, to make it appear that it was absolutely necessary for the harvesting of the crops to import men without families whose wages are filched from them by profiteering store keepers, who are charged exorbitant sums for cashing checks, for sending money orders.

How sad it is to see men waiting for work, standing in the market place waiting for hours to be hired, sober, industrious men, with a pathetically small paper bag containing a sandwich for their lunch, men with their short handled hoe ready to thin beets at truly backbreaking labor. They say America won't do stoop labor, but there were plenty of Americans there, and Lise Bowman who writes a letter in this issue follows the crops all summer with her husband and a little girl, of four. "I earned money too," the little girl said, and the mother proudly informed us she had earned two or three dollars, picking olives, and had bought her own shoes.

Where are the priests among the poor, following the crops and those who pick them? You can count them on the fingers of one hand. Assigned to parish work, in towns, there is little chance for close contact.

New York

Only a few days after I had returned to New York, I was on my way up Second Avenue to go to Nativity Church which is in the heart of the slums, where Puerto Ricans are crowded together, where store front churches abound and where some of the worst gangs of the city hang out. At night the streets are alive with children. They cannot go to bed until they are ready to drop with exhaustion because the rooms are too crowded. The parents go out to the service jobs in institutions, to the heavy jobs in laundries, to the hard and least paid labor. There are few parochial schools in these slums. But there was a boys' Academy and as I went to the eight thirty Mass, crowds of well dressed, well fed young students were crossing the avenue to make their nine o'clock classes. The contrast between their lives and the lives of the Puerto Rican boys they passed was painful. How many parishes, how many of the clergy are there in these sections of our great city of New York, and how many of the Puerto Ricans are they able to reach? Fr. Janner and his fellow priests break their hearts over their work. Two teen-agers had killed themselves these last months with overdoses of drugs, Fr. Janner told me.

A convent built in the slums for twelve nuns at the cost of $85,000. A family of twelve Puerto Ricans living in a two-room tenement house apartment. These things should not be. Billions of dollars in buildings, plants, as they have come to be called, including Church, school, convent and rectory, and nothing spent on the family, on youth.

Even worse, it is the family who pays for all this, the working man who wants his children to have a "Catholic education," who is afraid of delinquents, who thinks of the sisters and priests as a police force to keep his own children protected, and the Sacraments as an insurance policy against suffering in the life to come. A fearful view of the Church. Yet it is to the Church we must go or starve for the bread of life. It is the priest with his anointed hands who serves us in the great moments of life and love and death throughout our lives.

Catspaws

Another thing. As I passed through Texas there was an account in an El Paso newspaper of Catholic gangs going over the border to fight pro-Castro demonstrators. Was this a way of diverting their energies into safer channels? Perhaps there would be no police action against a gang of young toughs breaking up a meeting of Mexicans who were siding with Castro. They could indulge their desire for fighting with impunity. They were engaging in a holy war, they were fighting for religion, for the "Faith," for "Holy Mother Church." But on the other hand they might be catspaws building up anti Castro sentiment to prepare for the defeat of Castro and the taking back of the nationalized property. They might be fighting the battle of the rich, of the American corporations.

St. Catherine of Siena preached a Crusade, saying that it was better to go fight the heathen and regain the holy land, than for the Italian cities to be fighting among themselves. And on the other hand our Lord said through her, "I have left myself in the midst of you, that what you do for these, I will count as done for myself." And in this she was thinking of the poor.

And St. Teresa of Avila prayed that before her nuns became rich and lived in fine buildings, the walls would fall upon them and crush them. Yet she accepted money from her brothers who went to the New World to make their fortunes. Those fortunes were made by robbing the native population, enslaving them, even wiping them out completely (after baptizing them and anointing them first perhaps.) Hard not to be cynical, hard not to judge. Fr. John J. Hugo said that one could go to hell imitating the imperfections of the saints. He also said, that we loved God as much as the one we loved the least. What a hard and painful thing it is to love the exploiter. When I was interviewed by Mike Wallace on television, and he asked me, "Do you think God loves a Hitler and a Stalin?" I could only quote, "God loves all men. God wills that all men be saved."

One needs to read Raissa Maritain's essay on the "Development of Conscience in the Old Testament Since the Time of Abraham," published in *The Bridge*.

I realize that such a piece of writing as this is more like a meditation than a carefully worked out article, and I hope our readers will forgive me. It is because so many of them have asked me why we printed former articles about Cuba. After all, I am the editor of a monthly paper, presenting a point of view about what is going on in the world, and these events are vital happenings. They are matters of life and death. Our lives, the salvation of souls depend upon our thoughts, words and deeds in relation to them. Certainly our peace of mind does.

Down in South America, during Adlai Stevenson's recent visit, the heads of State indicated that they did not wish to interfere with the Castro regime which had to work out its own salvation in fear and trembling.

While these events are going on in Cuba there have been stirring events in Africa, in Laos. It is because Cuba is only 90 miles away and has now become a Socialist State that it is pertinent to write about it. But one must write also in the light of world history, and all that has happened in these stirring times. "It is not time for anyone to be mediocre," Pius XI said.

Yesterday I got a postal from Mike Gold, Communist columnist for the *Sunday Worker*, who is now in Moscow. I have known Mike since he and I were eighteen and twenty. His wife is a French woman and we collect rocks and sea- weed and shells on her occasional visits. Once they came with their two sons, and played French Christmas carols on their recorders for us, and once he brought me a poster of St. Anne of Brittany to hang in our dining room at the farm. (St. Anne, pray for them.) Mike has diabetes and he writes:

"I was invited by the Writers' Union here for a visit. Liz and I are also being given one of the famed 'cures.' They can't give one a new body but they sure restore some of the life juices. Our next stop is a sanitarium on the Black Sea— the water and the sun cure. All the best, *Mike* (friend of so- cialized medicine and Soviet Humanism.)"

Another friend said recently, "my son is studying medicine and another son the violin. I will have to work a long time to educate them. If they were in Russia they would have the best, they are such gifted children."

Another friend: "the only way my children can get a col- lege education is by entering the armed forces."

Fr. Joseph Becker, S.J., an old friend, told me as I passed through St. Louis that unemployment would increase, that there would be an increasing number of unemployables due to automation, and only those with a college education, and training in their chosen fields would be able to get work. Man needs work as he needs bread.

The Problem

So here we have the problem. The education of the peo- ple. Fifty percent of Cuba's millions were illiterate. No won- der Castro had to talk for so many hours at a time, giving background and painting a picture of what they were aiming at, for a multitude who could not read. He has pleaded for peaceful co-existence, and he has said that the Church has en- dured under the Roman empire, under a feudal system, under monarchies, empires, republics and democracies. Why cannot she exist under a socialist state? He has asked the priests to remain to be with their people and a goodly num- ber of Jesuits, God bless them, have elected to remain and do parish work instead of run schools. They know what it is to be persecuted and even by Churchmen too. They were sup- pressed by the Pope, expelled from Spain, in their own his- tory.

The word socialism has many meanings and Martin Buber used it one way in his great book (now a paper back) *Paths in Utopia.* In Russia it is understood as Marxist socialism as opposed to Utopian Socialism. And "atheism is an integral part of Marxism," Lenin said. If this is the type of socialism which will be taught in Cuban schools which are springing up all over the island, of course we are against it. But there is an atheistic capitalism too, and atheistic materialism which is more subtle and more deadly. The former editor of the *Osservatore Romano* has called attention to this cancer on our social body. Certainly we have kept God out of our own school system here in the United States. What is worst of all is *using* God and religion to bolster up our own greed, our own attachment to property and putting God and country on an equality.

We are certainly not Marxist socialists nor do we believe in violent revolution. Yet we do believe that it is better to revolt, to fight, as Castro did with his handful of men, he worked in the fields with the cane workers and thus gained them to his army—than to do nothing.

We are on the side of the revolution. We believe there must be new concepts of property, which is proper to man, and that the new concept is not so new. There is a Christian communism and a Christian capitalism as Peter Maurin pointed out. We believe in farming communes and cooperatives and will be happy to see how they work out in Cuba. We are in correspondence with friends in Cuba who will send us word as to what is happening in religious circles and in the schools. We have been invited to visit by a young woman who works in the National Library in Havana and we hope some time we will be able to go. We are happy to hear that all the young people who belong to the Sodality of Our Lady in the U. S. are praying for Cuba and we too join in prayer that the pruning of the mystical vine will enable it to bear much fruit. God bless the priests and people of Cuba. God bless Castro and all those who are seeing Christ in the poor. God bless all those who are seeking the brotherhood of man because in loving their brothers they love God even though they deny Him.

We reaffirm our belief in the ultimate victory of good over evil, of love over hatred and we believe that the trials which beset us in the world today are for the perfecting of our faith which is more precious than gold.

"Be glad in the Lord, and rejoice you just and be jubilant all you upright of heart." Because "All the way to heaven is heaven, because He has said, 'I am the Way.'"

The temperature is ninety degrees these days and there certainly has been a long continuing spell of hot weather. Right now at early morning, with the apartment door open, there is a current of air and one can catch a breath. The humidity is high and everything is so damp it is hard to handle paper or pen and one's reading glasses slide down the nose and get filmy. Walking down stairs the stair rail is sticky. August weather, in other words.

During the month we sent out an SOS to friends to help us pay the rent which comes due in frightening frequency. Now in a few days September first will be here. Rent for the 175 Chrystie Street place, St. Joseph's House of Hospitality, is $275. Then there are rents for all the apartments, eight or ten of them, I forget which. Hatty and Scotch Mary have an apartment on Spring Street, and Dianne, Jean, Sharon and I are on Ludlow. Our places are $25 and $21 a month, and our landlord who is a plumber, generously tells us he will give us a few days leeway. If we are evicted I understand landlords can charge an increase of 15 percent on the new tenants.

Rents and utilities remain our biggest problem. Ed Forand goes regularly to the market and gets free vegetables and fruits, and of course we are raising all the vegetables we can eat on the Peter Maurin Farm.

I am writing in front of the window of the little apartment on Ludlow St. very much like the apartment I had when the *Catholic Worker* started so many years ago. There is an ailanthus tree outside the window, an old tree stripped almost bare of leaves. Two doors down there are some beautiful maples, doing very well, and occasionally one sees tenants cleaning up the yard, a little haven of green in this slum area. It is a deep valley these windows look out on. The buildings are six-story walk-ups across the yards fronting on Essex street, and the Ludlow St. buildings are the same.

Essex street is famous for its markets, now under roof but formerly on push cart; and Ludlow street itself since we have been here, has been receiving every night great trucks from the south, from Florida, South Carolina, etc., bearing bushel baskets of small cucumbers and peppers for the innumerable pickle factories all over the East Side. The smell is delightful. When I come home from the office about eight at night, the glaring lights show a scene of unloading and loading. Men and boys stripped to the waist pass down baskets to others to load on small trucks to take elsewhere in the city. It is good to have this bright busy distribution center out in front of the house. Downstairs under me is a Chinese grocery store, and on the corner a kosher restaurant where one can get good barley soup, or in hot weather borscht or schav, which is a green sour-grass soup with sour cream, and served with heavy pumpernickel bread. Good for hot weather lunches.

Orchard, Ludlow and Essex streets, we report to former East Side residents, remain the same but further east on Grand street there is one great cooperative apartment house after another. A few blocks down Grand is St. Mary's Church, and a few blocks down Essex past Canal and East Broadway there is old St. Teresa's surrounded by privet hedges and fronted by small sycamore trees nursed and cherished by the old monsignor who has presided there for many years.

I sit in front of this typewriter to finish a column or so for the CW before going on retreat over Labor Day with the Charles de Foucauld secular fraternity at Mt. Saviour, Elmira, New York. It is only grim necessity which keeps me at this writing. I think longingly of the farm and the green fields and woods, the cool porch where Classie May sits with her infant Brenda Lee and sews. Or of the beach where four mothers and their children are enjoying the salt breezes and bathing, fronting directly on the water as they are. Here is a delightful letter I received from one of the Puerto Rican grandmothers who accompanied her daughter and the children for a ten-day holiday while the poor father had to stay in the city and work.

"Excuse me for the lateness in writing you this letter. I hope you are well. I thank you very much for the summer vacation we stayed at your country. We were there as if we were in Portorican countries. I think since I am old it is the best week I have gone. I am very glad since I knew you and if in any time you need me for something, call me."

AND MORE ABOUT CUBA

To cure unemployment and poverty in Puerto Rico, the United States had advocated birth control in Puerto Rico. The Castro government has not done this in Cuba.

Abortion and sterilization clinics have been set up in Japan to handle overpopulation problems and unemployment, with the tacit (?) approval of the United States. This has not happened in Cuba.

This last month, Archbishop Bernard Mels, Congregation of the Immaculate Heart of Mary and four of his missionaries were imprisoned in Leopoldville, after they had been manhandled and insulted, and twenty other priests beaten. There were reports that thirty of the 120 nuns of the archdiocese were manhandled. A third of the Congolese troops ran amuk and there was widespread rape in Luluabourg, Albertville and Kindu.

Nothing like this has happened in Cuba, though half the priests were deported and (we do not know how many nuns) and all the church property nationalized. None of the priests or nuns are leaving the archdiocese in Africa, although there is almost a complete exodus of teachers, recruited over the last few months, according to an account in the diocesan press.

The killing and dismemberment of the thirteen Italian airmen which took place during the month was because they were taken for Belgians. They were flying supplies to a U.N. garrison of 200 Malayans in Kindu, in the Kivu province. A drunken group of 80 soldiers of the central government perpetrated the crime. None of the 200 or so Europeans living in Kindu were harmed.

On the one hand the Holy Father and the hierarchy of the Church are begging for lay missionaries, for a papal peace corps, for skilled teachers, doctors, technicians to go into missionary areas and we are wondering if these new recruits are getting any teaching about the necessity of laying down their lives for their brothers.

We have reached that stage, in the evolution of peace in England and America when it is not expected of a priest or sister to take up arms to defend themselves on missionary work in foreign countries. (On the other hand, the seminaries are half empty in France, due to the Algerian war, and eighty-five priests on active duty in the army signed a protest against the torture of Algerians by French troops last year.)

On the one hand missionaries go forth ready to die. And on the other hand, we have now a priest defending the right of man to defend his life, to ward off intruders from his family air raid shelter by force of arms. Of course a man is not going to hell for defending himself with a lethal weapon when he has never been taught non-violence, love of enemy, bearing wrongs patiently, doing good to those who despitefully use him, giving up his cloak when his coat is taken, laying down his life for his brother, in other words, living the Gospel way. To speak of men making the supreme sacrifice when they have been trained to kill, to drop bombs on unarmed men, women and children, the sick and old, is blasphemy if we seriously considered it.

A new commandment (not a counsel) was given us by Jesus Christ when he said we should love others as he had loved us, and forgive those who tortured and killed us.

It seems to me a part of the training of all who are in the papal peace corps or in any peace corps, should be in overcoming fear, the fear which paralyzes the flesh and would lead a man to take to any implement handy to wipe out his opponent's threat.

The theologians who justify a man's right to defend himself, are preaching *casuistry*, dealing with *cases* which should be dealt with in the confessional, not in the pulpit or the press.

In Jail

Forgive me if I again speak of my paltry prison experiences. I do not mean to boast, but one must speak from *experience*, and one only meets closely those who have confessed to, or been accused of murder, in our prisons. We may have murderers around us, among the hundreds who come in from the Skid Roads of our country to eat with us, but we ask no questions—a man has to eat. One has felt violence imminent, when a crazed Negro threatened to go berserk when a Bowery woman pushed off the table his new hat which a relative had bought him to attend the funeral of his son who had died the week before. And murder was committed by accident in our Troy New York house of hospitality years ago when one man knocked another man down in a sudden brawl.

But it was in jail I met a gentle woman, mother of five children, who had endured countless beatings from her husband. She was in the cell opposite me, crowded in on an extra bed, which took up all the available room in the cell which was meant for one cot, and she lay there with a look of utter despair on her face and did not eat or move, hour after hour.

That was the last year we were imprisoned, and since we refused to pay bail, we were placed on the floor with women awaiting trial. In our corridor there were two kidnappers and five women accused of murder.

There was a kidnapper down the row who knelt down each night by her cot and said the rosary and some novena prayers, and she urged any of the other women there to join her. By the time Deane and I were imprisoned, there were eight or ten, kneeling around the bed.

It was only this praying which drew the new prisoner out of her despair. That touch of beauty in the midst of this place of horror in which she for the first time in her life found herself, drew her back into the current of life around her. She told me later of her crime, her terror as she felt her husband's hands close about her throat and before breath was choked off completely her clutching at the knife she had been using to cut bread with for her children, and her stabbing him in the side, to make him release his hold on her. It was instinctive, this seizing of any weapon. Could she be considered guilty? I don't know what disposition the judge made of the case, but I am pretty sure, with the testimony of neighbors and with good counsel, if she had it, her crime could have been called *self defense*. Certainly any priest would have absolved her in the confessional. It takes three things, all of them combined, to make a mortal sin, serious matter, due deliberation and full consent of the will.

I am sure it was of these things that Fr. McHugh was thinking as he wrote his articles in *America*. Frantic with fear for his loved ones at an impending raid, and undoubtedly for himself, having sacrificed much to build, at the persuasion of our "leaders," our own Governor of New York, even our President, what he considered an adequate shelter, a dungeon where he and his family were to be imprisoned for weeks, a man pretty certainly would kill when others, as frantic as himself, and without money to build tried to crowd in with him. I can only think he is as likely to be shot as to shoot. But providing he does kill the intruder, and does get out finally and find a priest, undoubtedly that priest, with his moral theology, will find him innocent of mortal sin and not in danger of hell fire, or rather of any more hell than the hell he comes out to. We are now living in a hell with our fears, our despairs, which are filling our mental hospitals, and skid rows around the country.

Unemployment

Peter Maurin was more preoccupied with unemployment than with any other issue and certainly if you consider the old adage, "the devil finds work for idle hands to do," we can apply it to our present arms race. It is only war and the threat of war that keeps as many people employed as we have today. And yet there is enough poverty and destitution in the world to keep our own economy busy providing for others and keep everyone here employed. "From each according to his ability and to each according to his need," Karl Marx said. And St. Paul said, "Let your abundance supply their want." "Bear ye one another's burdens." Love one another, for love is the fulfilling of the law."

Peter talked about a philosophy of work, which would mean, I take it, that we would accept dull work, and monotonous work, which was nevertheless useful work, as part of our human condition, necessary for the common good, and doing penance for turning from God by earning our living by the sweat of our brow. It would mean also that man would seek creative work too, and so fulfill himself as one made in the image and likeness of God Who is Creator. Fr. de Menasce said once that emphasis on sex is the result of man not being able to satisfy his creative instinct in *work*.

Chekhov

This last month I have been reading a lot of Chekhov, beginning with an article by Thomas Mann in which he quotes Chekhov as saying continually "am I not deceiving my readers, in not being able to answer his most important question?" "No other utterance ever had such impact on me; in fact it prompted my close study of Chekhov's biography," Mann writes. That question which Chekhov brings out in all his stories is "What is to be done? What is life for?" Chekhov's conclusion is that we are here to work, to serve our brother, and he was a doctor and wrote on the side in order to support himself through medical school and to support also his father, mother and brothers. He said toward the close of his life that much had been done for the sick but nothing for the prisoner so he set off to visit the far off prison island of Sakhalin, travelling by carriage over flooded countryside, and finally spending three months with the convicts, in the convict colony north of Vladivostok, a visit which resulted in many reforms.

Not to be a parasite, not to live off of others, to earn our own living by a life of service, this answered the question for him. And we have too that sureness of an answer—We must try to make that kind of a society in which it is easier for man to be good. "If you love me, keep my commandments," God says.

Man needs work, the opportunity to work, the tools to work with, the strength to work, the will to work. And when we see a Castro dealing with the problem of unemployment and poverty and illiteracy, we can only say—"We will see this good in him, that which is of God in every man," and we will pray for him and for his country daily.

Warships South of Cuba

I do not wonder Cuba protested the presence of warships in the waters near Cuba, facing the Dominican Republic. And that protest took the form of an assertion by Premier Castro that he was a Marxist-Leninist, and that he would work for a consolidation of his own party with that of the Communists. But even in the reports that came from radio and press there were discrepancies, and I should like very much to read the entire speech. The radio stated that he had been a communist all along, throughout his college years but did not wish to come out openly. The New York Times spoke of his "conversion" as recent. I should say it was as recent as the gunboats off the Dominican Republic.

Bishop Sheen's Quotation

I heard Bishop Sheen tell once the story of the two sons in the Gospel, a story which Jesus himself told. There were two sons, and the Father told the both to go out and to certain tasks. The one son said "I will," and then failed to do the work assigned him. The other said "I won't," and yet went away and did the Father's will. And which of the two sons found favor with the Father?

Marjorie Hughes was reminded of the parable in the Gospel of the man born blind who said to his questioners, after he had been hectored and badgered by men who said, " 'Give glory to God. We ourselves know that this man is a sinner.' He therefore said, 'Whether he is a sinner, I do not know. One thing I do know, that whereas I was blind, now I see.' "

The Cuban people are in that state now, and so are the poor and oppressed of South America, of all Latin America. One thing they know, and that is that work and schooling, land and bread are being provided, and that the Colossus whom they feared and hated, the Yankee of the north, had been defied.

We are not going to win the masses to Christianity until we live it.

1962

January 1962

☐ Dec. 25: "The brightness of your glory has made itself manifest to the eyes of our mind by the mystery of the Word made flesh, and we are drawn to the love of things unseen thru Him whom we acknowledge as God, now seen by men." From the preface in the Christmas Mass.

"What have I on earth but Thee and what do I desire in heaven beside Thee?"

It is joy that brought me to the faith, joy at the birth of my child, 35 years ago, and that joy is constantly renewed as I daily receive our Lord at Mass. At first I thought that following the prayers of the Mass would become monotonous and something for the priest to continue day after day, and that that was why people were silent and bookless. Some Quakers going to Mass with me once said, "Now I know what the Mass is,—it is a meditation." But it is an act, a sacrifice, attended by prayers, and these prayers repeated daily, of adoration, contrition, thanksgiving, supplication are ever there. One or another emotion may predominate but the act performed evokes the feeling of "performing the work of our salvation."

Christmas Eve and Christmas this year I went to the 11 o'clock Mass at St. Thomas, in Pleasant Plains, and was moved to the deepest gratitude that we are in a parish which has two such good priests. That is the greatest gift the Peter Maurin farm had ever received. We were included in the greetings in the parish bulletin, as "largest family in the parish."

Dec. 26: Setting out at 8, Stanley, Mary Hughes and I drove to Vermont to see the Hennessy family. Snow was heavy on the ground, and heavy in the sky tho not yet falling. We did not get there until 5:30 tho we only stopped briefly twice.

Dec. 28. Snow is falling.

Feast of the Holy Innocents. From early morning till late at night the house is riotous—Tamar's nine and two guests, an eight year old and a 15 year old. This morning they were out sledding after a hasty breakfast and now they are in again racing up and downstairs. The furnace fire went out and Eric is downstairs struggling with it. The fire in the kitchen stove and the Franklin stove in the living room are going good. The teen agers have their radio on, Nicky and Margaret, talking loudly are playing Monopoly. There is perpetual motion and perpetual sound from Mary, Martha, Hilaire, and Louise their guest. The house is in a turmoil of caps, coats, mittens, galoshes, scarves, toys and if anything is ever found again it will be thanks to St. Anthony.

The louder the noise, the louder the canary sings. In the kitchen, a mother hen and four chicks she had hatched unseasonably, chirp contentedly in a big box. Even now and then the hen knocks the cover off and comes out into the kitchen for crumbs. There are 3 cats, beautifully furry and Rex, the dog with long ears, beautiful affectionate eyes, a combination of brown beagle and cocker spaniel. He loves everybody, and sleeps with Eric and Hilaire, his head on their pillow. He has found food for himself up in the woods, a dead deer, and yesterday he dragged a leg up the driveway.

Today we are snowed in. "What shall we feed thirteen people for dinner," Tamar muses, and then remembers the 4 lbs. of ground deermeat, which a hunter sent her for holding his stray dog until he returned for it. There are two sacks of potatoes, plenty of squash, pumpkin, turnip, onions, bread and cake. There are two jars of hard candies, and some apples. All the home made cider has turned to vinegar.

One can only try to keep the kitchen orderly, and find a quiet corner to read, write, teaze or card some wool for a comforter.

A goodly amount of spun silk, and a great deal of cotton thread for the loom had come in at Chrystie Street and Tamar wove a silk scarf, and is going to set up the loom in cotton to make some material which she can afterwards dye. Weaving is her "tranquilizer."

Knitting generally is mine, tho I never get beyond scarves. I have made socks for the children, and once in a while achieved a good pair for an adult. One monstrosity I made which would match nothing and was due to be ripped out was seized by Anne Marie as an amusing gift (together with one of her own perfect ones) for a Worker Priest. I hope by now some friendly soul has re-knit it for him.

A friend who is married to a Japanese says that in Japan, knitted sweaters and socks are un-knit, steamed and re-knit to freshen them and prolong their life. In New York, the Italians who had brought woolen mattresses and comforters from the other side, take them apart and clean and recard them before they re-cover them. Wool is a live and healthy warmth.

As I washed and teazed wool for the comforter I had finished last month, during the days I had visitors at the beach house, I thought of God's goodness and the sacramentality of things . . .

July-August 1962

My New Book—the work on which has kept me from my other writing (except some letters)—is out of my hands, aside from reading the galley proofs. At least it is finished if I can keep out of the way of the particular editor to whom I have been assigned. I had thought all the work was done, the work accepted, the contract signed, and "just a few little odds and ends, loose ends, to be attended to." Ed Sammis was the editor Harpers assigned me to. He broke it to me gently. A few additional paragraphs here and there. And then he began to question me. "Who was Peter Maurin and what did he look like, more details about him. You make Ammon Hennacy come alive but not Peter." I'd have to do a few additional chapters! Of course I was glad to have this direction. It was good to have an editor who knew nothing about the beginnings of our work, who could draw from me all those details needed to make our work, its beginnings and its continuance understandable. So I worked steadily for months on the revision. I am rather like the sorcerer's apprentice when I get at the typewriter. When I am turned on, a flood of words come and hundreds of new pages poured out. All of which had to be sorted over by Mr. Sammis and woven into the narrative, as he said.

All the while I worked I kept reminding him, not that I wanted to complain, but that I was pretty well occupied by the life of the family, my own and the Catholic Worker family here in the New York environs, made up of scores of people in town and country. There were births and deaths, marriages, and engagements, and of course always the conflicts that go with community living. I would say that we are living in a hard school where from day to day there is a war going on in which we can only use the weapons of the spirit, and try to practice the non-violence we talk so much about. During the winter this conflict took the shape of a war between young and old, the twenty year olds and our senior citizens, as they are euphemistically called by the press. Since we were a community of need, it was the young ones, two of them, who in this case left to continue their work elsewhere. The next crisis was a moral one, not a simple one of techniques, or emphasis, or choice between two goods. A group of beats or those desiring to follow the life of beats, descended on us. This lasted some months. They came, they went.

My criticism was that they despised the life forces within man, that they were nihilistic rather than pacifist, that their contempt was directed against the very body of man, that temple of the holy Spirit, and that all the four letter words they used so glibly (and so reminiscent of our prison days) was to express this contempt, this hatred,—not only of the square, of the bourgeois around them, but of the life force in man himself. Also they lived and moved among the poor as though they were not there, taking their meager housing space, pushing in to table at the CW to get their share of the food, and so living that they disregarded the affront they offered the simple, reticent, decent and modest men among whom they lived.

All winter I had been reading Chekhov, his letters, stories and novelettes and the very basic philosophy of work that he expressed in his plays and stories gave me good ammunition in my talks about man's necessity to earn his living by the sweat of his brow, not to be a parasite on the social body, but mindful of the common good. I talked too on sex and chastity, and in addition to the Gospel teaching of Jesus, I cited Soloviev's book, "The Meaning of Love," but those to

89

whom I wished to speak were not there. I felt again the great gulf between youth and age. "You can only tell people what they already know," Ade Bethune had said to me once, quoting St. Augustine, (if anyone knows the exact quote I would like to have it). A priest wrote in and asked for a copy of my talk, and the letter was lost and I wish he would write me again if he reads this.

Another occasion for my speaking on the subject of sex, was to a group of non-Catholic students, participating in sit-ins and freedom rides, and puzzled by the changing standards of our times, especially relating to sex. Certainly sex and its place in life is as pertinent as the discussion of war, capital punishment, and the role of the State in man's life. I seldom speak at state universities or non-Catholic colleges without the question of overpopulation, birth control, abortion, and euthanasia coming up. The entire question of man's control over the life of others, over the life forces within man, is one of the most profound importance today. Kirilloff debated the question—Did God create me or is my life my own, to do with as I chose? And as an absolute gesture of defiance, an assertion of independence, a denial of God's existence, he took his life.

New Houses

My book, which the publisher wishes to call "The Cost of Love," and which I urge to be called "Loaves and Fishes," will be about Pete Maurin and the Catholic Worker, how it started, and continued through his life time and how it has gotten along since his death. It was good to bring the Catholic Worker story up to date, to let people know that we go on in spite of jail sentences, evictions, the comings and goings of people—that we are a family, and our very readers make up that family together with us at Chrystie Street and the farm. To let them know that there are other houses starting up. There is not only Ammon's House of Hospitality in Salt Lake City, but also the new one, St. Elijah house in Oakland, and St. Demetrius house in Boulder, Colorado. People come and go, houses open and close, but there are always readers of the paper, inspired by the charm of Lady Poverty and the means she offers, and by the love of their brothers to embrace this life and begin to study all it entails in non-violence and personalism.

Probably the book will come out next January. By then many other things will have happened and I will have to write another book. Perhaps a book about Brazil. I suppose the grapevine has spread the news that I am contemplating a trip to Brazil and making all my plans and suffering many delays. My book *The Long Loneliness* has been translated into Portuguese by Aimee Amorosa Lima and has been widely circulated these last few years. So our work is known there. The McCloskey articles about the Catholic Worker movement which was part of his Harvard thesis was translated into Spanish and circulated in the Argentine.

MORE ABOUT CUBA

Last month the National Council of Catholic Men, with the consent of the Bishops of the United States, were making a documentary on the Catholic Worker movement, a week's work of filming to be condensed into a one-half hour of television time on a Sunday morning in this coming September on the program, Look Up and Live.

One of the questions asked of a group of the editors sitting in the third floor office on Chrystie Street was, "Do you agree with everything that is written in The Catholic Worker?"

As I remember it, all of them answered "No," and I would have given the same answer myself, if I had been asked. But I was there just to introduce the others.

On another occasion the chancellor of the archdiocese of New York asked me if I saw everything that went into the Catholic Worker, for which after all I am responsible as editor and publisher. I told him yes, and that is true with few exceptions, when the paper was printed during my absence, and the material coming in late was used at once, assuming my approval. Perhaps on two or three occasions I disapproved of the emphasis given by the placing of material, as well as by the articles themselves. But no great harm was done.

Cardinal Hayes sent us word years ago, through Monsignor Chidwick that he approved our good work, and it was to be understood that we would make mistakes and the thing was not to persist in them. On another occasion Cardinal Spellman expressed approval of some of the aspects of our work, though it is undoubtedly true that there are many aspects of it which he is probably very dubious about, if not downright disapproving. The fact remains that we have been given, from the very first, the freedom which it is to be expected we laymen should take in handling temporal affairs, which after all is our province. That is a great gift. It seems to me that if the *Catholic Worker* did nothing else but indicate to critics the enormous freedom there is in the Church, which laymen so far have not taken advantage of, it is doing a good job.

A few months ago when I had a visit with Cardinal Leger in Montreal and he asked me about the position of the *Catholic Worker* in the church, I replied that we were a group of Catholics, engaged in writing and editing a paper dealing with the great problems of the day—the role of the State in man's life, war and peace, means and ends. That we had no chaplains, were in no way an organization included in Catholic Action, that we were under no bishop, and that we were therefore free to explore all possibilities of reform and restoration without committing the hierarchy to dangerous positions, and to try to rebuild the social order to make a better society "where it is easier for men to be good." To be good men, to be holy men is to be whole men, living a full life, developing all their capacities for good, using the talents God has given them.

The Cardinal had been looking at me from under his heavy brows, his deep set eyes scarcely visible. But when he lifted his head he smiled and commented, "St. John the Baptist."

We are among those who go ahead and prepare the way. This long preliminary is to indicate that we are Catholics in good standing, that we revere our clergy and are not hesitant to speak to the clergy. To print the criticism of others is not to mean that we are anti-clerical. We are reporting events and the point of view which led to these events.

Of course we are not in agreement with the most basic and fundamental point of view as expressed by our friend Mario Gonzales in his letter on Cuba. (It was our printer who put that bold black box around the letter which makes it stand out and which gives it so much prominence. And after all, it is a letter dealing with an issue of terrible importance.)

First of all we must quote Lenin, "Atheism is an integral part of Marxism." We therefore are not Marxist Leninists. At the same time, we admit to being fascinated by the story of the lives of both Marx and Lenin. We advise our readers to read such a book as "Three Who Made a Revolution" by Bertram Wolfe to understand what I mean. Having heard

Trotsky speak back in 1917 at Cooper Union and having interviewed him with another reporter from the New York Call who spoke Russian, I was doubly interested in the story of Trotsky, that tragic life ended by an assassin. To be interested in a Garibaldi, a Napoleon, a Castro is to be interested in men who have made and are making history, and to be inspired furthermore by their zeal, their study, their hard labors and to say again and again that until we ourselves as followers of Christ abjure the use of war as a means of achieving justice and truth, we Catholics are going to get nowhere, in criticizing men who are using war to change the social order. Too often, as Cardinal Mundelein said once, we will find ourselves on the wrong side.

We agree of course with the letter's utter condemnation of the Cuban invasion of a year ago, and the deception of the American people by both President Kennedy and Adlai Stevenson, who had too much conscience and not enough ruthlessness to be all-out villains and make a thorough job of it. So it failed, as it was bound to fail in the long run even if it had been successful at once. There are all manner of ways of resisting the enemy in an occupied country, and I am not talking about sabotage and destruction either. I am talking about the resistance the Christian ought to give, to be trained to give, with non-violence, with Christian love, with what cooperation can be given in all things which are for the common good.

What if men are stripped of their goods? "If a man takes your cloak give your coat too." It is good to be compelled to practice the poverty (not destitution) which is the ideal of the Christian life and most in conformity with the life of Jesus Christ. There is many a young priest throughout the world, and old ones too, caught in the System, going along with building laws, State requirements, involved with building operations, financing, interest, debts—wearing their lives away building ever bigger buildings and institutions while the institution of the family and the poor are left to the state to care for. There is too little personal contact with the poor. See Pius XII Christmas Message 1952.

Helen C. White's book, *To the End of the World* is about the French revolution but she confessed to me that she wrote it for our time. In that book there were priests and bishops who fled to other countries and tried to stir up armed intervention. And there were those who stayed, who went to prison. The head of the Sulpicians sat in jail and said, "Now I have the time to study St. Thomas!"

In our own day the persecution in Mexico was overcome by non-violence and civil disobedience. The French in Canada live in what to them is an occupied country and hold on to their language and religion and culture. It is the U.S. with press and cinema which corrupts them.

The Church cannot be destroyed, the gates of hell cannot prevail against it. At the same time we recognize the fact that in England the Catholic religion was wiped out so that only a remnant remained. All the Bishops but one went with the State at that time.

Over and over again we hear that such a technique as non-violence, voluntary poverty, suffering, and prayer and fasting are too heroic weapons to expect the laity to use. And yet in our time they are *compelled* to use them, and without the training and preparation necessary to such heroism. In the life of the family heroic virtue is expected, in accepting from the hand of God each child sent or accepting continence or celibacy within marriage. The teaching of the Church in regard to marriage and its indissolubility demands over and over again heroic sanctity. And in both cases without the help of the teaching of voluntary poverty and the mutual aid which maternity guilds and credit unions in the parish could give.

Above all, we need to hear more and more about the doctrine of the Mystical Body of Christ. "We are all members, one of another. Where the health of one member suffers, the health of the entire body is lowered." "An injury to one is an injury to all," the old I.W.W.'s used to say. We are all members or potential members of the body of Christ, St. Augustine said. And since there is no time with God, this includes Chinese, Russians, Cubans and yes, even those who profess Marxism-Leninism.

And why else did we print the letter besides our feeling that it presented authentic news from Cuba, giving the actual feeling of a great many of the people. It admits to the Leninist orientation and tells us that parochial schools are all closed and that the clergy have no newspapers and magazines in which to express themselves.

To speak frankly, this is a wonderful opportunity for the Catholic press to practice the silence of the Trappist, using another spiritual weapon. Baron von Hugel, a great Catholic layman and theologian said once that he was in danger of losing his faith if he read the diocesan press. I can understand such a remark when I read some of the hymns of hate and the Hearst-like editorials, in some of the papers.

In none of the letters sent to us in protest was there recognition of the fact that the writer, Gonzales, was as much opposed in his own way to the Marxist-Leninist position as we ourselves. His position is that of the anarchist, pleading for the principle of subsidiarity, calling for "secular monasticism," using that expression when speaking to the clergy in order to make them understand the idea of farming communes, or collectives, or cooperative farms.

What has not been done voluntarily has now been done with the revolution, by force of arms, by confiscation, though the Castro regime has offered to pay, over the years, for the property nationalized. (Little attention has been paid to such offers.)

I must assure Mario Gonzales that I would not be teaching "socialist morality of generosity and sacrifice," but would certainly try to speak always in terms of the generosity and sacrifice of Jesus Christ, our brother and our God.

Gonzales says, "a good Catholic can easily accept the 'materialist' doctrine of paradise on earth." He probably was remembering my oft-quoted line from St. Catherine of Siena, "All the Way to Heaven is Heaven, because He said, I am the Way."

As for the bitterness of soul expressed by Mario, I confess that I too have felt that bitterness, but at the same time felt self judged. I too am immersed in comforts, in luxury even, with enough food to eat, a roof over my head, even the means to travel, thanks to people who pay my way. I know that people look at me and judge me with the same harshness as the clergy are judged. "How hard it is to be what you want the other fellow to be" as Peter Maurin used to comment when criticisms were hurled about.

I must confess that righteous wrath as well as any kind of wrath wearies me. Rebellion too, I find exhausting. To grow in love, to rejoice, to be happy and thankful even, that we are living in such parlous times and not just benefiting unwittingly by the toil and suffering of others—rejoicing even that there is every sign that we are going to be given a chance to expiate here and now for our sins of omission and commission—and so to help the revolution and convert the revolutionaries. This is a dream worth dreaming, and the only kind of vision powerful enough to stand side by side with the

Marxism-Leninism which with its vision is working out in our day the Legend of the Grand Inquisitor.

Passports

I have obtained a passport with no difficulty, swearing that I would defend my country by those means which did not conflict with my conscience. The passport was sent to me three days after my application. But having been invited by a number of friends who have been to Cuba or who live in Cuba now, to come and see how things are going there now, I decided I would as a journalist apply for a Cuban visa. One of our readers, a rabbi from Boston, whom I had met at Fr. Robert Hovda's in North Dakota, wrote me that he had had no difficulty in getting a visa from the United States government as editor of a Jewish magazine. So I sent in my letter of application together with my passport three weeks ago and have heard nothing since. It should not take more than ten days, one of our experienced traveller friends assured me. So I wait.

Meanwhile, without the passport I cannot get my Brazilian visa. At that embassy I was assured that if one stayed only two months one did not need a visa. But the steamship line (Danish) which goes to Brazil sent me word this morning that they would not receive any passengers who did not have a visa to Brazil in their hands two weeks before sailing.

Change of Plans

More news has just arrived which makes me believe that it would be better for me to postpone my trip to Brazil until next April—but I am still trying for the Cuba visa and if it comes through (it is supposed to be even slower on the Cuban than it is on the American side), I shall be able to give more direct reports from these as to the cooperative farms, the family, the church and the clergy.

There is a good staff at both farm and beach and city, and I feel that this is a good time to do this travelling and writing, especially since God has sent me the means, most unexpectedly, to pay my fare. I am offered hospitality and can live on rice and beans so this will be no luxury trip. I ask our readers' prayers that the way will open up to me on these travels, this pilgrimage.

PILGRIMAGE TO CUBA—PART I

So now I am going to take our readers with me to Cuba, those who wish to read about it, even those who read what I write with doubts as to whether I am going to be truthful, or see the whole picture. I'm afraid there will be plenty of readers who will say that I am going to see only what "they" wish me to see. They will say that I will see only what I myself wish to see.

I have been thinking about that, because I wish to be truthful. But the trouble is if you have only managed to survive the filth, the misery, the destitution of our U.S. Skid Rows by seeing Christ in the people thereon, you've got yourself pretty well trained to find the good, to find concordances, to find that which is of God in every man. The trouble is that our country has severed relations with Cuba, a country the size of Pennsylvania, 90 miles away from Florida. I am afraid that I can only look upon this original breach of friendly relations as a cold war over possessions, what we claim are our own possessions in Cuba. When the revolution which we cheered at first turned out to be very radical, getting to the roots of the troubles of our day, and when a start was made to build a new social order (not within the shell of the old, as Peter Maurin always recommended) but by doing away as quickly as possible with the old, then the trouble began. The history of it is in all our journals, the history of the past as well as the history of the present.

The fact of the matter is that now Cuba is a Marxist-Leninist country, a Socialist Republic and we are supposed to have no relations with her. To get permission to visit Cuba, I wrote to the State Department and also to the Czechoslovakian Embassy which is representing Cuba in Washington. (The United Nations and the Vatican both recognize Cuba still, and of course England, Canada, Mexico etc.) If I wish to be in touch with my own country in Cuba I must go to the Swiss Embassy there.

One of our readers tells me to be sure and say that the U.S. granted permission first, and that there was more delay on the Cuban side. Someone else said that the Czechoslovakian Embassy had twice their own work to do now. I looked them up in the World Book, a very good encyclopedia which my grandchildren use in high school in Vermont, a thoroughly conservative and Republican state. It was printed in 1961 and stated that Czechoslovakia had outstripped all communist block countries in economic gains and was second only to Russia in granting foreign aid funds to underdeveloped nations.

When the permissions were in order I went to the offices of the Garcia Diaz line and got my ticket, tourist class, for eighty dollars. It is a big office on the ground floor of the Cunard building, and there were twenty-two desks there and only five of them occupied at the time. It was eleven o'clock in the morning. Unless I wished to go by bus to Miami and by plane from Miami to Cuba where there are two flights a day, this was the only way I could go by boat from New York. The Bull line used to go there, but now all trade has been cut off.

There was no one else but me there as I got my ticket, which when delivered turned out to be three pages like a bill of sale, the first for me, the second yellow sheet for the purser and the third the passage contract, a blue sheet full of finely printed rules and regulations, forty of them.

I read them all, and learned that I would be under the rule of Spain while I was on the boat, and probably sitting under a picture of General Francisco Franco. There is also a chapel on board, and though the trip will be midweek, I was assured there would be Mass on board. But the contract speaks only of Sundays.

There is medical care on the boat, I will be in a cabin with three other passengers, and rule sixteen says, "no passenger will pretend to use a cabin by himself unless he had paid for sole occupancy of same." So if there are no other passengers, I will keep strictly to my fourth of the cabin and not "pretend to use it by myself."

It is to be understood moreover that there may be delays in sailing and that the captain can change the route. Also the captain and company is not to be considered responsible for "total or partial non-execution of the transportation contract caused by the cessation of labor, total or partial strikes, boycott of patrons, workman, officers sailors or employees of whatever class, whether in the service of the Company or otherwise; or because of the disarming or total or partial stoppage of the steamers of the company, owing to a general or partial lockout, regardless of who are the promoters. It is understood that the expense and risk of such delays shall in each case, be borne by the passengers." Rule 9 says that neither the company nor the ship is liable for loss of, or injury to the passenger or to his property . . . occasioned by accidents, fires, explosion, peril of the sea, or any unforseen circumstances or by barratry, fault or negligences whatsoever of the Captain Pilot, sailors or members of the crew or passengers.

If I did not remember that the Spanish have been sailing the high seas for hundreds, perhaps thousands of years, I might begin to get worried at this point.

Furthermore, I am not permitted to trespass the limits of my class which is tourist. Rule 25 says that I must deliver to the purser, for his custody, "fire arms, munitions and any other dangerous articles, otherwise the passenger will be responsible for all the dangers resulting therefrom." Rule 28 says that passengers are responsible for all "injuries or prejudices caused during their stay on board."

At this point I stopped considering the rules and regulations and tucked the ticket away in the beautiful new passport case which Stanley V. bought for me as a going away present. I also have two ten dollar checks from friends and a Spanish missal from Fr. La Fontaine who is pastor at Holy Crucifix Church.

That brings up the question of money for travelling. Our lives are such open books at the Catholic Worker that we not only "have to give an account of the faith that is in us" as St. Peter told us to, but make an accounting of our expenses besides. So let me say here that a legacy enabled me to contemplate travelling, and the money which will come in for speaking engagements this winter will reimburse the office later. I shall travel as usual by tourist, bus, and so on and be grateful for hospitality offered.

To get back to my initial paragraphs and amplify them—of course I am going to see what I want to see, and that is the farming communes, whether they are state farms or collectives. I want to see how far they have gotten in diversified farming. I want to see how the family fits into the new economy, what the school situation is, what the church is permitted to do in giving religious instruction, whether any new churches are being built in the country districts or on the new collectives. I want to see a country where there is no unemployment, where a boy or a man can get a job at any age, when he wants it, at some socially useful work. "There is nothing better for a man than to rejoice in his work." *Ecclesiastes*.

Of course I know that the island is an armed camp, that all the people make up the militia. It is too late now to talk of non-violence, with one invasion behind them, and threats of others ahead of them. And according to traditional Catholic teaching, the only kind Fidel Castro ever had, the good Catholic is also the good soldier.

Several of our old editors have accused us of giving up our pacifism. What nonsense. We are as unalterably opposed to armed resistance and armed revolt from the admittedly intolerable conditions all through Latin America as we ever were. In Chile, land is being redistributed and reforms are taking place in many Latin American countries. But how much land, and to whom, and with what means to cultivate it? Is it good land, or waste land, and is the redistribution made in the spirit of Ananias and Sapphira? See the story in the first chapter of the Acts of the Apostles in the New Testament.

We are against capital punishment whether it takes place in our own country or in Russia or Cuba. We are against mass imprisonments whether it is of delinquents or counter revolutionaries. Incidentally Judge Liebowitz spoke of the rehabilitation of prisoners in the Soviet Union on his return from a visit to the penal institutions of that country.

No one expects that Fidel will become another Martin of Tours or Ignatius and lay down his arms. But we pray the grace of God will grow in him and that with a better social order, grace will build on the good natural, and that the Church will be free to function, giving us the Sacraments and the preaching and teaching of the Man of Peace, Jesus.

I know from long experience how few pacifist priests there are and how patrioteering is liable to incite the youthful middle class to such incidents as that of last week, when a group of students, in two yachts, shelled Havana, delivering sixty rounds into a suburb where Castro was supposed to be speaking. The State Department denies any knowledge of this attack, and considering the exposed activities of the CIA I would not wonder that the right hand does not know what the left is doing. And since James Donovan, famous lawyer, had just been sent to Cuba to negotiate for the release of more of the prisoners taken at the time of the invasion a year ago last April, it stands to reason that such a weekend attack must have been embarrassing to the U.S. State Department.

An assignment like this is interesting but also presents the greatest difficulties. I am most of all interested in the religious life of the people and so must not be on the side of a regime that favors the extirpation of religion. On the other hand, when that regime is bending all its efforts to make a good life for the people, a *naturally* good life (on which grace can build) one cannot help but be in favor of the measures taken.

The motive is love of brother, and we are commanded to love our brothers. If religion has so neglected the needs of the poor and of the great mass of workers and permitted them to live in the most horrible destitution while comforting them with the solace of a promise of a life after death when all tears shall be wiped away, then that religion is suspect. Who would believe such Job's comforters. On the other hand, if those professing religion shared the life of the poor and worked to better their lot and risked their lives as revolutionists do, and trade union organizers have done in the past, then there is a ring of truth about the promises of the glory to come. The cross is followed by the resurrection. Orwell said one of the tragedies of the present day was the loss of a sense of personal immortality. But are those to be believed who see their brother in need and do not open their hearts, their doors, their purses to them? Whatever we have over and above what we need belongs to the poor, we have been told again and again by the fathers of the church and the saints up to the very present day. But how much does a man need to cultivate the talents God has given him? To raise his family and educate them and to take care of his older ones. How much land does a man need?

The land in Cuba is very fertile according to the American Peoples Encyclopedia, and grows not only sugar cane. One and a half million acres was devoted to this crop in 1937 and American capital has spent millions on this industry. Tobacco was the second crop and is grown everywhere. Bananas, corn, coffee, tomatoes, lima beans, egg plant, pepper, okra, cucumbers, potatoes—the list is endless, and then from this out of date encyclopedia which can tell us much of Cuba in the past, we learn that 95 per cent of the crops are sent to the United States. The extent of the mineral deposits is unknown. Iron deposits believed to be 3 and one-half billion tons, held largely in reserve by U. S. Steel companies. "Copper, manganese, nickel, chrome, gold and asphalt—extensive. The U. S. was Cuba's chief customer. Raw materials were imported for manufacture by cheap labor." Canned goods, sugar, syrup, molasses, cigars, tobacco, canned fruits, lobster, condensed milk, peanut and castor oil, sisal rope and cordage, cigar boxes and pencils, shoes from alligator skins, sponges, mother of pearl, tortoise shell, paper, furniture, cement, brick, leather, starch, textiles, alcohol and rum. The list is endless. But why was everyone so poor?

Forests used to be one half of the island and now (in 1937) they were one sixth. Fish the year round and now provides large part of the food supply. There were railways, bus lines, cartroads and Cuba was an important point for steamship lines. There was a great influx of tourists. The Pan American and Royal Dutch Air Lines flew there.

Now there are no tourists, there is no trade with the United States.

When Columbus discovered Cuba (so named by the Indians) he found "mild, inoffensive tribes," ruled by chiefs who had religious beliefs in God and a future life. Cities were founded in 1512 and 14 by Velasquez: Baracoa, Santiago, Trinidad, San Cristobal de la Habana. The Spanish could not exact labor from the Indians so they were exterminated and Negro slaves brought in. Slavery was only suppressed in 1845.

According to the World Book, 1961, the rural population makes up 70 per cent of Cuba's population. Seventy per cent white, 25 per cent Negro and five per cent Indian.

Perhaps all these facts are known to our readers but I know I had to refresh my memory though I had read many books and articles about Cuba these last years. But what one reads in books is not enough. I will try to make the Cuban story come alive.

October 1962

PILGRIMAGE TO CUBA—PART II

When the *Guadalupe* sailed from Harborside, Jersey City, on Sept. 5, there was a chill in the air and the sea was rough.

But within a day the weather became very hot and so it has remained, day after day of fearful tropical heat, which keeps one bathed in perspiration from head to foot, which makes dressing a burden. Imagine trying to dress after a shower, without drying off! But I prayed for strength daily, to cover the assignment I had set for myself which would take a month. I could not stay longer if I wished to, because the visa granted by the Cuban government was for only thirty days. Our own government gave me leave to stay for three months.

To synopsize, the first three of those thirty days I spent hours each morning in various offices of the ministry of foreign relations, to get my credentials which consisted of a little green card with my picture on it, stating that I was of the Press. But the hours were fruitful. They asked me questions about the States, and I asked the questions about Cuba, about the revolution, about religion, state farms, schools and so on. I talked to Raul Lazo, to Olga Finlay, to Rodolpho Saracino and others and they all most hopefully asked me what I wanted to see in Cuba, and there was some talk of tours but none of it came to anything, which was just as well. It was far better that I should find my own way, pay my own way, and in the long run I "covered" the island, as much as is possible in a month.

St. Anthony was my guide and I called upon him continually. Recalling his unsuccessful foray into Morocco, among the infidel, I asked him to protect me, and all I found was friendliness and help everywhere.

The neatest favor he granted me was to enable me to slip under the barrier set up suddenly by the government preventing correspondents from leaving Havana, and ordering them to turn in all press cards which were now obsolete. But when the order came by individual courier on a motorcycle to each correspondent, at ten o'clock at night, marked urgent, to be opened in my absence by my host where I was staying, I was already sitting on my suit case in a long line in the bus station, in a mob of soldiers, campesinos, and their wives and children, all on the way to Oriente province, the furthest province away from Havana, an eighteen hour trip. It was a good thing I did not know of the new order since I had to sit there until four in the morning, because if I had I would have either had to obey or look upon each militia man with trepidation. (I would have obeyed out of courtesy to the country which permitted the entry of an enemy.) My

103

companion on the trip was a young man by the name of Charles Horwitz, graduate of the University of Chicago, who had worked at teaching in one of East Harlem's schools for the past two years. He aimed to stay for a year and teach in Cuba, but on the day of our return, he was picked up by security police and taken to the immigration office and held there for two nights—then put on a plane for Miami.

It took us a long time to find the reason for his detention. He was permitted to telephone us and to see one of our friends, and he said he was treated well. The reason for his expulsion was undoubtedly because he had been detained for his visa in Miami the month before and had talked too much to counter-revolutionaries there. He is an insatiable questioner and as such was invaluable to me on our trip inland.

I had, of course, no interviews with Fidel Castro, Che Guevara or Raul Castro or any other revolutionary leader. However I listened to some of them at a meeting in the Chaplin Theater which holds 5,000, five hours, until two in the morning. They all spoke loud and long and there was much audience participation. After a particularly rousing paragraph, and it could be for more faithful attendance at the schools set up all over the island as well as a call for resistance to United States aggression, the cheers and rhythmic hand-clapping and chanting began and continued until, in the case of Fidel, a motion from him meant a band blaring the opening chords of the National Anthem which quieted them at once.

But sometimes the interruption was to sing a ballad about the revolution or about the "year of alphabetization," specially composed for the purpose. These were the hymns of the new order. It is hard to get used to the words coined for the new regime. To "alphabetize" meant to teach someone to read and write. Just as in the case of Frank Laubach, the Protestant missionary and mystic, "each one teaches one" was being worked out religiously. To be an *analfabetico*, means to be an illiterate. My hostess in speaking of Marjorie Rios, said she had alphabetized Rosa, her maid. And every night in Havana every person, hotel clerk, waiter, dishwasher (who belong to the union of gastronomics) goes to school for an hour and a half. This goes for the entire island in every town, I was later to find out. In the case of the *gastronomics*, the first emphasis was on cleanliness.

This year is "the year of planification" which is an easier word to say.

That first meeting in Havana was a memorable one. I had been staying at a cheap little hotel off the Prado, which was formerly the red-light district. All hotels have been nationalized, and the prices set. Rooms were hard to get, since many hotels were occupied by students and couples coming in from the provinces on their vacations which are compulsory, one month a year.

I had talked to Lopez, the hotel clerk who got $150 a month, paid eighteen a month for rent on a little house which he would own in five years. I had talked to the waiters in the corner counter restaurant, and to the boys who cleaned the rooms. I did not know that slogan, "A tip makes the heart of a workingman sick," and had given one of the boys a dollar. He came back a few minutes later with a can of evaporated milk as a present to me! (About the food situation, more later.)

When I telephoned Lou and Lanna Jones, friends of Bill Worthy, of the *Afro-American*, they told me of this final meeting of educational leaders at which Fidel was to speak. (Everyone says "Fidel." There are pages of Castros in the telephone book.) They both worked in the ministry of education, one as a psychologist and the other as a social worker, and they would get an extra pass for me. We were accompanied by Helena Freyre de Andrade, a beautiful young woman whose grandfather had been·mayor of Havana and who was head of one of the departments.

The place was jam-packed of course, outside as well as in, and the first rows were reserved for foreign delegates, of which Ghana was most outstanding, and of others with special passes. We had seats in the third row, right under the rostrum from which Fidel was to speak. Confident as he was of his audience, he came last, not beginning until almost twelve. In my opinion, having heard him on radio many times and this time face to face, he is a truly great speaker, clear, distinct, and repeating the points he wishes to strike home over and over again. "He is the greatest teacher in Cuba" Lou Jones says. Like all people with enthusiasm, he tends to the kind of happy fervor we at the Catholic Worker are well used to.

"They love him so," Lou said solemnly, "that when he went to the scene of a bomb explosion, and a second explosion followed, the crowd threw themselves on him as in a football tackling, to save him! Once when he was speaking at one of the *concentrations*, (the huge outdoor meetings) it began to rain, and they would not let him continue speaking, because he had had laryngitis, chanting 'Cover your head, cover your head' and he finally had to do it."

I quote Lou because I have heard it said in the States that Fidel has gone insane with power, that he is a madman, used by the Communists, and now more recently that he is losing his hold on the people. He did not at all look like a madman to me. He is taller than those about him and he holds his head high. He has a trick of pulling himself up, taking a deep breath which throws his chest out still further, as though he were putting all he has into what he is saying.

This night, in that packed theater, heavy with heat and the smell of nardo lilies which bordered the platform and table at which sixteen people sat, President of Havana University, Marinelli, an old time Communist and outstanding educator, considered a man of integrity even by non-communists, Nunos Jimenez, who had fought with Fidel, and whose text on the geometry and geography is used in all the schools, and many others, I heard this leader of revolution, Fidel Castro, speak for the first time, and his talk was all directed to the youth of the country, for whom, he said, the revolution had been fought.

"Children are born to be happy," is a slogan one sees over and over again, and he pointed out that youth could best help the revolution by perfect attendance at school, by devotion to their studies, by emulating others who led, by self-sacrifice, discipline, self-abnegation. I heard these religious words, spoken with fervor, with passion even, and I kept thinking, "To seek for wisdom is to seek for God. The more we know of the natural world around us, in science as well as in philosophy, the more we know of God."

Television, radio, and each daily paper of course runs the complete speech of Fidel the morning after it is given. The presses are held up until the last words come in. And in this place, as of more interest to our readers and to show his style, I want to reprint some of another speech, that famous speech of March 13, which to Catholics seems to guarantee freedom of religion. Let me insert here that I went to Mass and Communion daily, that churches, but not schools are open, that almost 200 priests remain and more are coming in for those who left voluntarily (intimidated, insulted, in some cases threatened, but not coerced to go) that two minor seminaries are open, active catechism classes continue and the presence of sisters and an active secular institute of women rejoices the heart.

This speech was delivered to a University of Havana meeting, commemorating the fifth anniversary of the unsuccessful attack on Batista's palace. It was in the presence, Fidel said, "of the sons and daughters of the workers, the humble, of the masses from the countryside." During the ceremonies the master of ceremonies read, among other documents, the political testament of Jose Antonio Echevarria.

"He *began* to read it," Fidel said. "He read the first paragraph. He read the second paragraph. He began to read the third paragraph and when he was at the end of the third paragraph we noticed that without reading three lines he skipped to the fourth paragraph. Listen, *companeros.*" (This word is different from comrade, and means literally those with whom one breaks bread.) "Listen, *companeros,* and do not be hasty to pass judgment, nor even to blame the *companero.* It seemed to us that he skipped. And out of curiosity we read that part since he had skipped it. And it says—I am going to read the third paragraph 'Our pledge to the people of Cuba was given in La Carta de Mexico which united the youth in one line of conduct and action. But the circumstances needed for the student sector to fulfill the role assigned to it were not present at the right moment forcing us to postpone the fulfillment of our pledge.' From there he skips . . . 'If we fall may our blood . . .' and I read the three lines which are:

'We believe that the time has come for us to fulfill our pledge. We are confident that the purity of our intentions will bring us God's blessing so that we may bring the rule of justice to our nation.'"

Fidel commented that he asked the master of ceremonies when he finished reading about the omission. The *companero* replied: "When I entered I was given instructions. I told them that I was going to read this and they told me to take out these three lines."

"Is it possible, *companeros?*" Fidel cried out. "Let us analyze it. *Companeros,* could we be so cowardly, and could we be so politically warped, as to come here to read the political testimony of Jose Antonio Echevarria and be so cowardly, so morally wretched, as to suppress three lines?"

"It is known that a revolutionist may hold a religious belief. He may hold it. The revolution does not force anyone. It

107

does not go into his heart of hearts. It does not exclude the men who love their country. The men who want justice to exist in their country, justice which will put an end to exploitation, abuse and odious imperialist domination. It does not force them. Nor does it hold them in disgrace simply because they may have in their heart of hearts some religious belief."

He goes on to say that through out history exploiters have used religion as a counter revolutionary weapon. "Even the criminals who came to Playa Giron brought with them four priests, he said.

"But what fault is this of any good Catholic, a sincere Catholic, who may be a member of the militia, who supports the revolution, who is against imperialism, who is against illiteracy, who is against the exploitation of man by man, who is against all social injustices? What fault is this of his?

"Very well now. We write a revolutionary document. We publish it in several different languages. All the people support it. More than a thousand citizens, who are present when it is read, vote for it. It creates an extraordinary impression in Latin America. And what do we say? We say that in the struggle for national liberation, in the struggle against imperialism, all progressive elements, all patriotic elements, should be united and that in that front there should be not only the sincere Catholic, who has nothing to do with imperialism or with latifundismo, but also the old Marxist fighter.

"We declare this to the whole world and we come here with an unheard of display of cowardice to delete from the testament of a *companero* the invocation he made of God's name. While on the one hand we tell them that they have to unite, and that if they are patriotic and revolutionary in the fight against *latifundismo* and exploitation, no obstacle is posed by the fact that one is a believer. That one has a religion, is a Christian or any other—and that other may be a Marxist, putting his faith in Marxist philosophy—that that is not an obstacle: and we come here with this display of cowardice to suppress a phrase. This could not be overlooked. Because what is this? A symptom! A wretched tendency-cowardly, warped—of someone who does not have faith in Marxism, of one who does not have faith in the revolution, of one who does not have faith in his ideas.

"Into what is the revolution changed by this? Into a tyranny! And that is not revolution! Into what is the revolution changed? Into a school of docile spirits? And that is not the revolution. And what must the revolution be? The revolution must be a school of revolutionists. The revolution must be a school of courageous men. The revolution must be a school of unfettered thought. The revolution must be a forger of character and of men. The revolution must above all be faith in one's own ideas, application of one's ideas to the reality of history and to the reality of life. The revolution has to induce men to study, to think, to analyze in order to possess profound conviction, so profound that there will be no need to have recourse to such tricks.

"If we constantly speak of this, it is because we have faith in the people, because we believe in revolutionary ideas, because we know that our people are a revolutionary people, and because we know that our people will be more revolutionary each day, because we believe in Marxism-Leninism, because we believe that Marxism-Leninism is an undeniable truth. It is simple because of this, because we have faith in our ideas and in the people that we are not so cowardly as to be able to accept such a thing."

This was not all of his talk. And will it be shocking to our readers to learn that as I heard him speak three other times, the sound of his voice, his manner of oratory, his constant repetitions, reminded me of Peter Maurin? whose ideas, whose way of expressing himself, whose example of poverty and work, whose great message, if taken up by teachers throughout the church might have achieved in its time, the green revolution he was always speaking of.

But ours is the Way of the Cross, and not the least of the suffering is the recognition that so much of it is unnecessary, that it is the scribes and pharisees, the priests and the levites of the present day who are shouting "Lord, Lord" and denying Him, in His poor, denying Him in their acceptance of the armies of the State, denying Him in not working for that kind of society where it is easier for men to be good.

Fidel called for self-criticism, and he went on in his speech, more of which we will print in future articles, to criticize the young bureaucrat who pulls down a fat salary, and all those who pull down a salary of more than they need, while the *compensino* continues to work for a large and hungry family.

I will write more, of my visits to Guantanamo, Santiago de Cuba, the schools of Camilo Cienfuegos, that present of the army and built by them for the youth of the Sierra Maestre, of the visit to the fishing cooperative and new village at Manzanillo which used to be known as Red

Manzanillo; of Santa Clara, of the state farm or *granja* at Bainoa; of nursery schools, hospitals, including a huge mental hospital where the man in charge is a former fighter with Fidel, who is a devout Catholic and who said the rosary daily with the troops in the Sierra Maestre.

I will write of food of the body (there is no famine in Cuba) and of food for the soul, the conditions of the churches, and also of the Americans I met in Havana, including the exile Robert Williams and his lovely wife, who were finally driven out of Monroe, North Carolina, and of the events and charges that led up to it. And of the needs of co-existence with communism which will never be overcome by troops or embargoes, but only with the most true and strong love of brother, which is the only way we have of showing our love of God.

November 1962

PILGRIMAGE TO CUBA—PART III

On the way home from Cuba, through Mexico, I have spoken at San Antonio, Texas, the University of Minnesota Newman Club (twice) at a meeting at Mary Humphrey's in St. Cloud, at St. John's University at Collegeville, at North Dakota State College in Fargo, at Marquette University School of Journalism (twice), at the University of Chicago Calvert Club, and to small groups and at dinners which included a college president, nurses, nuns, family groups, and others.

"Do you think they will let you tell about Cuba when you get back to the United States?" a few people in the Ministry of Foreign Affairs asked me while I was still in Cuba. "They" meant of course our "imperialistic, capitalistic, militaristic government." We may be all of that, though I would hesitate to use those terms, being, as I am, a Catholic peacemaker and pacifist as well as a member of the Fellowship of Reconciliation. Those are not the terms one uses when trying to reconcile peoples. I convinced my interrogators that there was freedom of speech and of assembly in this country even though it sometimes resulted in lynching or prison.

110

I am going to try not to be the occasion of sin for our opponents in the future, which means that I will try and try again to think things out, study, read more, find more authorities for our positions, stimulate others to that same study, and so express myself that I will evoke in others what is really there to be evoked—a desire to do what is right, to follow conscience, to love one's brother and find what there is of God in every man.

Listening to Maurice Friedman who teaches at Sarah Lawrence and the New School and who is the author of many books on Martin Buber, I was converted to trying harder for the I-Thou relationship. That goes for fellow Americans, fellow Cubans and fellow workers everywhere.

My meetings convince me that there is an intense interest in Cuba, whether it takes the form of wishing to invade, or to overcome the barriers between us and resume friendly relations. I pray that what I write will bring about more understanding.

To go back to my voyage to Cuba, the fact of note was that the tourist class was filled with families returning with all their household goods. I went to Cuba on the Guadalupe and left on the Covadonga, ships of the Spanish Line which sail from Barcelona to New York, Havana and Vera Cruz once a month. The Guadalupe sailed in September and the Covadonga in October, and that was the last voyage. The Transatlantica announced that no more ships of that line would put in at Havana. This was before the crisis and it was almost as though they knew a week ahead of time of what was to come.

This morning I went to Mass at St. Rita's church where there are Masses each morning at 7:30; 8:15; and 9 a.m. and in the evening rosary at six thirty and Mass again at seven. There is also a holy hour each day at five thirty for the children. Perhaps it is a way of instructing them now that the Catholic schools are closed.

The side chapel was full of worshippers and I stayed for two Masses. One of the priests heard confessions before the Masses. Those who served the Mass were youths of sixteen or eighteen.

The main church was being painted though it seemed to me a very new church and I had been told it had been built by an American Augustinian who had built two other churches on the island and also had started a clinic. Since it is the feeling of many of the well to do and well educated

111

Catholic that one is a traitor to one's faith if one does not make the effort at least to emigrate, it is hard for those to remain. They had had the heartbreaking experience too of seeing their friends and brothers coming back with the invasion and being taken prisoner. Every appeal to youth is made on both sides, of course, and both sides think themselves serving a holy cause. There is no knowledge of any kind of pacifism and Catholic as well as Socialist believe that there is nothing nobler than for a man to bear arms for his country. "Youth demand the heroic," Claudel wrote.

After Mass I took bus number 32 down towards the ministry of Foreign Relations where I was supposed to pick up my credentials. I had been there yesterday morning and filled out forms, answered questions as to what magazines I wrote for as well as our own, and then was directed to get four photographs to be brought back the next day.

Raul Lazo, the young man in charge of the section for foreign correspondence asked me what I particularly wished to see and again I asked about the *granjos*, the *collectivos*, the schools, clinics, students picking coffee, housing cooperatives and so on. I said I should also like to go and see Guantanamo naval base,—just to stand there and look at it, the Hong Kong of Cuba. And then, I said, I should like to write to President John Kennedy and ask him to voluntarily relinquish it, as a great and unprecedented gesture of good will, which would have tremendous moral effect on the entire world. Of course he would be impeached at once. But such a mad gesture would not be without its effect.

Senor Lazo was young enough and serious enough to recognize my desire. After all, this is a country where a revolution was begun with a handful of men.

I had been escorted yesterday by Jean Curtis Hagelberg who is the lawyer Rabinowitz's representative in Havana. Her husband works for HOY, one of the three daily papers. She has three children and lives not too far from the ministry. She knows Gert Granich, Mike Gold's sister in law, an old friend of mine in Mexico where she lived for five years. She told me of the murder of one of the leaders of the peasants in Mexico, a communist. They came by night and took him, last April, and his family insisted on going with him, so all were shot, one a pregnant woman. The blood of martyrs is the seed of communism.

I was always getting lost in Havana when I travelled by myself. I took the bus, as directed but instead of proceeding east on the Avenue of the Presidents it turned south and began its meandering course through the city. When you pay your eight cents fare (two cents additional for transfer) you get a little ticket like a receipt and on the back of each one is a saying of one or another of the revolutionary leaders.

My ride was very pleasant and I finally made the conductor understand with the assistance of half the bus where I wanted to go. They identified me first as Russian then as American. I got off at the railroad station with a transfer and was told to take a 103 bus. I bought a copy of *Bohemia*, a monthly, which is only twenty cents. I opened to the picture of George Bernard Shaw with the inscription underneath: in Spanish of course, "The United States is the only nation in history which has passed from feudalism to decadence without any intermediate steps."

(There is a *Bohemia* published in the United States which is against the revolution.)

I bought also a copy of *El Mundo*, one of three dailies which cost five cents. *Revolution* was founded by Fidel. *Hoy* always was the communist paper, and *El Mundo* has 2 columns of Catholic news every Sunday though of course it is not a Catholic paper.

There was time between buses to look over the news stands in the station, and of course there are many such in every Plaza. The Russians are way ahead of us there. The stands are flooded with Spanish translations of every kind of novel, with history, science, theory and so on.

There was *Moby Dick* by Melville, *Anna Karenina* by Tolstoi; *Mother* by Maxim Gorki. There were Darwin, Engels, Marx and Jose Marti and many others, a wealth of cheap paper backs and many popular science books. There were the *Iliad* and the *Odyssey*. Also a history of the world by H. G. Wells. All kinds of stuff to testify to the hunger of the poor for knowledge.

In addition to the books, there are the popular slogans everywhere. "Eternal glory to the martyrs of Mondado." "Children are born to be happy." "The revolution is made for the children." And of course the little verses chanted by the students from all the trucks on the way to the Sierra Maestre.

I don't drink whiskey,
I don't drink tea.
I am going to Oriente
To pick coffee.

One bus I took gave me an interesting ride through the Central Park, past the Capital which is a copy of our own, past the statue of Jose Marti, along the harbor with its bars for sailors, pilots, navy, etc. everything looking incredibly poor and shabby now that the revolution has taken over. "But of course there still are night clubs, and they are good," one young girl from the militia said indignantly. All hotels are nationalized and there are no more red light districts.

One bus was marked *Old Havana* and we went through the most crowded sections and the narrowest streets I have ever seen except our own down town financial district in New York at noon.

But it was not the right bus and after half an hour I found myself back at the railroad station where I had a delightful drink of mixed fruit juices and took a cab to the ministry. I had another good drive along the Malecon where there was some fishing going on, and finally reached the ministry at eleven. There I received my card with my picture pasted on (by the stubby finger of the clerk) and was given an official stamp.

I had brought to Cuba some cartons of hospital supplies that the Medical Aid for Cuba had entrusted to me, so I called the National Hospital in Havana and was able to reach Dr. Juan Ortega, a young Cuban doctor who had been trained in New York and had practiced there for some years and had returned to work for his country with his wife and children. He was enthusiastic about the revolution and spoke eloquently on the necessity of dealing with the *whole* man, his work, his living quarters, his family, his problems of work and his talents and capacities.

Next day Dr. Ortega sent two young men, Lazaro Corujo, the administrator of the National Hospital and Rolando Aedo, who spoke English, having lived in Tampa for some years. He was the auxiliar casero, the paymaster. They drove me to the outskirts of Havana to the great new hospital and took me over the new buildings, through the wards and later we had dinner in the dining room where doctors, administrators, porters, orderlies, nurses, anesthetists, colored and white, all eat together.

The first week I spent at the home of Lou and Lenna Jones and at the end of the week I paid my first visit to a collective farm, or *granja* which was located near the Matanzas border some hours out of Havana.

I was driven by the Rios family, husband, wife and two

daughters and another friend whose brother was studying in Red China to be a jet flier. The mother and her fourteen year old daughter Pamela had been engaged in alphabetizing the winter before. They lived in the village for six months were returning to meet their old pupils and to find out about the continuation course that was going to begin in another month. We had lunch at Santa Cruz del Norte, a fishing village, and from there left the coast to go up into the hills, through lovely lush scenery to the village of Bainoa, a village of narrow streets, thatched huts, as well as better houses, a locked up church, a small factory where uniforms were made, and a country store where I bought a few cans of evaporated milk and a box of colored pencils from Russia. (There is little to buy in Cuba in the way of souvenirs.) Then we drove all around over rutted roads. It was still the rainy season and one can go ankle deep in mud.

According to published figures (American sources) the U. S. owned half the farm land, where 70 percent of the population lived and half the farming land was put to sugar cane, 45 millions tons being raised. The tourists were the second largest industry, 200,000 from the United States visiting yearly. Previously it took only two hours to fly and 6 and one half hours by auto ferry. It is hard to remember these things, isolated and poor as Cuba is now. Everywhere now there was evidence of the attempts to convert agriculture to more diversified crops. Cuba can support three times its population, Dr. Ortega had told me, explaining their utter condemnation of birth control.

It was good to be visiting in the homes of people as we did that afternoon. Marjorie, her daughter Pamela and Marietta, the other young woman, were all greeted by their first names and embraced and when I was introduced as an aunt mia tia, I was given the same welcome. We drank innumerable little cups of the black sweet coffee and news was exchanged back and forth. They knew that Marjorie was an American, so I as an American was accepted also, and somehow they did not associate us with their fear of an invasion. Radio SWAN broadcast constantly about impending invasions and the mothers grieved. But everyone, young men and women in the militia, were prepared to fight in this most hopeless situation which could only mean obliteration.

There on the land, where a great transformation was taking place in the economy of a country, there was not so much evidence of the militarizing of the country. I saw no women in militia uniform and the men and boys only when they had to go out to guard duty on the hills.

On one page of my note book I find I have written that there are 400 inhabitants in the village of Bainoa and on another page it is 700. Perhaps one figure is for the little village and the other for the entire *granja* including the people who live in the 64 new houses, for which they drew lots. All the new houses had three bedrooms; one for the parents, one for the young men and boys, and one for the girls. The bedrooms were large—I looked into one and saw two big double beds. The living room extended out on to the terrace and garden, which in turn looked away off to the horizon and the setting sun.

The houses were so much better than I expected (and more were being built) that I was surprised that there could be a refusal on the part of some of the small farmers to join. But it was a question of property which to them meant freedom. Freedom for themselves perhaps, but what of the others? "When we get to heaven," Peguy writes, "God is going to ask us first of all, 'Where are the others?'"

One small farmer had eighteen head of cattle, seven of them milk cows from which altogether he got 22 quarts of milk a day. Of course there had been a terrible drought last year when everything dried up and the cattle wasted away. But this year it is lush. This farmer had two pigs, and there were many chickens wandering around. Plenty of fruit on the trees and I suppose vegetables. His houses were primitive, made of the palm, some with dirt floors, but all swept clean and others had stone floors. His married sons lived with him. Hanging from the middle of the ceiling was a great kerosine lamp from China. There was no electricity, and this was used only when these peasants were being alphabetized, as they call it. They welcomed their former teachers with joy and affection and again we had to drink little cups of coffee, very strong and very sweet. We had to travel very slowly along the dirt roads, deeply rutted and bright orange like some of the clay in the South. It was good to be out on a Sunday where everyone was on the streets and resting and visiting and happy.

The revolution says, "Children are made to be happy," but St. Thomas says all men are meant for happiness. It was good to see so much of it around. It was evident in the home of the store keeper, another capitalist, whose sons worked with him, as those of the farmer miles down the road. One son especially kept dragging visitors in to see his three-month-old son. If he were asleep, he waked him so admirers could see his eyes, and it was indeed adorable to see how the baby flopped over into sleep again, either on the shoulder of the one who was holding him, or in the beautiful crib, made of several different kinds of Cuban woods, of contrasting colors.

I was always having a chance to admire Cuban furniture, beautifully made, capacious and sturdy, even in the poorest homes. (Everywhere there were little carpenter shops, in Cobre, Oriente province especially.) We admired the baby dutifully while the mother plucked the eyebrows of a younger daughter whose hair was done up in huge plastic cylinders, just like all the teen-agers in the States. The young wife still pale from the heat and her new responsibilities, talked babies and their health with her former teacher. They were very much petty bourgeois like the world over, store-keepers and prosperous, even though there was little on their shelves. We bought a few cans of evaporated milk and some cans of tomato juice and some Russian baby food like pablum, and I bought some Russian colored pencils to bring home to the grandchildren. There was also Russian canned beef on the shelves. There is indeed a shortage, yet none can say there is any starvation. (Every child under seven has its quart of milk.) It is rationing as we had it during the war, and I think better administered.

After visiting these two examples of still existing Capitalism, and later I found many such, I was pleasantly surprised at the beauty and comfort of the new houses going up everywhere in Oriente, Camaguey, Matanzas and Santa Clara provinces.

It was good we were visiting on Sunday and saw the men and talked to them, and to the girls too. Many of the women worked in the clothing factory in the town or in the tomato cannery when it was open. School starts October first and the school building on the granja rivals our own in the States. As we passed there were many chairs outside the school, showing that some meetings and classes were already being held out of doors on a terrace. The workers go to school nights, and one out of every twenty five will be elected to go to Havana to learn everything, including mechanics—how to take care of the machinery. The middle, educated, professional classes having abandoned the country, there is a crying need for administration.

117

There was the real hardship, the biggest problem. Everything that had come from America was breaking down and they could no longer get parts. Every now and then on the main road one passed cars and trucks which were broken down. And on every bus were signs—This engine from USSR. This from Czechoslovakia. The Czecho-Technicos were always, it seemed to me, as much in evidence as the Russ.

The *granja* we were visiting was called La Cooperativa Juan Abrahantes and later I read an article about it in CUBA. The Nov. 1961 edition in which the article appeared was called INRA then, and the title was "Ini Fidel se imagina mi alegria!" Even Fidel cannot imagine my joy! I drank coffee in dozens of houses, and we drove through the village, the surrounding country and through the cooperative proper, with its 62 houses, good roads, big truck gardens, pigs and chickens and beautiful flower gardens. And everywhere the houses were furnished with good hardwood furniture, with cane seats and backs for coolness, and everywhere there were rocking chairs. I told them all that President Kennedy had brought the rocking chair back into favor in the United States. There were shrines in many of the homes, but no church open nearby. The closed church I saw in the village was only visited by a priest every two weeks. Floors of these homes are tile, there is a laundry on a terrace outside the kitchen, and the terrace in front is shaded with trees and shrubs. Pictures I had seen had made these developments look like a Levittown, but they were far more spacious and cultivated than I expected. The men worked on the granja which is not truly a cooperative but a state farm, and the work was year-round work, not just for a few months a year. The private farm sold all its produce to the state. But there is private ownership in homes and one-half-acre plots. It was as I had envisioned it, and I was not disappointed. It is the model for agricultural reform in our own country where the *braceros* and migrant families suffer destitution most of the year like that of Latin America.

As I write this, still in Cuba, I look out the window at Dellis the Jamaican servant hanging out the clothes, and making room on the line where there are many clumps of ears of bright yellow corn, hung there not for decoration, but to feed the chickens which everyone has begun to keep in their gardens. When there are an influx of chickens on the market, people get them alive four or five at a time. My hostess had decided to keep a hen to see if she would lay. Sure enough her optimism was rewarded and there was an egg in the flower border. So she saved four more, and raised two tiny chicks and now she is getting perhaps four or five eggs a day. The corn is for the chickens and the children love to feed them. It is a comforting sound to hear the murmuring of hens, their triumphant call as they finish laying an egg, having performed their *trabajo productivo* as others in the revolution. There are fruit trees too, banana trees, mangos, lime and guava, and people have in some cases cultivated the empty lots. The becados, scholarship students, across the street from the first place I stayed, while waiting to be sent to pick coffee in Oriente cleared the large lot next to the big apartment house where they were quartered, and planted corn which has grown ten feet high. Pumpkin is a plentiful crop and we have eaten it as a vegetable every day since I came. Rice, bread, pumpkins, avocado, black beans, white beans, many kinds of beans, this is the diet, and plenty of sugar so there are sweets after each meal, cakes, puddings made without milk and so on.

It is the rainy season, the cyclone season, and every day there are periods of rain and thunder and lightning. The corn hanging on the line is getting wet again. The baskets of corn dragged into the porch attract huge black ants which swarm around the floor. The rain brings mosquitos and there are no screens. I am offered a mosquito net, but it is so humid in this season that I could not sleep so covered, and I turn thankfully to a small bottle of insect repellent. Dellis is washing, the little cook is getting lunch, and there is a gardener just now cleaning up the yard. All of these workers are going to classes at night. Voluntarily. There is a great hunger and thirst for knowledge. What are they thinking about? Probably of the time when all mothers will either take care of their own children, or put them in the nurseries provided and work in one or another branch of industry or agriculture or service job. The nursery I visited yesterday was named "Valley of Tenderness."

Certainly in the South of the United States there is a big servant class miserably paid and in addition despised. The insulted and injured. But in the States in the North there are very few who can afford anything more than a girl to come in to clean once a week, or to baby-sit occasionally. But here there are large numbers of people who are still living in former comfort affording several servants. And the rents are moderate from American standards. In one place I stayed, the family was paying seventy dollars a month. In another ninety, and this for luxurious apartments and houses in Miri-mar.

"And is it true that you will own this house after you have paid rent for a while," I asked. "Yes, we will own this in five years. It is a rather old house." But it is a dream of a home, with an enclosed garden with flowers and fruits.

We in the states are self conscious in the presence of a servant class and are uncomfortable at being waited on, but are quite happy with student workers and baby sitters. With everyone going to school in Cuba there is a new dignity to work in the home and one can think of functional rather than acquisitive classes. One Catholic mother was indignant at Fidel when he said in one of his speeches that the aim was to do away with prostitutes and servants as a class. "I will never forgive him," she said indignantly. "The idea of class-ing the two together!"

Among the Catholics I met there was complete freedom of speech and there was criticism as well as praise of the regime. It was in the field of education that parents were in a quan-dary. "How can we let our children go to schools where Marxism-Leninism is taught?"

I spoke to many Catholics and it was hard to answer such a question. I could only say as Fr. Ignacio Biain, Franciscan, said, "Have more faith in Divine Providence." And in one's own courage, in the effectiveness of prayer to build up cour-age. I told them of the courage of our own American Negro families who brought their little children with heroic cour-age through lines and mobs of jeering and insulting and threatening whites, in an effort to integrate the schools, and urged them to build up that same courage in their own chil-dren. And to find concordances as our own Holy Father has urged, rather than to seek out heresies, to work as far as one could with the revolution, and to always be ready to give a reason for the faith that is in one.

There is the singing of the *Internationale*, for instance, most of the verses of which can be joined in with enthusiasm. "Arise, poor of the world-On your feet slaves without bread-and let us shout all together-All united, Long live the International. 2. Let us remove all shackles-that tie human-ity-let us change the face of the earth-burying the bourgeois empire."

The third verse is the one where I would recommend that

the children sit down. It is—"No more Supreme Saviours-no Caesar, no bourgeois, no God. We ourselves have our own redemption."

The fourth verse is—"Where the proletariat-enjoy the good-it has to be the workers-who guide the train. Verse 5. The day that we reach triumph-there will be neither slave nor owners-and the fury that poisons the world-will at that point be extinguished. 6. Man is brother to man-let inequality cease-let the earth be the paradise-and homeland of humanity."

This is a rough translation which a Catholic mother gave me, who said wistfully, "We could well sing the other verses. We ourselves have been ashamed of our position in the face of poverty and ignorance, of not having done more about it."

A Weak Lay Apostolate

Fr. Matteo said once that the churches could all remain open in a persecution of the church, provided that religion was strong in the home. Groups should keep meeting together to discuss, not their oppositions with the revolution but Scripture, social justice, theology. I left Emmanuel Mounier's book, *Be Not Afraid* with them and all the others I had brought down in my too heavy suit case. There was nothing left of the Christian Family movement, the Young Christian Workers, Catholic Action, and it was better for them to meet and discuss the spiritual life rather than politics. The main thing was to have courage, to stand fast in one's faith, and find out every way in which one could lawfully participate. One example of courage was that of a young family man, a lawyer who was asked by the security police on his street to work with them in prosecuting "counter revolutionaries," a request which he refused. To be put in the position of a spy on people he might know, and to inform and be a party to their prosecution—this he could not do. When later he was persecuted by a woman member of the security police, he complained to the authorities, perhaps to Castro himself, and was upheld. The persecutions ceased and he attended block meetings, continued his work in the teaching field and gave an example of a man of principle. One day there was a story in *El Mundo* about St. Thomas More whom the Communists have long claimed as one of their own, perhaps because of his book, *Utopia*. I wish I could send the play, *A Man for All Seasons*, to my Catholic friends in Cuba who like Thomas More are Fidel Castro's good cooperators, but first of all, God's servants.

On the outside of one church in Guantanamo (the town not the base) I saw posters with quotations from Pius XII about the need for secular institutes, and I visited with the girls of one such secular institute in Havana where they lived in a big house together, sixteen of them and worked to help Fr. Iglesia with his catechetica groups.

In Santiago de Cuba I visited the shrine of our Lady of Cobre, an hour up in the mountains in the little mining town of Cobre (copper) and there I found a Sister Mercedes, one of the Social Service sisters, who was as serene and calm as though it were the most natural thing in the world to live under a Marxist-Leninist government, proudly calling itself socialist. They ran a guest house, which was like a most modern retreat house and it would have been a lovely place to stay and make a retreat. Retreats were still going on in Havana I knew. In Santa Clara I met a happy priest, Fr. Joseph, who reminded me of Fr. Roy. The priests at the shrine were still offering Mass each day.

Guantanamo Bay

When I mention Guantanamo, I must add that it was only a visit of a few hours to that town which looked to be comfortably off, probably thanks to the high wages of the Cuban workers at the base. But a young newly married couple told us that those who worked on the base were now forbidden to leave the base and that they had to take their vacations in Jamaica. This was long before the crisis.

One morning I went to what was formerly Camp Columbia, next to the air field, which is now transformed into the Ministry of Education, and built up into a school city called Liberty City. This is what has happened in every city I visited. The army was out. I saw the cavalry headquarters where Batista lived under guard, and which is now for the administration of scholarships. As you enter the gates of Liberty City, you pass a great building which houses the League against blindness, and next door the entrance to Tropicana Night Club, one of the most famous of Havana and now used by the workers. When we passed guards (against sabotage) you would say, "I am a functionary of the ministry," and we would pass in. The architecture of the Ministry of Education is a lively combination of tiles and cement blocks and all the barracks have been transformed into dormitories and classrooms by students. Everywhere in the city of course there are classrooms, even in the Havana Libre, the most luxurious hotel, formerly the Havana Hilton.

Lenna works for the diagnostic institute, and handles children and the teachers of children with special problems, and Lou is an educational psychologist setting up systems for evaluation and orientation.

I visited Batista's bomb shelter—or rather it was one for the generals I suppose, and one was reminded of Hitler's bunker where he met his end. It is air-conditioned, so well lighted one did not get the feeling of being underground. The map room was especially interesting with one wall covered with a map of Cuba with well-outlined sections showing where "Che," "Raul" and "Fidel" were in command of troops. Crosses marked the desire to obliterate these forces, and in the case of Fidel there was not only a cross but a hole where a cigaret had burned a circle on the map.

Work and Pray

I talked with one young woman who was a devout Catholic who up to the time of the March 13 speech which I wrote about in my October article had been most fearful about the revolution and its attitude towards religion. She wears a medal of the Blessed Virgin, and is a good and conscientious worker in the field of education, which Fidel considers the most important branch of the revolution. But she feels the pressures of her fellow Catholics who tell her she is cooperating with communism by working for the government. This girl told me that there are four churches open in her city, not a large one—that at the cathedral of the province there are four Masses and at the other churches three and two a day. That in the eastern part of the state of Matansas there are ten Canadian priests and twelve Sisters teaching catechism.

But if they do not teach together with their catechism an acceptance of voluntary poverty, manual labor, a devotion to the common good, the works of mercy as worked out by the government in housing, agriculture, clothing factories, hospital work, care of children in nurseries, harvesting of crops, studying to become literate and to cultivate their talents, catechism becomes principle divorced from practice.

Man is a creature of body and soul, and he must work to live, he must work to be co-creator with God, taking raw materials and producing for man's needs. He becomes God-like, he is divinized not only by the sacrament but by his work, in which he intimates his Creator, in which he is truly "putting on Christ and putting off the old man, who is fearful and alienated from his material surrounding. He must be taught those words of Catherine of Sienna, "I have left myself in the midst of you," Jesus said to her, "so that what you cannot do for me, you can do for those around you." And "All the way to Heaven is heaven, for He said, 'I am the Way.'"

Later I met a Canadian girl from British Colombia who had been picking coffee berries for the past two weeks. She was a sturdy, blond girl, well educated one felt and evidently from a radical Catholic background. She was here alone, and had been teaching English for a year. Thousands of students are being taught English and as many Russian, with intensive courses of four hours a day. How many are being sent to Russia? One student told me 4,000 are preparing to go.

The girl who was a *brigadista* in the granja which I visited Sunday, has not only a brother who is studying to be a jet flier in China, but one who is in the regular army. She herself works every day in the department of commerce studying the produce of Cuba and the foreign markets for it; her teaching is at night.

The Canadian girl had Canadian friends, who had come from Mexico and lived in a trailer.

Catechism

I have two copies of newly printed catechisms, printed on Cuban government presses and paper, for beginners and secondary students, I am not minimizing the importance of catechism, no matter how dogmatic—"Who made you?" "God made me." "What did He make you for?" "To know Him, to love Him and to serve Him." But it seems to me never too early to begin teaching a child—"How can you love God whom you have not seen, unless you love your brother whom you do see?" And how can you know God, to love Him, unless you use all knowledge to go to God, all beauty, all truth, all goodness? As it says in the *Acts of the Apostles*, God did not leave us without testimony of Himself, in the whole world of nature, the visible world giving evidence of the invisible world, "filling our hearts with food and gladness."

When catechism is taught with what Peter Maurin called a philosophy of work, and Catholic students can enter into work for the poor and oppressed and the illiterate, it is good. But if they are denied that work in education or other fields because of their faith, then they could undertake obscure and humble work by which to earn their living, becoming contemplatives in the world like the Little Brothers of Jesus, of Charles de Foucauld. With Peter Maurin's philosophy of work how religion will flourish and spread!

But of course too, there will always be persecution. The servant is not above his master. There is no redemption without the shedding of blood (one's own blood, not the blood of others).

The Canadian girl said, "There is no electricity in those county districts where we were picking coffee, so it is hard to teach. But the brigadistas go about in the dark with their pockets full of candles, and the alphabetizing goes on just the same." What dedication!

Another visit that day in the ministry of education with a man who was preparing art appreciation courses. "He who is without culture is not free," is another slogan in school rooms, on billboards and carved on bullfrogs.

Peter Maurin again and his synthesis of "Cult, Culture and Cultivation." He too insisted that education and culture was fundamental in building a new social order. But his clarification of thought began with Cult—religion, worship, man's acknowledgement of his Creator, source of all joy and strength.

So Little Time

Things I would have liked to have done and people I would have liked to have seen. I would like to have taken one of those little ferries, the launches which went across the harbor to Las Mercedes and to have eaten at the little restaurant in a boat on the shore. I would like to have visited the movie houses where the theaters were showing films from China, Czechoslovakia, Rumania, the USSR as well as other countries in Eastern Europe. To have seen the performances of *Lysistrata* by Aristophanes, and those put on by the afficionados, which meant in Cuban speech, not the lovers of the theater as we use it in terms of lovers of horse racing or bull fights, but amateurs, brought in to the theaters to play, sing and dance on the stages of theaters not only in Havana but in Santiago de Cuba, Manzanillo, Santa Clara and other cities.

I was not able to find our friend by correspondence, Mario Gonzales, parts of whose letter, three typewritten, single-spaced pages, we will quote from later. I would like to have visited Cedric Belfrage, former editor of the *National Guardian*, who was just coming back from South America when I was leaving.

I would like to have had a visit with Carlos Rafael Rodriguez whose daughter has become a Catholic. He is an old time Communist and is now head of the agricultural reform. I would like to have talked to Blas Roca, head of the Communist party there, whose brother, I heard has a chicken farm (looks like private property there).

I would like to verify the rumor, printed in a Mexico City newspaper circulated in all the hotels, that Fidel Castro has married again, a woman from Santiago de Cuba. I would like to write further on the cults among the Negroes in the city slums, and about the slums I saw but which are really unnecessary to describe as we have heard of them many times before.

And next month we will run the story of Robert Williams, the American exile, anything but a pacifist, who came to public attention a few years back by advocating that the Negroes arm in the South to defend themselves, and who was suspended from his position in the NAACP for a time. I grew to love him and his wife in my visits with them in Havana, and I would like to have our readers know them too.

December 1962

PILGRIMAGE TO CUBA—PART IV

Mail is coming through to me from Cuba quickly and it was good to receive clippings of two columns of religious notes, from *El Mundo*, entitled Mundo Catolico, written by one of the priests whom I met while in Cuba.

These notes were sent me in November by Mario Gonazales. In discussing the lesson of the Sunday, about tribute to Caesar, the priest takes the opportunity to point ou the role the layman must play in political life and the necessity for him to "penetrate all social structures, all civilization, with whatever regime, *sin compromisos con lo politico y lo idealogico.* To penetrate and to live with the pure forces of the spirit, of

126

love, of generosity, and with *la valoracion positiva*, in all that which is not intrinsically immoral." (I am not sure of my translating, and so I use the Spanish text.) The column ends with a prayer by the Archbishop of Santiago de Cuba, Msgr. Enrique Perez Serantes, a prayer for peace. And then there are the usual lists of feast days and special Masses said in the cathedral and other churches of Havana.

I must repeat again and again that the churches are open all through Cuba. That the cloistered Carmelites remain in Havana. That there are sisters visiting the prisons, teaching catechism, etc. That there is a secular institute of young women to teach catechism, that I brought back with me copies of two catechisms printed in Cuba, for first and second classes of children. That one of the priests has many catechism classes throughout the city, one estimate being five hundred groups organized for the teaching of the children. That there are two minor seminaries open and that young newly ordained priests are returning from Europe at the request of the Holy Father. That there are a number of Canadian priests working in Havana itself, and ten in Matanzas Province, and also Canadian sisters.

As for the food situation, there are severe shortages of course, and the situation will probably get worse, judging from Louis Jones' letter which speaks of the disruption of production. Here is a more detailed account of rationing, given me by one of the Catholic families. Where I was a guest there was a supplementary food allowance, and some of the families had received food sent to them by relatives in the States. I went with friends to shop and in many cases there were hours of waiting, but since each customer was given a ticket with a number on it, we were able to do other errands. There are long lines before the meat stores, and it seems to me the greatest hardship was in the meat shortages. A bad drought the last year cut down the crops and milk supplies, as well as the supply of meat. Russia has been sending canned meats, and so has China, but canned meat is not looked upon with enthusiasm any more than in the States where there was great objection years ago to the "Home Relief Beef" which we used to see during the depression.

I took notes in my little pocket diary of some of the rationing and my notes read as follows: Weekly, 1 and one-half lbs. rice per person; one-half lb. beans; three-fourth lb. meat; 1 and one-half lbs. potatoes; 1 lb. sweet potatoes; one-quarter lb. pumpkin; one-half lb. fish fortnightly; 5 eggs monthly; one-eighth lb. butter monthly; 1 lb. oil monthly; 1 lb. lard; 4 oz. cheese; 6 cans evap. milk; and to children under seven a quart of fresh milk daily. These were some of the figures given me by a friend who in general was against the revolution, and yet when others attacked it found good things to say for it, too.

Nothing was hard and fast in the way of rationing as far as I could see. Suddenly there would be a great many chickens on the market and they were given out alive, a half dozen to a family, and all over Havana the families were keeping them in their yards to lay eggs. Or sometimes there would be a notice that there was meat and there would be long lines of people waiting to get their share. There was a shortage of everything, and since the Cuban women love to sew and make their own clothes, and since cotton is the coolest thing to wear in the tropics there were great lines when it was announced that cotton goods had come in from China. Women complained that those who worked could not take advantage of the sales, so there was great discontent here.

In time of crisis people put up with shortages, and after all there seems to be plenty of beans and rice—I ate it twice a day all the while I was in Cuba; and it was the season for avocados. Fruit juices are sold on the street corners and they are delicious, the melon juice, the mango juice as well as oranges. At the bus stops when we were travelling, boys came on with pails of warm water, not too clean looking, containing tamales wrapped in their coverings of corn husks. I ate many of these with no hurt to my digestion, but I must confess I made an act of faith as I ate these unsavory looking morsels. Sometimes the tamales had some kind of sauce inside, generally they were like a thick cereal, a bit lumpy, with little but the corn flavor.

But when you are hungry, how good everything tastes! And if I sound as though my trip to Cuba were a happy one, I must confess I was happy because it was so much better than I expected, and because I was able to endure the heat, the travel, the getting around in strange places, and eating foods, and talk with people who spoke another language and who were all so friendly and kind, and who seemed to be so willing to love this individual enemy, for such they regard us from the Estados Unidos. On one occasion when a little boy came into the bus with his usual pail of tamales, the woman conductor who assisted the driver by collecting fares, helped all of us by passing out the tamales and bringing us our change. "Even the Americans are eating tamales now," she laughed and the entire bus laughed too in most friendly fashion.

I must recall too, the honesty of the people. At one bus stop I came back into the bus to find that Charles Horwitz had left his seat to go out, and had left behind his wallet which had evidently slipped from his hip pocket. There was a hundred dollars or more in it and his identification cards and other necessary papers, but there it remained; no one touched it. I could leave my transistor radio around in the same way, though one bus driver wanted to buy it from me.

Another thing—there is no drunkenness in Cuba. Coming from the Bowery as I had, it was amazing to me not to encounter any drinking in the plaza, in the bus stations, the bus stops, in the streets of the big cities like Havana, Santa Clara, Santiago de Cuba, Manzanillo, Guantanamo. When I commented on this, Marjorie Rios, an American woman married to a Cuban and living there for the last fifteen years, said that she too had never seen a borracho. Someone else added that the only ones were the Americans who used to flock there as tourists.

One of our readers, and a very dear friend, asked me after I came home, "Is there no criticism you can make about Cuba? Is everything so wonderful there, cannot you find anything against it?"

Of course one could find plenty wrong. It is a country racked by war, boycotted by its nearest neighbor and without many of the amenities of life. I could tell of water supplies breaking down, pumps not functioning in the big apartment houses, so that the tenants are forced to carry water from the first floor to fill the tanks of their toilets, the bath tubs and many pails for cooking. Of the disrupted service on the public transportation system, which leads by the way to slower and more careful driving by cab and bus drivers and by all private car owners.

Life is not easy in Cuba these days and the people are undergoing great hardships in every way. They are getting enough food to survive, but certainly not the kind of food they wish. They are just getting by, and undoubtedly food shortages make tempers short too. There is a great shortage of the professional classes, teachers, doctors, and so on. There is shortage of drugs necessary to save lives.

But there is just the same widespread efforts towards health and education and work for all, and the crisis has united the people so that there are not the problems of delinquency, and violence, drug and drink addiction, lack of work for the older and younger members of the community, lack of education in the past in Cuba's struggle for independence, Jose Marti, General Maceo and others, but none of these were faced with the problem of a *successful* revolution, and what to do about consolidating it, and building up agrarian reforms, housing reforms, building up production so that everything would not be going out of the country in trade but there would be food, clothing, shelter, health care, and education for all. In that, the problem in Cuba now is unique.

The Communists were the ones to throw themselves into the work of building up the country. Before the revolution, less than three tenths of one percent of the population was communist. Those who were, were highly trained and few. They had not been in favor of the Castro revolution, but when it succeeded, they threw themselves into the work of building up the country, with the help, of course, of their fellow-Communists in the USSR and other Socialist countries. What help the U.S. withheld was given them by others. So now Cuba is the first Socialist State in the Western Hemisphere. What to do about it? How to live with it? How to learn from it?

As I came through Mexico, spending ten days there on the way home, I spoke to the Maryknoll nuns in Mexico City, who are still forbidden to wear their own garb as are all the other nuns, and wear plain skirts and blouses like lay women. They told me there that no religion is permitted in the Mexican schools where they teach, no crucifix is allowed in the school room, and all religious instruction must be given outside of class, as in our own public school system. But in addition they have government text books, which they are forced to use, and there is one in particular which they have protested. It is only now, this year, that they have been permitted to teach from their own text (together with the text of the government which must also be used). It seems to me the Catholics in Cuba must learn from the Catholics in Mexico how to deal with and survive in a godless state and show the same courage the Catholics in Mexico have shown. The Catholic, the Christian, must outdo in zeal, in self sacrifice, in dedication, in service for the common good those who are following the teachings of Marxism-Leninism. So let us learn our lessons, and continue the struggle with the joy, which Leon Bloy says is the sure sign of the life of God in the soul. . . .

1963

April 1963

☐ It is the last day of March and the weather is so warm and mild and so many of us are recovering from flu that one cannot think of anything but how wonderful it is to sit on a park bench and bask in the sun. There should be benches on every street corner in the city. Down in our Italian section people pull out their chairs and sit out by the curb where there will be no danger of anything falling from the window sills of any of the five stories above them.

Children come from school and stop to buy ices, and children fret over too many clothes. But every now and then as you turn a corner, a wind springs up and you realize that at sunset it will be cold again. Buds are coming out on the bushes in the park, and in the swampy sections of Staten Island as people come to and from the farm, the call of the spring peepers is poignant.

Across the street from the three-story loft building which is our office, diningroom and all day quarters, the long park which extends from Houston street to Delancey which was the result of urban renewal many years ago and brought the displacement of many families, is still a shambles. Garbage, tin cans, litter of all kinds and also human beings, sitting on what is left of a stone wall. Children play in the midst of this litter. Five years ago we were displaced by the city, because of the new subway link being constructed from our home at 223 Chrystie street, three blocks north of us, and since then the park has been like this.

So much work could be done there, and nightly we hear about the unemployment problem among the old and the young, the problems of automation. But there is no money for the employment of the young or for more schools or playgrounds. Only for missiles, or for the exploration of space.

My roommate Marie ruminates on this every night. "Don't you think it's foolish, spending all this money on space?" she asks me. She used to gather newspapers from the trash receptacles all over the city every afternoon and come back in the evening to give us our choice. We didn't have much choice last month. I ask her for the *Wall Street Journal*, but she doesn't often get that. The few copies I saw in this time of dearth fascinate me. One issue told all about how complicated is the life of Roy Cohn, who prosecuted Hiss and who is or rather was, our staunch defender against communism. He does not have time for that now, except for an occasional foray into the field to keep his hand in. I heard him one night shouting down a lawyer from Northwestern University over the case of Morton Sobell who is still in Atlanta Federal prison. The lawyer was trying to talk about the legal aspects of the case and Morton's chances for freedom. Silence would be the only weapon against such an opponent as Cohn. Anyway, his affairs seem to be very complicated now and he is mixed up in all kinds of ownership in businesses, all of which was set forth by the *Wall Street Journal* in a front page right hand column and perhaps a Balzac could understand it but I could not. Anyway he did not seem to be prospering along these lines and perhaps that was why he was back on the radio, to get his hand in, or rather voice in on what had won him acclaim in the past. Also the *Wall Street Journal* told of peasant uprisings in Mexico.

I ask Marie for the *Christian Science Monitor* too, as there are nature notes, and feature articles about Maine and New England and rural life which make very pleasant reading in the New York slums. She has the *Post* now, Murray Kempton doesn't work there any more, but there are some interesting stories about a woman with eighteen cats and how she was sent away to a mental hospital, and about a vagrant who was picked up with $50,000 on him.

There is always so much happening. But it was too bad about the woman with the cats. "I do love little kittens," Marie said. "One time I was talking with a poor man on the Bowery and he said he did not believe in God, and I told him

133

that even if I did not go to the Volunteers of America every Sunday night where they talk to you about God, I would believe there was a God because he made little kittens. And puppies, and the birds." There is a pet store on Delancey that Marie stops by every day.

Berlitz

I like the atmosphere of the Berlitz school where you cannot speak a word of English but must speak Spanish for two hours a day with one or another teacher who may be from Spain, Chile or Cuba! Most of the time I had a teacher from Spain who had travelled and worked all over South America and Central America, who had fought in the Riff, who had had a most adventurous life and who enjoyed our conversations on pacifism, anarchism, farming communes, literature, and so on. My trouble is that I think in English and translate, but I am getting better, now that I have had seventy lessons. We go through the lessons in the book and talk about food, travel, the time of day, the weather, the amenities of life, and then discuss a little of the news of the day. I am beginning to feel confident that with patience, on the part of my hearers, and on my own part with myself, I will begin to understand more quickly. I already feel at home and enjoy mightily following the Mass each day in Spanish, in the missal Fr. La Mountain at Holy Crucifix church gave me. Someone said, that Fr. Louis Merton says, that the Bible in Spanish was most beautiful.

What cheers me in my study is remembering that Raissa Maritain wrote how she sat as a little girl, miserable in her French classrooms when her family first came from Russia to France and how suddenly she began to understand. And a priest told me that when he was studying in a French Canadian seminary where they teach in Latin, after agonizing months, he too began suddenly to understand. This sounds like a miracle to me. But Lou and Lenna Jones in Cuba said the same. Suddenly, after studying for months,—they understood.

There is something about going back to school again which is very stimulating. From the office, or from our apartments to the Berlitz school down near Trinity Church it takes only fifteen minutes to ride on the Broadway bus, and for those who work in the area it is simple. I saw Chinese, Japanese, French, Germans, and Americans all coming in to study.

This week end I brought Mary O'Neil (Roger's Mary) down to the beach house for a couple of days by the sea. She had been sick in the Women's and Children's Infirmary and Roger was taking care of the children at the Glen Gardner community. It was beautiful weather all day from the early morning "Get up, it is late o'clock," of little Johnny Hughes next door, until now at sundown. Johnny is wearing his first pair of suspenders which he calls his "red fenders" and which make him look, he thinks, like the firemen who came rushing down to the beach tonight to put out a brush fire just off the road which was threatening the beach houses. They have been on 450 calls in the last few days, and they look with dread on the Easter holidays when children will be home, and fires on the beaches are liable with a sudden shift of wind to bring sparks into the fields and woods at our end of the island. They blame too many of the fires on the children and forget the cigaret from the passing motorist, and the dumping of trash along the roadside, the broken glass which under the sun's rays starts fires amid the litter and dry grass. (I look at so much of this from the stand-point of employment and work teams now, and see so many places which could be made beautiful which are eye sores now.)

Vermont

I had a lovely visit to Vermont and saw the Hennessy family. All are well. Becky is 18, April third, and is going to college in the fall. The three oldest grandchildren work summers at what they can get to do, Becky in a summer resort, Sue baby-sitting and Eric on a neighboring farm, where he earned his living last summer, board and ten dollars a month. He short his first deer in the middle of the season last fall and Nick is still the best fisherman.

How wonderful these visits. Mary at twelve is the most competent and reliable of baby tenders, and Margaret reads to all of them, she is ten, and Martha is helpful in so many ways, sitting on the side of the sink washing huge messes of dishes for the family of nine children. The older girls can cook, bake, and do other household chores, but they have heavy studies. Still Sue gets in a lot of work in the house. And then there are Hilaire and Katey, who smiles always and says yes! When Nickie was little he used to say, firmly, "Not me!" but Mary always said, "Me too!" Katey is very soft spoken with her little "yes."

"We say prayers in school," Martha and Margaret tell me, "and we sing our grace at noon. Like this: In the morning it is the Our Father, and then Teacher reads us a prayer out of a book. She has three books. Then at noon we sing. 'O the Lord is good to me, and so I thank the Lord for giving me the things I need—the sun and rain and the apple seeds—O the Lord is good to me'."

Yes, they have prayer in the little public school in Vermont, and prayer in the home, and prayer and catechism with the sisters on Saturday morning.

Postscript

Joe Roach suddenly died,—one of the men on the farm, just after lunch, falling in his room by the side of his bed. The priest was called at once, and the ambulance, but Joe died while the priest was anointing him, with Jean Walsh, our dear nurse who tends all the sick at the farm at his side, and Monsignor Dolan, our pastor, saying the prayers for him of the last great sacrament. He was dead before the ambulance arrived a moment later.

Joe was one of the poor. He came to us when we had the farm at Newburgh a dozen years ago. He had a bad back injury when he worked on a farm upstate and was too crippled to work elsewhere. As far as we knew he had no compensation of any kind, and as with so many who were with us told us little of his family. But the police were able to locate a brother who claimed the body and will bury Joe in Newburgh in the plot of his family.

Joe was another Lazarus who had little in this life. He was poor in every way, having nothing of this world's goods, and little health of body. He had nothing when he died, and it is a humbling thing, going through the effects of one who has been with us for so long, to see how little accumulations there were, only the simple needs of a change of clothing, radio perhaps for the news and the sports, a few paper back books, a prayer book. He performed his religious duties, he earned his own living by the sweat of his brow, never failing to put in hours of work with us, washing pots, doing laundry, and he also served the poor,—all those who came to the farm in their need, or to conferences, days of recollection or discussion. As Peter always reminded us, we take into Heaven with us only that which we have given away in this life, and Joe had asked little for himself and had given what he had.

136

Let us pray for him and for all the other poor among our readers,—those who are poor in bodily health, or soul's health as well as for those who are the poor in this world's goods. May the love and affection Joe so craved for in this life be his now, "Heaped up, pressed down and running over."

May 1963

Low Sunday, Rome, Italy

What are we here for, why did we come, we fifty or more women from all countries, of all religious affiliations, and many without any particular belief, of many nationalities? It is a pilgrimage of course, a true pilgrimage, to the Holy City of Rome, to the head of the Church, and for us Catholics, to the representative of Christ on Earth, to present ourselves as though a first fruits of his great encyclical *Pacem in terris*, to thank him, to pledge ourselves to work for peace, and to ask too, a more radical condemnation of the instruments of modern warfare. We are to be part of a large general audience on Wednesday, a meeting of groups and of single pilgrimage.

Someone wrote in, "Might not the money for pilgrim fares have been better spent to serve the poor." But that was the question asked our Lord when He was anointed by Mary Magdalene just before he was betrayed.

My passage was paid for one way by a friend in Chicago and my return by another in Connecticut and in some places living in Rome is cheap. A Yale student I met last night said he was paying sixty cents a night for his bed in a hospice for pilgrims. Vincent MacAloon who runs the Notre Dame Club at Margot Brancaccio 82, is the one to get in touch with if you are going to Rome. Another Notre Dame student said Vincent had been a guardian angel to many.

We women are staying at the Pacis Domus, two miles from the Vatican, a great hospice on a slight hill, many buildings set up in a delightful garden full of singing birds. One tall cage has mourning doves crooning to each other, and also some very active turtles. There are pines and palms and primroses, beds of flowers in bloom and many trees just coming into leaf. Wisteria is in bloom and the air is fragrant. In San Sebastian House Marguerite Harris and I share a narrow little room with two beds, a wardrobe and a washbowl. There is not room for two to dress at the same time. But there are meeting rooms, and I am working in a room over the chapel, with French windows wide open on the fading light of evening.

Our breakfast is coffee with milk, and a roll and jam. Supper is soup, salad and bread and an apple. The menu has not varied. It is pilgrims' fare and it costs three dollars a day for room and meals. The hospice is filled with students from schools in England, France, Germany, and one table near us was labeled Louvain. Young men, boys with priests, young women and girls with nuns, the students in uniform and with busses to take them to see the wonders of Rome. But now Easter week is over and they all leave tomorrow morning and the place will be very quiet. Even conventions of men use the place, and they make just as much noise. There is a bar, where both drinks and coffee can be purchased and if you do not want the tiny cup of coffee with sugar, bitter and strong, you ask for Capuccino and get it with foaming milk, very good. Only the coffee bar is not always open. It has been closed all afternoon.

As usual with a diary, one works backward. David Kirk who is studying at Beda College met us at the boat in Naples and we had supper together at Santa Lucia. It was cool and grey yet clear, and it was beautiful to sit by the sea and eat spaghetti and return to the hotel by swaying street car. David left us to take the boat to Ischia where he was joining some other seminarians for their Easter holiday, living with some fishermen, and Marguerite and I went to the Church of Santa Brigitta named for St. Brigid of Sweden. There were many people in the church, and after praying at the shrine of the saint, we went to see the miraculous crucifix which had changed in the night from the crucified Christ to a glorified Christ the King, resplendent in robes and beautiful and serene of countenance. I prayed for our Lucille at the shrine of St. Lucy of course, and I am praying daily for all of the readers and writers of the Catholic Worker, and all who eat with us at our tables, all whom we encounter daily.

Mrs. Vaccaro, our landlady on Kenmare street will be pleased to know that I went to Mass at the Cathedral of San Gennaro, in a little chapel to the right of the main altar (if one is facing it) where everything was beautiful, stones, walls, altar with its sculptures and carvings. It is as though no one in Italy were unemployed, as though all they did was decorate everything with a keen sense of beauty and dedication.

When we bought our bus tickets next morning we thought we were going to travel on a regular bus. They say no one travels by bus in Italy, the trains are so cheap. But we found ourselves on a tour with some of the boat passengers, with a scheduled two-hour stop at Monte Cassino. It is a most terrifying trip with many hair pin turns up a narrow highway, so close to the mountain's edge that I could not bear to look down at the vast valley below, every inch cultivated. The monastery, destroyed by Saracens, Lombards, earthquake and the Americans in the Second World War, has been completely rebuilt. Nothing is ever as we have pictured it in our minds. I had expected an isolation like that of Mt. Athos or Sinai. Instead, the mountains are crowned with stone villages, ever so many miles apart and where the guide told of their destruction, she pointed out the completely new rebuilt town at the foot of the mountain on the plain. Even on Monte Cassino there are villas and gardens, terraced with olive trees and vineyards and at the foot of the mountain, the rebuilt town of Cassino.

What impressed me most was the people. It is spring, and there has been a hard winter and today the sun shone and everyone worked in the fields. They worked in groups, in little knots of three or four, not scattered over the field as we do. It was as though they held each other up, bore each other's fatigue, sustained each other. White oxen drew the ploughs, men and women dug around the fruit trees, the olive trees, the grape vines, and every twig and stem and pruning was garnered, and every blade of grass clipped for the cattle. Great round bolls of twigs were nested in the trees, off the ground, and women carried great loads of fresh cut grass on their heads.

We arrived at Rome at the end of the day, having avoided the Throughway all day, and settled ourselves at the *Domus Pacis*. The next day Hildegarde Goss Mayr and her husband Jean Goss arrived. They had been speaking in Milan and Turin and had been all night on the train, which was crowded, due to the elections coming at the end of this week. They said that as in the times of Joseph and Mary, people had to go to their home towns to vote, and the government paid their fare. Which meant crowded coaches. It is interesting to see the freedom of Italy, compared to our own country. When we landed in Naples, we saw a delegation of students with placards marching around the municipal square and distributing leaflets and shouting slogans. They were Communists. The Socialist billboards also displayed the hammer and sickle. There are any number of parties, eight perhaps, and at the Galleria in Naples, candidates were listed one after another on the bill boards with all their slogans.

While the Gosses rested, Marguerite and I went to the center of Rome, she to her dear Brigitta nuns and I to see our Catholic Worker friend and writer, Jim Douglas who lives with his wife on Gian Battista Belzoni street, up one flight, windows of the four room apartment looking out east and west over the city. There is a balcony where their two children, Billy and Peter can play. We had supper, and a Yale student came in who had worked in Mexico for the last two years. He is studying at Freiburg and will return for another year at Notre Dame.

I talked over the phone with Patrick O'Reilly Persichetti, a brilliant young pacifist anarchist, who, with Jim had prepared sheets of quotations from the Pope's *On War*, translated into German, Italian and English, thirty of each so that our women on pilgrimage, who are not Catholic can be briefed on the Papacy's efforts for peace and also the Catholic teaching on conditions for a just war. This pilgrimage is both pacifist and ecumenical.

Persichetti has translated Peter Maurin's essays into Italian and is going to do the same in Gaelic when he has time. He is manager of the Goldoni theater and we are going to have a meeting there, one for the women to show Peace films and later one for me, so I can speak to the American seminarians in Rome. Already I have received requests for meetings from students of the Divine Word Seminary, Holy Cross Seminary, and the American College. I had not thought I would be speaking in Rome.

There are many I must see, once our audience has taken place; Joe Calderon, one of our first friends in New York; Fr. Urban, Trappist from Gethsemane, who can speak and move about freely here in Rome.

I have had many requests from friends to visit other countries on this trip abroad, but I wish to remain in Italy a month and then return to my much loved little Italy in New York, stopping perhaps only at Lourdes on the way.

It is Monday, April 22, and we women have had preliminary meetings to get acquainted. There are two women from

140

South America and I can practice my Spanish with them. There is a beautiful young woman, from Hiroshima, and women from Canada, England, Norway, Belgium, Holland, Germany, France, Switzerland, Italy, Austria and the United States. There are two colored women, one from Jackson, Mississippi, active in civil rights and in Church work, and one from New Jersey who was brought up a Muslim and is now working with evangelists, for and with adolescents, among them many delinquents.

Virginia Naeve sparked the trip with the aid of Mary Pollard of New Hampshire and Hermine Evans of Chicago.

Today the Mothers for Peace—a group made up of Catholic Workers, members of Pax, Women Strike for Peace, Women's International League for Peace and Freedom, the Fellowship of Reconciliation, and others, women from Hiroshima, South America (Peru and Colombia), the United States (the majority), Austria, Germany, Norway, Sweden, Belgium, Holland, France and Italy!—were all received by the Holy Father in one of those vast audiences in St. Peter's together with groups from schools from many countries. We were at first disappointed (especially the non-Catholics) that we did not have an opportunity each one to speak to Pope John, but it was a perfect setting for the message he delivered on Peace, addressing us women, thanking us for our Peace Pilgrimage and message, and saying it brought comfort to his heart and blessing us, to return home to our labor for Peace. The speech was translated into French, German, Spanish and English at once, before he left the papal throne.

What an atmosphere of fatherly love and serenity he makes around him. And what a joyful pilgrimage this has been! I prayed again at Saint Peter's tomb, where I was fortunate enough to have a complete view of the entire scene, and there, sitting between a young scholarship student of voice from Nicaragua and a young Roman girl, a restorer of paintings, I prayed for you all, and received the Pope's blessing, which he said was for all our dear ones, and you are that to me, fortunate pilgrim that I am.

June 1963

I landed from the Italian Line Ship *Vulcania* at 45th Street New York, at eight o'clock in the morning to find Nina Polcyn of St. Benet's Book Shop of Chicago waiting for me with Stanley Vishnewsky, Tom Cornell, Terry Becker, Arthur J. Lacey (with dispatch case and letters), Joe Maurer, and Chris, Irish-American playwright and actor, and Cesare a young Argentinian. We had been getting only the most meager reports as to the Pope's health on board ship where the news was given out each day in Italian on a tabloid news sheet. Each morning at Mass the chaplain had asked our prayers for the Holy Father, and each afternoon at Benediction we had repeated those prayers.

We were still sitting at our lunch with people coming and going in the little apartment on Kenmare Street, when someone came in with news of the Pope's death at three in the afternoon. It had been a long agony and daily I had prayed the Eastern rite prayer for "a death without pain" for this most beloved Father to all the world. But I am afraid he left us with the suffering which is an inevitable part of love, and he left us with fear, too, if the reports of his last words are correct, fear that his children, as he called all of us in the world, were not listening to his cries for *pacem in terris*. He was offering his sufferings, he had said before his death, for the continuing Council in September, and for peace in the world. But he had said, almost cheerfully, that his bags were packed, that he was ready to go, and that after all death was the beginning of a new life. "Life is changed, not taken away," as the Preface in the Mass for the dead has it. And just as Therese of Lisleux said that she would spend her heaven doing good upon earth, so in his love, John XXIII will be watching over us.

It was on the day before I sailed for New York, May 22, Wednesday, that I had the tremendous privilege of being present at his last public appearance. He stood in his window looking out over the crowd in front of St. Peter's. An audience had been scheduled as usual for that Wednesday at ten-thirty, and the great Basilica was crowded to the doors when the announcement was made that the Pope had been too ill the night before to make an appearance that day but that he would come to the window and bless the crowd, as he was accustomed to do each Sunday noon.

I had had an appointment that morning for ten-thirty at the office of Cardinal Bea, to see his secretary, Fr. Stransky, the Paulist, about a meeting I was to have with the Cardinal that night and was leaving the No. 64 bus at the colonnade to the left of St. Peter's. I noticed that the people leaving the bus were hastening to the square. Word gets around Rome quickly and when I inquired I was told that the Holy Father would be at the window in a moment. I hastened to a good position in the square and was there in time to see the curtains stir and the Pope appear. I had not realized how tremendous that square was until I saw how tiny the Pope's figure seemed, up at that window of the apartment under the roof. Those rooms used to be servant's quarters and had been occupied by the popes since Pius X.

The voice of the Holy Father came through a loud speaker of course, and seemed strong. He said the Angelus (which we say before meals at the Peter Maurin farm, then the prayer to the guardian angels and ended with a requiem prayer for the dead.

It was the last time the public saw his face (many of the crowd had opera glasses, so one can use that expression). Questioning those at the little convent where I had been staying in Rome the last week, I learned the subject of the Pope's last talk, at his last Wednesday audience. He had urged all to read and study his last encyclicals, the call to the Council, *Mater* and *Magistra* and *Pacem in Terris*. He had said all he had to say, this was the message he left to the world.

"There is an immense task incumbent on all men of good will, namely the task of restoring the relations of the human family in truth, in justice, in love and in freedom; the relations between individual human beings; between citizens and their respective communities; between political communities themselves; between individuals, families, intermediate associations and political communities on the one hand and the world community on the other. This is a most exalted task, for it is the task of bringing about true peace in the order established by God.

"Admittedly, those who are endeavoring to restore the relations of social life according to the criteria mentioned above, are not many; to them We express Our paternal appreciation, and we earnestly invite them to persevere in this work with greater zeal. And We are comforted by the hope that their number will increase especially among those who believe. For it is an imperative of duty, it is a requirement of Love."

Yes, we will meditate on his words to us all, because he said he was addressing *all men of good will*, and we will know too, as we have known in the past, how difficult it is to apply these words to individual situations. We need all the gifts of the Holy Spirit, for our work, we need all the help of our guardian angels, and to make our non-Catholic and non-believing readers know what these words mean, we are printing together with this usual column of pilgrimage, definitions of the gifts of the Holy Spirit, as well as what the guardian angels mean to us who believe. And not to know these things, for those of us who do believe, means not to know the treasure we have, the resources we have to draw upon.

To report further about the trip to Rome which came about because a group of women, mostly of other faiths, and including those who did not believe, had called for this attempt to reach the Holy Father with a plea for a condemnation of nuclear war, and a development of the ideas of non-violent resistance. This very attempt brought out clearly how difficult are these attempts at unity and co-existence.

It is no easier to receive a hearing with Princes of the Church than it is to receive one from the princes of this world. There is protocol, there is hierarchy and blocs of one kind or another, there is diplomacy in what we generally consider to be the realm of the spirit. There is maneuvering for credit and recognition from groups and nationalities among the women themselves. This latter began as soon as the plane load of women arrived from the States and found that Hildegard Goss Mayr, Marguerite Harris and I had drawn up a preliminary paper, a one page message to be sent to the Holy Father. Because of the Pontiff's precarious state of health, the message had to be in the hands of his secretaries by eleven the next morning, Monday, in order that we be recognized at the coming Wednesday audience. There seemed to be no chance of a smaller audience, or any special recognition. But to be assured that our message reached him, it had to be short, complete and accompanied by individual letters from the women, and a summary of the make up of the pilgrimage. For this latter, Marguerite had worked valiantly every afternoon and evening on board the ship in our cabin on the way over from New York. She had typed up many copies of concise biographies of the American women concerned and had them ready for that first meeting.

But the acceptance of that one page message caused the most trouble. It meant a meeting that lasted from the time the women assembled until two o'clock in the morning and though it was finally accepted as revised, there was renewed discussion early the next morning, another meeting right after breakfast and then the hasty departure to meet the Cardinal who was going to bring it to the attention of the Holy Father.

This was only the first of continual meetings, meetings about the letters to be presented, about other people to see, influences to be exerted, meetings as to whether one sector or another of the group of sixty or seventy women were being properly understood or treated. The language barrier made everything harder. We were from so many countries, so many faiths, so many backgrounds. Some of the women had so little money that they actually did not have enough to pay the extra costs of lunches and the one sightseeing trip that we all took together which came only to about seventy five cents apiece. Certainly there was too little time for us to get acquainted with each other. But I think most of us have lists of the women who were there, and most of us hope to see each other again and perhaps get acquainted better through correspondence of one kind or another. There is so much peace literature being gotten out and one thing it does is to draw us together. Most of us felt we knew Virginia Naeve, for instance, just through all her short notes by which she kept us together before the pilgrimage began.

The day of the audience arrived and the big busses came to the door, and it did not seem that we were being treated as of any more importance than the bus loads of school children who were coming from all over Europe during their Easter holiday to see Rome and attend the large general audience which took place each Wednesday at St. Peter's.

We waited as everyone else waited outside in the square, two of our members in wheel chairs. We passed through the gates showing our unprivileged tickets, and back past the bureau of excavations and through one of the side doors and around into a section already packed with people.

Klare Fassbinder, the leader of the German group had managed four special tickets; the Japanese representative, dressed in her lovely costume and bearing gifts for the Holy Father, and the two women in wheel chairs were put near the front. But the large body of pilgrims of our group were far to the rear, and unable to see over the heads of the multitude. It was only by searching around individually that we were able to get a better view. Two other women and I were pulled by a gay young Italian girl up into one of the tribunes where there was a tremendous view of the crowd and where we would be able to see the Pope come in and ascend the throne, but that space was only cleared a little because a huge pillar was in the way of seeing the Holy Father himself, when he was seated before the altar, ready to speak.

It was long to wait. Probably people were standing two hours and it was not until twelve-twenty that finally there was a surge in that vast mob and a sudden silence followed by almost a roar of greeting. Borne aloft on his chair, (and how could any have seen him if he were not conducted in this way,) the procession proceeded around the columns and then the Pope, blessing all, was conducted up to his throne where he sat while a list of all the groups of pilgrims was read aloud. As the names of the villages of Italy, and the schools on the Continent, and of England and the United States was read out, applause came from various parts of this vast group. And our pilgrimage was not mentioned!

But then the Pope began to speak and the words that fell from his lips seemed to be directed to us, to our group, speaking as he did about the "Pilgrims for Peace" who came to him, and his gratitude for their gratitude and encouragement. The young woman who had helped us find our places was translating his words as fast as he spoke them and writing them down while two of us read over her shoulder. She kept beaming at us, and all those around us, seeing our buttons, large almost as saucers, bright blue and bearing the legend "Mothers for Peace" in Italian, also smiled and indicating the Holy Father and us in turn, seemed to be letting us know that he was speaking to us especially.

It seemed too good to be true and if all those around us had not kept assuring us he was speaking to us, I would have considered it but a coincidence. Our messages had reached him we felt, impossible though it had seemed they would. I wrote these things in the post-script to my account in the last month's issue of the CW, but I am calling attention in more detail this month to our difficulties.

We were truly an ecumenical group made up as we were of all faiths, of believers and unbelievers, and I had no doubt but that a few of the women, perhaps one or two, were working with the communist peace groups too. This did not disturb me, though I would prefer that those of that political point of view were more open about it so that there were more chance of frank discussion about our oppositions and points of concordance. One can understand however the economical disadvantage, the loss of jobs, that such openness would lead to.

This infiltration, (the very word "infiltrate" has a connotation of hostility and fear so that I do not like to use it, but it is the only one which conveys the idea of secretiveness) is bound to go on in a movement which is reaching such proportions as the peace movement. In the past such groups with whom the CW has always cooperated, the War Resisters League, the Fellowship of Reconciliation, the American Friends Service Committee, the Peacemakers, the Women's International League for Peace and Freedom, have been free from Communist membership. But undoubtedly with the thousands now participating in mass demonstrations around the country, this is no longer true.

It was because of this "certainty," an American priest stationed in the Vatican told me, that the pilgrimage of women was not officially received. I could only reply that if we understood the Holy Father' last pleas, he wished a closer association, a seeking for concordances, and the opportunity to discuss oppositions. How could we know our brother, keeping so aloof? I would like to go through that encyclical on peace and count the number of times the word trust was used, how many times we were urged to work together for the common good. We were to go into the world as sheep among wolves, Jesus himself said, and St. John Chrysostom commented on that by writing that if we ceased to be sheep we no longer had the Good Shepherd with us. What have we to fear?

"That such trust would be used for political purposes by the Communists," was the only reply that I got.

However I was assured by "Vatican sources" (I am using the customary newspaper terminology but I mean Fr. Stransky,) that *The Catholic Worker* was not under suspicion, though some of the women of the pilgrimage had been told that we were a Communist group in Geneva!

That last evening I had my interview with Cardinal Bea and the opportunity to tell him more about the peace pilgrimage and about the women of many churches who made it up. After all, he was the Cardinal who according to all accounts is one of the most important and influential men in Rome after the Pope and I was grateful indeed for the opportunity I had for an hour's conversation with him in his apartment in the Brazilian college out on the Aurelian Way. He asked after *The Catholic Worker* in particular and details as to our work and told in turn of his very happy visit to America and the many engagements he could look forward to on a return visit.

I think it was seventy engagements to which he had been invited, and if he came again, perhaps, his secretary said, he could also visit *The Catholic Worker*.

I asked about the coming council and the probabilities of there being a more exhaustive discussion of the morality, of the theology of war and peace today, but I am afraid I got no definite answers save the assurance that these things would be part of the *schema* on the Church and the world.

Unfortunately I lost my notebook, the diary of my trip, so my report may not be as exact as I would like it to be. I remember the Cardinal's speaking of the *Focolari*, and how impressed he was with their movement which has grown from its beginnings in the bomb shelters during the Forties so that now it has spread all over the world.

My general impression was, all during my stay in Italy, that the clergy did not know too much about any lay movements in the world that questioned either the injustices of the social order by direct action, or that tried to educate the people in the ways of peace, which would include refusal of conscription or the payment of taxes for war; and in the racial struggles the confronting of the enemy with non-violence and a sharing of poverty which would be the beginning of true courage, the readiness to face suffering and death.

I came away from Rome more convinced than ever that the particular vocation of *The Catholic Worker* is to reach the man in the street, to write about the glorious truths of Christianity, the great adventure of the spirit, which can effect so great a transformation in the lives of men if they would consent to the promptings of the Spirit. We must write about men like Mayor Giorgio La Pira, a Sicilian whom I met in Florence, who is a third order Franciscan, who lives in poverty and simplicity in a small hospital room, who took (by right of eminent domain perhaps) the unused homes of the rich and gave them to the poor, who preaches and teaches the poor as St. Francis did, and who is so beloved in his city of Florence that he has been voted into office time and again, and also by the Communists of his city.

"No, I am not afraid of the Communists," he told me. "I went twice to Russia, the second time purely on a pilgrimage to visit some monasteries." I met this extraordinary public official while I was in Florence on the invitation of Jean Goss of the European Fellowship of Reconciliation to speak to a small group of Protestants first, then later at the Major Seminary where George Lorimer was my interpreter. Jean Goss himself was speaking those nights to large audiences and he too had to have an interpreter because he spoke only French. He is a warm and ardent speaker and I had heard him (with interpreters) and was much impressed.

July-August 1963

An invitation for me to speak in Danville, Virginia, came last month so I set out July 8th to fill the assignment. Actually I was not asked as editor of *The Catholic Worker*, as a writer, a reporter. I was asked by Mother Teresa of the Society of Christ The King, to come and take her place because the newly assigned young priest did not think that it was fitting that a founder of a religious group of social workers, known for the past twenty years in the community should be taking her place by the side of a crowd of Negro demonstrators on the steps of City Hall in Danville.

Mother Teresa had spoken on the radio several times besides. The priest is the only one for miles around; the next nearest church is Lynchburg, and it is one of the difficulties of the Church in America, that one is dependent for the Bread of Life on the one priest who may be completely hostile to one's point of view. In the big cities this does not matter. There are a number of priests in each parish and any number of parishes in each city. But in Danville there is one Catholic Church and one priest. One wishes to be friends.

Mother Teresa heads a small group of sisters who do social work among the poorest of the Negro and white population, town and rural. They do what comes to hand and if it is a baby, left on their doorstep or a family of half a dozen children whose mother is in a mental hospital for five months, or a group of families back in the country to be instructed in the truths of religion,—they are ready. While I was with the sisters, there was a baby, carried about with them, taken to Mass in the morning, sitting in a little stroller in their kitchen or garden while they worked.

"We have learned about mothers from them," Mother Teresa says happily. St. Teresa of Avila advises that every convent have a baby in it to humanize the nuns.

It is an all day bus trip to Danville. The bus leaves at 8:30 a.m. and arrives at 8:45 at night with few stops on the way. It is the through bus to New Orleans. Mother Teresa met me at the station and drove me out Route 4, down Industrial Avenue, past tobacco warehouses, past a sewage plant, past a street of shanties and then a row of slightly better houses, and finally up a rutted road to the top of a hill where the sisters have put up half a dozen buildings, including a guest house, a community house, work shops, a library and so on. They began with barracks and the sisters do the building themselves. A tornado in 1953 destroyed some of their houses, and they are working on another now. There are fruit trees, a vegetable garden, lovely grounds under a great spreading oak (many of whose limbs were torn away by the tornado), and across a little valley, a good barn and milk house. They have two Guernsey cows, and have an abundance of milk, butter and cream.

It was not long after I arrived that a group of the young people from SNCC (Student Non-Violent Coordinating Committee) arrived for a late supper. There was Cynthia Ann Carter from Danville; Roland Sherrod from Petersburg, Va., Ivanhoe Donaldson from New York, Bob Zellner, field secretary of the Alabama SNCC, Mary Elizabeth King and Sam Shirah from Atlanta. We ate the good farm products (there were steak and hot dogs besides) and students told me of the happenings in Danville. Stories of which had been publicized all over the country, but they still could scarcely convey the horror of the brutality which had been inflicted on a helpless, unarmed crowd of demonstrators.

Before I left New York, and it was not too heartening to hear it, Bob Gore had told other members of CORE that in all the country, the police of Danville had been the most terrible. And on July 12 Martin Luther King told a mass meeting in Danville that he had seen brutal things done by the police elsewhere in the South, "but seldom, if ever, have I heard of actions as vicious and brutal as those done by the police here." Dr. King's Assistant, Wyatt Tee Walker, called Danville the worst area with Gadsden, Alabama and Savannah, Georgia, a close second.

This is what happened the week before:

The group of demonstrators which included prominent ministers and their wives, parishioners and many young ones, were driven by deputized police into an alley between a parking lot and the City Hall and there the fire hoses were turned on them with such force that they were thrown to the pavement and in one case a woman's clothes, (skirt and blouse), ripped off her, so that she was exposed with nothing but step-ins and naked from the waist up. Women taking refuge under parked cars were dragged out and beaten with clubs and kicked. Arms were broken by the force of the blows. Men, women and children were all beaten unmercifully and deliberately. It was fear run riot.

"Deliver me from fear of their fear," I prayed as I listened, using the words of St. Peter which had been part of the epistle of last Sunday's Mass, thinking of the hysterical fear of guilty whites, fear of the past, of the future.

"Trouble was, they deputized untrained policemen, men who were garbage collectors and street cleaners and other workers for the city," the students told me, as many others told me again and again. And when they said "untrained," I thought of what I had read of how police are trained to strike blows that will not be seen, that will not kill but will render the opponent unconscious and so on. But these men were striking as though to kill by their blows and many of the demonstrators had to be taken unconscious to the hospital. At present writing two are still there, one in Duke Hospital and one in Richmond.

The local hospital, Winslow, has 25 beds for the colored and the other hospital in this town of 47,000 has 750 beds for the whites. Winslow is a city hospital, free, a fact protested by white citizens who point out that they pay fourteen dollars a day at Memorial which had started as a hospital for the needy and had been given gifts of a million or more.

What I was invited to do in Danville was to speak at a mass meeting the following night in the High Street Baptist Church where Rev. L. W. Chase is pastor. The meeting began with songs and hymns and the hymn singing was hearty and beautiful.

"Are we weak and heavy laden, cumbered with a load of care? Precious Saviour still our refuge, take it to the Lord in prayer. Do thy friends despise, forsake thee, take it to the Lord in prayer. In His arms He'll take and shield thee, take it to the Lord in prayer."

There were other hymns and prayers and the invocation was surely a crying out to the Lord, a singing and a sobbing of a prayer, rhythmical, so that it became almost a litany. Rev. James Dixon prayed with all his strength.

And then there were the Freedom songs, many of which have been composed in jail, coming from the heart, from the suffering, from the open bleeding wounds of a people who have known indignity and sorrow for generations.

The Freedom songs were more lively than the hymns and clapping accompanied them and a light tapping of the feet. *"Keep on walking, talking . . . Ain't gonna let no injunction turn me round, walking up the freedom way."* There were many verses and many refrains. The singing lifted the heart, strengthened the weak knees.

There were many speakers but they were brief; William Canada told with complete lack of emotion how he had spent nineteen days in jail. Authorities kept denying he was there, and he was sought for by his family in hospitals and there was no knowing where he was until he was released. Despite beatings he had been put to work in the quarry.

Bob Zellner talked of Moses and how he led his people out of Egypt and how tired people got of the struggle so that they wanted to go back to bondage; it was forty years before they saw the Promised Land. And he compared the non-violent struggle of the Negro to the clamorous attack made on the walls of Jericho, which, he reminded them, had come tumbling down.

Claudia Edwards of Arkansas, one of the task force of CORE, urged the Mothers to join me in a picket line in the downtown area the next morning. She herself, she told me later, was going to buy her some jail clothes in an adjoining town since they were boycotting the downtown area in Danville. Jail clothes meant a pair of jeans or dungarees and a slightly heavier shirt so that if the hoses were turned on them again, her clothes would not be swept off. I saw her the next day at noon and she looked small and wiry, and very much alive. The next afternoon she and a dozen others lay down before the gates of the Danville Mills against which they are urging a world-wide boycott, and the police let them lie there and deployed the trucks to another gate. There were not enough of them to cover all the entrances to these great textile mills which have subsidiaries all through the South, and a world wide market. Ten thousand are employed by the Mill and only 500 Negroes.

There were speakers urging registration for the vote, so that next morning 47 went to the polls and registered, and they went together so that they would not be intimidated. There was only one woman, very nervous, to register them, so it took a long time, and many could not join our picket line at the noon hour. The rule is that at first registration, one pays not only the year's poll-tax but for three years previous, and this added burden keeps many from registering.

Lawyers spoke on the progress made in the courts. Leonard Holt from Norfolk and Arthur Kinoy from New York, both warned their audience, (there were five hundred there,) that the work could not just be done in the courts, that the people had to keep up their demonstrations, had to continue their struggle in the streets.

Reverend A. I. Dunlap, just recently appointed vicepresident of Kittrell Junior College, made a statement of purpose and since he was directly in front of me and spoke so that he kept his audience in gales of laughter I could not get the gist of his talk which was also very brief.

I was the speaker of the evening and I do not know whether I would have had the courage to speak, outsider that I was, if I had not been there to represent Mother Teresa whose work was known and loved by them all. Besides, the singing lightened my own heart, dissolved my own fear, so that I could tell them of the Women's Pilgrimage for Peace and the Pope's encyclical *Pacem in Terris*.

There was no end to what one could say about that Encyclical. There was the part where he said "He who possesses certain rights, has likewise the duty to claim those rights as marks of his dignity, while all others have the obligation to acknowledge those rights and respect them."

I took that statement on a poster placard on the streets of Danville the next morning when we picketed for an hour and a half before the hostile or indifferent stares of hundreds of people during their lunch hour.

There was a notable absence of Negroes but some of those who shopped said they were from the country and did not know about the pleas of their fellow Negroes to keep out of the downtown area and not to buy from stores where Negroes were not employed in fair ratio to the whites.

There was much to quote from Pope John: what he had to say about the rights of conscience; about unjust laws; about the place of women, the part they had to play in the world.

And I told my listeners too, that after so many years of work in the Peace Movement, I had come to the conclusion that basic to peace was this struggle of the colored for education, job opportunity, health, and recognition as men. That while we talked of averting war, we were in the midst of one of the strangest wars in history, where the side which had declared the war were using no weapons but those of suffering. They were praying; they were marching; they were doing without (by boycott); they were in a way offering their own flesh, their suffering, their imprisonment, for their brothers. "A new *commandment*" (not a counsel) "I give to you, that you love each other as I have loved you." And that commandment of Jesus means the laying down of life itself for one's brother, colored and white.

It is the Negro who is leading the way, and it is among the Negroes that the ranks of the martyrs is increasing. They are uncounted, unknown, many of them. Medgar Evers leads them, going out as he did with foreknowledge of his doom. He fell, and his brother is taking his place. Others are unknown, unsung heroes. Something is happening in our midst that we do not recognize. We have eyes and see not, ears and hear not. The last are becoming the first. "He hath put down the mighty from their seat and hath exalted the humble."

It is hard to feel that the color of our skin in a way separates us from this mass of people whom we have injured. It is with too little and too late that we are engaging ourselves. But even if it is at the eleventh hour that we are called to serve, we can respond.

We can pray too that we may be "counted worthy to suffer," a fact the apostles rejoiced over when they put up their non-violent struggle for the Faith, and were imprisoned and beaten. I felt that I had not been counted worthy when I learned that the Danville police have been imprisoning all the pickets since I left, besides all those who have been engaged in sit-ins. The jails have been filling up.

I talked to some of the women who had been beaten by the police and their deputies and the savagery was incredible. The only thing they were spared were the humiliating stripping and searching that all women are subjected to in the Women's House of Detention in New York.

On the picket line which I participated in through the downtown streets of Danville, I was preceded by Mrs. Chase, wife of the minister of the church where I had spoken the night before, and Mrs. Lawrence Campbell whose husband is the executive secretary of the Danville Christian Progressive Association and minister of one of the other leading churches of the city.

The very young among the Negro students have led in the integrating of public facilities, lunch counters, hospitals, libraries, theaters and housing in many places, and have engaged in minds and hearts of youth in Danville also. It was fascinating to see and hear these young ones, some of them only fourteen, talk of the work and the struggle ahead.

Just as in Birmingham, many of these young ones have already seen the inside of the prisons. Comparing them to the gangs of unemployed teen-agers who are looked upon with fear and trembling by the householder everywhere, one can only see in these young ardent souls great hope for the future.

John Davis was one of the first from Danville to take a position of responsibility in these activities. In an interview at the office of *Liberation* in New York, he told how a group of young people were arrested for trespassing when they sat on the steps of Charcoal House, a segregated restaurant, after the manager closed the place in the face of their picket line. When they were arrested there were two news men present and Chief of Police McCain warned the police to handle their prisoners with care, but when they arrived in the jail cells where there were no witnesses they were kicked and "cursed in most vile language."

Ivanhoe Donaldson who drove down from New York was halted by the police outside Danville and arrested for driving with faulty brakes, handcuffed, taken to the police station, and struck in the face several times. Another student from Brandeis University who came to help the SNCC group was beaten so badly with clubs that Mother Teresa said it was a wonder he had any sense left. The police kept saying, one of the young colored girls told me, "Is you a white man or is you a nigger?" and when he would not answer, they kept beating him.

This same little one, who looked no more than twelve years old, had been thrown into prison too, together with a crowd of others, and "the prison was so full that they had to put us in the side with the white people,—so we integrated the jail!" Truly this is also a children's crusade. It is not that they have been led into it,—it is hard to keep them out.

An Emergency Food Drive has been announced by representatives of SNCC and the Congress of Racial Equality (CORE) in Danville, to help ease hunger due to the cutting off of unemployment compensation and loss of jobs which occurred in reprisal for participating in demonstrations.

"There are also many families where one or both parents are in jail, and they have vowed to remain there without bail.

155

Food is needed for their children," according to Rev. L. G. Campbell. Staples such as flour, canned milk, and canned vegetables and meat are needed for immediate distribution. "We are making a special appeal to all friends of justice for small and large packages to be sent to 226 North Union St., Danville, Va., said Avon W. Rollins, Executive Committee, SNCC.

Besides the relief that is needed and the money for all the expenses and legal fee of these committees (they are doing a lot of work and not spending much on literature) there is the problem of the building of a kind of social order which can handle the problems of automation, the building of a new society within the shell of the old. The continuation, in other words, of Peter Maurin's program of Farming Communes and Agronomic Universities throughout the country. Besides teachers, students, workers and scholars, all are needed who have funds to invest in land and enterprises, those who know how to plan and those who know how to build, those most especially who know how to teach,—to work with others. There is not much room for the individualist, but much need for the personalist, in the communitarian society where the aim will be the common good; the need to make the kind of social order "where it is easier for man to be good," as Peter Maurin said.

There is time to talk about these things in prison, in meeting halls, in times of unemployment and tension. We each have our vocation—the thing to do is to answer the call. We each have something to give.

Late News. Rev. Chase of Danville whose wife led the Mothers for Freedom picket line in Danville in which I took part, was arrested. Police came at four-thirty in the morning and kicked in the door of his home and dragged him out in pajamas to the local jail. Later in the day eighty more pickets were arrested, including Mrs. Chase, his wife.

September 1963

Cuba and Sex

I am reminded some more of Cuba when I read an article last month in a pacifist paper entitled "Forget about Gandhi!"

The author writes about the "indigenous, improvisatory

character of Negro non-violence;" and about "the asceticism and puritanical practices of the Black Muslims with their bitterness and overtones of violence." But "In Birmingham the motto seems to be: Let's eat, drink and make love tonight, because tomorrow morning we will be in the white man's jail. One man told me with obvious glee, that when some of the imprisoned demonstrators were released from jail because friends or relations had posted bond for them, he heard one of them say: 'Don't worry; I'm just gonna take a bath and get some sugar from my honey. Then I'll be right back in.'

"When the Committee for Non-violent Action" the writer continues, "organized an integrated peace walk through a portion of the South last year, it required all participants to take a pledge of celibacy and abstinence from alcoholic beverages for the duration of the project. But a pacifist who went South last month to take part in a Freedom Walk, and who fasted during his entire imprisonment, told me that the day before they went out to face almost certain brutality and arrest they had a gala party at which the whiskey flowed like water. 'Pacifism was never like this,' was his happy comment just before he set off for the South once more, thoroughly prepared to face whatever mortifications of the flesh lay in store for him but obviously feeling liberated by the realization that he would not be required to add his own mortifications and punishments to those imposed by his opponents."

There is a certain arrogance about this writer's attitude giving the white man's stereotyped picture of the Negro. And also evidence of his own belated adolescent retreat from the Protestant Puritanism of New England forebears. I am reminded when I hear these middle aged liberals sounding off on sexual and other fleshly freedoms, of some of the men of the same middle-class, middle-aged liberal background who used to hang around Greenwich Village probing into and inciting the young people about them, to a free sex life as though hoping youth would not miss those ardors that they perhaps feel that they had missed. Or perhaps they had not missed them but their pleasure in sex had been dimmed by just that sense of sin natural to man when he lets his lower nature take over irresponsibly. Some men have incited their own children to gratify their desires and to get rid of the fruit of their intercourse by abortion, as I know happened in two families. It is one thing not to judge others, and it is still another thing to expect men and women to live according to

157

right reason, to seek wisdom and live by it. The wisdom of the flesh is treacherous indeed.

Cuba is held up to us as an example of the Puritanism of the Marxist-Leninist, and dismal pictures of her are painted. No more houses of prostitution, no more gambling halls, no gay bars. When someone implied that Fidel Castro might have a mistress (to use old fashioned language), the students with whom I was talking during my visit to Cuba last September looked shocked. "There is no time in his life for that kind of playing around," they said. And the girls looked as though mud had been thrown at their idol, regarding such a question as a desecration of a hero.

There is the story in Scripture of King David who had remained behind in Jerusalem when the army of Israel were fighting in the Ammonite country. One day he had risen from midday rest and was walking on the roof of his palace, when he saw a woman who came up to bathe on the roof of the house opposite, a woman of rare beauty. She was the wife of Urias who was away at war. King David sent for her and when she was brought to him, "he mated with her." When she found that she had conceived, she told King David. Whereupon the King sent for Urias, and when he arrived from the scene of battle, he questioned him for a while asking him how the battle was going and so on, and then told him to go home and refresh himself. "So Urias left the palace, and the king sent food after him from the royal table; but Urias slept the night at the palace gate among his master's attendants; go home he would not. Then David, learning from common talk that Urias had not gone home, said to him, Thou art newly come from a journey; why wouldst thou not go back to thy house? What? answered Urias, here are the ark of God and all Israel, and all Juda encamped in tents, here are my Lord Joab and all those other servants of my master sleeping on the hard ground; should I go home and eat and drink and bed with my wife?"

King David kept him a few more days, made him eat and drink until he was bemused with wine, but still when he left at night he slept at the palace gate. "So David sent for his General Joab to put Urias in the first line where the fighting is bitterest, there to die by the enemies' hand."

Recently during the Profumo scandal in England there was much talk as to how much freedom a man should take to himself in public life, how much freedom to love, to drink and make merry.

158

Certainly food, drink and sex are good, in their proper order, in their place. In time of battle, such a strange and mighty battle as is going on now between armed and unarmed forces in our country and we too on the unarmed side with our Negro brothers, the weapons of the spirit certainly do not include the strong drink and sexual license celebrated by this pacifist leader.

I know one of the white demonstrators who told one of our group that when he was arrested he was so "hung over" from a party the night before that he was glad to be arrested and thrown into jail, that he could not have walked another step in the march he was undertaking. He was one of those too, who wished to get "some sugar from their honey" before they went on to jail. A far cry from Urias!

I have been asked to express myself on these matters, especially since there has been a pamphlet published in England by the Quakers which is said to condone premarriage sexual intercourse "if the parties are responsible." My reaction is that of woman who must think in terms of the family, the need of the child to have both mother and father, who believes strongly that the home is the unit of society.

Sex is a profound force, having to do with life, the forces of creation which make man god-like. He shares in the power of the Creator, and, when sex is treated lightly, as a means of pleasure, I can only consider that woman is used as a plaything, not a person. When sex is so used it takes on the quality of the demonic, and to descend into this blackness is to have a foretaste of hell, "where no order is, but everlasting horror dwelleth." (Job x.22) Aldous Huxley has given us a glimpse of this hell in "After Many a Summer Dies the Swan," showing the sexual instinct running riot like cancer cells through the body, degenerating into sadism and torture and unspeakable violence. I speak in extreme terms I admit. But long long before I was a Catholic I felt how prevalent was the demi-vierge attitude. I certainly felt that the teaching of Jesus, "He who looks with lust after a woman has already committed adultery in his heart." There is no such thing as seeing how far one can go without being caught, or how far one can go without committing mortal sin.

On the other hand, the act of sex in its right order in the love life of the individual has been used in Old and New Testament as the symbol of the love between God and Man. Sexual love in its intensity makes all things new and one sees the other as God sees him. And this is not illusion. In those

159

joyful days when one is purified by this single heartedness, this purity of vision, one truly sees the essence of the other, and this mating of flesh and spirit, the whole man and the whole woman, is the only way we know what the term "beatific vision" means. It is the foretaste we have of heaven and all other joys of the natural world are intensified by it, hearing, seeing, knowing.

When I became a Catholic forty years ago, I felt with joy that my faith brought me what scripture calls "a rule of life and instruction." So I recommend the Gospels which are so potent, so grace-bearing, that the priest says when he has finished reading the Gospel, "By the words of the Gospel may my sins be blotted out."

I finish this writing down at the beach house with the waves pounding on the beach in a foretaste of an equinoctial storm. It is only September 6th and there are probably two more months of warmth ahead, and these months are quiet months as no other months are quiet. One rests between the tumult of summer and winter. In October I shall be travelling. I hope with the money I earn speaking, to travel still further, to England to attend the peace conference at Spode House. So expect a couple of travellogues these next two months, but not much letter writing will be done. I shall take to postal cards!

November 1963

All Saints Day, 1963
Taena Community,
between Stroud, Cheltenham
and Gloucester, England

It is good to spend the Feast Day with this community of families which had its beginnings in 1940 and through three moves, and various vicissitudes, has continued until now, and will, God willing, continue. There are twelve adults and twenty-three children. Three single men, a farmer, a potter and sculptor. There are not enough workers of the land for these 130 acres, with its 35 cows, 45 sheep and 80 chickens, 15 acres of wheat and 5 of potatoes, so they hire a lad, David, and recently a group of girls from a reform school nearby came to harvest the potatoes.

Barbara goes out to work as county nurse, George Ineson

as an architect, Tom as an accountant, but now he has been in the hospital with a stroke. Say a prayer for him.

I have slept at Ronald and Hilary's home these last nights and there is in the house besides me, two single men and eight children, and Hilary's mother who is visiting. Hilary, a tall young woman who met her husband in Germany in Quaker Relief Work, and has spent her entire married life in community, does all the cooking, washing and caring for eight children. It is an old stone farmhouse with no, God forbid, central heating. The kitchen is a large room facing south and all the cooking is done there, so the place is warm. But the washing up is down a short flight into a half basement, and the lavatory up one flight, and the bath up another. We all eat together at table, and the older children, Benjamin, Rebecca and Robert, are very keen. We have animated discussions about interracial problems, and Guy Fawkes Day which is November 6. They have prepared a man-sized effigy with a clown-like face, all stuffed with straw, dressed in a man's suit, a most startling figure to come upon, lolling in an easy chair in the living room. Rebecca sits on his lap and Rachael wags his head, but he will not be treated so kindly next week when he will be burnt on a huge pyre already prepared for him in a meadow below the house. It occurs to me to be shocked at this, and I suggest that the children have a trial and pardon the dynamiter but they will have none of it. He must be burnt and all over England on what has become a children's holiday, the fires will be burning. For the last weeks in London the children in the slums have been parading their Guy and soliciting pennies for Guy but after he has afforded them all these treats he must crown their enjoyment by going up in flames. Fireworks of all kinds complete the picture.

All is green and beautiful still here in England. Flowers in profusion, nicotiana, calendula, snapdragon, blue gentian, stock, and many others, and it has been raining these last few days and the colors are the more brilliant. Many of the trees will stay green, but those with leaves turning, are in rich browns, and yellows, but not the flaming colors we are used to in our New England states. It is not cold yet, though the nights are sharp. But we are glad of the heaters, paraffin (kerosine) and electric. The foundations of the house I am in are very old, sixteenth century, and the house has been built on. The rest is seventeenth and eighteenth. Full of drafts of course, with high ceilings. I had wanted to get up to Yorkshire to see where Charlotte Bronte lived, but could not make it. But it seems to me that this house, though larger than the one described as the Brontës', must be rather like it. There is another tiny old cottage, where silversmith Philip Lowery lives with his wife Angela who was brought up in the community at Ditchling. I have dined also with George Ineson and his wife Connie twice and with Barbara McNulty, a public health nurse. We had a gathering one evening and four or five former members of the Bruderhof were there and also some Quakers. Most of the talk was about community and the need for such oases in a world where such problems as large scale farming, migrant labor, automation, unemployment, juvenile delinquency and old age exist. Peter Maurin used to say, "There is no unemployment on the land," which made everyone angry, so that they pointed out to him the dire situation of the migrants who wandered from state to state looking for work. These terse statements of his always started things off. Given the land, rented or owned, there is always work.

For thirty years people have criticized us for "standing for the family farm" pointing out that it did not work. Of course it does not, given no capital, a large family and no help. But Peter has always talked of the farming commune and the agronomic university, and that is still what we are most interested in. It is good to visit such a community as Taena. Of course there are family differences, controversies, differences in temperament as there are in every community, and of course there are those that deny that there is a community, and insist that they are a group of separate families, each on its own. When I think of Upton, Massachusetts, South Lyons, Michigan and Marycrest, New York, where families have raised their children, and kept going with a great deal of mutual aid over the years, I am overcome with admiration at the hard work, the endurance, the continuing vision of these families.

When I visited Donald Attwater at Penzance the other day, he gave me a copy of *Saints of the East* to read, published in England by Havril Press, London, in 1962 and I have been dipping into it on my trip.

Theodosius of the Caves (Pechersky) was the father of Russian Monasticism and the monastery at Kiev is open again today, though it was closed for a while during the first years of the Soviets. Perhaps that is the monastery that Mayor La Pira of Florence, Italy, visited on pilgrimage.

Theodosius emphasized the importance of community life, I read today, and one of his monks declared that a "Lord have mercy on us" prayed from the heart collectively by the community is of greater religious value than the whole psalter said alone in one's cell. His monastery had a hospital for the sick and the disabled, they had a hospice for travelers and every Saturday a cartload of food was sent down to the city jail.

All communities overflow in good works, even in England where the State is trying to take care of all. Audrey Henson gave me a book of R. H. Tawney's to read which deals with England today and I must certainly study the socialization which Pope John so recommended. Michael Harrington, whom I ran into in London at the American Express, used to talk to us about the modification of socialism in England. (He was leaving for Paris next day, and was going to Poland. He was without collar and looked as though he were wearing the same suit he had when he lived with us on Chrystie street, and he looked young and happy.)

Spode House

This has been the last week of our trip. Eileen Egan and I, to explain belatedly, came to England to attend the annual meeting at Spode House, a Dominican retreat house north of Birmingham where, with Dom Bede Griffiths, we had been invited to speak. It was a large and most interesting meeting, and Father Conrad Peplar and Father Simon Blake were most friendly hosts. Those were the two priests we saw the most of. Dom Bede was the priest who received the group which began the community which became Taena, into the Church, so they were happy to have had a visit from him before the conference began.

I cannot give all the details of my trip. I spoke at another meeting of the Pax group in London, to gatherings at Bob and Molly Walsh's at Oxford, to the anarchist group at the Dryden room of the Lamb and Staff pub in London, had lunch at the House of Lords with Lord Longford, a socialist peer, had tea with Lady Cripps whose daughter married an African whose husband is now in prison in Ghana, and whose grandchildren, two of them, are doing most adventurous things in Thailand and Kenya; visited Denis Knight and his beautiful family in Tunbridge Wells, stayed overnight at Sennon Cove near Land's End, saw Penzance and Donald Attwater's wife Dorothy and their two daughters, lunched on fish and chips, had tea with Eric Gill's brother Cecil Gill in Cardiff. For eight years, before his conversion Cecil had been a medical missionary in New Guinea.

There was a dinner, and then a gathering of all kinds of people engaged in good works at the home of Victor Gollanz and his wife. There was a boat trip up the Thames to Greenwich, starting from Westminster Bridge in front of Scotland Yard, and in Greenwich we saw the Cutty Sark, a great sailing vessel made of teakwood, and so great a boat it dominated the streets around. Tea in Greenwich and then by bus to Hempstead where we had a meeting with the secular fraternity of Charles de Foucauld.

And now I write at Taena, tomorrow going on to Stanbrook Abbey to see Emily Coleman whom we knew as Emily Scarborough when she wrote the Peter Maurin Farm column for the CW eight years ago. Then to London, and Cambridge for a day, and then to Southampton and the boat for home. I will think of many other things that I should have told, such as my afternoon with Hugh Brock, editor of *Peace News* who drove us out to see Muriel Lester, former head of Kingsley Hall who had the privilege of putting up Gandhi on his visit to England in 1931. We saw Epping Forest, Hemstead Heath and visited the graves of Karl and Jenny Marx in Highgate Cemetery.

December 1963

The gigantic nature of the struggle in which we are each one of us engaged, a struggle between the forces of good and evil was clearly shown to us this last month by the assassination of our President. This story of horror is still unfolding in the daily press. It is not for us to reiterate what all are reading in their daily papers and listening to on their radios. And all who read and listen are relating what occurred to all that went before, the recent past with its murder of little children in Birmingham, bombings and shootings in the South, the assassinations of the president of Viet Nam and his brother-in-law. Violence in the rest of the world more or less accepted as "a fact of life" inevitable in the struggle for a better world, but resulting in shocked grief and bitter tears by our own people when it happens to us.

I was in Chicago when I heard the news. I had just gotten

off the bus from South Bend, where I had been speaking to Notre Dame students, seminarians, Brothers, and parishioners at the liturgical fair held in St. Therese' parish. I had gone to Nina Polcyn's whose guest I always am in Chicago, and she had left St. Benet's book shop on South Wabash to go to Mass with me at the Paulist church and then to lunch. The news came to us then over the radio and we could only sit and weep at the senseless violence that had erupted again, this time striking down a young and vital leader of a State, a husband, son and father.

Two days later, as we came from the liturgy in Fr. Chrysostom's Eastern rite church on West Fullerton, we heard the news of the second blow struck, another assassination, even more horrible than the first in that it took place in a police station, where men are supposed to be mindful of "law and order," the protection of the weak and the innocent, and where all men are presumed innocent, so it is said, until they are proven guilty. To this we had come. To these low depths we had fallen.

Yet here we are at this happy season, the time of the birth of Jesus Christ into the world as an infant in a manger, and "the government of this world is on His shoulders," and we know that God can bring good out of evil, that all things can work together for good to those who love God, that the time of rejoicing comes almost simultaneously with the time of sorrow, of repentance, that there is no "time" with God, that we are living in eternity this moment, and that "all the way to heaven is heaven, because He said, I am the Way."

1964

April 1964

MYSTERY OF THE POOR

☐ On Holy Thursday, truly a joyful day, I was sitting at
the supper table at St. Joseph's House on Chrystie Street
and looking around at all the fellow workers and thinking
how hopeless it was for us to try to keep up appearances.
The walls are painted a warm yellow, and the ceiling has
been done by generous volunteers, and there are some large
brightly colored ikon-like paintings on wood and some colorful banners with texts (now fading out) and the great
crucifix brought in by some anonymous friend with the request that we hang it in the room where the breadline eats.
Some well meaning guest tried to improve on the black iron
by gilding it and I always intend to do something about it
and restore its former grim glory. Better still would be to
have the glorified Christ, robed and crowned and colorful,
which we have hanging in the diningroom at Peter Maurin
Farm. Nina Polcyn of St. Benet's bookshop in Chicago, long
associated with Milwaukee, Chicago and New York houses,
promised crucifixes for every room in the new place we will
move to in a few months.

I looked around and the general appearance of the place
was as usual, homelike, informal, noisy and comfortably
warm on a cold evening. A close observer would however,
notice that many of our guests had a habit of hiding shoes, a

coat, a pair of socks in the most unlikely places, something in reserve to take back to their rooms at night. If they did not forget them. In the cat's box under one cupboard there was a pair of shoes as well as our pet cat, a good ratter.

"Don't touch it," Ed Forand warned, "the shoes are someone's and the cat is guarding them!" He was cheerfully ladling out a most delicious stew, with much gravy over plentiful mashed potatoes. He likes to cook, he says, and takes the job twice a week. Clare Bee, our English volunteer, has it two nights, and Chris two, and Monica one. Another aspect of our work which distinguishes our editors from all other editors. They cook a community meal each night for as many as seventy-five people.

The atmosphere at Chrystie Street is a cheerful one, and Ed Forand has a great deal to do with that. He is unfailingly energetic and happy. When he is sick he has the good common sense to take time off, and his work is varied enough to relieve tension. Early morning after Mass and communion he is at the market collecting vegetables and fruits, all of which are free. Mondays he takes off for rest or recreation. He visits Church during the day to renew his spiritual energy. He makes a monthly day of recollection when we are fortunate enough to get a priest, at Peter Maurin Farm. This month we had Father Berrigan and next month we will have Father Janer. Baron von Hugel says that we should live our good lives on three levels, the spiritual, mental and physical to be healthy and equalize the stress.

But enough of Ed. This that I am writing is an appeal and I wanted to start with a most cheerful note. Because when I looked around Good Friday and saw the marks of the Cross on all around me, my heart tightened with compassion. Our old friends who have been with us fifteen or more years, are getting older, and the marks of pain are on their faces, and in their movements. It is a miracle that some have survived the truly fearful operations they have had to have. How can Bill, sick as he has always been, continue with the dishwashing every noon? And one of our waiters who was all but dying a few years ago, had managed to survive and keeps on helping us. There are many of course who cannot work, who have not the physical ability or facility for work. How to start now to give a philosophy of work, which Peter Maurin always used to talk about. And how to judge another's crippling pain? Looked at with the eyes of a visitor many of whom are our readers who get the 74,000 copies of the paper which are mailed out each month, our place must look dingy indeed, filled as it always is with men and women, and some children too, all of whom bear the unmistakable marks of destitution and misery. Aren't we deceiving ourselves, I am sure many of them think, in the work we are doing? What are we accomplishing anyway for them, or for the world or for the common good? Are these people being "rehabilitated," is the question we get almost daily, from visitors or our readers who seem to be great letter writers. One priest had his catechism classes write us questions as to our work after they had the assignment in religion class to read my paperback book, *The Long Loneliness*. The majority of them asked the same question, "How can you see Christ in people?" And we only say: It is an act of faith, constantly repeated. It is an act of love, resulting from an act of faith. It is an act of hope, that we can awaken these same acts in their hearts too, with the help of God, and the works of mercy, which you our readers, help us to do, day in and day out over the years.

On Easter Day, on awakening late after the long midnight services in our parish church, I read over the last chapters of the four Gospels and felt that I received great light and understanding with the reading of them. "They have taken the Lord out of His tomb and we do not know where they have laid Him," Mary Magdalene said, and we can say this with her in times of doubt and questioning. How do we know we believe? How do we know we indeed have faith? Because we have seen His hands and His feet in the poor around us. He has shown himself to us in them. We start by loving them for Him, and we soon love them for themselves, each one a unique person, most special!

In that last glorious chapter of St. Luke, Jesus told his followers, "Why are you so perturbed? Why do questions arise in your minds? Look at my hands and my feet. It is I myself. Touch me and see. No ghost has flesh and bones as you can see I have." They were still unconvinced, for it seemed too good to be true. "So He asked them, 'Have you anything to eat?' They offered Him a piece of fish they had cooked which he took and ate before their eyes."

How can I help but think of these things every time I sit down at Chrystie Street or Peter Maurin Farm and look around at the tables filled with the unutterably poor who are going through their long continuing crucifixion. It is most surely an exercise of faith for us to see Christ in each other.

But it is through such exercise that we grow and the joy of our vocation assures us we are on the right path.

It is easier most certainly to believe now that the sun warms us and we know that buds will appear on the sycamore trees in the wasteland across from the Catholic Worker office, that life will spring out of the dull clods of that littered park across the way. There are wars and rumors of war, poverty and plague, hunger and pain. Still, the sap is rising, again there is the resurrection of spring, God's continuing promise to us that He is with us always, with His comfort and joy, if we will only ask. "Ask and you shall receive, seek and you shall find," He said. And Pascal adds to His words, "You would not seek me if you had not already found me."

You must excuse me if I seem to be writing an Easter sermon, out of place for a woman to do, but I must keep trying to explain what we do, year in and year out, and to ask your help again. We are not mailing out an appeal this spring because sooner or later, when the long delays are over, and the lawyers and real estate men and the surveyors get through to our sale (and there is tremendous volume of buying and selling now that the Verrazano bridge over the Narrows is nearing completion) we expect we will have enough money to get our new place up the Hudson, and enough to carry us through the summer besides. We have never yet sent out an appeal when we had money and I am afraid we were having delusions of grandeur this last month when we did not send out our usual March appeal. Actually, when we pay our rents, almost a thousand a month, for our apartments in the neighborhood and for the furnished rooms and apartments for Millie and Julie and Katherine and so on; and when we pay the gas and electric, and the bread and meat bills, and Tony the grocer, and all the daily odds and ends of medicines, carfares, stamps—we would not have had enough for the envelopes, paper, mailing and so on for that usual semiannual appeal which takes up the slack and keeps us running. So I am writing this appeal instead, and trust that our readers, before all their money dribbles away, will send some off to the poor. "Let your abundance supply their want," St. Paul said. "Bear ye one another's burdens." "Love one another," St. John pleaded. And "love is an exchange of gifts," St. Ignatius said. So please, will you make this gesture of love? Where is no love, will you put love, and so make this increase in the sum total of good in the world? It is about the most peace-making thing you can do—the most radical thing, since it gets at the roots of the trouble.

The mystery of the poor is this, that they are Jesus, and what you do for them you do for Him. It is the only way we have of knowing and believing in our love. The mystery of poverty is that by sharing in it, making ourselves poorer by giving to others, we increase our knowledge of and belief in love.

A grateful heart for your help, which has always been forthcoming, is just one more thing to thank you for.

May 1964

I am writing this column, at the beginning of the thirty second year of the Catholic Worker, at Tivoli, New York, where we are making new beginnings of a farming commune, agronomic university, house of hospitality, all combined in one, because that is the way it has worked out over the years.

Peter Maurin

Peter Maurin, to inform those who have come lately to a knowledge of *The Catholic Worker* and its program of action, is the founder, the instigator, the teacher of us all. Peter died in 1949, on May 15th, the anniversary of the feast day of St. John Baptist de la Salle, who was born in 1651, and founded a new congregation which he called the Brothers of the Christian Doctrine. Peter and many of his brothers became Christian Brothers in France and he had his training with them, though later he found that his vocation was a unique one of direct action, emphasizing both the freedom and the responsibility of the ordinary layman. He was a forerunner and he is still a forerunner. We are spending our lives trying to work out his ideas, and we are learning the hard way, by trial and error. There is very little we say or write that we do not have to give an accounting for, here in this life. "Do you know what you are talking about, do you really mean what you say?" our Lord seems to ask us, as we live with "the people," as distinguished from the masses so often swayed hither and yon in our day by the demagogue. Living as we do with bread lines, with the people who come to us, off the streets, of all races, colors, creeds, of all intelligences one might say, we see how we ourselves have to learn, continue to study, to work and pray for the help of the holy Spirit. We sure have to grow in patience. While on the one side we receive acclamations, on the other side, it is denunciations.

People are always thinking we have accomplished what we are holding up as an ideal, and the simple ones who come to us keep wondering why we have not already built that kind of society where it is easier for man to be good, as Peter Maurin expressed it. It is a wonder, with all their expectation and disappointment, they do not go away, but bad as we are, it is worse outside, someone said; or "though I am unhappy here, I am more unhappy elsewhere," someone else said. And so we are really not a true communal farm, a true agronomic university, but a community of need, a community of "wounded ones" as one girl who came to us from a state hospital, expressed it. I myself have often thought of our communities as concentration camps of displaced people, all of whom want community, but at the same time want privacy, a little log cabin of their own, to grow their own food, cultivate their own gardens and seek for sanctity in their own way. This kind of sanctity of course has for most of us as little validity as the sense of wellbeing of the drug addict. "Man is not made to live alone," as we are told in the book of Genesis.

But as it is, work is our salvation. There is scarcely one among us who does not want to contribute by his work to the community, and since there is little choice in the work to be done, ordinary humdrum work for the most part, governed by the circumstances which arise each day, we are, willy nilly, being sanctified, but not in the way we wish, not by our own efforts. Jim washes dishes, and nobody likes the way he washes them. Tom cooks, and no one likes the way he cooks. Another is general pot washer, and carries trays to the sick and he is criticized for his mournful disposition. If you say it is a fine day, he tells you there will probably be a freeze-up tomorrow. I remember another in our midst, many years ago who used to say, "It is no use ploughing that field because we probably won't have the money to put into seed, and if we did we would probably have a drought." (But each one with his many superficial faults, has also profound virtues). If you laugh at such a whimsy, you are liable to offend as though you were making fun of someone. Oh, community is a wonderful thing, as all the religious orders in

171

the world know so well. There is not much room for complacency or a sense of accomplishment, looking around after thirty-one full years of work.

Day of Recollection

Father Janer, S.J., who has charge of Nativity Mission across the "park" from us on Forsythe Street, who deals with Puerto Rican gangs in our slum area, gave us a day of recollection during the month, and made it clear to us just what we were accomplishing. "When you have done everything," he said, "you are still unprofitable servants. You can give all you have to the poor, you can give your body to be burned, but all this is nothing—without charity, the reason for it all. God is love, love is the reason for all we do, the highest reason, on the highest plane. We may talk about freedom and justice, but the reason for them too is love, love of brother, by which we show our love of God. It is when we have done all we can on the natural plane seemingly without result, that we can say, 'Now I have begun.' Because God takes over, and since we believe in the doctrine of the mystical body, all our sufferings lighten the load which is being carried in Africa, in Asia—all over the world. We are lightening the sufferings of the East Side, of Harlem, of Appalachia.

All this is paraphrase, of course. But I can speak from my own experience of its truth. Suffering borne in this way has certainly a depth of joy, a hard core of joy, because we know that "unless the seed falls into the ground and dies, it remains alone. But if it dies it bears much fruit." We must give up our life to save it. So we can look at the little we have done in thirty-one years with peace and joy and leave it in God's hands to make of it what He will.

I have said these things, and written these things many times, not only in regard to our own work, but also to the whole struggle for social justice and racial justice. Every time hand bills are passed out on the street, every time one walks in a picket line, or sits down in factory or before a factory gate, or at the world's fair, or in front of the Waldorf, every time a voice is lifted to call attention to man's joblessness, his homelessness—these acts are expressions of faith, hope and charity. We cannot be silent.

Another thing Father Janer said struck me. He looked out of the chapel window at the brown fields, and the forsythia bush in bloom, and the maples with their touch of red, and the willows, pale green down by the brook, and he said,

172

"What if it all should stop! What if spring progressed just so far, and then nothing happened! What a frustration that would be!" He went on to say that if we did not develop spiritually, no matter how much we might accomplish in the material order, we were like a spring which never developed into summer, we were like plants that never matured, like trees that did not bear fruit.

To have such a day of recollection is a good way to begin our thirty-second year.

Our New Venture

I suppose I have been writing the foregoing in fear and trembling because with a new venture, it will seem to our readers that we are accomplishing much in the material order. We have been building up to this move for a long time. We began in 1936 with a small farm on Mammy Morgan's Hill outside of Easton, Pennsylvania. We bought the adjoining farm. Later we sold one, and deeded the other to two of the four families who lived on it. Of the four families, three remained; the other moved to the western part of the state. We bought another farm, much larger and more expensive, at Newburgh, New York, and lived and farmed there until after Peter's death. For a number of reasons we moved, one of them the constant presence of the jet planes which zoomed off Stuart Field nearby, one of which exploded and landed on a field near the house a year after we vacated it. Our next farm was at Pleasant Plains, Staten Island, where we had over twenty acres of field and woodlot, a large house and barn and outbuildings. The building of the new bridge over the Narrows, thus starting a real estate dealers' field day, has resulted in our moving again.

Knowing that we would receive over a hundred thousand dollars for a property for which we paid sixteen thousand, I began to look for a place where we would have room not only for our farm family but for our courses and retreats in the summer, and which of course could be used for the same during the winter.

The Sunday New York Times brought to my attention a real estate ad about property on the Hudson, twenty-five acres, with three large buildings, one completely furnished and habitable, in the past a resort, school, land army headquarters, boys' camp, orphanage. Originally it had been the mansion of General dePeyster, an old brick building not used now for many years. It was after his death that the orphan-

173

age and school were built. We are in the village of Tivoli, in the township of Red Hook, just north of Bard College and the Christian Brothers at Barrytown, and perhaps an hour's drive or less from Poughkeepsie.

On St. Mark's Day, April 25, the day of the major litanies, Hans Tunnesen, who has been with us since the first farm at Easton, Ed McLoughlin, Tom Hughes, Joe Domensky and Alice Lawrence and I drove up from Staten Island, and joined John Mastrion, former owner, and his partner who were already here, putting in a new boiler. The electricity was turned on, all the pipes tested, the pump started to fill the reservoir at the top of the hill. The bottled gas heater was turned on, and we started our first meal in the apartment which occupies one wing of the building. The men took cold bedrooms upstairs and Alice and I slept in the warmer quarters of the apartment which will be occupied by one of the three families which are coming to us this summer.

With the twenty-five people which make up our community at Staten Island, and with three new families which are arriving, one of them for the summer (a professor from Purdue with his wife and children, to help us get started) and Martie Corbin and Rita and their three from Glen Gardner, and Lorraine and her three, our community will about fill the place. We will have a job getting the other two buildings in shape for permanent use. As it is, we can use some of the room for the summer courses which we expect to have.

One course is sure, and that is a retreat to be given by Father Marion Casey from Belle Plaine, Minnesota, beginning Sunday, July 19 and ending the following Saturday. There will be on the weekend of the Fourth of July a discussion led by William Horvath and Ruth Collins, about the rent strike and the possibilities of cooperative ownership and rebuilding of old tenements in Harlem. This will be one of a series we hope, of weekends to discuss this idea.

We are thinking, as we institute these courses, of such other enterprises as the Brookwood Labor School which graduated A. J. Muste and Walter Reuther and many labor leaders; of the Putney graduate school of Vermont, of the Highlander Folk School. It was a Negro woman coming from a course at the Highlander who started the explosion in Montgomery Alabama when she refused to relinquish her seat in the city bus after a long day's work at a sewing machine. She would never have thought of making protest for herself, but the sessions at the Highlander Folk School gave her the courage to think of the common good and the sufferings of her fellows. So, in a way, the action of this one woman led to the rise of Martin Luther King to world prominence so that now there is no part of Asia or Africa which has not heard of him. Who knows what Nyreres will begin to see their vocations at the little school we are beginning at Tivoli, New York.

We hope too, to have one weekend retreat a month all through the year, and several long retreats in the summer, so that we may learn to appreciate the gifts of the Holy Spirit and begin to release some of those spiritual forces which will keep up with and control the gigantic strides which man has taken in the physical order.

"Go forth and stand upon the mount before the Lord," the word of the Lord came to Elias as he abode in a cave. "What dost thou here, Elias?" he said to him when he had fled the world in fear. "Go forth and stand upon the mount before the Lord. And behold, the Lord passeth. And a great and strong wind before the Lord, overthrowing the mountains, and breaking the rocks in pieces: the Lord is not in the wind. And after the wind an earthquake; the Lord is not in the earthquake. And after the earthquake a fire; the Lord is not in the fire, and after the fire, the whistling of a gentle air."

This is from the Douay version of the Bible of the year 1609 and that in turn was from the Rheims translation, 1582, and it is not so graceful a translation in our ears, but we know what it means.

Elias took courage and went forth and found Eliseus ploughing and cast his mantle upon him, and he was no longer humanly speaking alone.

So too, here at Tivoli, after study and prayer, the manual labor of hospitality and the suffering of community living, we can go forth and send others forth "to speak truth to power," in the gentle air of non-violence.

June 1964

I have been reading Fr. Boyer's *Life of Newman* for some months now and have gotten to the part where Newman and his little band are starting the Oratory in Birmingham, England. I visited there last fall, when I went to England to speak at Spode House, the Dominican Retreat center near

Birmingham. Canon Drinkwater who had visited us in New York obtained a car and chauffeur and drove us to these hallowed spots, holy to me because of their association with Newman. The writings of Cardinal Newman were introduced to me by Father John J. Hugo of Pittsburgh, himself in a way, another Newman struggling against the inertia, apathy, and even corruption of his own day.

St. Philip Neri, who founded the Oratory in Rome, was born in Florence in 1515 the same year as St. Teresa of Avila, in Spain, and he lived all his life in Rome. He was one of the most influential persons of his time. According to my missal, "he was a man of original character and happy disposition. He had a great love of God and of people of all conditions. He lived as a pilgrim touring the streets of Rome for fifteen years, exerting powerful influence on many people. At 36 he was ordained a priest. He gathered around him about 20 priests who formed the congregation of secular priests of the Oratory."

One of the things I remember reading about St. Philip Neri is how he knelt in the window of his Rome dwelling and looking out over the city prayed for it. Ever since reading that, I have followed that practice, and enjoy it. I do this because I am half the week in New York, and half the week in Tivoli at our new farm.

The City

We have three women's apartments on Kenmare Street in New York and they are full, with cots which can be set up in the kitchen for extra and unexpected guests.

My front corner room looks down over the crossroads of Mott and Kenmare and receives the morning sun and plenty of breezes which dispel to some extent the fumes from the traffic outside. Kenmare St. leads directly east to the Williamsburg Bridge and west to the Holland tunnel, and of course the traffic is enormous. Perhaps the new Verrazano Bridge, with its cross-Staten Island expressway to Goethels Bridge leading to New Jersey will handle this traffic when the new Bridge is completed this year. But our city fathers are still trying to get the go ahead signal to demolish our neighborhood in favor of a cross-Manhattan expressway to handle the traffic problem. There is ninety million dollars involved, to be put up by the Federal government, to the city's ten, and this great sum will not lightly be relinquished. If it only could be put into better housing for the poor of the

East side! Housing where there are no automatic lifts, where murder, rape and other violence have been committed, where there are enough community servants to man the elevators, halls, the playgrounds and work as recreation directors and camp leaders and exploration guides to siphon off the unemployed youth hungry for movement, hungry to satisfy their curiosity about the world around them. (We know one such leader in Springfield, Vermont where my daughter lives, who has a science club and takes the members all over the state to visit factories, power plants, museums or to climb mountains.)

But no, there is money for arms and for traffic but not for the poor and unemployed,—nothing for youth!

Last night I sat at my window and watched the world passing by, trucks from all over the country, and where is Marianna, Florida? Trucks laden with furniture, lumber, animals, sacks of saw dust, potato chips, fruit and vegetables, gasoline, milk, cement, cane syrup, garments, lowing cattle. There was an occasional horse and wagon, noisy on the cobblestones which pave the street. There are traffic lights on each corner so there is the shifting of gears, the roar of motors. When the traffic flows uninterrupted, there is the clatter and the bounce and the jangle of empty trucks over uneven pavement. There are police cars, police ambulances, fire trucks, chartered busses going to and from the World's Fair. There are trucks gathering up waste fats from all the butcher shops around to bring to soap factories in Brooklyn. There are sanitation department trucks that make a noise like an air raid siren as they grind up the boxes and furniture and tin cans and garbage collected daily from all the battered ash cans which stand in rows in front of each tenement. And there are people bringing down bundles of trash to push into these already crowded cans, old women marketing with their shopping bags, young women pushing baby carriages, still other young women in stretch pants, pink pants, purple pants, green pants, orange pants. Clothes hanging from fire escape to window on short lines, crowded together. Bed clothes airing on window sills.

We have lived long in this neighborhood, Mott Street, Spring Street, Chrystie Street; all our ten apartments are in this section where Chinese, Puerto Rican, Negro, Italian, Jew —all Americans, live in comparative peace. We all feel safe here in this radius surrounding the Bowery because we know each other and are known. To a certain extent, that is.

On the other hand, the Daily News features each day scenes of violence and crime, all the tragedies which are taking place among six million or eight million or more people. This ceaseless news of violence repeated every hour, on the hour, on radio, and then dished up again with pictures when the Daily News comes out in the night, builds up the fear which is growing up in our midst, a fear almost deliberately stirred up by the press, which makes whites fear Negroes and the rich the poor, and one neighborhood another. There is wild talk of people arming themselves, first tear gas pencils are suggested, and now guns! Are the newspapers building up to rioting like that of the Know Nothings in the last century? I write these things because I believe that each one of us participates in building up an atmosphere,—whether it is of fear or of the love which casts out fear.

Tivoli

One of the letters which came in this morning was from a Holy Cross Brother who writes that thirty years or more ago he was Boys' Director of what was the Leake and Watts Farm School, a branch school of their larger home in Yonkers. He went on to say that he thought this same property which we purchased was ideal for us and is looking forward to reading more about it.

One of the questions that has been asked was "How did you find it?" It was by reading the real estate ads in the New York Times. Once realizing that we were selling the entire farm at Staten Island, though we thought at first we were selling only some acreage which we did not use and which had brought up our taxes to astronomical figures, I set out to look for a place. We had thought of selling part and keeping house and barn and gardens. But there was trouble with the fire department for having a chapel in the barn. We had no permit, they said. There was trouble with the building department who said we could not put up a fire escape on a wooden dwelling. We did it anyway, risking a fine of $250. New England and Canada are filled with wooden houses with outdoor stairways. The building department also told us we could have only one family and four extra people in the house. If there were no family brood, one person would count as a family. Which would mean only five people. I hesitated to write about this idiotic interpretation of the law in our regard since I continued to break it. But what a relief to get away from such harassment. How easy it is to understand the grief of the small landlord and store keeper and business-man in this day of corporations with their corporation law-yers.

Another reason for our moving was the sudden realization that we were going to get a large amount of money for our sale of the property. This was shocking not only to us, but to our friends. To think that we were going to "make money" in this speculative fashion—there was something immoral about it. There was the capital gains tax. Were we going to pay it, the twenty-five per cent which goes to the federal government and which in turn goes for "defense" and moon shots, and the making of poison gas and all kinds of fearful missiles? A certain amount of course goes for the upkeep of our huge veterans hospitals where the wrecks left over from former wars are cared for or kept in dead storage. A certain amount goes also for "foreign aid" which usually means too our occupation of territory for missile bases, and for alliances. Not much money is given without strings attached.

The thing to do was not only to rejoice in our windfall but to spend it as quickly as possible. I certainly felt that God, our Father, who is a personal God, a personal Father, who sees our needs, who foresees the means we must have to do the kind of work we envision, directly intervened here.

We could have inherited money or unencumbered prop-erty. No one would have objected to this. I could have writ-ten a best seller, perhaps. The fact of the matter was that we were caught in a land boom. A piece of property which we paid $16,000 for could be sold for $175,000. This was the prospect before us.

The sum before we were through all the negotiations was whittled down to a smaller amount. First of all there was a payment of $25,000 on the signing of the contract almost a year ago. Five thousand of that went to a lawyer who was extricating us from a mistake which would have permitted another speculator to have the property on a ten year mort-gage with a comparatively small down payment and "no interest." Charles Butterworth and I were sued for seventy thousand dollars and five thousand dollars or delivery of the property, which suits dragged on for months until they were dealt with out of court on the payment of fifteen thousand dollar settlement. I felt this was theft on the part of the un-scrupulous real estate dealer, but "business is business."

Actually, $12,000 was contributed by a new buyer. We paid $3,000 to the first dealer and three thousand to the first

179

agent. Which made six thousand less on the $175,000 offered. The twenty thousand left over after the initial payment to the lawyer went to pay an accumulation of bills which had plagued the CW family for some time. It costs us a thousand dollars a month in rents in the city and another seventy thousand or more dollars a year to keep our two large households going in city and country which means the total support of sixty people, not counting our breadline and the daily petty cash outlay which is anything but petty.

The new farm, which comprises sixty-five acres cost $78,000 and a nine passenger International Harvester station wagon will set us back another three thousand five hundred. We sold the mortgage at an eighteen per cent discount which lops off another ten thousand or more. But we have no interest to pay and no interest to take and since we sold the mortgage to the very people, a family which bought the place, we are not putting them in the position of paying interest. But we have not converted them by any means from the desire to make money on the Staten Island property by chopping it up into lots and building on it houses similar to a greater or lesser degree to those you see advertised in other developments to sell for $19,999 with a long term mortgage which will all but double the price. Indeed, one buyer of such a house once said to me that the house he was buying would fall apart before he had the mortgage paid off. These jokes one sees portrayed in cartoons where the wall of one apartment collapses when leaned against to show some young couple at table, or some young lady in the tub, are an indication of what is happening on the building line. A grim joke indeed.

I have not all the figures handy, but what with penalties, fees to two agents, discounts and so on, not to speak of our purchasing of our new home for cash, there will remain enough of the money to pay all debts and get through the summer on.

For a time we wondered what to call the new place which boasted of three buildings. The old de Peyster mansion which is at present uninhabitable aside from two little apartments built into it for summer guests, will eventually be repaired. On one great cornerstone the words *Beata Maria* were chiselled and on another *Watts*, the names of two of the de Peyster children evidently. So we thought at first of calling the place Beata Maria, as we had called the farm at Easton. That was too hard for many of our readers and visitors to remember, so we decided to call the whole place, the *Catholic Worker Farm*; the first old school house, the *Peter Maurin House*; the second *Beata Maria*, and the third house in which we are living, *St. Joseph's*. Catholic Worker Farm at Tivoli, New York, will be our address.

Originally there had been the mansion of one of the river barons, then the stables were remodelled into the school dormitory building where our Holy Cross correspondent worked over thirty years ago.

The school building was used and so was the mansion. We have already started the library and chapel in the Peter Maurin House. And in St. Joseph's house, everyone from Peter Maurin Farm and from the beach houses are by now almost moved in. Stanley has set up his press in one dusty room of the mansion; and the two apartments will be occupied by Lorraine and her sons and a professor from Purdue and his wife and children who are coming to help us get started this summer.

After the school no longer functioned at Tivoli, the land army took over during the Second World War, and again the dormitories were used by young people who worked in the crops up and down the Hudson valley. Then I understand the Jehovah's Witnesses took over and ran the place as a camp and farm for a time. The last owner was John Mastrion and his family, who ran the place as a resort for families and the place was beautifully built up with a new roof, rooms for families, big dining room and kitchen, recreation room and swimming pool.

When I read the ad in the New York Times, it said "suitable for a religious group" and since they mentioned three houses I thought that here would be room to grow and to house the groups that came to us for discussion and retreat so many times during the year.

The fact that the Good Friday over a year ago had seen two hundred young people descending on Peter Maurin Farm to spend the day and night before going on with their pilgrimage to the United Nations; and that the Labor Day week end crowd was made up of one hundred and forty peace workers, made me the more convinced that this was something we needed. So after visits in December and January, and actually no visits to any other places, a down payment was made and then all we had to do was to wait to get the money in hand to complete the purchase. In the spring Mr. Mastrion, his son and some of his relatives came

181

and put in a new boiler in the main house and started it to working, and stayed to show us how to operate the pool, the pump and the reservoir. He and his family had been coming up summers for the past eight or nine years and they were sorry to leave the place, but the father, for whom the place had originally been purchased, had died, and so the family wished to concentrate their work in the Sheepshead Bay area where they lived and the New York City area where John Mastrion worked in construction. We found him generous and cooperative to a degree, and are intensely grateful to the family for all the loving work they put into this project not only when they themselves were the owners, but for us, to get us started up there. I told them when they left us, when their work was finished, that I would be remembering them when we said our nightly rosary and compline together. And they assured us they would remember us too.

This is not too complete an account and is written with many interruptions and distractions and again we beg our readers to excuse us for long delaying the answering of letters. During the course of our moving from the Peter Maurin Farm, the beach houses, and some folk from the city also to the land—the transferring of files, past and present, trays of mail, answered and unanswered and to be filed,—all have gotten into an awful hodge podge and a lot of sorting out of papers will have to take place. But on the one hand, Marquette University Library is receiving our archives. If they are not already discouraged at the masses of material they have received, we can ship a lot more off to them. And on the other hand, I am reading a delightful book, *Maryknoll's First Lady*, by Sister Jeanne Marie, published by Dodd Mead and Company and learning about all the hard beginnings and paper work they had to do, and so am less discouraged at not having been more successful even after thirty years in getting our own files in order. Will we ever, undisciplined laymen as we are, be any more orderly? Just now some students came in, and after an hour with them, I must stir up my desk still more to find some lost sheets and articles to go off to the printer. It is the same with Tom Cornell, with Martin Corbin, with all editors of wide interests, it would seem. Humans and books and papers are inextricably mixed up.

Let us hope that this is our last move, in the rural area at least. Stanley, the Melancholy Slav, says that doubtless the state will decide some day to put a Throughway along the river. But I doubt it. Expressways and urban renewal may mean other moves in the city but we will be in our same district, God willing, for many years to come.

July-August 1964

THE CASE OF CARDINAL McINTIRE

Of all hostilities one of the saddest is the war between clergy and laity. We have written and spoken many times of all the aspects of war, the beginnings in our own hearts, the hostilities in the family between husband and wife, parents and children, children and parent. The entire conflict of authority and freedom. *The Catholic Worker*, pacifist and anarchist in philosophy, has had to discuss and write about all these things, in particular, and in general.

The works of mercy are works of love. The works of war are works of the devil,—"You do not know of what spirit you are," Jesus said to his disciples when they would call down fire from heaven on the inhospitable Samaritans. This is to look at things in the large context of modern war. But as for the hostilities in our midst, the note of violence and conflict in all our dealings with others,—everyone seems to contribute to it. There is no room for righteous wrath today. In the entire struggle over civil rights, the war which is going on in which one side is nonviolent, suffering martyrdoms, every movement of wrath in the heart over petty hostilities must be struggled with in order to hold up the strength of the participants.

"Let us but raise the level of religion in our hearts, and it will rise in the world," Newman wrote. "He who attempts to set up God's kingdom in his heart, furthers it in the world." We cannot all go on Freedom Rides, or take part in the COFO program in Mississippi, as young students are doing. (Marie Asche, who worked with us last summer, has gone to Mississippi). But we can sustain them by our contributions, money, prayers, and by works in our local area along these lines.

This is what seminarians and the Catholic interracial group have been doing in Los Angeles, not only this year but for

183

many years, only to meet with prohibitions from the hierarchy, prohibitions of meetings, to setting up interracial councils, and so on. This silence and non-cooperation on the part of the priest and bishop and cardinal, this more than silence,—this censure, this prohibition, has increased the separation of clergy and laity, and has built up a wall of bitterness.

Last month a young priest in the Los Angeles diocese wrote a letter to the Holy Father, asking for the removal of Cardinal McIntyre from the work of the diocese. His letter was given to the press all over the country and was reprinted by both secular and Catholic press.

When I read the accounts in the dailies and some of the diocesan press, I thought of *The Caine Mutiny*. When I read the book, I compared it with the stories of the sea in Joseph Conrad's novels. The reasonable interference of the sturdy mate in the more recent book brought him to trial on the charge of mutiny. One of the things that struck me most forcibly in the latter book was the difference between the worker mate and the intellectual officer who needled him into making complaints and then would not back him up, who urged him to save the ship and crew by disobeying orders, and then would not testify for him at the trial.

When a friend was criticizing one of the Cardinals as being backward and restrictive of the freedom of the laity at that time, I was reminded of the book I had just read and I asked him why he did not go to the Chancery office and state his complaints, his remonstrances. The laity have a freedom to express themselves that the clergy do not. The late beloved Fr. La Farge, S.J. said in one of his last books, that the trouble with the church in America was a bullying clergy and a subservient laity and when I quoted that statement in regard to an incident which happened at the CW house of hospitality in Chicago, one of our readers wrote in angrily holding us to be the author of the statement of Fr. La Farge.

I had not intended to write at length about this Los Angeles incident since so many of the diocesan papers and weeklies gave it ample coverage. But I recalled letters I had received in the last year, asking my advice as to what to do, letters from the laity and from the seminarians, east and west, —and when I recalled too my long acquaintance with Cardinal McIntyre, (shall I say friendship?) I decided I would write at length, and personally. What I say about him, I could say also in one way or another about Cardinal Spellman and Cardinal Cushing.

Another reason why it is good to write at length is that the problem has to do with war, with race, with poverty, voluntary and involuntary, with spiritual teaching and our dissatisfaction with it. And what we can do about all these things. One of the newspapers in New York talked about the indignity which the young priest was forced to submit to, the kneeling before his superior and promising obedience. I do not know what the ceremony was, but I imagine it is that one that occurs at every ordination, when the candidate for the priesthood kneels and placing his two hands within the hands of the bishop, swears obedience. One never hears a Catholic objecting to this. We lay people kneel to receive absolution, to receive a blessing, to receive all the sacraments, as coming from God, through the priest. The non-Catholic does not realize what a relationship of love and loyalty there is between the layman and the priest, the priest and bishop. In all the great events of one's life, birth, marriage and death, and for the unmarried the confirming of their vocation. For the times of sin and sickness, there is absolution and anointing, and at the moment of death, the holy oils and the prayers of priest and the people. It is our Faith which lends strength and dignity to our paltry and tragic lives, "In Thy hand are strength and power and to Thy hand it belongs to make everything great and strong."

I first met Cardinal McIntyre back in the late twenties when I was filled with the longing to be a Catholic and could not because of marriage difficulties. One goes to a priest in the chancery office to straighten out these difficulties and Cardinal McIntyre who was then a monsignor was the one assigned to me to take care of my inquiries. His office was not a private one. His was one of a long row of desks on either side of the room, far enough apart so that one could talk privately. There was always a long line of people waiting in the outer office, and one by one, we were ushered in. There was never any haste about these interviews. He always gave me most courteous and sympathetic attention and I remember times when I was there at noon and he had a sandwich and a glass of milk brought to his desk. He said the Angelus when the clock struck twelve. I remember thinking how hard these young priests had to work, the tales they had to listen to. They had to be lawyers, psychologists, priests, all in one. Between him and Father Hyland, another young priest at Tottenville, Staten Island, I was helped along the way, over a period of several years, and was baptized.

When five years later I started *The Catholic Worker* at the instigation of Peter Maurin, I did not ask permission,—I did not discuss it with the chancery office. My contact with these young priests made me realize the more what I had always felt,—that Catholics lived in a world of their own, quite apart from the rest of the population. They did represent the Irish, the Italians, the Poles, the Hungarians and all the rest of the immigrant Catholic crowd who seemed so apart in every way, not just by religion, from the rest of the white, Protestant and generally middle class people from whom I sprang. I felt the order, the discipline of their lives, even if it meant a twenty minute Mass on a week day, in complete silence, and a three quarters of an hour of worship on Sunday with news of bingo parties and coal collections scattered in with announcements of requiem Masses and banns of marriage.

I had been writing articles for *The Sign*, for America, the Jesuit paper, and doing clerical work for Fr. Joseph McSorley the Paulist and when I spoke to them of my venture, all three editors, Father Harold Purcell, Fr. Parsons, and Fr. McSorley all advised me to launch out, but not to ask permission. It would not be given, was implied. But I understood why. How make the hierarchy responsible for such an unproved venture? They might be held responsible for debts to be contracted—perhaps that was also understood to be part of the question.

At any rate the first issues of the paper came out and were greeted with enthusiasm by clergy and laity alike. The circulation soared, enough contributions came in so that hospitality could be provided for the down and outs that made up our first staff.

Workers and scholars alike were down and out in the depression, and we have always been the lame, the halt and the blind, the off scouring of all, to use St. Paul's phrase, all through the years. "The gold is ejected and the dross remains," one of our friends said of us. We were greeted by those who did not know us as a pack of saints, and the legend continued to grow, such a term giving an easy way out to those who felt themselves to be happily more publicans than pharisees. Our standards were too high, could not possibly be lived up to, but it was good to be reminded of them. Such principles would not work, they showed pride and presumption in a way, but they evidenced the longing in every human heart for the lost Eden of the past and the Paradise we all hoped for in the future. We were Utopians, in other words.

Well, we have hung on to our personalist communitarian philosophy over the years, and it has been called anarchism, pacifism, communitarian socialism and many other things. But through all the years, there was never any criticism from the chancery office in New York about our philosophy even when it led us to jail in New York, New Jersey, Chicago, Philadelphia, Baltimore, Washington, Omaha—wherever there were demonstrations about race or war.

The Baltimore House of Hospitality was closed as a public nuisance. It was inter-racial when it was against the law to have both black and white under the same roof in a hostel. Civil Disobedience began for us then.

Irene Mary Naughton was arrested for picketing in an inter-racial demonstration at Palisades Amusement Park. This was in the forties and was just the beginning of CW involvement. But still the chancery offices never interfered. They never committed themselves either.

We were too busy to worry much about the attitudes of individual priests in chancery offices or parishes. Somehow or other, I had always realized that the church was made up of every political viewpoint as well as of saints and sinners, that there was room for all, that people were the product of their environment. Then too I had my own family to remind me, a conservative one in many ways. My own father was most intemperate in his remarks not only about the "foreigner" but about the Negro, coming from Tennessee as he did, and there were my Georgia cracker cousins, hard shelled Baptists, fundamentalists, Campbellites, religious bigots and racists undoubtedly. And yet one could not hate them. They could not prevent one from going one's own way. So it was the same with the Church, the family of the Church. Churchmen became conservative; had to hang on to the gains made in a country which spoke of Hunkies, Dagoes, Spiks, Micks, greasers and so on. These despised ones showed that they could make it too.

But the people didn't get much more "instruction" than the Asians St. Francis Xavier reached with the teaching of prayers, and the pouring on of water in Baptism. Get to Sunday Mass, make your Easter duty, don't marry outside the faith,—the grace of the sacraments would do all the rest.

This was my first impression of the church until Peter Maurin opened my eyes to the splendid literature of the church, the social teaching, and I travelled and found like-minded people all over the country. From the first we had the advice and instruction of good and holy, and learned priests,—all of which gave us courage.

We were called to the chancery office occasionally. At first I saw only Monsignor McIntyre, and later it was Monsignor Gaffney. It was always over some trivial matter. After a few years, I felt that I understood the technique. I would get a letter reading, "Dear Dorothy, if you happen to be in the neighborhood, would you please drop in." I very seldom was in the neighborhood of Fiftieth street,—all our work being on the east side, but I took care to go at once. Monsignor McIntyre would greet me in most friendly fashion, and then press a button for a stenographer. She would bring in a file, and he would open to a letter, one of a long pile of letters, and holding his hand over the signature, he would say, "We have received a complaint about something in the last issue of the CW," and he would read out some line like "Would you have your daughter go to the marriage bed with a Negro?" (I remember that line well. This was from a satirical article by Robert Ludlow.) Quite often the sentiments objected to were from his writings.

There was never any comment. But a few friendly inquiries about the work. I do not recall how many times I had these meetings with Monsignor McIntyre.

I remember once asking him for the use of an unoccupied rectory on the east side. Insurance problems, probable trouble with the board of health and the fire department and building department stood in the way, however.

But he tried to help us. Before we got our Peter Maurin Farm on Staten Island, I found a place on the beach down near Tottenville that I wanted very much to buy and Bishop McIntyre, sympathizing with our money problems, offered to back or sponsor a bank loan for us for fifteen thousand dollars but that deal fell through because of the usual housing, health and fire department restrictions, on our work.

No comment was ever made by the by-then bishop or archbishop about political views. When we started to run articles like "War and Conscription at the Bar of Christian Morals," by Monsignor Barry O'Toole of the Catholic University and "The Crime of Conscription" and "Catholics Can Be Conscientious Objectors," by Fr. John Jr. Hugo of Pittsburgh, Bishop McIntyre merely commented, during one of these aforesaid visits, "We never studied these things much in

188

the seminary." Shaking his head, and adding doubtfully, "There is the necessity of course to inform one's conscience." And I assured him that that was what we were trying to do.

A recent paperback call *The Essential Newman* carries part of Cardinal Newman's correspondence with Gladstone in which he discusses *conscience*, and he is reported to have said that if he were called upon to propose a toast on such a subject, which was unlikely, he would propose—"to conscience first, and to the Pope second." This was at a time when there was great discussion of new dogma, infallibility of the Pope.

Bishop O'Hara of Kansas City once said to Peter Maurin, "You lead the way,—we will follow." Meaning that it was up to the laity to plough ahead, to be the vanguard, to be the shock troops, to fight these battles without fear or favor. And to make the mistakes. And that has always been my understanding. This business of "asking Father" what to do about something has never occurred to us. The way I have felt about Los Angeles is that the lay people had to go ahead and form their groups, "Catholics for interracial justice," form their picket lines, as they are only now doing, and make their complaints directly, to priest and cardinal, demanding the leadership, the moral example they are entitled to.

How can any priest be prevented from preaching the gospel of social justice in the labor field and in the inter-racial field? One can read aloud with loud agreement those messages from the encyclicals, which are so pertinent to the struggles which are being carried on. One can tell the gospel stories in the light of what is happening today. Do the poor have the gospel preached to them today? Do we hear that resounding cry, "Woe to the rich!" Do we hear the story of the rich man sitting at his table feasting while the poor sat at the gate with neither food nor medicare? How many priests have read Fr. Regamey's *Poverty* or Shewring's *The Rich and the Poor in Christian Tradition*?

It is voluntary poverty which needs to be preached to the comfortable congregations, so that a man will not be afraid of losing his job if he speaks out on those issues. So that pastors or congregations will not be afraid of losing the support of rich benefactors. A readiness for poverty, a disposition to accept it, is enough to begin with. We will always get what we need, "Take no thought for what you shall eat or drink,—the Lord knows you have need of these things."

If more seminarians spoke out, even if the seminaries were emptied! (It is said the seminaries of France were half emptied because of the Algerian War, which went on for so long.) If more young priests spoke out while they continued to work hard and continued to "be what they wished the other fellow to be," as Peter Maurin put it,—what happy results might not be brought about.

But often the critical spirit results in desertions, from church and priesthood and seminary, and I suppose that is what the hierarchy fears. We have plenty of experience of the critical spirit and have seen the ravages that can be wrought in family and community. We have had many a good worker leave because he could not stand the frustrations, because "those in charge" did not throw out troublemakers, or *force* people to do better. The critical spirit can be the complaining spirit too, and the murmurer and complainer does more harm than good.

If we could strive for the spirit of a St. Francis, and it would be good to read his life and struggles, we would be taking a first step, but it is only God himself who can make a saint, can send the grace necessary to enable him to suffer the consequences of following his conscience and to do it in such a way as not to seem to be passing judgment on another, but rather win him to another point of view, with love and with respect.

"You have heard that it hath been said, an eye for an eye, a tooth for a tooth. But I say to you, Resist not evil: but if one strike thee on thy right cheek, turn to him also the other; and if a man will contend with thee in judgment and take away thy coat, let go thy cloak also unto him, and whosoever will force thee to go one mile, go with him another two. Give to him that asketh of thee, and of him that would borrow of thee turn not away. You have heard that it hath been said, thou shalt love thy neighbor and hate thy enemy. But I say to you, love your enemies, do good to them that hate you; and pray for them that persecute and calumniate you, that you may be children of your father who is in heaven who makes his sun to rise upon the good and the bad, and raineth upon the just and the unjust. For if you love them that love you, what reward shall you have? Do not even the publicans this? And if you salute your brethren

190

only, what do you more? Do not also ask the heathen this? Be you therefore perfect as your heavenly Father is perfect."

Hard sayings indeed and no wonder that St. Peter said, in another context, when Jesus said that it was harder for a camel to go through the eye of the needle than for a rich man to get into the kingdom of heaven. "Who then can be saved?" "With God all things are possible."

When a man, black or white, reaches the point where he recognizes the worth of his soul (what does it profit a man if he gain the whole world and suffer the loss of his soul?)— when he begins to realize what it means to be a child of God, a son, an heir also, the sense of his own dignity as a child of God is so great that no indignity can touch him, or discourage him from working for the common good.

It is for this that our shepherds are to be reproached, that they have not fed their sheep these strong meats, this doctrine of men divinized by the sacraments, capable of overcoming all obstacles in their advance to that kind of society where it is easier to be good.

Let Catholics form their associations, hold their meetings in their own homes, or in a hired hall, or any place else. Nothing should stop them. Let the controversy come out into the open in this way.

But one must always follow one's conscience, preach the gospel in season, out of season, and that gospel is "all men are brothers."

This teaching is contained in all the work of the Confraternities of Christian Doctrine. It just needs to be applied.

September 1964

We have just finished making a retreat at our Catholic Worker farm at Tivoli, and as usual we come out of the retreat with what the world would call an upside down way of looking at things.

When I wrote recently about personal responsibility, the work of the layman and the work of the clergy, the controversies on the West Coast, the article brought a number of letters, some with bitter comment and some indicating that they had obtained better perspective on the situation and a more loving attitude. During our retreat we read Jorgensen's *Life of St. Francis,* and here are some less known words of the universally beloved St. Francis.

"Then the Lord gave me and still gives me so great a confidence in priests, that if they even persecuted me, I would for the sake of their consecration say nothing about it. And if I had the wisdom of Solomon and travelled in the parishes of poor priests, yet I would not preach without their permission. And them and all other priests I will fear, love, and honor as my superiors, and I will not look at their faults, for I see God's Son in them, and they are my superiors. And I do this because here on earth, I see nothing of the Son of the highest God, except His most holy body and blood, which the priests receive and which only they give to others. And these solemn secrets I will honor and venerate above everything and keep them in the most sacred places."

In August on the feast of the Transfiguration, Peter, James and John went up on the mountain with Jesus, and saw him transfigured, shining in glory. This vision given to them to sustain them during the suffering of Jesus, faded and the words of the Gospel read, "They saw only Jesus." Each year when I read this short phrase I have thought of it as a word to hold close to my heart to help me to regard properly all those most degraded ones we come into contact with, whom we see lying abandoned in gutters, and all those whom the world call the unworthy poor. And I thought this year how it applies to all, also to those in high places, to those who are in honor as well as to those in dishonor. "They saw only Jesus."

I am not judging them who have cried out in criticism. Doubtless we need a Savonarola as well as a St. Francis. God gives us our temperaments.

I am not minimizing the evils of the sins of omission on part of clergy and laity in California, Louisiana, Philadelphia, Rochester, or almost any other city you want to name. I am not minimizing the sufferings of the Negro, in whom Christ is crucified over and over again. But I am trying to call attention to the attitude of Jesus, who should be our model. He said of the oppressors, whether foreign or local, whether priest or intellectual, or worker, "Father forgive them for they know not what they do." He said, "Put up your sword," and that sword can be of tongue or pen.

Bernanos said, "Hell is not to love any more." Righteous wrath and indignation is usually not loving. Jesus said to love our enemies.

But to speak of the whole problem on the natural plane, it

seems to me an enormous waste of energy to direct our attacks against the hierarchy instead of attacking the problem of the poverty of the Negro, his joblessness, his homelessness, the insult and injury which is inflicted on him. It is a temptation of the devil, a diversion of our energies. Direct action would be to rent and sell to Negroes in our own neighborhoods, or take in a Negro family as an immediate work of mercy, to find work, to start an industry, a pilot project—in other words to use one's energies and imagination. Some actions would be fruitful and some would raise persecution and as much of a hullabaloo as the letter writing on the West Coast. Direct action, rather than the indirect action of asking why the hierarchy behaves as it does, would be more to the point.

The Catholic Worker is controversial also in its attitude to the war on poverty. To attack poverty by preaching voluntary poverty seems like madness. But again, it is direct action.

"The coat that hangs in your closet belongs to the poor." And to go further, "If anyone takes your coat, give him your cloak too." To be profligate in our love and generosity, spontaneous, to cut all the red tape of bureaucracy! "Open your mouth and I will fill it," says the Lord in the Psalms. The more you give away, the more the Lord will give you to give. It is a growth in faith. It is the attitude of the man whose life of common sense and faith is integrated.

To live with generosity in times of crisis is only common sense. In the time of earthquake, flood, fire, people give recklessly; even governments do this.

The trouble is most people do not see the poverty. Right now, in the Hudson Valley, the fruit is being picked by crews of Negroes from the South who have been moving up along the coast, and they are invisible to the eye, living back in the woods, on dirt roads, working deep in the orchards. With every migration some are left behind to work in the storage plants, in the packing sheds, and they have the worst houses, crowded together in rural slums. Sickness and destitution put some on the welfare rolls, and they are generally despised by the righteous tax payer. This is our attitude toward poverty when we do see it.

This morning, Tuesday, feast of the birthday of Mary, mother of Jesus, the lesson from *Morning Praise and Evensong*, (compiled by William Storey and published in paperback by Fides Press, Notre Dame, Ind.) was from the Sermon on the Mount:

"You have heard it said, 'An eye for an eye and a tooth for a tooth.' I, on the contrary, declare to you: do not meet evil with evil. No, if someone strikes you on your right cheek, turn to him the other as well. And if a man intends by process of law to rob you of your coat, let him have your cloak as well. And if someone forces you to go one mile with him, go two miles with him. Give to anyone who asks you, and if someone would borrow from you, do not turn away.

"You have heard it said: 'Love your neighbor and hate your enemy.' I, on the contrary, declare to you: love your enemies and pray for your persecutors, and thus prove yourselves children of your Father in heaven. He certainly lets his sun rise upon bad and good alike, and makes the rain fall on sinners as well as saints. Really, if you love those who love you what reward do you deserve? Do not tax collectors do as much? And if you have a friendly greeting for your brothers only, are you doing anything out of the common? Do not the heathen do as much? Be perfect then as your Heavenly Father is perfect."

This really was the subject of the retreat that Father John J. Hugo gave us here at the Catholic Worker Farm at Tivoli. It is the ideal, the goal, at which we aim. We fall far short of everything we profess, but we certainly don't want to water down the doctrine of Christ to fit ourselves. We can keep on striving toward it. "Lo, the Bridegroom cometh, go ye forth to meet him." We have to go towards him. We have to do our share. For the rest, "His grace is sufficient for us, we can be confident."

We had a good liturgical retreat, centered around the Mass. We said Lauds and Vespers, we sang beautiful hymns, compiled by a researcher and musicologist who works with Father in his parish. Labor Day was the feast of St. Joseph the Worker, and the Nativity of the Blessed Virgin followed, and we have just now said goodbye to Father, who is driving back to Pittsburgh and his parish. Retreatants came from San Francisco, from Maine, and points in between, and a few are still here. Our usual population of about thirty go on about their daily tasks.

To Vermont

And I too am setting out this morning for Vermont, where I will continue to take care of the grandchildren for the next four months. I was there for the week before the retreat, because Tamar's course in practical nursing has already started in Brattleboro (and she loves it).

I have had a week already of cooking and washing up and sewing and the general enjoyment of eight of my own, (Sue was still working at a summer resort near Rutland and I must pick her up there tomorrow) with half a dozen other neighboring children, much playing of Beatle records, not to speak of two melancholy ballads about a devil woman and a jack and a king. But after tomorrow they will all be in school and the quiet Fall will begin.

October 1964

Beloved, Joy be with you always!

"Joy is the most infallible sign of the presence of God," wrote Leon Bloy. And we have had our share of joy in these last months. The expansion of our work with the new Farm in Tivoli and temporary relief from the pressing burden of debts which followed the sale of our Peter Maurin Farm have given us a sense of exhilaration, of re-birth and great hope for the future. We did not mail out our semi-annual appeal last spring because we were not in pressing need. But now, as we face the winter, our joy is still with us, and we live more closely with "Lady Poverty," as St. Francis called her. Our bank account is low and the normal state of affairs at the Catholic Worker again prevails: living from one day to the next, trusting in God's Providence evidenced so long for us by the love and almsgiving of our readers and friends.

Our family has grown. We have now about forty residents at the Farm and about sixty people at Chrystie Street, and the daily soup line grows longer, now that winter is coming. Rents for the Center and for the ten apartments on Kenmare and Spring Streets cost us over one thousand dollars a month, altogether. We are laying in a supply of winter overcoats to be distributed as soon as the weather turns. And by the time you read this message, we shall literally depend upon your charity for our day to day existence. "Love is an exchange of gifts," St. Ignatius said, and we certainly feel a sense of love and gratitude to you when you answer our appeals. St. Teresa said she was so grateful a person that she could be bought with a sardine. All small gifts add up and we surely need them.

195

To help the poor! This is a great and fearful work. It is through the poor that we achieve our salvation; Jesus Christ Himself has said it in His picture of the Last Judgment. It is through the poor that we can exercise faith and learn to love Him. It is a great relief to read the lives of such saints as St. Vincent de Paul when doing this kind of work. An article some years ago said that he had contact with refugees, convicts, thieves, assassins and bandits, as well as with professional beggars, swindlers, prostitutes. "He saw quite clearly, and sometimes said, that many of these poor people were filthy, physically repulsive and suffering from loathsome diseases, that sometimes they were dishonest, drunken, hypocritical and ungrateful; but to use his own phrase, that is only one side of the medal. Turn it, and with the eyes of faith you see that each is stamped with the image of God and is a brother of Jesus Christ." . . . "The poor are your masters, he said, and thank God you are allowed to serve them." We too see in ourselves our measure of sin and decay of mind and body, but the more we can look at the good side of the coin, the better off we are ourselves, finding Christ. Our faith will grow through such an exercise of love.

It is a joyful experience, to serve the poor, and to be poor ourselves. As our family sits down at the second floor of St. Joseph's House here on Chrystie Street, folding, labeling and mailing the paper, or as they scrape vegetables on the first floor for our evening meal, each is giving something, sharing with his fellows, no matter how humble his gift. There is therapy in work, and joy in sharing, a sense of belonging for those who are the outcasts of our society. There is also the gay exuberance of our young volunteers, students taking time off from their studies to work with us, to learn the problems of poverty and the social order. At the close of our day, when we gather to sing Compline, the night prayer of the Church, we are reminded each evening to remember our benefactors, and so we do, begging God's joy for all of you.

With love and gratitude,

Dorothy Day

November 1964

This is the month when we pray for the dead and read over again The Dream of Gerontius, and the teaching of St.

Catherine of Genoa on Purgatory, who said that next to Heaven, that was the happiest place one could be because one is sure and secure. If the pains of separation are the most we have to bear, and they will be proportionate to our love, there must be great joy there. These are matters of faith, and a mystery . . .

Here and there in my missal, my little office, lay breviary, Imitation, I have lists, some of the dead, and some of the living, and when I remember the dead at Mass I always add, "all those listed in my prayer books." Eternal rest grant unto them, O Lord, and let perpetual light shine upon them.

There are lists of saints in the Mass, and time out for us to remember the living and the dead. And my dead include martyrs on the labor movement, Harlan county miners, Memorial Day massacre victims, the five little children killed in Birmingham, and all those tortured and lynched by all our fellow human beings who give themselves over to those black forces of evil—of cruelty and hatred and lust for murder, which rise within them and take possession of them. Oh, God, you must—you will—wipe away all tears from their eyes, you must make up to them for all the agony they have endured, which their families have endured.

Even as I write the mail comes in and with it a letter returned to me marked DECEASED. It was a note I had written to Madeleine Krider, a former neighbor in Staten Island, so she must now be added to the list. She was one of our benefactors, coming to our aid when we were forced to buy the first house on Chrystie street when we had to leave 115 Mott street and could not rent another. Many of our readers helped, and one of those who came in to the office to leave a donation was Madeleine, who offered to loan us three thousand dollars without interest for as long as we needed it. She did not have much herself, making her living by cleaning up and renting bungalows at Midland Beach so that she could live at home and take care of her mother who was bedridden with arthritis. She herself lived in one of the bungalows, a little narrow, vine-clad cabin-like affair, one of a row built before there was a building code, on tiny plots of land, put up mostly by the owners themselves. She had worked hard at manual labor, and she lived poor herself but she said that our paper made her feel ashamed at being a landlord and living on rents. Not many months passed before she came to see us again to tell us that in reading the Sermon on the Mount, part of which we had quoted in that month's issue of the

197

paper, she had been struck by the statement that when one loaned one should not ask a return of the money, so she wished us to consider the matter closed.

Later on, her mother dead and her own health deteriorating, she decided to sell the few little houses she had and go down to a tract of land she had bought in Florida, west of West Palm Beach, and build there a place which we were welcome to use with her as a house of hospitality for any who needed a change of scene from New York. She invited various members of our Staten Island community to visit her, but they all clung to the familiar community in and out of New York, so she had to work with the poor down there. She had had built for herself a small cement block house, divided by a breezeway, so that she could occupy one part and her guests, when she had them, the other. At first nothing worked out. She took a few alcoholic women but was not able to handle them, and they too preferred the freedom of their lives in town. Then she discovered the town dump as a place where one could encounter the poor. She herself retrieved furniture and lumber which others had thrown away, and during one of her visits, she met a little family: the wife dying of cancer and the husband and son trying to take care of her in the truck in which they lived. They were migrants, spending all their time in Florida, which is a vast state. She took in the family, and the woman stayed until she died in that little house set in a pine grove, so near to and yet so far from the homes of the wealthy.

Then she began visiting the migrant camps and helping the Puerto Ricans and Negroes who worked the crops, collecting clothes and food for them, and trying to teach catechism to their children.

On one occasion of sickness among relatives in New York State she came north again and the story St. Francis told, "This then is perfect joy," came very much to my mind. She arrived at what was then St. Joseph's Loft on Spring street, where we were daily being insulted by neighbors because of our guests from the Bowery and where on one occasion Judy Gregory and I had had eggs thrown at us as we came from Mass on a Sunday morning.

Madeleine came in the evening and there was no one there who knew her, and I was on the farm on Staten Island. She was unostentatious in her dress, a tall thin woman, nervous in manner. She was referred by whoever it was in charge of the office, then to the Salvation Army, where she could get a bed for the night for thirty-five cents, sharing a huge dormitory with the derelict women from the Bowery. I was not too much surprised at this, since on several occasions I myself had been taken for a Bowery woman, both at the Municipal lodging house and at a Catholic nursery where I was abruptly dismissed by a busy young nun at a day nursery. I had gone there trying to get the child of a young unwed mother taken care of, but before I could even make my wants known I had the door shut in my face with the curt remark, "Go away, I can do nothing for you!" I could well understand a young nun in the midst of some crisis with a score of tiny children being hasty and thought nothing of it —was even glad to be so closely identified with the poor as to share the insults and contempt they encountered.

But Madeleine—sick as she always was! And our benefactor! But she went where she was told, and shared the lodging of the poor, overwhelmed with compassion for them, and only wishing she could do more to help them. As though this encounter with our hospitality was not enough, when she came to Spring street for a cup of tea the next morning she met with more rudeness. She asked for a cup of hot water and was brought coffee instead, which she gave to an old woman sitting next to her. When she went over to the sink to get some of the boiling hot water from the faucet, the dish washer snarled at her, "Don't you like the way we wash dishes around here?"

But she finally got the cup of hot water to make her tea from the tea bag she carried in her purse, and she got the directions to Staten Island and visited us there and when she told me the story, she felt only sadness at the way poor, old and unattractive women are treated. As for herself, "This then was perfect joy," bringing her a bit nearer to the sufferings of Christ and by her very sharing, lightening to some degree the burden of others.

I thought of these things when I received that terse message from the postoffice, "Deceased." I have no way either of knowing whether it was really true, because we only exchanged notes yearly. I knew she had gone to a nursing home some months before. Death is always taking us by surprise.

For those who will say, "Dear Lord, I believe, help thou mine unbelief," such stories of the deaths of his little ones are anything but cheerless. "This day thou shalt be with me in

Paradise," Jesus said to the poor criminal dying in agony nearby on a cross.

"What is it I love when I love Thee?" St. Augustine asked. I have only an old translation here at Perkinsville, but I will copy the passage and maybe it will induce our readers to go back to this wonderful book.

"Thou hast stricken my heart with Thy word and I loved Thee. Yea also heaven and earth and all that therein is—behold on every side they bid me love Thee. But what do I love when I love Thee? Not beauty of bodies, nor the fair harmony of time, nor the brightness of the light, so gladsome to our eyes, not sweet melodies of varied songs, nor the fragrant smell of flowers, and ointments and spices, not manna and honey, not limbs acceptable to embracements of flesh. None of these I love when I love my God. And yet I love a kind of light and melody and fragrance, meat and embracement of my inner man, where there shineth unto my soul what space cannot contain, and there soundeth what time beareth not away, and there smelleth what breathing disperseth not and there tasteth what eating diminisheth not, and there clingeth what satiety divorceth not. This it is which I love when I love my God."

Lord, increase in me this love. Take away my heart of stone and give me a heart of flesh. In Thee have I hoped, let me never be confounded. I believe, help Thou mine unbelief. I pray this for all of us, in the words of Scripture itself, uttered by the Word made flesh who dwelt among us, and who told us—"Ask and you shall receive."

1965

January 1965

☐ People always want news so I will begin with that. News of each other, I mean. Somewhere in the correspondence of St. Ignatius and Francis Xavier, one writes to the other, "I am so eager for news of you that I even want to know of the fleas that are biting you." So I will start by giving an account of myself. It is so impossible to keep up with all the mail and do any other writing that I skipped writing the *On Pilgrimage* column two months of the four that I was in Vermont. So I announce now my deep gratitude for all the letters and Christmas cards and the help that we have received for our work, and beg our readers to excuse me from correspondence now until I get the new book I am working on finished and in print. How long that will take, who knows. Living in community takes much time, also speaking engagements and traveling. So I do beg our friends, our large Catholic Worker family who are scattered all over the United States and even further, to excuse my silence and to take this column for a letter, a report. Be assured however of prayers. I doubt whether I ever read a letter without saying a prayer for the sender. I do, however, see all the letters which are addressed to me and pass them on to be acknowledged, and answered as best we can.

Vermont

When my daughter talked to me of her opportunity to take a year's course in practical nursing, with four months of her training in Brattleboro and eight months in the local hospital of Springfield, Vermont, we both recognized it as an opportunity of a lifetime to get training for a specific job. Her education in crafts in Canada and in agriculture and care of animals at Farmingdale, Long Island which had fitted her for her twenty years of married life and the raising of a family on the land, had not fitted her to hold down any job.

With children all day in school women have come to feel the isolation of the home, the lack of community facilities such as day nurseries. They know they have a contribution to make to the common good. Their talents are unused and undeveloped. And above all, there is the crucial need to earn money to help support and to educate and provide training in turn for the young ones.

She could only take the course offered by the government under the Manpower and Retraining Act if I could go to Vermont and stay for four months with the seven children of the nine who were home. When she returned to spend the last eight months at home while she worked from seven to three at the hospital in Springfield, she herself could take care of the children, all of whom were in school except Katy who is a little over four. It is planned that she join the family of a cousin for a few months until a permanent nursery school can be found locally.

I had dreaded the four months as a time when anything could happen and I thought of Sue's broken arm from tobogganing the winter before, and how Nickie had practically put out a tonsil when he fell off the porch with a sharp pencil in his mouth, and how Mary had been bitten by a baby rat she had found, not to speak of all the other dire happenings in Catholic Worker families all over the nation. When you get old you know too much. One must learn to mortify the interior senses which include the memory. I had always taken that to mean most especially never to remember injuries and grievances and hark back to them, or let them accumulate, and here I had to apply this basic teaching to my imagination which conjured up all kinds of trouble ahead.

Well, I had a wonderful time. It was unalloyed joy, those four months, to live in the midst of the beauty of Vermont and the beauty of children.

Tamar was home week ends, so I had longer visits with her than I had had for years.

Trave

It is four years since I have taken a long trip south and west and I plan to set out again on February first. I am to speak in Austin, Texas, February 22, in San Antonio, February 23, a day or so later in Houston, and then on to Tucson to speak at the University of Arizona. I want to visit the Oakland House of Hospitality and also the Salt Lake City House, and I have been invited also to Oklahoma City to speak there. I do not yet know my exact schedule but I hope to travel by car and go to North Carolina first, to Conyers, Georgia to visit one of our former editors, Jack English, now Fr. Charles, and then on to Natchez, Mississippi to visit friends and readers there. I do not as yet know my exact schedule but mail will be forwarded to me.

The City

Meanwhile I have had a week in December, and all of January to enjoy the farm at Tivoli and its warmth and space, and in the city to share the poverty and cold of those at Chrystie Street and Kenmare St. Chrystie Street is of course St. Joseph's house of hospitality and it is as bright and colorful as paint can make it over these joyful holidays. As for Kenmare Street, where the women have four apartments, unheated, with cold halls and wind whistling through cracks around the windows,—it is hard to get used to after four months in the country, in a house as warm as toast with a Franklin stove in the living room besides, burning good pine logs.

But here at Kenmare St. we go to bed with a hot water bottle at our feet (an empty pint is just the proper size) and a wool cap on our heads and a muffler around the neck. When you are heating with the gas oven you want to cut it off at night, and besides that the cold comes through the bricks if your bed is against the outside wall. Next time Hiroshi, Placid or Michael come in for a cup of tea and some bread and butter of an evening (our dinner is at five thirty and by nine people are in the humor for a snack) I'll get them to move all the furniture in my room so that the bookcase and desk are against the outside wall, and the bed against the wall between this apartment and the next which houses four young women. With these little apartments, we have both privacy and community which works out better than our other women's houses of hospitality of the past which we have had as part of St. Joseph's house as a whole. We are decentralized indeed and in a way scattered among our neighbors who are also drawn into our community through their charity. They give us furniture when they are buying

203

new. They give us delightful Italian dishes on feast days; we find clothes hanging on our doorknobs and Missouri Marie returns the charity by writing letters for the Italian woman upstairs who speaks English perfectly but cannot write it, and by doing the shopping for the landlady when she is ill, and so on.

I suppose it would be politer not to allude to people around the CW as German George, Polish Walter, Ukrainian Mike and Missouri Marie. And thinking of my sister-in-law who was formerly Teresa de Aragon, I will Americanize a European custom and allude to George German, Walter Poland, Mike Ukraine and Marie Missouri hereafter.

To go back to the subject of cold. There is an Arab saying "Fire is twice bread." Certainly it is a hard and miserable thing to be cold. It is hard to work. It is hard to keep clean. It is hard to forget the body, this cumbrous instrument of the mind and soul. When the senses are all at peace, satisfied and content, the exercises of the mind and soul seems to be going smoothly. I have thought a good deal along these lines in connection with poverty and destitution and the attitudes of those who suffer these affronts in a prosperous land. I have thought of them when people talk of the demands of labor for higher wages and shorter hours. There have been occasional critical comments about the Catholic Worker—why do we emphasize these material things? Why are we frozen in these attitudes, these positions about poverty and the social order? It is because we must be like the importunate widow before the unjust judge, like the man who came to borrow some loaves to feed his hungry family and knocked at the door of his friend until he got what he wanted from him.

We emphasize the material because we are working to make that kind of a society in which it is easier for men to be good. And while the triple revolution of automation, civil rights and peacemaking is going on, we have to rack our brains, use our imagination, seize upon every opportunity, every encounter, to enlighten our own minds as well as those of others, to inflame our own hearts as well as those of others, that we may all be working for the common good, and towards that Eternal Good for which all hearts long . . .

When I left New York on February first, it was snowing and not so cold. It had been ten below zero the day before. Stanley Vishnewski from Tivoli was going to meet me at the station to bring me some things I had forgotten, but his train was an hour late, so I missed him. Clare Bee, Ed Forand and Walter Kerell saw me off. My sister had provided me with sandwiches, so I had supper on the train and my fare and berth was paid for by one of our readers, Ditte Shafer, of Tryon, North Carolina, so I travelled in great comfort.

When I woke up I was in North Carolina, with its yellow and red earth and green cover crop on the fields and brilliantly green pine trees (all the other trees were bare). I read the psalms for matins and lauds in Father Frey's little book, Confraternity edition (5300 Ft. Hamilton Parkway, Brooklyn 15, N.Y.). I include the address so that our readers can get them and be comforted as I was, sorry as I was to leave home and family on another trip. I needed the strength and courage that the psalms always give.

As I write I am passing row upon row of Negro shacks like corn cribs, and then there are fields of junked cars, and the earth over and over is wounded with erosion. All these things hurt. Of course I am surrounded by squalor on the Bowery, and moral squalor too, but here people are closer to the earth, and so much alone with their poverty and pain.

In Tryon, I visited Ditte for two days, spoke at the beautiful little church there and met Father Kerin, who is principal of the Catholic high school in Atlanta and drives down once a week to offer Mass. It was cold that night, around the zero mark, and Father Kerin had made the extra trip for the meeting, a long drive. The next day there was a morning meeting, after Mass at Brevard, and the mothers of the parish came. Early Thursday morning Father Charles Mulholland, an old friend, came far out of his way from Brevard to Tryon to pick me up, and we drove first to Highland, over the steepest mountain roads, which were icy at every turn—roads that climbed thousands of feet and wound down around the mountains into Alabama. At one point we were four thousand feet up and stopped at a little church at Highland, where three of us assisted at Mass in the warm living room in back of the church. Water had frozen in the pipes, but one of the parishioners had prepared a good breakfast after Mass, all complete with home-made coffee cake, which warmed us for our trip. Then we set forth to drive to the Trappist Monastery of Our Lady of the Holy Spirit, at Conyers, Georgia, east of Atlanta. We got there at three p.m. and Father Mulholland had to start back to Brevard after a brief rest for coffee.

It is strange to write of good conversations at a Trappist monastery, but the season is still the joyful one of Epiphany and I was permitted to speak to Father Charles and Father Peter, both of them long associated with the Catholic Worker. Father Charles was formerly Jack English and Father Peter was Victor Assid. Part of the new look is that from now on Trappists, the new ones at any rate, are going to keep their own names, and the lay brothers now dress the same as choir monks.

The next night I spoke to the community in the crypt and I was happy to speak, begging the prayers of this power-house for those in Alabama and Mississippi that I am going to visit, as well as for myself. I spoke and answered questions for an hour and a half, and before I went to sleep in the little guest house on the lake near the entrance to the monastery, we enjoyed visiting with the Sherry's, Gerald and Evelyn, who had come out from Atlanta, and getting first impressions of the work of the Council, which Mr. Sherry had attended for some weeks.

Mr. Sherry is editor of the diocesan paper, and before he and his wife left he gave me a list of questions which he begged me to answer and mail back to him as I proceeded on my way. So now that I am settled before a typewriter at the Holy Name of Jesus Hospital (integrated) in Gadsden, Ala., I can add these pages to what I have written for him and send them on to Martin Corbin to include in my February *On Pilgrimage* column. There is always the need for recapitulations.

INTERVIEW

Q. Can you explain briefly the aims and purposes of the Catholic Workers movement?

A. The aim of The Catholic Worker movement is really to further what Peter Maurin (the founder and leader of the movement in 1933) called the *Green Revolution*. He wanted to make the kind of society "*where it would be eas-*

ier for men to be good," he said. That involved us of course in a program of action, which began with 1) clarification of thought through discussions, courses, retreats, work camps, which go on at our Catholic Worker farm at Tivoli, New York throughout the year, and 2) the running of houses of hospitality where there can be the direct action of the works of mercy, running a breadline, clothesroom, hospice where immediate needs can be taken care of those who come to us. That has meant the building up of a family around the country of people from all walks of life, of different backgrounds, people of every race, color and creed. The leaders of the work are Catholic. There are probably about ten or twelve houses and farms around the country, each autonomous. But the readers themselves throughout the country try to carry on what Ammon Hennacy calls a one-man revolution.

Q. Is there such a thing as Christian Communism?

A. Peter Maurin wrote an essay, to the effect that there was a Christian communism and a Christian capitalism, in which he made his point very clear. The quotation "*Property, the more common it becomes, the more holy it becomes,*" is from the writings of St. Gertrude. It was Eric Gill who said, "*Property is proper to man.*" And St. Thomas said that a certain amount of property is necessary to lead a good life. It would take a book to answer such a question.

Q. How do you think the Church can best assist the War on Poverty?

A. By teaching Holy Poverty—a philosophy of poverty and a philosophy of work. If children took the lives of the saints seriously, they would realize their capacity for spiritual and material action and the importance of their contribution to the Green Revolution. The plight of the migrant and agricultural worker would be alleviated by farming communes such as the *kibbutzim* of Israel or the collectives and communes of China and Russia and Cuba. Joan Robinson, British economist teaching at Cambridge, has written favorably about Cuban and Chinese communes. In his book *Paths in Utopia,* Martin Buber says that only a community of communities deserves the name of commonwealth. A great deal of study of cooperatives and small-scale enterprises, as well as a sense of personal responsibility, is necessary in this war on poverty. You find the workers in the interracial movement in the South, determined to begin a war on poverty right where they are, through mutual aid, the use of talents and physical resources, study groups, adult education and so on, before they call in the government for aid. They are starting from the bottom up.

Q. What do you think is wrong with the present approach in this regard?

A. Everyone is saying the problem is too vast for any but public agencies and large-scale government help. People are waiting for Church or Government, or in general for George to do it. We begin with ourselves and give what we have, and the movement spreads. This is the dynamic, organic approach.

Q. What do you think is the minimum that Catholics can do in view of the needs of the times?

A. We should not think in terms of minimum. Aim at perfection. Aim high, and we will get somewhere. God can take the loaves and fishes, if that is all we have, and multiply it. But the thing is to *want* to give all. A new commandment Jesus gave us, to lay down our lives for our brothers. If we are ready and willing, God can show us what we can do. We are living in a time of crisis. In war the State asks men for everything, to lay down their lives, to endure hardship, loss of family, "blood, sweat and tears."

Q. People have accused you of supporting the Communist takeover in Cuba; would you clarify your views on this?

A. With John XXIII, our beloved late Holy Father, I think that where the social aims of Communists are Christian aims they should be supported. Our own bishops have also said this in one of their annual messages. Interracial justice, education for all, medical care, housing for the poor, twelve months' work a year instead of four months—these are good aims. And I can only report what I saw in Cuba, the churches open, retreats and days of recollection being given, catechisms printed, instruction going on. The Catholic schools have been confiscated, yes, but if we listen to Our Lord, Who said, "*If they take your coat, give them your cloak too,*" we could meet such things with holy indifference. These things have happened many times before. All the land taken from the papacy has meant no diminution of her influence in the world. At no time in history have people listened so warmly to the Popes in their encyclicals.

Q. Do you think that the work of the Vatican Council has in any way justified your pioneer work in the dialogue with the community?

A. We are tremendously interested and encouraged by the

work of Vatican Council II and are looking forward to the work of the last session, hoping that Article 25 in Schema XIII will be made even stronger, so that they will condemn not only nuclear weapons but all weapons of modern war, napalm, blockbusters, chemical and biological war, as well as nuclear war. And we hope that the teaching on the meaning of *conscience* will be made clear. Of course we rejoice in the liturgical reform, and thank God for such prelates as Archbishop Paul Hallinan, for their pastoral letters, informing their people as to what is going on.

Q. What is in your opinion the root cause of the tremendous gap between haves and have nots?

A. One can't answer this question without taking into consideration the entire history of the United States, man's nature, his fall and his redemption. To put it simply, the root cause of the gap is man's greed, avarice, acquisitiveness, his fear of insecurity, and the lack of attention to the teachings of Jesus and the saints throughout the ages.

Q. What must the lay apostolate do in the light of Vatican II to keep it abreast of the call to aggiornamento?

A. Read and study, listen and learn. We have to know God in order to love and serve Him. We have to know our neighbor likewise. As I travel through the country, I am trying to learn what is going on—all the exciting things that are happening—the strength, the courage, the vigor of the struggle going on in the South. They are teaching the rest of the country.

Q. What is the future for the church in America?

A. I'm hoping that young Catholics will become more and more involved in a cause which increases their love of brother (and they will be growing in the love of God). Here is Gadsden, my first stop after Conyers, Georgia, I find a young Negro Catholic, born in New Orleans, Bennee Luchion, who is involving the whole community, not just in a fight for justice but in the building up of a center where arts and crafts, puppet shows, clothes center for mutual aid, education classes to fight illiteracy to help men get jobs, and many other activities, are going on. He has been jailed six times for taking part in demonstrations. I saw him for the first time in church this Sunday morning, going to the communion rail and getting his throat blessed after Mass. Some one said afterwards that he came here without a cent, lives in one place after another, is fed by the community and is involving everyone. And thank God the Catholic community is involved!

It is impossible to write all my impressions on the trip I am making in such a column as *On Pilgrimage*. I must write some longer articles later on various aspects of the problems I have encountered. Fortunately, tapes were made of many of my talks and if it is possible I would like to get copies of these tapes which will serve as notes. Meanwhile all this can be is a diary, and a diary which works backward, at that.

I write today from Tucson, Arizona, and by the time this March issue of the paper reaches our West Coast readers I will be home again, in New York, or perhaps on my way to Puerto Rico where I have been invited to speak to some university students who are nationalists but on the non-violent side.

I am staying now with the James Allens, who have a family of ten, and eight of the children, all very articulate, are at home. Mealtimes mean discussion on all kinds of topics, from the new morality, the new look in the church, the population explosion, the anarchism of the home and the kind of anarchism Ammon Hennacy talks about, war and peace, man and his destiny. And in the midst of this life, an old man, the grandfather, lies peacefully dying. Today he was anointed. It is hard to write at such a time, but this is my job.

Arriving only last night by Greyhound from Albuquerque, I find it very warm here. When this is written I am going out to sit under a tree and read. Mail follows me, but travelling, speaking and just conversations leave little time to answer mail. I'll catch up on that later.

Albuquerque

Here I visited the Resers, in the house which Al has over the years enlarged and which looks down an unpaved country road and across to the far horizon of the mountains through which I had come. It is as though Albuquerque was in a large shallow bowl and we were on one rim of it looking across the city to the mountains opposite. Years ago Al started the house of hospitality in Chicago together with Ed Marciniak. John Cogley lived there while he went to college and at the same time ran the house. All three had known each other from boyhood. Al came to the Southwest for his health. (He would have died had he stayed in Chicago.)

Catherine works part time for Catholic Charities. The oldest son is married, with kids, and he works cleaning out and welding the insides of trailer truck tank cars. Isn't this dangerous work? Certainly all work has its risks, but there are safety devices. They steam out the tanks first before the men go into them. (I just read of a dozen seamen overcome by gas fumes in a tanker. They got out, all but one, and when a fellow worker went in to rescue him both were killed.) Bill has the Great Books, which I dipped into while I was there. Pete, his cousin, works as mailman and takes courses at the university.

"They sure need a house of hospitality around Albuquerque," Al said. "The Salvation Army takes transients in for one night and Brother Matthew for three."

The Catholic Worker may not be able to take in many but those who come become a part of the community and make it such a place as Orwell recommends in the concluding pages of "*Down and Out in Paris and London.*" If there were only many more of them! These are means in a war on poverty not much regarded.

Oklahoma City

Stayed here with Sister Nativity who lives in an old rectory which has been turned into a Montessori center for the children of the district. Sister was formerly in charge of a hospital but has chosen this work among the poor.

About a mile away there is a slum section separated from the rest of the city by a river on one side and railroad tracks on the other and there is a small house no better than the Negro houses around where two priests live together with Vincent Maevsky who spent some months with us last summer. He is going to college and also cooks the meals there. There is poverty there but not destitution, so that it looks like something which will continue and not be just a flash in the pan, just a romantic gesture as so many attempts "to live poor" are. Vincent, for instance, lived in an apartment of two rooms on Spring Street last summer which he and two others called the Sacco-Vanzetti house and where they took in so many that every bit of available space was taken up and the young extremists took to the comfort and privacy of the roof during the summer months. This sort of thing is a gesture which needs to be made no doubt but it never lasts because it is humanly unendurable for donor or recipient of hospitality. I don't know how many of these splinter

211

offshoots of the CW house have happened in the past, as a result of our own attempts to think of the common good, and to use some measure of common sense and as a protest against our failures in charity too.

Jacques Travers seems to have some balance. He teaches, earns his living, and shares his apartment with two others, one of whom many might give up as hopeless cases who may walk off with all his possessions as he has done in the past with others. For the other who is a former professor, he is providing a home in his old age, who had nothing before but a room on the Bowery (for which, by the way, the Catholic Worker has been paying slightly more than a dollar a night for many years).

But such unspectacular hospitality is not for the very young ones who like to make the grand but not lasting gesture. However, if they had a true vocation for this work of love, sharing what they had very simply, they would have persevered through hell and high water, as the saying is. Meanwhile it is a school for them, an exercise and they can only learn by doing. They have yet to find their true vocation. Even so, as an act of love, it is of uncalculable value.

It was good to see Vincent and to learn that he will be with us again this summer, to give out clothes, mind the door, ladle out soup, in addition to other more exciting adventure like picket lines and sit-ins. We visited also with Fr. McDole, who was one of a group of priests who went to Mississippi last summer.

I came to Oklahoma City from San Antonio, a long trip which took from seven a.m. until eleven p.m. and then we sat up, Sister Nativity, Vincent, Fr. Vrana and I, until two-thirty talking and enjoying sister's fresh coffee cake and coffee. Jean Walsh had been with them at Christmas time and it was her enthusiasm for their work which led me to go so out of my way to be with them. We had a good meeting the night after I arrived and the seminarians who had just come from a Shrove Tuesday day of recollection were able to attend. I also had time to visit St. Patrick's church, which is of great beauty, and built by the parishioners themselves, with the guidance, of course, of contractors and other experts.

San Antonio

Back in San Antonio I had had a meeting which was crowded to the doors and even outside, and thanks to microphones, I could reach them all. In fact the meetings in Austin and in San Antonio were marked by so great an interest in the poverty program of the government on the one hand and the Vietnam situation on the other. Thanks to John Howard Griffin who has also been giving a series of talks to capacity audiences, they were also keyed up about the civil rights issue and the problems of jobs for Negro and white.

Undoubtedly they were worried, some of them, about their own future work. I heard one student say to another, "Do you realize how easy it is to lose your security clearance —what would happen to you then?" In the way of job opportunity, I suppose he meant.

One of the young men who had stayed with us one summer and who taught afterward in the Aleutians lost his "security clearance" after two years of teaching and has not to this day the slightest idea why, and now can get no more work as a teacher. He loved his work too, and loved the Aleutians and had only admiration for the fearlessness of the young men who flew under the most hazardous conditions (in their work of surveillance, I suppose). We were talking about war and the challenge war presented to the young when everything was asked of them in the way of sacrifice. It is a time when we need to read again that conversation of the young airman in Bernanos' famous story, *The Diary of a Country Priest.* We printed it once in the CW during the Second World War.

In San Antonio, the sick young man who was president of the Young Republican Club distributed leaflets containing an attack on my moral reputation but it was an audience which did not heckle though there was a good hour of questions afterward. Undoubtedly in most audiences there were many who represented most conservative and unimaginative thinking, but they were serious and courteous and undoubtedly could be reached in discussion. We are too often belligerent pacifists who talk only to ourselves and to each other. "God will that *all* men be saved."

Thanks to my hostess, Encarnacion Armas, I was able to have a close look at the truly destitute sections which surround San Antonio. On the one hand there are the air bases, five of them, not to speak of an army camp within a hundred miles, of from 45,000 to 60,000 very young draftees or enlisted men, and the knowledge and sight of all the money spent on war, and on the very small amount spent on the poor in comparison, and that to be spread over five years,

213

makes for bitterness of heart. "In peace is my bitterness most bitter," one of the prophets said.

"The poor are the first children of the church," Bossuet said, but to look at the unequal distribution of the Church wealth one would never know it. The amount spent on wall to wall carpeting and expensive furnishings in the offices which have to deal with the fact of destitution is a scandal in the church, which cries out to heaven. As I see it I think with refreshment of the barracks used as a convent by the Missionary Servants of the Most Blessed Trinity in Gadsden, Alabama, and of the two slum priests in Oklahoma City, and of the Benedictine Monastery at Weston, Vermont, and of the Little Brothers in Detroit, and the Little Sisters in Boston, Chicago, Washington and Montreal, and all the others working among the poor and not trying to get hunks of government money with which to begin from top down to alleviate poverty. One worthy voluntary project for some publisher to do would be to reprint Conrad Pepler's book—*Rich and Poor in Christian Tradition*.

Before San Antonio there was Austin, where I spoke at St. Edward's University to a very large audience and where I met Fr. Trebtoske again, who used to work with us in New York before he went to the seminary. He is in a Mexican parish where they have a fine center for the children, bright and gaily painted, spacious, light and airy, better than anything that I saw in San Antonio where the Bishops' committee for the Spanish speaking is located. The Montessori method is used to teach the children and the children come after school every day.

Of course one sees the results of the cursillo everywhere, this course in Christianity which results in a sense of community, a sense that we are all one, and responsible for each other.

In Houston I visited Rose Badami, member of the Legion of Mary who started a house of hospitality for girls in difficulties of one kind or another. There needs to be more delicacy exercised in this kind of work, such as was done once by two young Christian Workers in New York, directed by Fr. Wendell, O.P. where they took in girls who were friends of theirs as well as girls out of prison and none visiting them knew which was which. The house in Texas is the first work of this kind I have seen undertaken and I hope it grows, but one must have a sturdy endurance and a lively faith that God will repair our own failures to remember that we are but unprofitable servants and these guests are His guests, and not our own. We are there to wash their feet, as it were, and preferably in silence, which St. Brendan said is two thirds of piety.

Fr. John Sheehan, Basilian, had me speak at St. Thomas University before I left. He was formerly in Rochester and taught the sons of our Catholic Workers there. He reminded me of the work in Toronto where the state university is combined with the Institute of Medieval Studies run by the Basilians. We could learn much from them as to how Church and State work together in the field of education. We learned much in the early days of our work from Fr. Carr and Fr. Phelan, both of the Institute.

Mississippi

And now to get back to Mississippi about which I must write later an entire article, and with care lest I endanger our friends there by some indiscretion. When you visit friends who have been threatened, whose homes have been watched and in one case bombed, you are anxious not to add to the burden they bear of danger and suffering. Each time they speak out they are in danger and their children are in danger.

You come from Mass in the morning and see bright shiny pick-up trucks with rifle racks in the window behind the seat, with two or three rifles, and no license plates on the car. This I witnessed too, morning, noon and evening when this violation in regard to plates was clearly visible. Then you hear of a young man whose car was being refueled arrested on charges of speeding, assaulting an officer and disorderly conduct because he tried to use the men's toilet, and he a Negro.

Ave Maria, the weekly magazine published at Notre Dame, Indiana, carried a series of articles written by the editor, who was accompanied by an Episcopalian priest, in which he told of the terror he experienced there. John Howard Griffin is lecturing on his experiences in Mississippi. Father Hesburgh, president of Notre Dame, was a member of the United States Commission on Civil Rights which was conducting hearings on whether the Negro was receiving police protection in his attempt to register to vote, or whether his rights were being interfered with. I spent one day at the hearings overcome with horror and shame at the tale of brutality which unfolded. Kidnappings and beatings, eyes gouged out, dismembered corpses found in bayous, two full pages of the names of Negroes murdered in Mississippi, these things came out under the questioning of lawyers and educators which made up the commission.

Even as the hearings went on, the COFO house in Laurel, Miss., was burned to the ground. Men who testified at the hearings had to be given a guard to escort them home, and how safe they would be there was a question. Many who testified were born and raised in the same place. And many had worked and raised their children to go north to college.

During the hearings I met Clarie Harvey of Jackson, Mississippi, who had been one of the women with whom I made a peace pilgrimage that last month of Pope John XXIII's life on this earth. We had lunch together, a group of us in an integrated restaurant in Jackson. In Natchez, though there was token integration of one day, the only counter is in the Kress chain where Negroes can be served. The great struggle is the fight for voter registration now. There are no Negroes in the parochial schools yet in Mississippi.

Incident: We had dinner with Fr. Mahoney, S.S.J. who gives shelter to a COFO worker who was escaping a few cars full of masked men. The next day the filling station attendant across the street from his house stood out in front cracking a bull whip, practising with it, as it were. He seemed highly skilled.

Incident: Fr. Thompson, a Negro, across the river in Ferriday, La., visited his friends the Foleys in a white neighborhood. Bob Foley teaches in a white parochial school, not yet integrated. From then on no white neighbor speaks to him or his Louisiana-born wife and children. He is from the north—didn't know better. Cars come, filled with grim white men, and park in front of the house, with glaring headlights. Telephone calls in the dead of the night. Then near midnight a bomb exploding in the middle of their front lawn. Though there was a police station down the street, no officer came out. No evidence of interest by white neighbors.

Incident: We went to lunch with Fr. Thompson. He told us of a Negro shoe repairman who lived down the street who had been set on fire after being soaked with gasoline. He lived five days.

Incident: Powell Hall, Methodist minister with a wife and five children, demoted from one post for preaching integration, now in Kingston, Mississippi, went to town in Natchez and leaving his children in the library to browse, went to a gas station to refuel. He was picked up by the police for vagrancy.

This sketchy account has been written with many interruptions, one of which was to view the brutal breaking up of the Selma, Alabama march. Lord Jesus, son of the living God, have mercy on us.

April 1965

My winter pilgrimage to the West Coast began on February 1 and I returned to the East coast on April 4th in time to write this column. Thank God, I will be home for Holy Week and can be in the midst of the Catholic Worker Community for that holy season, commemorating the death and resurrection of Jesus, a week of penance and a week of rejoicing too. . . .

West Coast

At the invitation of Father Philip Straling I spoke at the Cardijn Center in San Diego, and I met there the young priest, Father Victor Salandini, of San Ysidro, California, whom I had met four years before in El Centro when I stopped on my way west to find out more about the lettuce strike which was going on in that great desert reclaimed by irrigation. Three of the San Francisco diocesan priests had been there and had prayed with and sung with the strikers, and for that work of mercy they had been rebuked by the San Diego diocesan authorities and their own chancery office and subsequently transferred to other sections of the diocese, and later still to other parts of the United States and Latin America. If young priests want to see the world, they have only to speak out in the agricultural conflict, which is still convulsing the West Coast.

Even more so this year with the repeal of the law permitting the importation of Mexican Labor, the *braceros*, who had lived in camps without family and were submissive "arms" of the growers. That is what the word *bracero* means. It is the local unemployed who are trying to work the crops this year, for the first time since the Second World War, when the braceros began to be imported in such great numbers, and now a subtle war is going on, with every attempt being made by the growers, the Associated Farmers, to make it appear that there is not enough local help to be had. Father Salandini, whose own family are growers, is already speaking out against the injustices practiced against the workers in the fields.

The last time I passed by, four years ago, I was driving alone in an old Ford, the gift of Father Clement Kern of Detroit, and when I knocked on the poor rectory of Father Victor's Mexican parish (I had been turned away from the other parish when I had asked to see the priest to talk of the strike), he welcomed me and invited me to lunch with him at the kitchen table, but he confessed on this 1965 meeting that he had thought I was "on the road," and looking for some kind of a handout! It was a poor Mexican parish of course, and I suppose I was expected to belong at the other parish on the other side of the tracks.

Tia Juana

San Ysidro is on the way south to Tia Juana, and there was a strike going on over the pitifully small wages. In Tia Juana, destitution was everywhere evident. There is a new order of sisters there, with a novitiate where young Mexican girls are trained to go out and work in these slum sections. Alice LaBarre, at whose house I stayed in San Diego, drove me there for a visit.

My next stop was up the coast at Santa Barbara, where I had been invited to speak by the Franciscan Brothers at their seminary at the old mission. It was too bad that I could not stop at Los Angeles, but already I was behind my schedule. The hardest part of these trips is that I am not able to accept all the invitations to visit old friends along the way. The Catholic Worker family, one might almost say the Catholic Worker community, has grown so over the years that one could spend a year on the road, and sometimes I think that is the way I will end my days,—just traveling around, but in a car next time so that I will not be dependent on bus schedules and can get off the beaten track more.

At Santa Barbara, Frater de Porres, some other brothers, Jo Miller and Eula Laucks met me at the crowded bus station and I was able to attend and speak at a panel meeting that night at the local high school, where a discussion of *Pacem in Terris* was taking place. It was just after the great meeting of world leaders held in New York to discuss the encyclical, which I had not been able to attend, and it was good to get a resume of that historic gathering. The next morning there was a glorious Mass at eleven at the chapel of the Brothers, where the singing of the introit, gradual, offertory and communion verses was accompanied by guitars and the entire congregation participated whole heartedly in the singing. Remembering the love St. Francis had for music, I could only think how he would have approved of this work of worship this day, this full-hearted assent to the truths of our faith. There was a meeting after the Mass, and a night meeting to and after the Sunday Mass the next day, another lunch at the Brothers, and an informal meeting with them until three o'clock. That morning, Cardinal McIntyre was dedicating the newly built church at which we participated at the Mass. I waited to pay my respects and tell him I was happy to see him looking so well and vigorous. Our exchange was cordial and it was neither the time nor the place to speak of profound and urgent matters that face the Church today both at home and abroad. He knows how we feel about the undeclared war in Vietnam, the tortures and devastation going on there, so opposite to the works of mercy for which we have always stood. I had been invited to speak after lunch on Monday at the Center for the Study of Democratic Institutions in Santa Barbara. The discussion in the morning had been about world law, about revision of the Constitution as well as the drafting of a world constitution, and I could only tell the assembled thinkers of "the law and order" one found in the slums, urban and rural. Truly one could say of law that like love in practice, it is a harsh and dreadful thing compared to law (or love) in dreams. John Cogley, who has been with the Center for some time, introduced me. The night before, John and his wife Teddy had been guests with me at the Irving Laucks' home, and we had had plenty of time to talk about the new generations and their attitudes, about travel, about common memories, with no stress or strain over opposing positions or differing emphases.

After the lunch I went to see Miguel, the artist whose studio was near the Center, and was delighted and astonished to find that he was the same Miguel who had stayed with us at Maryfarm, Newburgh, some fifteen years before.

At three in the afternoon there was a demonstration and walk through a mile of streets in downtown Santa Barbara to the steps of the City Hall. I participated in the march and the speaking, the first time I had ever spoken outside. We were expressing our sympathy for Selma and the entire South, for the reception the demonstrations had received at the hands of the police on their first march towards Montgomery, and for the first deaths in that struggle, those of Jimmy Lee Jackson and James L. Reeb, the first a Negro and the second a white Unitarian minister.

Oakland House

There has been a House of Hospitality in Oakland for some time, but I had never visited it and was looking forward to seeing it. Bob and Susan Callagy gave me hospitality and took the time to drive me around. They have written some of the letters appearing in the CW about the work out there, and seem to have a complete, overall feeling for it. They are another example of how a family, given the temperament, the health and the energy necessary, can take care of work, family duties and such an apostolate as this at the same time. There are five children and enough other young families in the movement so that they babysit and exchange hospitality.

The children go to a progressive school in which the parents too take active part. Perhaps they will write some time of the school, its beginnings, aims and make up. Callagy, as everyone calls him, was in the Marines in the Korean War, and he said that on the wall of the barracks there was the slogan, *"Better a small war than no war at all."* The indoctrination they received was that it was war for its own sake, war to make men, not to destroy them, or rather to make them by showing them their power to destroy. That seemed to be the kind of schooling they received. We were talking about the present war and wondering if the men involved knew what they were fighting for. Callagy told of the tanks of napalm on low-flying planes, or spraying the jellied gasoline on the defenseless. It clung to skin and clothes and could not be put out or brushed off, but it burned until skin itself dropped off. And of course in this last month there has been the use of nauseating gas, and tear gas, and the gas which brings about diarrhea and chest pains and disables the opponent, man, woman and child so that they are incapable of fighting. "They get them young in the Marines," Callagy said, "seventeen, eighteen, before they know what anything is about."

One peace offensive which Callagy has engaged in was the rebuilding of a church in Mississippi last summer. He and four others drove in a pickup truck and with their tools, a good record player and plenty of symphonies and folk music, they rebuilt the church to the sound of music, in five days, if I remember rightly. Someone asked if they had not been afraid, but five stalwart carpenters with tools in their hands, tools for construction, not destruction, filled with the strength and joy of youth, to the tune of great music, would be formidable adversaries. The symbol of Mississippi, a college student in Texas said, was the pickup truck, with a three-shot-gun-carrying rack behind the driver across the window, and no license plates on the car. At night of course, with dimmed lights. I saw many of them while I was there for two weeks.

I visited Mike Gold and his wife Elizabeth and was glad to hear that she was helping in one of the tutoring programs at the Oakland House. I spoke at the House of Hospitality where Hugh Madden presides. He is too militant to be another St. Francis, too gregarious to be another St. Benedict Joseph Labre, but partakes of the virtues of both. My talk there could go on only until nine since a crowd of men were waiting to unroll their bedding and go to sleep on the floor. Many of them knew the old Industrial Workers of the World halls and agreed with me when I spoke of the need for such mutual aid, such centers run by the men themselves. Susan Callagy, Dorothy Kaufman and others collect food from the markets and keep the soup kettle full. It is never so much a problem of food as of housing and warmth.

When I finished speaking at the place I went across the street to the women and children's center, which is in an old frame building, more than half a century old, with a few stores and tenants upstairs, and a large yard in back and to one side. It was big enough for a clothes center and for the mothers to gather together for sewing and for children's painting classes. Several of the families have the children home for dinner every week or so, and other times the mothers. It is a solid Negro neighborhood, extending for five miles around. There is certainly a good group that make up the Catholic Worker crowd in Oakland and Berkeley and I'd like to mention all their names, but my notes are in another suitcase sent ahead of me and not yet reclaimed.

The next day I spoke at the University of California at Berkeley, on the famous campus where there has been so much stir these last months, some of it caused by a few who seem to distract attention from the real issues by their own craving for attention. I did not feel that I could cope with such a crowd as the one that throngs the square at noon each day (although Ammon Hennacy was quite happy to take them on), a crowd which can go from speaker to speaker as they do in Union Square. Instead I had the use of one of the halls and there was quiet enough to sense the deep concern of the students in regard to the problems which confront us in the South, on the West Coast and in Vietnam.

Stockton

The next morning, Carol and Francis Gorgen (with their baby) drove Mary Lathrop and me to Stockton, over the smooth green hills where flocks of sheep grazed, and into the city of Stockton, where the agricultural workers congregate and where the buses are always crowded with migrants going up and down the long valley for work. Last time I was west, I had gone at 4 a.m. to the center of town with Andy Aerano, one of the organizers, to see the shape up, the trucks, the government agencies who were registering these workers in the fields. Mary Lathrop had herself shipped out from here to work in the fields and was familiar with the whole set-up. Last year she wrote stories about it for the *CW*.

We had a luncheon meeting that day with some of the young priests serving their internship in pastoral theology with Father Alan McCoy at St. Mary's. Here is another parish like that of Father Kern's in Detroit, where two of the Catholic Worker Houses are situated: St. Francis House and St. Martha House.

In Father Alan's parish there are a breadline, showers, clinic—all kinds of social services—not to speak of the superlative service of the *cursillo* movement. *Cursillo* is a retreat (made once only for the lifetime) which results in community, a retreat given by priests and laymen and fortified by prayers of communities all around, a course which results in conversions, rather a turning to God with the whole heart and soul and mind and strength. Community means that the *cursillistas* keep in touch with each other and help each other in any way they can. It all began as a retreat for the Spanish-speaking, originating in the island of Majorca, and was brought here to the Southwest by airmen who came to learn to fly jets. Strange beginnings!

To Salt Lake City

After another meeting that night with some of the parishioners, we had a good night at the David Brewers out on Eight Mile Road in their delightful octagonal house set in the middle of a wide valley of utter flatness, covered over by the blue bowl of the sky. I set out the next morning after Mass by train to Salt Lake City to see for the first time Ammon Hennacy's Joe Hill House of Hospitality and St. Joseph's Refuge. Ammon faithfully and dutifully has both names on a big sign on the front of his house, which was described in the last issue by Peter Lumsden, who came to take care of it for six weeks while Ammon was travelling on the West Coast and speaking up and down California. (I met Peter Lumsden in California a few days before.) Mary Lathrop, who helped Ammon start the house a few years ago, painted murals on the walls of the original house, which was a storefront on Postoffice Place, and helped support it by her work. She painted pictures not only of the execution of Joe Hill, the labor martyr of I.W.W. fame, song writer for the Wobblies and a legend in the labor movement; but also of the Holy Family, of which St. Joseph was the protector.

Ammon was there when I arrived after a thirty-six-hour trip. Peter Lumsden had gone on to Oakland and I had seen him there, and I understood that, on his way home he was going to pick up Murphy Dowouis, half Irish and half French, or Cajun as Ammon always calls him in his column. Both Cajun and Utah Phillips, also a folk singer, played and sang at my meeting that night at the Newman Club at the university. There were a number of priests present and a good gathering of students. Ammon circulated the *Catholic Worker* and his literature against capital punishment, but he had no more books to sell. There are none left of the first edition, and he has five hundred dollars worth of orders for more picked up on his speaking trip. But the printer won't print more until he has more money, and Ammon already owes him $1,500. He has not charged enough for the book; $3 does not cover the cost of the book, and the mailing adds up to a lot. His friends should all be sending him offerings to help balance the books.

Pat Rusk had been staying in the house helping, and she was setting out with me the next morning, but she was going to New York via St. Louis. Just as we were leaving another young woman arrived. Ammon is the exceptional person who can attract both female and male admirers by the horde, and his own faithfulness to friendship is rewarded by theirs to him.

A Long Trek
By now it was cold again and I was glad of my warm coat, which I had carried through the heat of Mississippi, Texas,

Arizona and California. There was snow everywhere, and a blizzard as we sped over the roads of the state of Nebraska, narrow roads, and every time a trailer truck passed us there was a great cloud of snow impeding our vision—mine and the driver's—since I was sitting on the front seat. Windows on either side of the bus were all frozen up and mud and snow-splashed and one could see nothing. It was good to be in front speeding through the night on the way to Minnesota.

This too was a thirty-six-hour-trip, and I was happy when I arrived in snowbound Minneapolis to find Michael Humphrey, his wife Mary, his brother-in-law and his sister Susan waiting for me to drive me the sixty miles to St. Cloud. I was amazed at the drifts, in some places sixteen feet high, which I saw around the houses where the wind had piled it. At the Humphrey place the narrow walk was hard to get through with a suitcase. Mass next day at the Newman Center of the State Teachers' College, where Mary and Susan attend classes. Some of the Humphrey and most of the Doyle children go to the elementary school connected with the college. The Mass was beautifully participated in and the Gelineau psalms were sung. In the evening to the movie, *The Pumpkin Eater*, which Mary, mother of a large family, especially wanted to see. It was very hard for us to get the point of the movie. What was going to happen to the wife after the sterilization and abortion? Was the husband going to quit his philandering? Was the wife going to become a gibbering idiot with nymphomaniac tendencies like the woman she encountered in the beauty parlor in the hair dryer?

After the movie we went to the home of Fredric Peters, where there was to be a meeting of families, which was late because it was a job getting all the children to bed. Their house is large and right on the Mississippi, which of course was frozen over and snow-covered and could not be distinguished from the fields which stretched out beyond it, except that there were banks on either side. There were many students there as well as married couples and the meeting lasted until after two a.m. The Petters, who have the largest dress goods shop in town, and Barbara White, who is a genius at sewing, had between them made me a beautiful maroon-colored dress of wool crepe, which was all ready for me on my arrival. A frivolous note to introduce to this account of a wandering apostolate perhaps, but an indication of the generosity shown me on my journey. Eric Gill has a lot to say about clothes and their meaning in our lives. He recalls the

224

meaning of clothes in a little homily for the Stations of the Cross where Jesus is stripped of his garments.

Barbara White made two other dresses for me during my three-day stay, fitting and finishing one which Mary Humphrey, who has made dresses for me in the past, had all but completed. Mary is coming to stay with us at Tivoli this summer with some of the children, and we will put her to work making sleeping bags for the next winter. Not to speak of flannel shirts for the men of the staff.

The next day, Jim Palmquist came over and fixed the furnace, which had been out of order for a week all during the zero weather so that we did not have to all camp out in the living room, dining room and kitchen, which is one long L-shaped room. Michael brought wood and the Petters sent coal, so we luxuriated in warmth again. Jim himself has a family of seven. Three more inches of snow today and zero weather at night.

We drove that night to the home of Herbert Burke, who is a professor at St. John's, Collegeville, where we saw another movie, a Japanese film called *Ikuru* (To Live) and is about a bureaucrat dying of cancer, and how he ends his days accomplishing a great work of mercy, building a park in a slum section of Tokyo.

His attempt to "live" under the guidance of a benevolent Mephistopheles (who said he would not charge him anything) and his finding the meaning of life through a young clerical worker who had left her stupefying job in his office to work in a toy factory (no sex undertones, just contact with the poor and simple) was profoundly moving. Somehow she convinced him that he should return to his office and work at what he wanted most to do, not allowing himself to be strangled by routine difficulties. The story of his going from bureaucrat to politician, from office to office, his humility, importunity, and insistence, was moving indeed.

After the movie, a meeting again with the crowd of students from St. John's, most of whom were Dr. Burke's pupils. Again we were up until two a.m.

The next day, my last in Minnesota, we were snowed in for fair, though there was in the afternoon a two-block walk to show solidarity with the civil-rights drive in Selma and to commemorate the death of the three victims, Jimmie Lee Jackson, James L. Reeb, and Viola Gregg Liuzzo.

It was a day of visitors from morning till night, so that there was scarcely time to eat (the kids, it seemed, were liv-

ing only on the cake they had baked for these same visitors).
To bed early and up at four-thirty to catch the 5:40 train to
Milwaukee. It was one of those trains with a Vista Dome, but
the uniform whiteness of sky and field was hard on the eyes.
No evergreens to brighten the landscape.

Milwaukee

I was so tired on arrival that I went to the Abbot Crest
hotel, right across from Gesu Church and down the street
from the Library where the archives of the *Catholic Worker*
are stored under the good care of Father Raphael N. Hamilton, S.J., who used to work in the history department of
Marquette. Prof. William Miller of the history department is
writing a book on the history of the *Catholic Worker*. They
were using the meeting, selling tickets to build up a scholarship fund for students from the South from Xavier University in New Orleans especially. The meeting was overflowing,
I was glad to see, and it testified to the students' concern with
social and racial problems. Smear leaflets were passed around
outside the building. I had forgotten to mention that these
leaflets were the usual thing at many of the meetings
throughout the country, and were labeled sometimes as being
issued by the Young Republicans, Catholics on Guard, etc.
etc.

I was happy to visit Florence Weinfurter at the Cardijn
Book Shop, just across from the University, where I met
Tim Dunn, from Sheed and Ward, who lived in Westminster, Maryland, and knew the Hennessys and the Ordways
there. He said he had just seen Hazen Ordway again and that
his oldest son is in the seminary. I also saw Donald McDonald, dean of Marquette School of Journalism, who is going to
the Center for the Study of Democratic Institutions, just as
John Cogley is leaving to work on the New York *Times*.

It was good to visit with David Host too, also on the faculty of Marquette, who spent a summer with us in the early
days at Charles Street, in New York. Had dinner with Dr.
Miller and his wife and family out in the country, an hour's
drive from town, where he has planted a field of pines and
added to his house.

By this time the snow was melting so fast that brooks were
running from the high fields in back of the house and flood-
ing the road below the house. The sound of running streams,
the glow in the willows and fruit trees, yellow and rose, and

the sound of birds, all this meant the end of a long winter and spring. And getting closer to home!

Pontiac

I spoke on April first at Marquette, and early the next morning I met Nina Polcyn and Sister Cecilia at Evanston railroad station, and with Mary Margaret Langdon driving us, we made the seven-hour trip to Clarkston, Michigan, where Father Martin Carrabine, former great leader of the apostolate, is invalided at the Jesuit novitiate there. I had known him since the first years of the CW; his Cisca groups had papered the city of Chicago with copies of the *Catholic Worker* every May Day, and from these groups of his had come leaders for the lay movement all over the country. Father Bernard Cooke, S.J., whom I had just heard speak at Marquette, had called him unique—that he had given a leadership and an impetus which had never been duplicated since.

Father Carrabine was delighted to see us and recognized us, although it was very hard for him at first to articulate, and a short visit that night was all he could take. But the next morning we had two more visits, one before and one after the eleven o'clock Mass—three visits, just as on a Pilgrimage, one of the others said. Father had given us all retreats and had been close to us for years. He was one of these priests who was always available, always encouraging, who seemed to see Christ in each person he met. He took the thousands of high-school students and young college students who thronged into his cramped offices as though he enjoyed the visits of every one of them, no matter how early they came, or how late they stayed. He was stationed at Holy Family Church on the West Side of Chicago and when the House of Hospitality was thriving on Blue Island Avenue, we were in his parish.

During the organizing drive in the stockyards, and during the strike in Little Steel in '36, he stood by us valiantly when the *Catholic Worker* was barred from many parishes and schools because John Cort had written the headline, *Cops Murder Ten Pickets in Chicago Riot* in what came to be known as the Memorial Day massacre. There was no television then to show the shooting of fleeing pickets.

Strong and compassionate, steadfast and faithful was Father Carrabine to all the laity, in the field of labor, and race relations. He was the soul of the apostolate in Chicago and never neglected to emphasize the privacy of the spiritual.

And now I am home again and can take up the tasks of correspondence and visitings, and talkings at home, although I hope to spend these last ten days of Lent in holy silence, a fasting from speech which Gandhi strongly advocated. In my Lenten missal there is a holy card bearing this note: "Two-thirds of piety consists in silence." (Rule of St. Brendan, 483-577 A.D.) . . .

May 1965

PETER MAURIN, PERSONALIST

We are usually driving back and forth to the farm at Tivoli, but on the few occasions when I have taken the train from Grand Central station, I have enjoyed the view from the river side, and been oppressed by one aspect of the view from the land side. That is, the ugly habit of people to use as dumps the back yards of their houses as well as the swampy places and creek beds of the little streams flowing into the Hudson. In Yonkers especially there are some rows of houses that evidently front the street and where the front yards are probably well cared for. But garbage and trash have been thrown down the cliff side that leads to the railroad tracks and Hudson River, so that it hurts each time one sees it.

Suddenly I thought one day of one of the jobs Peter Maurin had undertaken on the first farm we owned at Easton, Pennsylvania. It was a job which illustrated many of his ideas but also his love of beauty, his sense of the fitness of things. It also illustrated what he used to call his philosophy of work.

There were two farms, actually, at Easton, the upper and lower farm, and it was on the lower farm that most of us were housed and where we had our retreats every summer. There was one old house, two large barns, one of which we used for the animals, and the other of which we converted into chapel, meeting room, dormitories, and at the lower level, a long kitchen and dining room. The entire barn was built on a hillside so that on the road level the entrance was into the chapel and dormitories. It was below that, on a much lower level, that we had converted cowstalls into a long concrete floored room which made up the kitchen, in one corner and long dining room which could seat thirty or more guests. It was only later that we had electricity and running water in that kitchen. For several years we used lamplight and water from the spring house across the road.

At the very end of this large building, connected with it by one stone foundation wall, there was a foundation built up with field stone ceiling-high, which was overgrown with weeds when we first saw it that first summer, which was so hectic that we saw no further than that. We were too busy caring for the dozen children from Harlem and the numerous guests, most of whom were sick in one way or another.

But the winter disclosed the painful fact that this beautiful foundation, overlooking the fields below it and the Delaware river valley far below that, was actually filled half way to the top with all the debris of years. The tenants of the farmhouse before us had used the foundation as a convenient dumping ground for garbage, tin cans, old machinery, discarded furniture, refrigerators, washing machines and other eyesores such as I complain of seeing from the windows of the train. (What to do with all this waste, all these old cars and machines, is one of the problems of the day.)

Peter Maurin surveyed this dump and before we knew anything about his project, he was hard at work at it with wheel barrow and pick and shovel. He had undertaken, with no assistance, to clean this Augean stable. Actually we had no plans then, nor did we for several years, for utilizing the foundation and making an additional house on the property.

Fortunately, the ground sloped so steeply down back of the barns that Peter's engineering project was feasible. By dumping the refuse over the back and covering it with fill (another laborious job since he had to wheel loads of this heavy clay earth from the wooded hillside further down the road) he widened the foot path in back of the barn so that it became a narrow road around the back of the barn and in fact a little terrace where it was possible to sit and survey the long sloping valley below, a scene of incredible beauty, since we were high on what was called Mammy Morgan's Mountain, overlooking the conjunction of the Lehigh and Delaware Rivers.

I do not know how long this great task took Peter Maurin, the sturdy French peasant with the broad shoulders, the strong hands which were the hands of the scholar, more used to handling books than the shovel. He had taught in the

Christian Brothers' schools in France in his youth and though peasant-born had received a good education.

Philosophy of Work

I write this account of a piece of work which I remembered only because the sight of the dumps from the train window which had flashed by in one short instant had brought it suddenly to my mind so that I knew I should write about Peter in connection with it. It started a long train of thought which had to do with many of our problems today and Peter's solutions. I will try in this short space, and no matter how inadequately, to summarize them, although each of the points he used to make could be expanded into a day-long discussion.

First of all, it must be emphasized that Peter Maurin was a deeply religious man. He never missed daily Mass, and many a time I saw him sitting quietly in the church before or after Mass. When he lived on Fifteenth Street he walked to St. Francis of Assisi noon-day Mass. When we moved to Mott Street, where he lived for fifteen years he walked to St. Andrew's near City Hall to go to the noon-day Mass there. He never rushed, but walked in most leisurely fashion, his hands clasped behind his back, ruminating no doubt, paying little attention to shops (except for bookshops) or to passersby or even to traffic.

He read and studied a great deal, delighting to find new authors who could contribute to what he called the new synthesis of Cult, Culture and Cultivation. Cult came first, emphasizing the primacy of the spiritual. (Poor proof reading overlooked the error "*privacy* of the spiritual" in last month's issue.) He never talked personally of his own spiritual life but recommended to us such writings as Karl Adams's *Spirit of Catholicism*; Pius XI's 1927 Encyclical on St. Francis of Assisi and the Rule of St. Benedict.

He recommended the writings of the saints as they had to do with their practical lives, what their faith led them to be and do. When Ade Bethune came to us as a high-school girl with drawings of the saints, Peter urged her to picture the saints as workers, and she drew pictures of Our Lady feeding the chickens, sweeping a room, caring for a host of children; not someone to be worshipped but to be followed. Ade and others who followed her in this tradition (Carl Paulson in his stained glass) pictured St. Benedict planting a field, St. Peter pulling in his nets, St. Martin de Porres feeding a sick man.

Work, according to Peter was as necessary to man as bread, and he placed great importance on physical work. I can remember a discussion he had with the great scholar Dom Virgil Michel, who was the pioneer of the liturgical movement in this country.

"St. Benedict emphasized manual labor, as well as intellectual," Peter said. "Man needs to work with his hands. He needs to work by the sweat of his brow, for bodily health's sake. We would have far less nervous breakdowns if men worked with their hands more, instead of just with their heads."

As a result of Peter's emphasis we were called romantic agrarians, and without paying attention to Peter's more profound vision, national leaders in the field of social justice and civil rights insisted on misunderstanding our whole message, which was one emphasizing the necessity of farming communes, rather than individual family farms, cooperative effort rather than the isolated and hopeless struggling with the problem of the land and earning a living from it. He cited the cooperative effort of Fr. Jimmy Tompkins and Father Coady of Nova Scotia, and the cooperative teaching of the Extension department of St. Francis Xavier University in Antigonish, Nova Scotia, where there is still active leadership in the cooperative movement. He was deeply interested in the *kibbutzim* of Israel.

Work, Not Wages

A philosophy of work meant an abolition of the wage system. An explanation of that phrase would mean another long article. It would mean "Work, not wages," a slogan which Peter delighted in, as he did all slogans which made man think. (There is a new slogan now "Wages, not work.")

It is to be remembered that the first plank in Peter Maurin's program for the world was "clarification of thought." I remember John Cogley's comment one time that all slogans, all such phrases, became cliches in time, and Peter, the Frenchman, tried to keep up with the slang phrases of the day and to probe to the root of them as to what they meant, what they signified at the time. I remember one of his essays ending in a long list of such slang phrases, the last of which was "So's your old man!" capped by the sardonic, "So what!"

Once when I looked around our crowded house of hospitality and asked Peter if this is what he meant when he talked about houses of hospitality where the works of mercy could be performed at a personal sacrifice, by practicing voluntary poverty, which meant in turn stripping one's self of the "old man" and putting on the "new" which meant Christ, so that we could be other Christs to our brothers, in whom we were also to see Christ,—Peter sighed and said, "It arouses the conscience." . . .

July-August 1965

One wakes early in the city on hot summer mornings, and this morning I began my day by going on with my reading of Pope John XXIII's *Journal of a Soul* (McGraw-Hill). I had reached page 84, "Notes made during the spiritual exercises after the Babylonian Captivity" (which is what he termed his time in the Army). He wrote of knowing what hell was like, now that he had lived in barracks. "What blasphemies there were in that place, and what filth. Would hell be any better? What if I were to end there, while my fellow soldiers, the poor wretches, who grew up surrounded by evil were sent to Paradise—no wonder I tremble at the thought. . . . O the world is so ugly, filthy and loathsome! In my year of military service I have learned all about it. The army is a running fountain of pollution, enough to submerge whole cities. Who can hope to escape from this flood of slime, unless God comes to his aid. . . . I did not think any reasonable man could fall so low. Yet it is a fact. Today, after my brief experience, I think it is true to say that more than half of mankind, at some time in their lives, become animals, without shame. And the priests? O God, I tremble when I think that not a few among these betray their sacred calling. Now nothing surprises me any more; certain stories make no impression on me. Everything is explained. What cannot be explained is how it is that You, O most pure Jesus, of whom it is said 'He pastures his flock among the lilies,' can put up with such infamous conduct, even from your own ministers, and yet deign to come down into their hands and dwell in their hearts, without inflicting on them instant punishment. Lord Jesus, I tremble for myself too. If 'stars of the sky fell to the earth,' what hope have I who am made out of dust? From now on I intend to be even more scrupulous about this matter even if I become the laughing stock of the whole

232

world. In order not to touch upon impure subjects, I think it is better to say very little, or hardly anything at all, about purity. We have this treasure in earthen vessels. I have reason to tremble. 'Is my flesh bronze?' "

In his letters to the rector of the seminary at Rome, young Roncalli is far more moderate in his expressions; the editorial note which introduces the two letters explains that at that time there were no military chaplains to give spiritual assistance in the barracks and that his letters, while commending the courtesy of the officer in command and the good nature of the Italian soldier, bear out what he wrote in his notes "with all the frankness of an innocent soul brought face to face with the reality of the moral crisis in which most young men, especially those who live the communal life of the barracks, find themselves involved. In such circumstances the weaker and less noble, one might say the most melancholy characteristics of youth come to the fore."

"Nevertheless," young Angello Roncali wrote, "every day I am more convinced of the great benefit I shall draw from this year's experience, for the glory of God and to the advantage of the Church."

Now, half a century later, the Vatican Council at Rome is taking up this issue of war and peace, and the rights of conscience, as well as the formation of conscience in regard to the means used in modern war.

There was still time this morning to read a chapter in the Gospel, and I opened to the 22nd chapter of Luke, which begins with the story of the Last Supper, Jesus' taking bread and wine and saying: "This is My Body, this is My Blood," and then crying out: "Behold, the hand of him who betrays Me is with Me on the table." . . . "And they began to question one another which of them it was that would do this. A dispute also arose among them which of them was to be regarded as the greatest.

"And He said to them, the kings of the Gentiles lord it over them; and they that have power over them, are called beneficent." (The newest version says 'Benefactors'.) "But you, not so: but he that is the greater among you, let him become as the younger; and he that is the leader, as he that serveth. For which is greater, he that sitteth at table or he that serveth. Is it not the one who sits at table? But I am among you as one who serves. And you are those who have continued with me in my trials. And I dispose to you, as my Father hath disposed to me, a kingdom. . . . And turning to

Simon He rebuked him saying, 'Simon, Simon, behold Satan hath desired to have you, that he may sift you as wheat. But I have prayed for thee that thy faith fail not, And thou being once converted, confirm thy brethren'."

Simon Peter protested that he was ready to follow him to the death, but Jesus sadly told him that before the cock crowed Peter would deny him three times. He reminded them of His sending them forth without purse or scrip and asked them did they want for anything? They said "Nothing." And He went on; "But now he that hath a purse let him take it, and likewise a scrip, and he that hath not, let him sell his coat, and buy a sword.

"For I say to you, that this that is written must yet be fulfilled in Me: *And with the wicked was he reckoned*."

The apostles said, "Behold here are two swords. And he said to them: it is enough."

I thought about these very mysterious passages in the half hour I stayed in church after my communion. Often I have thought of how the apostles were afraid and hid themselves behind locked doors. And I thought too of how even after Jesus' death and resurrection they were still hankering after a kingdom, a worldly kingdom and the subjugation of their enemies. It is all there in the pages of the New Testament, in the Gospels and in the Acts of the Apostles. It is not easy reading, the New Testament, any more than the Old is.

I am thinking of it now, in connection with the Council, this last session on which so many hopes are placed.

Certainly Jesus knew that since He *was reputed among the wicked*, He was always going to be entangled with the things of this world. Christ is our head and we are His members. We are other Christs by our incorporation into the body of Christ. We involve Him even in our sin. "He became sin for us," according to St. Paul. He knew we were going to go after material things. (A certain amount of goods is necessary to lead a good life, St. Thomas Aquinas said.) When the Jews fled Egypt they took with them (as restitution for unpaid wages?) the belongings, the gold and silver of the Egyptians. To this day we have an increase of wealth in the Church until persecution takes it from us, or until we voluntarily do penance, deprive ourselves, deny ourselves and follow Him in serving our brothers. To this day we have the sword and the spectacle of brother fighting against brother, German and Italian Catholic against French and English and American—Catholic, Protestant, Orthodox, fighting each other. "The time will come when you will think you are serving God in putting one another to death."

It is as though He said, "Very well, take your scrip, your purse, your sword. Each one of you must have a personal encounter with Me, your risen Lord, your Jesus, your Master before you understand." Just as Mary Magdalene, Thomas, Peter, James and John did. "I have loved you with an everlasting love even when you are denying me. You will each one of you, loved uniquely by the Father, have to be visited by the Holy Spirit before you will understand. You have your freedom to make your choices. It is a matter of your individual conscience, your individual conversion. Ask and you will receive. Seek and you will find."

My comfort is that a thousand years are one day in the sight of God, and so Christianity is two days old, we have scarcely begun, we are still defending God and Country (putting them on an equality) by our wealth and our weapons.

Our prayer and our hope is that from the chair of Peter, from the College of Cardinals will come during this last session of the Council, a clear statement, "Put up thy sword," with the healing touch of Jesus in such a statement to the ears of those who, hearing, do not understand.

The apostles didn't take the sword, they cowered in fear instead and could scarcely believe that they saw Him again. They were still asking Him about when the earthly kingdom would come despite His clear statement that His kingdom was not of this world which is a testing ground, a place of trial, a school of Christ, as St. Benedict had it.

But after the Holy Spirit enlightened the apostles they went to martyrdom, embraced the cross, laid down their own lives for their neighbors, in whom they were beginning to see Christ.

"Inasmuch as ye have done it unto one of the least of these my brethren you have done it unto me."

We long with all our hearts for such a statement from the Bishops, clear, uncompromising, courageous. We know that men in their weakness, like the apostles, will still take the sword, will still be denying Christ in their brother the Negro, the Vietnamese.

But the teaching of Jesus has indeed been answered again and again over the ages, from the apostles to the present day and again and again these called by the Holy Spirit and

235

touched by grace have laid down their lives for the Faith that God is our Father and all men are our brothers.

"A new commandment I give unto you, that you love others as I have loved you," that is to the *laying down* of one's life. The commandment of love, which is binding on us all, in Old Testament and New, was finally heard by Peter, once the denier, and by Franz Jagerstatter in the Second World War. And by how many others through the ages whose histories have never been written? Our God is a hidden God, and such stories are hidden too in the lives of the saints.

We read in the life of Theophane Venard in Vietnam of how he considerately shed his clothes before his head was chopped off so that the executioner who was paid for his deed with them would not be receiving blood-stained garments. Such was his love for his enemies, remembering Jesus' words, "Father, forgive them for they know not what they do." We think of the martyrs of Uganda, Protestant and Catholic, when we read the history of Africa and her exploitation.

Christ is being martyred today in Vietnam, in Santo Domingo and in all places where men are taking to the sword in this world crisis. He will be crucified to the end of time. He is with us in His humanity until the end of time.

Weapons of Peace

One of our Catholic pacifists asked me to write a clear, theoretical, logical, pacifist manifesto, and he added so far, in these thirty-three years of *The Catholic Worker*, none had appeared from my pen.

I can write no other than this: Unless we use the weapons of the spirit, denying ourselves and taking up our cross and following Jesus, dying with Him and rising with Him, men will go on fighting, and often from the highest motives, believing that they are fighting defensive wars for justice for others and in self-defense against present or future aggression.

To try to stop war by placing before men's eyes the terrible suffering involved will never succeed, because men are willing (in their thoughts and imaginations at least) to face any kind of suffering when motivated by noble aims like the vague and tremendous concept of freedom, God's greatest gift to man, which they may not articulate but merely sense. Or, in their humility (or sloth,—who knows?) men are quite willing to leave decisions to others "who know more about it than we do." Without religious conversion there will be few Franz Jagerstatters to stand alone and leave wife and children and farm for conscience's sake. But as Jagerstatter said, it was God's grace that moved him, more powerful than any hydrogen bomb.

This month I saw the film *China*! and two years ago I visited Cuba and saw the changes the Marxist-Leninists were making there. Living so close to misery and vice, destitution and homelessness, hard and cruel labor, sickness of mind and soul and body at *The Catholic Worker* as we do,—seeing all this aspect of life each day in city and country, one is tempted by such a vision of a *forcible* working towards the common good.

If the Chinese and the Cubans are working for justice, and a better life for the masses, are they not also working for Christ, though they do not know him? But as Harold Robbins, the distributist, wrote in *The Sun of Justice*:

"Freedom is the primary and supreme reason for the existence of mankind. That He should be freely loved and served seems, as far as our thought can penetrate, to have been God's chief reason for calling us into being. At the cost of this freedom God could have established and maintained a world full of *order*, but not of justice, for free will is of the essence of human justice."

It is on these grounds that we stand opposed to war. Upholding this freedom for Communist and Capitalist, the East and the West.

September 1965

When Pope John was journeying in North Africa before he was made a Cardinal, he wrote that his trip brought home to him vividly "the problem of the conversion of the people without the faith. The whole life and purpose of the Church, of the priesthood, of true and good diplomacy is there: Give me souls: take all the rest."

And I thought to myself, "We are the Church too, we the laity," and this is our problem also. This is why we are opposing war, and right now the war in Vietnam. Souls are being lost. War is a sin against Love, against life. God is Love, and He wills that all men be saved. The whole purpose of our life is Love. Why did God create us? Because He loved us. Why do we love him? Because He first loved us.

237

And God so loved the world that He gave His only begotten Son to us, to show us our salvation, knowing that in the exercise of our freedom we were going to continue to crucify Him to the end of the world. We are doing it now in Vietnam, in the death of every man woman and child. "Inasmuch as ye have done it unto the least of these my brethren ye have done it unto me."

In his *Journal of a Soul*, Pope John wrote: "While the war rages, the peoples can only turn to the Miserere and beg for the Lord's mercy, that it may outweigh His justice and with a great outpouring of grace bring the powerful men of this world to their senses and persuade them to make peace." "The two great evils which are poisoning the world today are secularism and nationalism. The former is characteristic of the men in power and of lay folk in general. The latter is found even among ecclesiastics."

This last month I have been reading many of Pope John's Encyclical letters—realizing that he will always be known for *Pacem in Terris* and *Mater et Magistra* (*Peace on Earth* and *Mother and Teacher*). Gordon Zahn reviewed the *Journal of a Soul* in *Peace News* and said that if the pious practices and devotions which were played down in most appraisals of what Pope John has meant for the modern world were capable of producing such a world figure we should pay more attention to them.

Last night I read *Poenetentiam Agere* and wished we could print the entire plea for penance, "an invitation to the faithful" to prepare for and make fruitful the work of the Vatican Council, which is this month beginning its fourth session.

I could not help thinking how little penance we have done these last years, how little mortification, how little dying to self, which is what mortification is. To mortify is to put to death, to do violence to oneself. "You have not yet resisted unto blood," St. Paul said. "Without the shedding of blood there is no salvation." Blood means *life* in Biblical terms. Some years ago I saw a man die of a heart attack before my eyes, and his skin became like wax as the blood stopped moving in the veins and seemed to drain back to the heart.

If our cause is a mighty one, and surely peace on earth in these days is the great issue of the day, and if we are opposing the powers of darkness of nothingness, of destruction, and working on the side of light and life, then surely we must use our greatest weapons—the life forces that are in each one of us. To stand on the side of life we must give up our own lives. "He who would save his life must lose it."

Combining these thoughts of penance, mortification, and sex, I can only write what I truly believe, and that is that outside of marriage, and to some extent inside of marriage, there must be a fine regard for chastity and purity, and emphasis on their necessity.

"Puritanical" has come to be a term of opprobrium, used to describe those who regard sex as purely an animal instinct, characteristic of brute force and energy, indeed somewhat filthy, mixed up with the plumbing operations of the body. Little children get things mixed up in this way.

But a young person falling under the attraction of another human being for the first time discovers the transforming quality of sex, and sees it truly for the expression of love that it is, used throughout the Bible as an illustration of God's love for man. There is nothing higher, nothing sweeter, nothing more beautiful than this love. It is sung in the Canticles of Canticles, it is told in the Book of Osee.

Sometimes the Scriptures seem full of one great love song in the midst of tragic and gory history. Sexual love is seen as a mighty force in man, his creative power. Man is co-creator with God, made in the image and likeness of God. What a gift of oneself then is this celibacy that is embraced by clergy and religious, and by laymen—in some cases willingly, in other cases unwillingly. When marriages are broken up by death and separations the unwilling celibate (since there is no element of self-will in it) has the power to offer this great gift to God—no trivial gift this sex, so often used in life as a plaything.

Puritans probably started out by considering everything as dross compared to the love of God. Indeed, St. Paul used still stronger words—he considered all as dung, and for using such words he suffered the same criticisms as the Puritans do.

But we all surely know the eye is not satisfied with seeing, nor the ear with hearing and it is the same with the other senses. To look for satisfaction is to find only momentary well-being and fulfilment, and in the end satiety may result in the loss of all desire and striving, and a deadening of all sensitivity.

Aldous Huxley presented a vision of hell in his novel "After Many a Summer Dies the Swan," where he portrays sex turned to sadism. Looking for a paperback by Dr. Benjamin Spock on the treatment of abnormal and crippled children. I was horrified to see how sex and sadism seem to be the theme of so much of our paperback literature. Sex and war, which is the opposite of the works of mercy, are closely allied.

In the Book of Maccabees, the young men were supposed to be in the state of grace before going into battle. Nowadays, young men going on leave before battle are given contraceptives. And our country calls itself Christian. What a misuse of life forces!

The best thing to do with the best of things is to give them up, some spiritual writer said. Give up your life to save it. Sow in order to reap. Sow blind sex to reap love, a transfiguration of the senses.

To take this position is not to consider sex wicked and secret and ugly. Secret and solitary sin is ugly, as D. H. Lawrence pointed out, because it is solitary, it is unnatural, directed to solitary pleasure, not a natural sharing with another of a human and natural need. It is misusing something great and powerful—a lever that could move the world toward life, not death, that horror of nothingness toward which it seems to be moving.

This plea for penance, a giving up of so great, beautiful, powerful and even terrible a thing, is an offering worthy of God, if indeed any offering can be considered worthy. It is seeing sex in its context, marriage in its perspective. It is a plea for penance. It is a plea for purity of all the senses, through voluntary mortification, a word used constantly by Pope John, who said, "Many importunately seek rather frantically earthly pleasures, and disfigure and weaken the noblest energies of the spirit. Against this irregular way of living, which unchains often the lowest passions and brings eternal salvation into grave danger, it is necessary that Christians react with the strength of the martyrs and saints, who have always given testimony for the Catholic Church.

"In such a way all can contribute, according to their particular status, to the better outcome of the Second Vatican Ecumenical Council, which must bring about a reblossoming of Christian life."

October 1965

Rome

"We have two days in each one here in Rome," a young Jesuit from Malta told me. "That break in the day from

12:00 until 4:00, which bothers tourists and catches them unawares, brings about this multiplication of days. I wake up at 4:00 a.m. and so get in a good day's work and am ready for lunch and my siesta. Then I begin again and work until midnight, with a break for dinner around 8:30." The signs on the shops say: *Open 8-12, 16-20*, or the equivalent. Of course many of the Council Fathers do not have this relaxed way of dealing with time. Mass at St. Peter's is at 9:00; the session lasts until 12:30; a press briefing is held until 1:30 or even 2:00; there is a brief lunch; panel discussions in many languages at 3:00; conversations that go on until after 5:00—and then I suppose they rest until dinner. I have had the joy of meeting many friends, bishops, priests and lay people from all over the country, here on the streets of Rome and at these meetings, not to speak of luncheons and dinners. As usual my life is full of contrasts, dining out with bishops and at home on a hard roll, a paper cone of olives and a piece of mozzarella cheese. You can live cheaply in Rome as a pilgrim if you know the simple *trattoria*, hot shops and pushcarts, and you see many a dignified citizen lunching on a sandwich as he walks along the streets. There are even the restaurants of St. Peter, supported by the Vatican, which the guide book *Europe on Five Dollars a Day* warns are for the poor and not for tourists.

The room in which I am writing reminds me very much of our own Italian section in New York. It is a small room with a very high ceiling. The immense window takes up the whole rear, and through my Venetian blinds I can look down one flight into a large courtyard divided into two parts by a wall, over which a luxuriant grapevine climbs. Pots of ivy, roses, and other plants fill one court, and the other, directly under me, is festooned with clotheslines. The sheets hanging from them help reflect the light up into my room. The windows are wide open (they are tightly closed at night), and there are shelves of plants under some of the windows and little birdcages hung next to others. Children play in the yard, and there are fountains and tubs of water for washing clothes at each end. Sometimes you can hear the fountain running all night. Rome is famed for her glorious fountains, which play on beautiful sculptured figures in every *piazza*. There are always people taking their ease around these fountains, and children bathe in them in the summer. It is hot now during the day, but there is an autumn chill in the air and at night a wind springs up.

My room costs seven hundred lire a day, which amounts

to a little over a dollar. (A dollar is worth six hundred and twenty lire.) Bus fares are fifty lire, and I pay two fares each way to get to St. Peter's and back. The streetcars and buses are crowded and, because of the double-day, there are four rush hours.

I would not like to think of driving here, but I am getting quite accustomed to the rhythm of traffic, thanks to the reassuring briefing I received from Vincent McAloon, the head of the Notre Dame Alumni Center (Largo Brancaccio 82). Mr. McAloon gave a discourse on how to cross a street that was so inspiring that I have been able to proceed with confidence in the midst of the wildest assault of foreign cars from all directions it has even been my confusion to see. I go stolidly ahead, and, miracle of miracles, cars make way, dash fore and aft of me. In the two weeks I have been here, I have yet to hear the clang of ambulances. As one Dominican brother explained, "You present them with your life, these drivers, and they graciously hand it back to you."

And what of the Council? They have scarcely gotten into the thirty-thousand-word pastoral constitution on the Church in the Modern World, which will eventually, after debate by the Fathers and subsequent revisions, be promulgated, either as a new constitution (in which case it will be doctrinal and claim the assent of clergy and laity) or as a "declaration" (which term might lessen the authority of the text). It is clarification of this kind which is being attempted at the afternoon panel discussions. Father John Courtney Murray was the chief consultant at the first week's panel. Ten other theologians took part, including such diverse authorities as Monsignor Francis J. Connell, editor of the *American Ecclesiastical Review*, Father George Tavard, and Father Frederick McManus, the last two most sympathetic friends of ours. The panel meets in a small theater with a main floor and a balcony, so there is plenty of room. Every effort is made to answer the questions of the press and other people attending.

Last March, John Cogley wrote in *America* that he felt "on the outside looking in," that there did not seem to be a genuine confrontation of laity and clergy, bound together in the service of the same cause, the Church's *aggorniamento* or renewal. "Secular wisdom was missing." The Fathers of the Council and their theological advisers "are at their least impressive both substantively and rhetorically when they attempt to deal with thorny practical issues like nuclear war or the population problem . . . clerical and lay mind are both necessary to shape a total Catholic response to the modern world, which is one of the aims of Vatican II . . . but the Council's emphasis is overwhelmingly on the former . . . the layman is an intruder of sorts and sooner or later recognizes the fact."

This may be true during the Council sessions in Rome, but when I read the document on the Church in the Modern World, which notes the "interventions" of thousands of clergymen who commented on the original draft, it seemed evident that laymen had, however indirectly, contributed their thought on the vital questions of the day, whether they are represented by the revolutionary tin miners of Bolivia, the hard-pressed families, youth "stirred to rioting" or women no longer accepting their lack of status in the Church and the world. The result has been calls for discussion from both sides, so the document seems a tortuous affair, veering this way and that. It is hard to see how the work of discussion, clarification, and voting will ever be accomplished. But Cogley went on to write of the sense of mystery and the awe he felt during the assembly of the Council and of his conviction that in a group coming together with such lofty aims the presence of the Holy Spirit is indeed felt.

New Friends and Old

I arrived at Naples on the Raffaello. I have a great love for St. Raffaello, patron of travellers, to whom Ernest Hello, the French mystic, once addressed a prayer beginning: "Lead us to those we are looking for, those who are looking for us." I was led at once to the Notre Dame Center I mentioned earlier and to Vincent McAloon, who found me a place to live and who directs me daily on my involved journeys around Rome. At this center of hospitality I have received my mail and here I have met Dr. Joseph Evans and his wife Hermine, of Chicago, Richard Carbray, who teaches at Rosary College, and James Douglass, who teaches theology at Bellarmine College, in Louisville, Kentucky. Douglass has been meeting every day with bishops to discuss the paragraph in the schema on the Church in the Modern World that deals with the weapons of modern war. I too have been watching and praying about article 101, which concerns the rights of conscience of Catholics, humanists, and all others averse to the use of violence. I have with me three hundred copies of the summer issue of the *Catholic Worker*, which was dedicated to the bishops of the Council. Thanks to the American

Pax Association and its secretary Howard Everngam, this issue had already been sent to the bishops of the entire world.

I have also met Donald Quinn, the editor of the St. Louis *Review*, who is here with his wife, Bob Hoyt, the editor of the *National Catholic Reporter*, and Monsignor Francis Brown, the editor of the Steubenville *Register*. I had dinner with Monsignor Brown, Bishop Shannon, of St. Paul, and Frank McDonald, a Notre Dame man now at Oxford, who is spending this time at Rome because he is learning Italian and is fascinated by the Council. The bishop talked about tradition, quoting T. S. Eliot, and Frank, who could be included among the rebellious youth whom the Council schema says must be listened to and taken into consideration, was deeply impressed. I thought of how rare such men as Bishop Shannon are, men who show respect for all others and listen to them with sympathy. In his *Journal of a Soul*, Pope John XXIII paid tribute to one such priest, Father Francesco Pitocchi, who was always ready to listen to the poor. I am thinking of myself as I wrote this, and of how those as old as I do not listen enough, with warmth and loving kindness. Not that one should not speak. Certainly I myself find it easy to talk to someone who talks readily, just as I relapse into silence before the silent.

Among other great ones of the clerical world with whom I dined were Archbishop Thomas D. Roberts, Bishop John Wright, of Pittsburgh, and Bishop Joseph Brunini, of Jackson. And I briefly encountered others, whose hospitality cheered me, like Bishop Paul Hallinan, of Atlanta, Bishop Delargey, of Auckland, New Zealand, and Bishop Eustace Smith, O.F.M., of Beirut, Lebanon. I had lunch with Mariella Benziger and her sister, with Janet Kalven, of the Grail, with Father Riches, who is a convert and a cousin of the two Fathers de Menasce, whose writings in the *Commonweal* have impressed me so, and with Sister John Baptist, from California. And I paid my respects to His Beatitude, Maximos IV Saigh, Patriarch-Cardinal, who offers his liturgical worship in Arabic and Greek.

I met Trappists too, priests and students who are permitted to speak and visit while in Rome. Father Lamb is a friend of Father Charles English, one of our former editors, and we had a pleasant day together before he went back to his studies. He gave me the address of the Little Sisters of Jesus, whose place is on the Viculo de Onofrio, in a poor section across the Tiber. The headquarters of the Little Sisters is on the grounds of the Trappist Monastery at Tre Fontana, which I visited last time I was in Rome on the pilgrimage of women for peace.

But I must pay tribute to St. Anthony and to the honesty of the Italian people. When I arrived in Rome from Naples, I tried to telephone Vincent McAloon from the terminal. I was not able to reach him and was about to get into a cab when I realized that I had left my bag hanging on the telephone. Ruth Collins had bought the bag in India and given it to me a year ago, and it contained my passport, purse and travelers checks, not to speak of books and so on. Praying desperately and with my heart pounding, I rushed back to the telephone and found three men standing there, a soldier and two porters. *"Dove? Mi bolsa?"* I gasped. I was answered with beaming smiles and led away by one of them to a counter for tourists, where I was given my bag, to the happiness of all. Two thousand lire sounds like a big reward, but it is about three dollars and fifty cents, a very small sum in comparison to what I had almost lost. It was a happy introduction to Rome.

A week from now I shall begin the ten-day fast for peace, initiated by Chanterelle del Vasto, in which a score of women from all over the world will take part. Certainly prayer and fasting are needed today, our own work to overcome the spirit of violence in the world.

November 1965

There were thirty-five bishops on board the *Raffaello* on the way to the Council in September and a great many priests, so there were Masses morning, noon, and night in the little chapel. Bishop Mark McGrath, of Panama, concelebrated every afternoon at five o' clock with other priests and on several occasions I had the opportunity to talk to him about Schema 13 and the paragraphs concerning war and peace and conscientious objection. Father Allan Cormier, a young Holy Cross priest, was on his way to study at Strasbourg (one of his teachers will be Yves Congar) and he had introduced me to the Bishop, who said he had met me when he was an undergraduate at Notre Dame. He remembered we had a house of hospitality at South Bend, run by

Julian Pleasants, who now teaches at Notre Dame and continues to carry on some of the traditions of the CW, in that he lives on the land, keeps a cow, and is near a few other families with like interests who are both workers and scholars. Bishop McGrath receives the *Catholic Worker*, and I gave him *Reconciliation Quarterly*, published by the Fellowship of Reconciliation, an unusually good issue, with articles on the Church and State and conscientious objection in Italy and a comment on Pope Paul's talk to the Belgian soldiers. There were also very good articles in the *Jesus Caritas* Booklet No. 23, including those by Yves Congar and Stanley Windass and one by Father Rene Voillaume, Prior of the Little Brothers of Jesus, on "The Christian in the World Today."

The Council opened with a penitential procession on the feast of the Holy Cross, with the Pope, cardinals, bishops, and clergy proceeding from the Church of the Holy Cross to St. John Lateran, the Mother of all the churches of Christendom. It was a most solemn procession, with litanies and the Parce Domine sung and the loud speaker system was good, so every word could be heard. Before the singing began, the women around us were reciting the rosary together, and later during the procession there were the litanies. I was with Doctor Joseph Evans and his wife Hermine, of Chicago, and James Douglass, with whose writings our readers are familiar and who teaches theology at Bellarmine College, in Louisville, Kentucky.

The procession made me think of Vincent McAloon's description of the funeral of Palmiro Togliatti, the secretary-general of the Italian Communist Party, who died last year. There had been a procession of Communists which proceeded for three hours through the streets of Rome, past closed churches, a somber and silent procession, startling in black but lightened with red scarves and red flags, and dramatized as they passed workingmen's clubs and headquarters, by their silence and upraised clenched fists. I wondered why all the churches were closed; perhaps it took place between twelve and three in the afternoon, when they are all closed anyway.

Later that night at dinner, Hermine Evans told us of her visit to the home of Franz Jagerstatter and her talk with his widow and now married children. The widow gave Gordon Zahn a few bits of Franz's bones, which had not been consumed by the flames of his cremation, and Gordon gave one to Archbishop Thomas Roberts, who put it in his pectoral cross. Archbishop Roberts prepared an intervention on Jagerstatter which he was not permitted to deliver at the Council; instead he delivered it as a eulogy at a press conference held in the hall of the communications commission, which was large enough to accommodate quite a gathering of newsmen from all over the world.

For non-Catholic readers who do not understand the significance of relics, one need only substitute the word *souvenirs* and remember how we all treasure mementoes of those we love which we keep to remind ourselves of them.

When my friends from Chicago had left Rome and Jim Douglass was busy visiting bishops, I often got to bed early, after a seven o'clock Mass at St. Mary Major, and read two books, one of them the life of Pope Paul VI, *Apostle for Our Time*, by Rev. John Clancy, who is now, I believe, teaching at St. John's University, in Brooklyn. It is a fascinating book, which shows the wide experience our present Pope had in dealing with the practical affairs of the huge diocese of Milan, and tells how he said Mass in the factories and helped rebuild the working-class sections. I felt that *Time* magazine had treated him unfairly indeed by giving the impression that he was a man at home only in the State Department of the Vatican, protected from the life of the real world about him by his desk and paper work. With all the talk of reforming the seminaries today, it was interesting to find that Pope Paul had never lived in a seminary, but carried on all his studies while living at home in the midst of a family where the father and brothers were engaged in journalistic and political work. Both by his reading and his work he kept in contact with and took part in the work of his times.

Manzoni's Novel

For lighter reading there was the great Italian classic, *The Betrothed*, by Alessandro Manzoni, with its engrossing story of war, famine and pestilence, and the touching romance of the Bergamese peasant and silk weaver and his betrothed. I had wanted to read it because Pope John quoted from it in his *Journal of a Soul*, speaking of the stirring sermon of Cardinal Federico Borromeo and his rebuking the peasant priest for his cowardice. It is a stirring book and the new translation in the Everyman edition is an excellent one.

One day I had lunch with Father Bernard Law, editor of the diocesan paper of Mississippi, and later we visited the shrine of St. Benedict Joseph Labre, which is in a little church not far from Notre Dame Hospitality Center, which is located at Largo Brancaccio 82. The center is surrounded by places you want to visit on foot; St. Mary Major, St. John Lateran, the Colosseum, the great railroad station and bus terminal, and the open-air markets. Jim Douglass and I had dinner with Bishop John J. Wright at the Piazza Navona, and the next day lunched with Cardinal Eugene Tisserant's secretary, Father Riches, who has a little parish outside of Rome. He had heard me speak at Santa Clara, California, where he had taught for a period, and we talked together as fellow converts. He and his cousins, the two de Menasce priests, are converts, originally from Alexandria, Egypt, and educated in Rome. The next day, Archbishop Roberts, his unofficial peritus Richard Carbray, and I went to pay a call on His Beatitude, Patriarch Maximos, at the Salvator Mundi hospital on the Janiculum Hill. On the way I saluted the statue of Garabaldi, who was God's instrument in relieving the Papacy of those encumbrances the Papal States, and preparing the way for the great part the Church had played in this century. Never when she was a great temporal power was the Church listened to with such attention as she is today. One might say the work of detachment has only begun. As I passed this great equestrian statue I could not help but think of the words of Bishop P. N. Geise, of Indonesia, who said that we must seek poverty, live poorly, build poor buildings, take in the poor where we are. He himself gave up his Dutch citizenship. The Bishop of Mwanza, in Tanzania said; "The world is not divided into the East and the West but into the haves and the have-nots. Only a wealthy country can afford the luxury of all this private ownership."

Our meeting with the impressive Patriarch Maximos was a brief one. He said that he would speak in season and out of season, in the Council and out of it, on the subject of peace. I think he was the only one at the Council who invariably spoke in French instead of Latin. But with his double dignity of Patriarch and Cardinal he could do as he pleased. Later, when he heard of us twenty women who were fasting for peace, and praying for the light of the Holy Spirit to descend on the Fathers, his comment was "Water nourishes!"

Another evening there was a dinner at the convent of the Canadian Sisters of the Precious Blood to honor Archbishop Roberts on the anniversary of his 56 years as a Jesuit, 40 years as a priest and 28 years as an archbishop. There were three bishops at the dinner, one from Peru, one from Southwest Africa, and one from the Amazon. Guests included Dr. Gordon Zahn, Professor of Sociology at Loyola University in Chicago, author of *In Solitary Witness*, the life of Franz Jagerstatter (reviewed in the July-August and September issues of the *Catholic Worker*), Father Joseph Small, S.J. from Seattle, and two Maltese Jesuits, Father Ghigo and Father Tonna, who were in charge of distribution of all news bulletins. It delighted me to see the small, narrow cells, formerly occupied by the Sisters, in which the bishops stayed on either side of the long sitting rooms, which was also the corridor between the row of little bedrooms. The bishops' quarters were comfortable, but certainly not luxurious.

Vatican Radio
It was interesting to visit the Vatican Radio, where Father Ellwood Kieser, Paulist, made a taped interview with me for his program *Insight*, which is broadcast in California.

There was a happy meeting with Barbara Wall, of whom I had heard much but whom I had never met. She with her husband Bernard started the English *Catholic Worker* many years ago, perhaps before their marriage, and now they are grandparents. Bob Walsh took over the CW and the Walls published a magazine called *Coliseum*, probably the first venture in lay intellectual discussion of theological, as well as sociological, problems of the day. Bernard Wall is a man of letters and his wife is a novelist as well as essayist, journalist, and translator.

Cardinal Suenens
The only time I spoke in Rome was informally at one of the regular Monday afternoon meetings held at the headquarters of Cardinal L. J. Suenens, of Belgium. The guest was Frank Duff, founder of the Legion of Mary, which has spread from Ireland throughout the world and is doing significant work in Africa and the Chinese People's Republic. Fearing that some of those present might dismiss the Legion as merely a pious organization with little social emphasis, I told of my encounters with the Legion in prison, when one of the correction officers in the New York Women's House of Detention started a Legion group on her own time and did more than anyone else I encountered in the prison to

bring some reminder of the beauty of religion into the lives of the women there.

October First

The fast of the twenty women, which I had come to join and which was the primary reason for my visit to Rome during the final session of the Council, began on October 1st, which was a Friday. The night before I had enjoyed a feast with Eileen Egan, who was on her vacation, and an Indian bishop, at one of the most famous restaurants in Rome, as the invited guest of Signor Rossi, who operates the Scoglio. I felt rather guilty at prefacing a penitential fast in this way— thinking of St. Augustine's and Tolstoy's discourses on the greedy appetite for food, which continues through old age.

But Eileen reminded me that after all penitential Lent was prefaced by *carnevale*, which means farewell to meat as well as a celebration. So I enjoyed the pleasant evening, and certainly felt all the better for it those first two days of my fast, which are supposed to be the hardest.

The next day, very early, I checked out with my suitcase from my little room on the Via Napoleane 111, proceeded by cab to the American Coffee Shop on the Via Conciliatione to check my bag, and then on down to the great square in front of St. Peter's to wait for Barbara Wall and Eileen Egan at the end of the Colonnade. We were going to Mass together on that First Friday morning.

Without tickets we could not have got in, since all the Masses which preface the meetings of the Council are packed to the doors. The laity receive communion not at the main altar but at a side altar. All around there were confessionals, frequented, I was edified to see, by bishops and cardinals, with their scarlet and purple robes billowing out behind them on either side of the open confessionals, taking as long, I noticed, as nuns, who I always thought were scrupulous indeed, judging by the length of their confessions.

But I was able to go to confession on that last visit I paid to St. Peter's, and I felt with joy and love that warm sense of community, the family, which is the Church. How the Council has broken down barriers between clergy and laity, and how close the bishops seem to us when they are together from all parts of the world, at home in Rome, and not set apart alone and distant on episcopal thrones and in episcopal palaces!

The Mass that morning was in the Syriac rite and was

sung, so it was not until ten that I arrived at the Cenacle on Piazza Pricilla, which was on the other side of Rome in a district that I had not yet visited, on the edge of the suburbs. There we gathered in the garden, twenty women, and a few of the male members of the Community of the Ark, including Lanza del Vasto, whose wife Chanterelle had initiated the fast. He led us in the prayers that we would say each morning as we gathered together after Mass, the Our Father, the peace prayer of St. Francis, and the Beatitudes. Afterwards, the trained members of the community sang. Then we went to our rooms, which were on the third floor of the old convent, looking out on gardens and sky.

Each day we followed a schedule. There was Mass at seven-fifteen and then prayer together. From nine to twelve we kept to our rooms in silence, reading, writing or praying. During the day we divided up our time in the chapel so that throughout the day and night there was always one of us keeping vigil. At noon we went to the garden and read together. Readings included a book by Martin Luther King, and an account of the work of Father Paul Gauthier, who founded the Companions of Jesus the Carpenter, in Nazareth. Most of us had some sewing or knitting to do. The wicker chairs were comfortable, the garden smelled of pine trees and eucalyptus and sweet herbs, and every day the sun was warm. Other members of the Ark, who were running an exhibit on non-violence, came and told us news of the visitors to the exhibit and of the Fathers of the Council they had talked to.

At four in the afternoon there were lectures by priests, and at six a French doctor came daily to see how everyone was getting along. Two of the women were ill during the fast and had to keep to their beds, so the lectures were held in Chanterelle's room. Prayers again at seven or eight, and then silence and sleep—for those who could sleep.

As for me, I did not suffer at all from the hunger or headache or nausea which usually accompanies the first few days of a fast, but I had offered my fast in part for the victims of famine all over the world, and it seemed to me that I had very special pains. They were certainly of a kind I have never had before, and they seemed to pierce to the very marrow of my bones when I lay down at night. Perhaps it was the hammock-shaped bed. Perhaps it was the cover, which seemed to weigh a ton, so that I could scarcely turn. At any rate, my nights were penitential enough to make up for the quiet peace of the days. Strangely enough, when the fast was over, all pains left me and I have not had them since. They were not like the arthritic pains, which, aggravated by tension and fatigue, are part of my life now that I am sixty-eight and which one accepts as part of age and also part and parcel of the life of work, which is the lot of the poor. So often I see grandmothers in Puerto Rican families bearing the burdens of the children, the home, cooking and sewing and contributing to the work of mother and father, who are trying so hard to make a better life for their children, so I am glad to share this fatigue with them.

But these pains which went with the fast seemed to reach into my very bones, and I could only feel that I had been given some little intimation of the hunger of the world. God help us, living as we do, in the richest country in the world and so far from approaching the voluntary poverty we esteem and reach towards.

Kind Visitors

I must not forget to thank the visitors who came: Richard Carbray, Bishop Shannon of St. Paul, Abbot Christopher Butler, of Downside Abbey, Barbara Wall, Eileen Egan and Mrs. Stephen Rynne (Alice Curtayne), who wrote the lives of St. Catherine of Siena and St. Brigid of Ireland and is now covering the Council for an Irish paper.

On the night of the 10th of October, the fast, those ten days when nothing but water passed our lips, was finished, but hard though it was, it was but a token fast, considering the problems of the world we live in. It was a small offering of sacrifice, a widow's mite, a few loaves and fishes. May we try harder to do more in the future.

December 1965

It is a happy thing to feel gratitude, so we thank our readers for these feelings of ours, as well as for the help they have sent us to pay our bills, and for the good letters upholding us in a difficult time, making us realize how widespread the *Catholic Worker* family is throughout the world.

Every night, as a small group of us go into the house chapel to say the rosary and compline, we pray for the individuals who have asked most especially for prayers and for the living and the dead, believer and unbeliever, our own family, as well as our correspondents. And we pray with deep gratitude for those who send us help to enable us to do the work of hospitality.

In the daytime you can see the wooded hillside from the chapel windows, where one of the men from the Bowery has cleared away underbrush so that the stone walls which terrace the hillside here and there are visible. The setting sun on these terraces colors the rocks a deep rose, and the trees come alive with light and color. My room faces the river, not the hill, and as I write this morning I look out at the Hudson River and marvel at how the Atlantic tide reaches all the way up to Tivoli and covers the rushes, which in turn cover the mud flats across the river. Bits of driftwood float upstream. The channel is on our side, and just now a great oil tanker went by under my window.

Downstairs in the room below me, Agnes Sidney, who is eighty-five, is bedridden. Brother Raphael, of the Christian Brothers in Barrytown, saw to it that we had a hospital bed, and six young novices brought it over last week and set it up so that Agnes can face the river and look out at tanker, freighter and barge. Her husband, long dead, was barge captain and she herself lived for thirty years on barges, sometimes making the perilous journey from New York to Boston, via coal barge.

The happy news on the radio this morning is that the Vatican Council has passed with an overwhelmingly majority vote, the Schema on the Church in the Modern World, included in which is an unequivocal condemnation of nuclear warfare. It was a statement for which we had been working and praying. We will report further on the details of the condemnation of modern war in next month's issue.

As to the questions this condemnation will raise in the hearts and minds of all men, Catholic or otherwise—I can only feel that such questions and the attempts to answer them will lead to more enlightened knowledge, more enlightened conscience on the part of all men. It will lead, as Peter Maurin was always fond of saying, to clarification of thought, a state of mind which should precede all action. I am sure that he thought that our action very often trod on the heels of thought too quickly and so was very imperfect. But I always felt, with St. Francis of Assisi, that we do not know what we have not practiced, and that we learn by our actions, even when those actions involve us in grave mistakes, or sin. God brings good out of evil, that evil which has come about as a result of our free will, our free choice. We learn, as the saying is, the hard way. But the promise remains: "All things work together for good to those who love God," or who want to love Him, who seek to love Him. As Pascal said: "You would not seek Him if you had not already found Him." In other words, the promise is there, "Seek and you shall find, knock and it shall be opened to you." And to repeat again, since there is no time with God, the promise, the finding, and the seeking go together. Even when one is following a wrong or ill-informed conscience.

For me, this answers the question as to whether we, at the *Catholic Worker*, think that a man is in the state of mortal sin for going to war. I have been asked this question so often by students that I feel we must keep on trying to answer, faulty and obscure as the answer that each one of us makes may seem to be. To my mind the answer lies in the realm of the motive, the intention. If a man truly thinks he is combatting evil and striving for the good, if he truly thinks he is striving for the common good, he must follow his conscience regardless of others. But he always has the duty of forming his conscience by studying, listening, being ready to hear his opponents' point of view, by establishing what Martin Buber called an I-Thou relationship. I suppose this is what priests mean when they talk about loving one's enemies, trying to reconcile the teachings of the Gospel with war. The intention, they feel, is to bring about peace and initiate rational discussion around the conference table, and from there on try to establish a relationship of love by building hospitals, repairing the damage done by war, restoring prosperity to a country exhausted and ravaged by war. (Because our modern wars are always fought on the soil of others.) But what means are being used to accomplish these good ends! The means become the ends, a Benedictine writer, Augustine Baker, brought out forcibly.

And even those *good* ends. Cardinal Leger's richly provocative talk, published in this issue of the paper, brings out that we are always trying to make others like ourselves, so convinced are we that we white, Anglo-Saxon, (Protestant usually goes with this in opposition to Negro, Catholic, and Jew though we Catholics have taken on the same formula) are right.

It seems to me that those of the hierarchy who opposed

the inclusion in Schema thirteen of this condemnation of nuclear war were leaving out of account Divine Providence, when they thought that without these weapons of destruction we could not face up to the threat of Communism's taking over the world. The idea of arms being used as deterrents, to establish a balance of terror, and so keeping the world at peace was long ago condemned by Benedict XV, who spoke of "the fallacy of an armed peace." Abbot Christopher Butler brought out the fallacy of such reasoning even more strongly in the quotations from his intervention at the Council which we printed on page one, first column, of the October issue of the *Catholic Worker*. (We are continuing to use other interventions, as they are called, from other members of the hierarchy in the paper, for the sake of clarification of thought on this all-engrossing problem of war.)

The primacy of conscience in the life of a Catholic is more and more brought out by the deliberations in the Council and by the very conflicts that take place there. The promulgation (a solemn word) of the doctrine on religious liberty is an example of this. When I was in Rome, one bishop (it may even have been an archbishop) said to me: "You need not worry about the problem of conscientious objection to war, since freedom of conscience is already thoroughly established in the schema on religious liberty." I always hesitate to name the bishops when I am quoting them, for fear of not being entirely accurate. We would not think of printing their letters of commendation of our "good work" when they send us their frequent contributions, knowing that they would seem to many an endorsement of our position, when it is actually our works of mercy that they are commending. Of course we consider enlightening the ignorant and counseling the doubtful works of mercy, as indeed they are. As for "rebuking the sinner" we are told not to judge, by our dear Lord, and we are only too conscious of our own all too imperfect state. However, our positions seem to imply a judgment, a condemnation, and we get the "holier than thou" accusation often enough.

Whenever this question of conscience comes up, the question of obedience immediately follows, obedience to Church and State, even when commands are not personally directed at us lay people, nor obedience exacted of us, as it is of the clergy. We have pointed out again and again the freedom the *Catholic Worker* has always had in the Archdiocese of New York. We have been rebuked on occasion, when we advised young men not to register for the draft; when we spoke of capitalism as a cancer on the social body, as Count della Torre, the former editor of *Osservatore Romano*, did; and on only one occasion, for our use of the name *Catholic*. This last reproach came up again in a news report recently, and we can only repeat what I said to our former chancellor, Monsignor Gaffney, (God rest his soul) that we have as much right to the name *Catholic* as the Catholic War Veterans have.

As to my oft-quoted remark that if the Cardinal asked me to stop my writing on war, I would obey, which has been brought up quite a number of times recently, I will try to clarify it: First of all, I cannot conceive of Cardinal Spellman's making such a request of me, considering the respect he has always shown for freedom of conscience and freedom of speech. But in the event of so improbable a happening, I have said that I would obey. "What becomes of your obligation of conscience to resist authority? You have quoted St. Peter's saying that we must obey God rather than men."

My answer would be (and it is an easier one to make now that the Council has spoken so clearly) that my respect for Cardinal Spellman and my faith that God will right all mistakes, mine as well as his, would lead me to obey. A respect augmented by the way he has carried out his physical duties in connection with military ordinariate, in visiting the soldiers in far-off parts of the world. This Christmas, as during the Korean conflict, he will be in a war area, since there is not a spot in Vietnam which can be considered safe. We have been a troublesome family to the chancery office, and I am sure that there are plenty of bishops around the country who are glad we are not in their dioceses. It is fitting, of course, that the Christian revolution (it has scarcely begun in its pacifist-anarchist aspects) should struggle on in New York as it has these last thirty-three years. Let us pray that it continues.

As to what change will be brought about by the pronouncements of the Council? None immediately, just as there was none when Pope Pius XI spoke out against Fascism in Italy. (And was it not Cardinal Spellman who flew out with that encyclical, which was suppressed in Italy under Mussolini?) Popes speak out, as Paul VI did recently at the United Nations, but wars go on. There are cheers and rejoicings, and seeming assent to what they say, but action does not seem to be influenced, *that is, immediately*. They are respected for what they say because of their lofty position. But a Father Daniel Berrigan, S.J. is "given another assignment" to Latin America. But in the long run, these words, these pronouncements, after much blood had been shed, influence the course of history, which progresses more and more towards a recognition of man's freedom, his dignity as a son of God, as made in the image and likeness of God, whether his is Communist or imperialist, Russian or American, "North" or "South" Vietnamese. All men are brothers, God wills that all men be saved, and we pray daily, *Thy will be done, on earth as it is in heaven.*

Meanwhile, to go from the general to the particular, I rejoice that Father Berrigan has this new assignment. He has done magnificent writing on race relations and war, he has spoken and walked on picket lines, and undoubtedly he needs some rest, some time to think, to research, to learn more about solutions to the problems that make for war, such as world poverty and hunger. If we had peace tomorrow, in Vietnam, the problem of poverty in Latin America would still be there, fermenting more violence and hatred, more use of force. Are pacifists in this present war going to be pacifist still when revolts break out throughout Latin American countries? Are we going to have trained and resourceful people ready to deal with these problems? And above all with accent on the primacy of the spiritual and knowledge of "the little way?"

A Jesuit priest from Madras, India, came in the office to visit us the other afternoon. When he spoke of the war in Vietnam he spoke as one nearer to it than we were, and he reiterated the familiar argument: If Vietnam is lost to the Communists, all Asia goes too. One of the Midwest senators answered this argument very successfully in an address printed in the *Saturday Review* last April.

But from the Christian point of view (and in this case from the Jesuit point of view) when he asked "What are we to do?" I could only point to the example of St. Ignatius, who first of all laid down his arms, then went to support himself by serving the poor in hospitals, and then went back to school to study. Peter Maurin not only emphasized such a "simple" program, but pointed out that we should study history by reading the lives of the saints, which throw a light on what is happening in the present day. He also had a famous essay, "They and We."

People say: They don't do this, They don't do that, They

don't do that, They ought to do this, They ought to do that. Always "They" and never "I." The Communitarian Revolution is basically a personal revolution. It starts with I, not with They. One I plus one I makes two I's and two I's and two I's make We. We is a community, while "they" is a crowd.

When a mother, a housewife, asks what she can do, one can only point to the way of St. Therese, that little way, so much misunderstood and so much despised. She did all for the love of God, even to putting up with the irritation in herself caused by the proximity of a nervous nun. She began with working for peace in her own heart, and willing to love where love was difficult, and so she grew in love, and increased the sum total of love in the world, not to speak of peace.

Newman wrote: "Let us but raise the level of religion in our hearts, and it will rise in the world. He who attempts to set up God's kingdom in his heart, furthers it in the world." And this goes for the priest too, wherever he is, whether he deals with the problem of war or with poverty. He may write and speak, but he needs to study the little way, which is all that is available to the poor, and the only alternative to the mass approach of the State. Missionaries throughout the world recognize this little way of cooperatives and credit unions, small industry, village commune, and cottage economy. And not only missionaries. Down in our own South, in the Delta regions among the striking farmers of Mississippi, this "little way" is being practiced and should be studied.

From California comes news this month, not only of the strike in the Delano region of the grape pickers, well covered by the *National Catholic Reporter*, but a letter too of co-op development in the California Valley. "We have visions of a complex of co-ops in the California Valley, owned and controlled by the farm workers. It will be interesting to see how long it takes vision to be translated into reality."

Dom Chautard, in his *Soul of the Apostolate*, in answer to the question as to how to find workers in all these vineyards, called attention to our Lord's words: "Pray ye therefore, for workers." So right where we are, at this moment, we can pause for a moment and send up such a prayer.

The Lord knows we need to around the *Catholic Worker*. Sometimes it seems that the more volunteers there are around the place, the less gets done. I have letters from six volunteers on my desk now. Not only are all the beds full, so that we cannot put them up for the Chrystie Street work, but also, it seems in regard to these we already have that their interests in peace keep them from the clothes room, or from the paper work connected with the thirty or more subscriptions which are coming in each day. Paper work is scorned and yet it is an essential when you are dealing with the people who receive the eighty-five thousand copies of the paper which go out each month. Paper work, cleaning the house, cooking the meals, dealing with the innumerable visitors who come all through the day, answering the phone, keeping patience and acting intelligently, which is to find some meaning in all these encounters—these things too are the work of peace, and often seem like a very little way.

But as Pope John told the pilgrimage of women, Mothers for Peace, the seventy-five of us who went over to Rome to thank him for his encyclical *Pacem in Terris*, just the month before his death, "the beginnings of peace are in your own hearts, in your own families, schoolrooms, offices, parishes, and neighborhoods."

It is working from the ground up, from the poverty of the stable, in work as at Nazareth, and also in going from town to town, as in the public life of Jesus two thousand years ago. And since a thousand years are as one day, and Christianity is but two days old, let us take heart and start now.

1966

January 1966

□ Fr. Joseph McSorley, C.S.P., my first spiritual director, gave me Caussade's *Abandonment to Divine Providence* to read many years ago. We, who are such activists, need more of this teaching. No danger of Quietism with *Catholic Worker* enthusiasts. A little more quiet, a little more time to read and digest might help. When I was becoming a Catholic, I had only such books the the *Confessions of St. Augustine* and the *Imitation* to begin on. There had always been Scripture, and even in childhood I almost had the feeling of partaking of a sacrament in holding it and reading. The first time I went to jail with the suffragists in Washington, at the age of eighteen, and asked for the only book I knew they would give me to read, I wept over the Psalms—wept with joy at their comfort. And at the same time felt ashamed at turning to religion when there was nothing else to turn to.

Of course, there were, and always will be, great gaps in my understanding of such questions as the problem of evil in the world and God's permission of it. I cringe still at Ivan Karamazov's portrayal of "a God that permits" the torture of children, such torture as is going on today in the burning alive of babies in Vietnam. Theologians debate situation ethics and the new morality (leaving out of account the problem of means and ends) while the screams of the flaming human torches, civilian and soldiers, rise high to heaven. The only conclusion I have ever been able to reach is that we must pray God to increase our faith, a faith without which one cannot love or hope. *"Lord, I believe, help thou my unbelief."*

. . . Sometimes it seems to me that every kind of warfare is carried on around the *Catholic Worker*. There is the war between young and old, colored and white, and class war, between the haves and have nots. Only this morning, on hearing that I was going to New England for a week, one of the poor women staying with us said bitterly, "It costs a lot of money to travel around the way you do." (Since this charge has been made by some of our readers, I must explain that we are paid for most of the talks we are asked to give.) But what resentment between those who have no money in their pockets and those who have—between the worker and the scholar, in other words.

Peter Maurin was well acquainted with these conflicts and lifted them all to a higher level, and I suppose I should put this conflict over the way the Mass should be said under the heading of the authority and freedom conflict. The priest has the authority and in this case he did not exercise it. He wanted, I suppose as St. Paul said, "To be subject to every living creature," as Jesus was in His crucifixion.

We went to press on February 16th last month, and that same day I went with Ruth Collins to see a house on the East Side which is just what we need for our House of Hospitality. The cost is thirty-five thousand dollars, a modest sum when one considers the cost of houses today for a family alone. Our family is an oversized one, and this house will mean two large apartments for men, one for women, offices for the work and the usual dining room and kitchen. We have ten thousand dollars, which we can use as a down payment but the rest will have to be mortgages, including repairs to conform to the Building Code. If we can raise what seems to us to be an enormous sum of money, we can pay it off each year in payments which will be less than what we are paying now for the rents of Chrystie Street and the ten apartments, not to speak of the heating of five apartments and of the loft building at Chrystie Street. We have already paid enough in the last five years to have bought the house as it is, that is without repairs. St. Joseph, pray for us. In these inflationary times it is no longer possible to live as we did at the beginning of the *Catholic Worker*. To try to be poor in an affluent society is hard indeed.

This is truly a period of pilgrimage; since March 15th I have been invited to many places. First of all, by Bishop John J. Wright, of Pittsburgh, to the National Inter-Religious Conference, held in Washington from March 15-17. The keynote address, by Dr. John C. Bennett, president of Union Theological Seminary, stirred immediate controversy, which continued throughout the meetings, especially at Workshop No. III, which dealt with: "Forms of Intervention: Moral Responsibilities and Limits."

As far as I know, this was the first conference of its kind held in the United States that dealt with the specific issue of Vietnam, and many of the participants tried to keep discussion of this undeclared war out of the meetings. Dr. Bennett's paper was more than twelve typewritten pages long and it was distributed to the hundreds of people present on the opening day of the conference. The subsequent discussion did not give the paper the attention it deserved. That is the trouble with such conferences. There are too many workshops, too many meetings, so many speakers, making the sessions too long. Everyone tried to keep to the time schedule, but a day beginning at 9:00 a.m. and ending at 10:30 or 11:30 p.m. and including luncheon and dinner with more speakers, is too much. There were many first-rate minds present, Catholic, Protestant and Jewish, clergymen and laymen although there were too few Catholic laymen. One who did participate was Dr. Gordon Zahn, whose point of view was opposed by representatives of the Catholic Association for International Peace, which many of us feel is subservient to the State Department and overly loyal to the administration. However, they have performed a service in helping start this discussion of *peace* with other religious leaders. We hope that the Conference will continue in existence and meet more frequently and that there will be greater participation by those Catholics who believe in nonviolence and personal responsibility. We hope too, that the thoughtful position papers, such as the one drafted by Rabbi Jacob Agus, Tilford Dudley, of the National Council of Churches, and Arthur I. Waskow, of the Institute of Policy Studies, will be sent to the participants well in advance of the next meeting.

While in Washington I attended another conference involving a score or so of thinkers from the fields of education, health, religion and science. This conference was personally sponsored by Dr. Leonard J. Duhl, of the National Institute of Health, and was held in the faculty lounge of Georgetown University. The program is somewhat similar to that of the "think" group at the Center for the Study of Democratic Institutions, at Santa Barbara, but they meet informally only twice a year to converse and exchange ideas, and I do not know whether they publish papers. Peter Maurin would have been interested in such gatherings for the clarification of thought.

In Hartford, Connecticut, I spoke at the monthly meeting of the Catholic Graduates Club. I also spoke to the priests and seminarians at St. Louis de Montfort Seminary, at Litchfield Connecticut, who have a storefront and apartment in a slum area of nearby Waterbury. They are anxious not only to help the poor directly but to study the problem of poverty and their duties in regard to it. They are learners. The sung mass was most beautiful.

At Regina Laudis, the Benedictine monastery at Bethlehem, Connecticut, I had a happy visit with my godchild Sister Prisca. We talked of Shakers, and herb gardens, and worship and hospitality, contemplation and meditation, authority and obedience, and voluntary poverty. It is a happy place. Norman Langlois, his wife Margaret and six of their nine children live in a rambling house in Bethlehem proper, which has a population of perhaps a hundred. Norman gave me some money to plant three trees for him; according to a Russian saying, this planting will save his soul. I hope that other friends will bring a few trees with them to plant when they come to visit our farm at Tivoli. Fruit or nut trees, ginkgo trees or sycamores or pines—we love them all. (Speaking of gifts, if anyone has a trailer in which a family could live and which is not being used, we could store it. We know three families right now who would like to camp out on our property in Tivoli this summer if they could have the use of a trailer. In the summer there are often more people who want to come than we can accommodate.) Norman and his brother Donald used to run a house of hospitality in Burlington, Vermont. When the truckmen in that area were on strike they used the house as their meeting hall and headquarters. Donald, who still lives on a farm near Burlington, says that he may start another house now that his children are growing up.

We (Pat Rusk is accompanying me on these trips) drove to Hyde Park, New York, in time for an evening meeting at the Episcopal Church. The parish was hospitable (there was a pot luck supper) and there was little opposition, except from the young incoming pastor, who differed strongly with our C. W. position on Vietnam and criticized my interpretation of Scripture. Since Hyde Park is only three-quarters of an hour from Tivoli, we drove home to gather our clothes and papers together for our long trip to Minneapolis, St. Louis and points in between. On the following day, we drove to New York and arrived just in time for me to attend a meeting of some of our Associates, together with lawyers and real-estate friends, to discuss the buying of a new house in New York City.

That night, Ammon Hennacy, who was making a short visit East, spoke at our Friday night meeting, and the house was packed to the doors. The next morning after Mass he came over to the Kenmare Street apartment (he had stayed the night before with Bob Steed on Mulberry Street) and spent the rest of the morning with us. He had lunch in Chinatown with Bob and Walter Kerell, brought us back a few orders of chop suey and stayed around for a while longer. Marge Hughes and Johnny came over to greet him. That evening there was a supper party for him at Janet Burwash's and the next day he was to go up to Tivoli and on to Worcester, Massachusetts.

Next morning Pat and I started out for the Midwest. Early the following evening we arrived at Bill and Dorothy Gauchats' Our Lady of the Wayside, which is now a house of hospitality for children rather than a farm (although there is a goodly piece of property surrounding their big home).

It was a joy to visit the Gauchats and see the work they are doing for little ones, seven children, all under seven years of age, who are retarded or spastic or afflicted with cerebral palsy. There is one child of two, blind and deaf but with a "thinking" look, and one wonders how he will ever be able to communicate with others. They adopted one spastic child to save him from being institutionalized. He is now eight and although he cannot articulate words, he is able to write notes to other members of the family by using the hunt-and-peck system on a special typewriter, which has a guard over the keys to keep his fingers from slipping.

The Gauchats are writing a book about their work with these children, in the hope that it will be of help to parents of similarly afflicted children and induce them to keep them in the home as long as possible. A very special love for such little ones grows in the heart, and the other children of the family learn compassion. Dorothy has helpers, of course, but above all she has the help of her husband after his working hours and the help of her own devoted children. We are looking for a publisher for this book, which is half completed.

When we left Lorain, Ohio, we found a spot along the shore of Lake Erie where Pat looked for shells while I just sat and rested and prayed by this great inland sea. It rained and snowed intermittently all through Ohio and Indiana that day, and it was good to arrive in Chicago and go home with Nina Polcyn, who operates St. Benet's Book Shop, and seize upon my mail, which had been forwarded there.

Passing through Ohio, we had learned that the Lorain Catholic Interracial Council had invited a guest speaker: Ida Cousino, of the National Farm Workers Association, who showed slides of the grape strike which has been going on in Delano, California, since last September. Then in Chicago we learned that the Chicago C.I.C. was sending a doctor and a team of workers to the strike area. This morning, we had as breakfast guest Monsignor John J. Egan, of Presentation parish (a new assignment, as pastor in addition to his job as one of the consultors of the archdiocese, and his previous commitment as director of the Office of Urban Affairs), who brought us the good news of the end of the strike. The heads of the Schenley interests, who control the growing and marketing of the major grape crops in California, have agreed to negotiate within thirty days. There are thirty other growers who have not yet followed suit. DiGiorgio officials propose a secret vote of farm workers to see if they want the N.F.W.A. to represent them.

"Does this mean that the owners have abdicated in favor of worker ownership?" Pat asked. It does not, of course, but it does mean that the first steps have been made to provide an adequate wage, so that the workers in the field may begin to enjoy a more human life, may begin to think. Nonviolence has been taught and practiced throughout the strike, and the only violence has been on the part of the employers and the scabs.

The report came while a march from Delano to Sacramento was in progress. Men, women and children, three hundred of them, walked through the vast valley, with the banner of Our Lady of Guadalupe at their head. Today some priests and laymen flew to the West Coast to make the last lap of the march with the victorious workers, in what is now a procession of thanksgiving rather than supplication. There has been superb coverage of the strike in the *National Catholic Reporter*.

News of the eviction of twenty-two hundred people from their homes in Mississippi comes in a report from the Snick Shop (65 Main St., Worcester, Massachusetts), which goes on to quote from the Delta Ministry of the National Council of Churches estimate that from ten to twelve thousand more people will lose their homes this winter or spring. Farm workers are not covered by the Federal Social Security system or by unemployment compensation. The Snick Shop sells magazines, Negro history books for children, Freedom Song albums, and cloth and leather goods made in the Poor People's Co-ops of Mississippi. (See article elsewhere in this issue.) The Friends of S.N.C.C. (Student Nonviolent Coordinating Committee) in Worcester are assuming the responsibility of helping the people in Lowndes County, Alabama, where conditions, they say, are as bad as in Mississippi. We call this project to the attention of our New England readers.

Tonight we go to Monsignor Frederick Hillenbrand's church in Evanston for Holy Thursday services and the Mass. We'll spend Good Friday in Milwaukee and make our Easter vigil there. Then on to Minneapolis for a three-day conference with the University of Minnesota Newman Club, and after that to St. Louis University for a talk on April 18th.

May 1966

Martin Corbin, managing editor of the *Catholic Worker*, has set the second Wednesday of the month as the day on which we go to press, which means that I must write this column today to be in-time for press day, which is a week from tomorrow. Time was when we came out two weeks beforehand, before May Day so that on that great anniversary of the *Catholic Worker* (we begin our 34th year this May) we could, all over the country, get out on the streets with it in all the cities all over the country where we had houses of hospitality.

Now that May first is the feast of St. Joseph the Worker, it is more than ever necessary to think of the paper as a message, a reiteration of Peter Maurin's teachings, since he was the founder of the CW movement and taught us what he liked to call a philosophy of poverty and a philosophy of work.

Peter was a French peasant, educated by the Christian Brothers, himself a Christian brother-teacher, who left them to become a teacher to the poor and the worker. He came to this country in 1909 or thereabouts, traveled over Canada and the United States as a migrant and unskilled worker, lived in cities in flophouses, ate at cheap beaneries, taught on park benches and city parks and street corners.

"If you wish to reach the man in the street, go to the man in the street," he said. To Peter, a philosophy of work meant that all men should accept work as not only doing penance for sin, since they had to work by the sweat of the brow, but also, as co-creating with God, taking the material things of the universe and developing them. *"Man is made in the image and likeness of God, Creator."*

All work should be in some sense a development of the works of mercy, having to do with food, clothing and shelter, health and education, re-creation, and should be not only to earn a living, "by the sweat of one's own brow rather than by some one else's" but to earn a living for others who suffer from involuntary poverty and destitution. Poverty can be of mentality; the feeble-minded and retarded and delinquent; there are the lame, the halt and the blind; and there are the spiritually destitute. "Let your abundance supply their want," St. Paul said.

Poverty is an interior thing, a personal thing. One can only judge the practice of poverty in others by the generosity they evidence in sharing not only their material goods, but their physical, mental and spiritual wealth, and the generosity they evidence in giving their time, that most precious possession in this too short life.

But we have written these things over and over, in one way or another, and this issue must be a real On Pilgrimage, telling of the travels Pat Rusk and I undertook this last month. It is exactly a month since we set out from New York in our 1958 Volkswagen, which right now is said to have many things wrong with it and yet after a night's rest keeps steadily on.

Many years ago I would have been afraid to take a long trip with anything but the best car, and since I never had that, I trusted to buses. After seeing the *Grapes of Wrath* in the movies, and the valiant pilgrims to the West Coast from the dust bowl area driving in ramshackle old trucks, I can dare anything.

I have had clutch rods come out in my hands, gas pedals go down through the floor, batteries fall out into the roadside, windshield wipers fail in cloudbursts, lights go out, fanbelts break, etc., etc. (Some of these things happened after inspection!).

These failures always seem to happen in some safe place or just as I drove up the homestretch. Many a time when something unaccountably went wrong and I was just able to pull over to the side of the road, giving the car a rest seemed all that was necessary.

With a good book in the car one could only regard these halts as little unexpected gifts of time to oneself, time to relax and rest a while. Stanley Vishnewski's brother, who works in the Bethlehem Steel plant in Baltimore, operating a crane or some such giant machinery, was the one who told me that machinery and cars needed a rest too once in a while. And Peter Maurin always said that machinery should be the extension of the hand of man. I've known people who beat and yank and tear at machinery in anger when it does not respond to their touch and I soon learned on this car to shift gears gently, but very firmly, jiggling around a little when they seemed stuck. (Clutch is slipping, garage man said.)

Maybe, Pat says, the above paragraph will induce someone to buy a rebuilt, or even a new engine and clutch for us. Our brakes are all right and tires too. Though there was something wrong with the oil-feed-line yesterday and the green light showed for an hour, it is all right today, these last hundred miles. How all women need instruction when they use a car! But we all learn the hard way in this life.

This day found us back in Avon, Ohio, again at Our Lady of the Wayside Farm, which is no longer a farm, but another house of hospitality on the land. I cannot count nor tell of all the people Dorothy and Bill Gauchat have taken into this large red brick house—unmarried mothers, alcoholic old women, a priest in trouble, and so on. Bill was the founder of the Martin de Porres House of Hospitality in Cleveland, which was located in a slum residential area facing the gigantic factories on the other bank of the Cuyahoga River, which flows through Cleveland. Bill is a graduate of St. Michael's College in Toronto. Dorothy, who came as a high-school student to help the house in those days, and later was an apprentice of Ade Bethune in Newport, looks like the heroine in *The Sound of Music*. After their marriage they moved to the farm in Avon, which used to be across the street from their present location, and there they were raising their family (eventually six children). They had cows, chickens, fruit, vegetables, and they dispensed hospitality in the two or three little guest houses on the place, usually occupied by migrant Mexican families who later settled on their own bits of property and worked in the industrial plants in nearby Lorain.

The work they are engaged in now is still one of hospitality and is of tremendous significance for our day and age. It denotes a respect for life, and for man's wisdom, for science and the possibility of developing cures for the conditions they are trying to alleviate. At a time when the world seems careless of human life, and the instruments of death are ever more horrible, the Gauchats are caring for little ones who would otherwise be left to deteriorate and suffer in state hospitals for incurables: spastics, cerebral palsy victims, the deaf, dumb and blind, the retarded, the encephalitic. And they have been doing this now for years. They are permitted by the state to harbor only seven of these little victims. One wishes that the standards set for the individual practice of the works of mercy would be enforced in the state hospitals for these poor afflicted ones.

I could not help but think as we visited the Gauchats on April 4th, and now again on our way home, May 4, that their work in this area will be like the few loaves and fishes blessed by our Lord and increased to feed five thousand. Dear God, let this alleviation of pain and suffering here help to alleviate the pain and suffering which we, in our inhumanity, are inflicting in Vietnam. Last night we saw the first part of *The Mills of the Gods*, a TV documentary on Vietnam. We saw the burned children and women in hospitals, evidence of the napalm (see the story in this issue of Redwood City, Calif. and the proposed manufacture of two hundred million tons of napalm in a factory they wish to build there.) We saw the torture by Vietnamese of Vietnamese, with our American soldiers and officers looking on. "That never would be permitted in France," that is, the showing of such a scene, or the filming of it, the French observer said, recalling the torture of prisoners of war in Algeria.

If I did not believe, if I did not make what is called an act of faith (and each act of faith increases our faith, and our capacity for faith), if I did not have faith that such work as the Gauchats' does lighten the sum total of suffering in the world, so that those are suffering on both sides in this ghastly struggle, somehow mysteriously find their pain lifted and perhaps some balm of consolation poured on their wounds, if I did not believe these things, the problem of evil would indeed be overwhelming.

The next stop I made was in Chicago, where I stayed with Nina Polcyn; a story about her appeared in the *National Catholic Reporter* last month. She was associated with the Milwaukee House when it was running. The group there seemed to go off in all directions, so that you find former Milwaukee CW's like Nina, running the St. Benet's Bookshop in Chicago (300 S. Wabash); Ruth Anne Heaney teaching and living on one of the farms started by Catholic Workers in Rhineland, Missouri; Michael Strasser teaching at Duquesne in Pittsburgh; Ammon Hennacy in Salt Lake City, Alba Ryan in Maine, the Humphreys in St. Cloud, Minnesota, two priests, a Maryknoller in Japan and a Dominican in California, and so on and on. Anyway, Nina dispenses hospitality and news of the apostolate and is a center both at home and at the bookshop for all kinds and conditions of apostles. I went through Chicago going and coming and was present for a few hours of discussion at the home of the Heyermans (Helen Heyerman is Nina's sister) and there were representatives of almost every lay group in Chicago present. We had to leave early to have dinner at Monsignor Egan's.

Monsignor John J. Egan is now stationed in Presentation parish on the near West Side in what was once an Italian parish and is now predominantly Negro, I think. There were a number of priests there from a neighboring parish, and a Glenmary priest, Father Lester Schmidt, who had been "taking the plunge," they called it, spending the preceding week on West Madison Street (the skid row of Chicago) many times without sleep because most of the hotels were filled up or would not have him. This idea of The Plunge was started by an Anglican priest a year ago and was a student venture designed to enable men and women to experience some of the desperate misery of destitution and homelessness. Father

Schmidt, who was in shirt and slacks in that warm rectory, looked desperately tired with his head in his hands most of the evening, perhaps to shade his eyes from the blinding glare of electric lights, that I thought he was some friend of Monsignor Egan's who was having a breakdown. I could not help but think of a young man released from a mental hospital who attended our Christmas party at Chrystie Street a few years ago and sat through all the jubilation with his face in his two cupped hands and his head bowed.

Saul Alinsky

Monsignor Egan's guest that evening was Saul Alinsky, who to me represents the man of vision, one of the truly great of our day, in a class with Danilo Dolci and Vinoba Bhave. Thank God we have some heroes today in the social field whose vision illuminates the hard work they propose. Most of our aims are too small. I often think of Teresa of Avila, who said that we compliment God by asking great things of him, and I do ask Him to make this vision of Saul Alinsky grow in the minds of men who hear him.

I know that several articles about Saul Alinsky have been published in *Harper's* within the last year and that another of his books is coming out soon. The book I remember of his is *Reveille for Radicals*, published twenty or more years ago and which tells most vividly of the Back of the Yards movement in Chicago, where churches, settlement houses, unions, corporations, institutions, were drawn together in a common aim. Since my own radical interests were sparked by Upton Sinclair's book *The Jungle*, Alinsky's book interested me, and because he thought in terms of building from the ground up, rather than from the top down, on the principle of subsidiarity, he followed what I considered the philosophical anarchist position, rather than the Marxist socialist one.

Right now he is in the news for his attack on the poverty program, and because he has been called in by such cities as Rochester and Kansas City, Oakland and Detroit and other areas for consultation as to how to handle the gathering tensions between white and black.

What interests me about him is the largeness of his vision. At a time when there is much talk about air pollution and water pollution, he proposes that vast sums be set aside to tackle the national scandal of water pollution, for instance. He envisages something like the Tennessee Valley Authority with the use of the billions to build villages, schools, hospitals, roads, and all else needed (and this I suppose would mean decentralization, and a work which would be so vital that even the least worker would be caught up in the importance of the task on which he was called to work. It would do away with the sense of futility which is present in so many, the war on poverty projects, and the constant suspicion of political chicanery and corruption. It would truly be the rebuilding of the social order and the supplying of work at a time when automation and cybernation is the nightmare of the day.)

Alinsky's attacks on Sargent Shriver makes news, of course; his condemnation of the niggardliness of the funds allocated to the war on poverty and the consequent focussing of attention on the vast sums spent for destruction are a good thing. And when it comes to personal attacks in his public speeches, I heard him speak on the way home when we were passing through Detroit and I found humor but not malice in his presentation. He is not a demagogue.

Of course—and I am as firmly convinced of this as I am of the necessity for our own work—it will take the example of such people as Danilo Dolci besides to point the way. Until each individual stops dumping broken down washing machines, refrigerators, cars, empty cans and assorted non-organic, unassimilable material down the banks of our brooks, ponds, streams, lakes and rivers (not to speak of the outhouses still built over streams in the slums of our villages), we will not have such projects and reforms as Alinsky proposes. A Danilo Dolci would be sparking a strike against unemployment and destitution by getting a group of men together as he did in Sicily, to work on roads and fields. This resulted in world publicity when the men were all arrested for this unheard-of remedy for lack of work. Even working an idle field is confiscating property not their own. The sacredness of private property is not yet challenged by any but the Marxist . . .

June 1966

After finishing this column news comes to me by 'phone that Nicole d'Entremont (one of our editors), Terry Becker, Diane Feeley and Raona Millikin (who is engaged to Jim Wilson) are all in the Women's House of Detention, serving five-day sentences for their civil disobedience. Nicole and Diane, who refused to take bail, served an additional three days after their arrest. Whether or not our readers approve of the disobedience which brought about the arrest, which was a sit-down on Fifth Avenue in front of the Armed Forces Day parade, it is certain that visiting the prisoner is one of the works of mercy enjoined upon us by our Lord Jesus Christ. In several countries, Brazil, Belgium and Switzerland, the little Sisters of Jesus of Charles de Foucauld live in prisons for varying periods, to share the life of the prisoners, to lighten in some small way the heavy burden of misery. Just as the conscientious objectors who worked in mental hospitals during the war did something to improve the conditions of those hospitals, if only by their compassionate kindness, so these Catholic Worker prisoners who see in their brothers and sisters the suffering Christ, are helping to lighten the sum-total of anguish in the world. They are reminders, they are news, good news, of another world. They are the gospel in other words, and carrying it to its ultimate meaning, they are the Word, they are other Christs. They would be abashed to think of themselves in this way, but I am speaking in terms of the ideal, unashamedly and unafraid of ridicule saying what we would want to be.

Saul Alinsky spoke last month of how difficult it is to know what poverty is really like, even by going to jail to be a prisoner for a time. It is true that we must take ourselves as we are, and recognize that with our education, our families, our backgrounds, it is impossible for us to know what destitution really is. But by attempting at self-discipline, reducing our wants, curbing our constant self-indulgence, learning what it means to work by the sweat of our brow, and by enduring the contempt and insult only too often met with, we are learning a kind of poverty. When we do not recognize the importance of ourselves as sons of God, when we do not in faith esteem ourselves and recognize the importance of our work, no matter how small it may seem, we are likely to be crushed by the criticism of others and take refuge in the do-nothing attitude. I once heard a psychiatrist say, man craves recognition more than food or sex and that when he does not get it he feels poor indeed. This is a real poverty to be endured. But it is good to be considered a fool for Christ, as St. Paul said, remembering always the folly of the Cross.

I write these things, hoping still that next issue Nicole or

Terry will write about their prison experience, the first for each of them.

Morton Sobell

It too often happens that our program of work and the energies that arise in a community of the poor like ours, keeps us from participating in all the meetings that are being held by groups to which we wish to give our support. One such meeting is the Morton Sobell meeting, to be held on Friday, June 17th, at 7 p.m. at the Hotel Sheraton-Atlantic, Broadway and 34th street, in New York.

This meeting marks the thirteenth year since the execution of Julius and Ethel Rosenberg. Before the rally there will be a Truth Exhibit, with a dramatic display of new evidence now before the courts pointing to the innocence of Morton Sobell and the Rosenbergs. Those who cannot get to the meeting can write or wire Attorney General Nicholas Katzenbach, Justice Department, Washington, D.C., asking him to free Sobell or agree to a hearing on the new court motion.

We have written about the case before, but to those who are new readers we recommend the recent book published by Doubleday, *Invitation to an Inquest*, by Walter and Miriam Schneir. The Rosenbergs were executed on the charge that they were engaged in a conspiracy to transmit information relating to national defense, to the Soviet Union. Sobell was illegally convicted on the same charge. The New York *Times* reviewer of the Schneirs' book concluded: "There was not enough evidence to condemn the Rosenbergs to death. And I wonder if a jury would find them guilty and a judge sentence them to death if they were tried today." The St. Louis *Post-Dispatch* said: "This book is disturbing reading for any American . . . Were the Rosenbergs victims of an era? This book at least establishes that the question needs to be answered." Sobell already spent sixteen years of a thirty-year sentence in prison, six of them in Alcatraz.

I will never forget the evening the Rosenbergs were executed. There had been many appeals, and Pope Pius XII himself had asked for clemency. But it was the time of the Korean war hysteria, and feelings ran high. Picketing of the White House had led to counter-picketing by youths demanding their execution.

As the hour approached, it was unbearable to think of these young parents being put to death, notwithstanding the

274

protests of the world. On their last day I thought often of Ethel's agony at being parted from her children, and as I bathed one of my own grandchildren I kept praying over and over again for fortitude and courage for her, virtues which both of them had maintained, but I was thinking especially of Ethel at this time. And believing in a personal God, who is our Father, I begged this strength for her, the one last thing I could do. The next day, when the unbearable story of the execution was published, one of the newspapers carried a story of her last gesture. She walked firmly and confidently to the electric chair, accompanied by the woman prison guard. Before she took her place in history and in the chair, she turned to the guard, kissed her, and thanked her for her kindness during her last days.

I am always being surprised at the readiness to respond evidenced by some of our public officials when we wrote them as we are always being urged to do. (We do not write often enough, illiterate and slothful generation that we are.) When Morton Sobell was in Alcatraz I wrote to James V. Bennett, Commissioner of Federal Prisons, and begged that Sobell at least be transferred to a prison in the East, so that his wife and children could visit him more often.

The reply was friendly enough. Mr. Bennett thanked me for the tone of my letter, complained of the abuse he usually received from people who wrote him in petition, and went on to say that Mrs. Sobell did not seem to have any difficulty in raising the money to visit her husband, and that as for the children visiting him, he questioned whether the children should visit such a father, convicted traitor as he was. I did not publish the letter at the time, not wishing to discourage people from writing their appeals to government officials, and I hope I am not misquoting him now. I am still surprised at the intimacy, not to say petulance, of the response. I speak of it now in order to encourage people to write to Attorney-General Katzenbach. We should continue to make our voices heard and attend any meetings we can in the cities in which we live.

City and Country

All of the foregoing was written in the city, at one of the five Kenmare Street apartments, which make up part of the house of hospitality in New York. Visitors from Spring Street, where there are five more apartments, kept coming in. Besides the noise of traffic outside the windows there was the noise of all the comings and goings in the house, not to speak of the boy upstairs, who has all his friends in with their band instruments to practice. We turn up the radio as loud as possible—a symphony of course, which we enjoy, but it does not help us to think.

The following pages were written Pentecost Tuesday, at ten o'clock of a very rainy evening on a Greyhound bus, on my way in to New York, where Pat Rusk was to meet me at eleven forty-five to help me carry my suitcase and typewriter to the house of hospitality. I always carry a stenographer's notebook with me for just such idle hours. My account begins:

I had to leave my car in Vermont because it broke down, badly, I am afraid. I always come away from Tamar's with gifts from one or another of the family. "Grannies are nice because they always bring presents," Kathy, who is five, comments, and it works the other way too. The presents I was bringing back to the community were a great wooden bowl, suitable for a community salad, and two little bowls, from the Bowl Shop at Weston, Vermont. There was also a soapstone griddle, which Eric, eighteen, gave me. He works after school and on Saturdays and holidays, in the only factory in Vermont where they make soapstone griddles and stoves and comes home looking as though he had been sprinkled with talcum powder from head to foot. When he works in the village garage he comes home looking black. There was also a pot of catnip for Peggy at the Tivoli farm, a present from Martha, who loves cats just as Peggy does. Martha, age ten, is going to be a veterinarian, she says.

This bus ride, which enables me to sleep for an hour before I started this, was good because I was sleepless last night, what with my sciatica. I had stayed awake reading Dickens' *Bleak House* and after three hours' sleep got up refreshed enough to drive to Bellows Falls with Tamar and Becky, who is home from college for a week now. We went to Bellows Falls to offer a Mass with Father Miller at the home of Mr. Norman Harty. Norman Harty, who lost a leg in World War II works in the post office from eleven p.m. until seven in the morning. He is a man of profound faith. Once, when the rosary was being discussed and its importance minimized, he said that it was something that he had held on to when he lay wounded. I thought of the many times I had held to it as to a lifeline, in times of misery or peril or in sudden crises.

Abbot Marmion says that praying the Stations of the Cross give fortitude, so I use both devotions.

I was most happy with that simple and reverent Mass, with the beauty of the red vestments, the white linen cloth, the beeswax candles, which with the lilacs outside took the place of incense, so that sight, sound, smell, taste and gesture engaged all the senses, and body and soul both were engaged in worship.

We did not have music, of course, though I have been at similar Masses where both guitar and recorder were used and which added unutterable beauty. But Father Miller's enunciation was clear and distinct, his voice pleasing,—no gravelly or nasal tones to grate on the ear. (I remember Joan Overboss at the Grail saying once, "Everyone must sing and those who can't, just sing a little lower." The same would go for speech.)

Another neighbor at the Mass has two sons in the Merchant Marine, young officers on freighters and tankers bringing munitions and oil to Vietnam. After witnessing the famine victims in India during one of his trips, one of the sons went back on board ship and wept all night.

I could not help but think of Don Milani's statement in his defense against the charges made against him of advocating resistance to conscription for war. He said that even those who cooked for troops contributed to war. How involved we all are, what with the hidden taxes we pay for war, the high standard of living all of us enjoy, even when we refuse to pay income tax, so much of which goes for war, and when we build prisons for draft refusers.

We are all exploiters, as Orwell said in one of his essays. Workers who consider themselves exploited are the exploiters of others. The general strike in Belgium, when the workers revolted against the austerity regime that followed the loss of the Belgian Congo, was evidence of this.

One of the most stirring statements Pope Paul has ever made was his call for a new economic order, and new institutions. Who will rise up to work out a just and wise solution to the problem of the money holdings, the investments, the money power of the Church, which is an occasion of suspicion, mistrust and of actual scandal to the world.

Which reminds me to recommend the books of Seymour Melman, who is a professor of engineering at Columbia and has written on the problem of converting the war economy to a peacetime economy. As it is, communities fight for government contracts, even for the manufacture of napalm, gasoline jelly, for noxious gases, not to speak of bombs, planes, helicopters, trucks, and all the armaments that go into devastating wars. How many countries we arm—to keep the peace, as they say. What insanity!

If we keep coming back to this subject always in these pages, it is not only because Peace is the most important cause of our time, but because too, I have found on my travels so many people who not only do not question the morality of war (any more than an Eichmann questioned the morality of the extermination of a people) but do not even know that napalm is a fire that burns the flesh from the bone and that there is nothing that can put it out.

God did not forgive the sin of ignorance, as Father Paul Hanley Furrey pointed out once, recalling the 25th chapter of St. Matthew.

Lord, when did we see you burned with napalm? Inasmuch as ye did it to one of these my littlest ones you did it unto me.

My only comfort sometimes is that saying of Our Lord's: "God wills that all men be saved." "Ask and ye shall receive." May His will be done.

September 1966

I am in the city this week and some one came to visit with a great bag of good ripe tomatoes which had to be stewed up right away to keep them from spoiling. Marie in the back apartment came in with some clean jars and a sharp knife and announced she would help cut out any bad spots. After all she came from a farm in the midwest and knew all about canning. Pretty soon the delightful smell of stewed tomatoes filled the air. My hands smelled of them. At the farm last week Alice and I peeled a peck of peaches to make what we called at home an upside-down cake and then too my hands smelled of fresh peaches. In the fall around Tivoli the wonderful smell of ripe apples fills the air. These are some of the delights of the harvest season, always a happy time around the Catholic Worker after the almost overwhelming work of the summer months with its visitors, students, families and children.

While we worked at the tomatoes which Mike and Louis

had brought from friends on Staten Island, Marie talked very frankly of panhandling. She enjoyed doing it, and she said the Bowery was the best place—people would always give you a nickel or a dime there. One man seeing her accept a nickel gratefully, handed her a dollar and hastened away before she could thank him. With this money she buys little extra treats such as sardines, evaporated milk and jars of apple sauce. On one occasion she came in one morning when I was about to leave for a trip and gave me a sandwich and an orange for my lunch, which she had bought from a man on the Bowery who was selling them both for a dime, a lunch provided him by the Municipal Lodging House and which he was probably exchanging for the first dime to pay for a 35c bottle of wine, called Sneaky Pete by the men around us. Marie earns bits of money from the neighbors for whom she runs errands or does a bit of work, and this too is always spent on others. It is so good, everyone knows, to have a bit of money to spend and even if board and room and clothes are provided at the Catholic Worker, not having a penny to spend means an involuntary poverty which many of the young ones feel. So they go out to sell the paper on the streets, and such selling means a direct encounter and questions asked and countered or answered by the seller.

Today is the feast of St. Nicholas of Tolentine who preached sermons on the street corner, my missal says. I still use a missal because I want to hold fast to those prayers in the canon of the Mass, and because I want to know the feasts, the saints and heroes we celebrate, also sometimes the priest is not a clear speaker. Yesterday was the feast of St. Peter Claver who is the patron of all the priests who work with the Negro and who struggle for civil rights, who hunger and thirst after justice, and the epistle and gospel are inspiring. The Maryknoll missal has all the psalms and here is prayer for every occasion, the prayer of the Israelite, the prayer of the Christian.

This morning I was inspired myself to preach a sermon on a street corner, a strong sermon against drink which is the curse of so many of those we live with and sit at the table with. St. Paul talks of abstaining from what causes your brother to stumble. We concede of course that wine is good and lightens the heart of man, as Scripture says, but we live in the midst of the tragedy drink has caused, and to use the most difficult but the only potent means to help, inflict suffering on ourselves by sacrificing this little enjoyment, put to death that bit of self that demands this indulgence and justifies it as being harmless. We had just received an account in the letter from the mother of a young man, who with his wife and unborn child was killed in an auto crash caused by two young drunken drivers also killed. And there was the drinking and perhaps drug addiction on the part of three teen agers which led to the brutal beating and murder of Al Uhrie last month, on East Fifth Street, a young man who was one of the gentlest and most consistent pacifists in his daily life that we ever knew. His wife and five months old baby are now living with us in Tivoli. When one is surrounded by many sorrows, one's own is lightened a little, leveled off a bit perhaps by the way folks try to take care of each other. I cannot believe that people are so captivated by drink that they will not give up their own harmless indulgence for the sake of others around them. It must be that they do not have faith in the weapons of the spirit or recognize their power. How to explain it, to make it clear. St. Ignatius said love is an exchange of gifts. St. Teresa said that we could only show our love for God by our love for our brothers. Jesus said for us to pray thus: *Our Father.* So we can say, Father, I love my brother and I love you. I want to offer you a sacrifice, and beg you in return to send Arthur or Louis the grace to overcome the most dangerous failing they suffer from. Give us this day our daily bread of strength to suffer for each other these little ways of sacrifice, as well as the daily pinpricks of daily living which can become a martyrdom in a family and grow into hate and violence.

I thought these things at Mass this morning, and I had to say them when I encountered someone for whom I thought the words important.

October-November 1966

I first met Peter Maurin just after the Feast of the Immaculate Conception in 1932, when I had returned from reporting the Hunger March of the Unemployed, which was a march on Washington from all parts of the country by seamen, shipworkers, textile workers, miners, and other workers, demanding social security, unemployment insurance, old-age pensions, aid for dependent children, and so on. (We have these things now because of the demonstrations, marches and other pilgrimages which took place then, and, think with hope of the present-day pilgrimages of the migrant and agricultural workers of California and Texas and the peace parades, sit-ins, teach-ins, vigils and the pamphleteering and leafleting which are going on today.) I have written before about praying at the Shrine of Our Lady in Washington and of how I came back to New York to find Peter Maurin waiting for me with the suggestion that I use my journalistic background to get out a paper to reach the man in the street.

But I have never written about my solitary pilgrimage in September of that same year to the shrine of the Jesuit martyrs at Auriesville, New York. I had read in the *Catholic News* of a pilgrimage, which was to be sponsored by St. Michael's Church, to leave from Grand Central Station on a Sunday morning, arrive at the shrine for Mass at noon and return to New York after Benediction at four p.m. The cost was minimal. I had never made a religious pilgrimage and I knew nothing of this shrine, which was in the process of being built up as a popular place of pilgrimage. It was long before the mitigation of the rule of fasting, so I set out early with no comforting coffee and nothing to eat, as did the entire train load of St. Michael's parishioners. I read about the Jesuit martyrs long before I became a Catholic, in the compilation of their reports that Edna Kenton had edited. She was a friend of the old *Masses*, where I worked long before. I had never heard, however, of the Indian girl, Kateri Tekakwitha, who was born at this site, and I was fascinated when I read her story in pamphlet form. I had brought no lunch with me as the others had, and there was no place to purchase anything, because the one lunch stand was soon sold out. So I spent a day of penance there at Auriesville, with nothing to eat until I returned home after eight o'clock that night.

One never knows exactly what one's needs are, or what graces one receives on such occasions, but I often felt that this day of penance influenced my writing the next months so that Peter Maurin, reading the articles I had written dealing with the problems of poverty and unemployment, came to me with his message and his teaching, in answer to the prayers I said that day, and the day at the shrine of the Blessed Mother in Washington, where I prayed most especially for the hunger marchers, to whom I felt more akin than I did to the thousands at the shrines.

A few weeks ago, I again made a solitary pilgrimage to

Auriesville, on my way back from speaking engagements at Rochester and Geneseo, New York. The shrine was all but deserted that late afternoon. The cafeteria was closing for the year that very day and the woman in charge showed me where her guest house was, up the hill. I was the last guest she was going to take that season, she said, as she and her husband were going down to Florida. I slept well that night, after a supper of a cheese sandwich, an apple and coffee made with hot water from the faucet. Mass was at seven the next morning, in the huge octagonal auditorium, with many altars. I was one of only three participating at the Mass.

I remained for a time in front of the statue of St. Isaac Jogues, thinking of that former pilgrimage so long ago. And suddenly it came to me: I had been going around the country, and yes, to Mexico, Italy and England too, speaking for many, many years now, telling the story of the Catholic Worker movement and its perennial philosophy of work and poverty, as the basis of peace and as an expression of the love of God and love of brother. For thirty-four years I have spent months of every year in travelling and speaking, and I never left our house of hospitality in New York, or one of our farms, without a wrench, without a sickness at having to go. And yet I was convinced that this was my vocation. Years ago, Father McSorley, of the Paulists, who was my first spiritual adviser, had told me to go where I was asked. I enjoyed all the trips, the meetings with all our groups and speaking at all our houses over the years, and I learned much from the encounters I had with other speakers and other groups, priests and people. I never came back without feeling enriched, and convinced too, that we were on the right path.

But this morning, as I left the Auriesville shrine, I felt, with sudden peace and certitude, "I am not going out to speak any more. I am going to write. I am going to write the pamphlet on the works of mercy which John Todd asked me to write when I met him three years ago in England. I am going to write the four articles for *Ave Maria* which they requested for the coming Advent. I am going to finish that short article for the *Jesus Caritas* bulletin, and most of all, I want to write the book I promised Harper's, *All Is Grace*."

William James once wrote that when you make a resolution, you should proclaim it or publish it, and that this will give you strength to stick to it. So I publish this. I am going to stay home.

But I still had two engagements to keep, made last summer, and one of them was to speak on a panel at Brandeis University on *Poverty and the Church*. Judith Gregory met me at the bus station just in time for dinner and the meeting, and later I spent the night at her apartment, which she shares with three other young women in Cambridge. When I spoke to her of my resolution, she gave me a wonderful quotation from Thoreau's journals (all fourteen volumes of which her mother had read):

Thinking this afternoon of the prospect of my writing lectures and going abroad to read them the next winter, I realized how incomparably great the advantages of obscurity and poverty which I have enjoyed so long (and may still perhaps enjoy). I thought with what more than princely, with what poetical, leisure I had spent my years hitherto, without care or engagement, fancy-free. I have given myself up to nature; I have lived so many springs and summers and autumns and winters as if I had nothing else to do but LIVE them, and imbibe whatever nutriment they had for me; I have spent a couple of years, for instance, with the flowers chiefly, having none other so binding engagement as to observe when they opened; I could have afforded to spend a whole fall observing the changing tints of the foliage. Ah, how I have thriven on solitude and poverty! I cannot overstate this advantage. I do not see how I could have enjoyed it, if the public had been expecting as much of me as there is danger now that they will. If I go abroad lecturing, how shall I ever recover the lost winter? (Vol. VII, Sept. 19, 1854.)

Rochester and Geneso

The other engagements I had were at the University of Rochester and at the State College at Geneseo. Eloise Wilkin gave me hospitality in Rochester. She is an illustrator of children's books and a doll designer too. I enjoyed my stay there with her and our drive to the Trappist monastery near Geneseo the next day to visit the monks before my evening meeting. This is the simplest of all the Trappist monasteries I have visited; I forgot to ask if they had building plans. I hope not. It does seem to me that in times like these, when there is famine and homelessness in the world, there should be a moratorium on the building of bigger church institutions. However, the monastery seems to be the same as when I visited there years ago and the monks number thirty-six, I believe. They work for their living by the sweat of their brow, not only by keeping up the place and raising beef cattle for sale, but also in baking thirty-five thousand loaves of bread a week (thanks to modern machinery) for sale in Rochester, Buffalo, Syracuse and Elmira. When it is baked trucks from a big baking company come right to the gates and take it away for delivery. I was very glad to hear about this, because Monks' Bread is now sold everywhere and I had heard they had sold the franchise. What has happened is that they have sold it to a big flour company, which distributes their mix, on each bag of which the monks are paid a royalty, which the monks give to the poor. I know that we benefit by their charity regularly. My own complaint at this time is that the entrance to the chapel is inside the enclosure, so that women visitors are not able to be present at the singing of the divine office. I was glad to hear that there will be at least that minimum of building; the making of another entrance. As it was we went down to the retreat house through the rolling fields and visited the chapel there. I love this part of New York, where you can look way off to the horizon in every direction and overhead that great blue bowl of sky! Abbot Jerome is a Biblical scholar, and I should have liked much to have remained for a longer visit, but I had a supper and speaking engagement and Eloise had to return to Rochester. We had had such a pleasant visit together that I hated to see her go. She had come to our Pax conference this summer and is one of those who works at prayer for peace, saying much of the divine office each day for that intention.

What interested me before about Piffard, New York, the location of the monastery of Our Lady of Geneseo, is the knowledge that enormous salt mines are worked all through that district. Indeed the salt strata run all the way from Lake Ontario to West Virginia; three hundred and fifty men are employed around Piffard and Restof. It is the largest operating salt mine in the world and the local pastor told me that half a million people could take shelter in it. There is already a narrow-gauge railroad, the Geneseo and Wyoming, called locally the Gee Whizz. Looking into the *Encyclopedia Britannica* for more information, I found nothing about salt mines themselves but a great deal about salt and the commerce in it. There is a long history of religious use, and bread and salt has always been a symbol of hospitality. Salt has been used to seal covenants and is so mentioned in the Book of Numbers. Soldiers in the time of the Roman Empire used to be paid in salt, and I recall the expression still heard, "He is not worth his salt." After reading this one can understand a little better the significance of Gandhi's Salt March.

On the first day of October, my oldest grand-daughter Becky was married to John Houghton of Newport, New Hampshire, which is the town of his birth and of his father's before him. The wedding took place at St. Mary's church, in Springfield, Vermont and the reception was at Weathersfield Center Church, which is much used for such receptions and where the yearly town meeting takes place. This historic church is on a country road and surrounded by maples and elms and pines in all their glory. Myrtle Baker baked the wedding cake, Mrs. Bullard guided everyone in all the arrangements, her daughter Sue drove the bridal car, the bride dressed at the Foley home down the road and Foleys and Bullards and Bakers and of course friends and relatives of the bridegroom were the guests. The church hall was so beautifully decorated with fall leaves by Judy Barton that the Pierce sisters, who were using the hall for a tea that afternoon, begged that the decorations be left. With all the joy and the excitement no one noticed how it was raining, not even the bride. I am so much there as I write this, sitting by my window in Tivoli, that I was startled at hearing the New York Central 9:30 train go by the window, wondering, with a start, where I was and what was that noise. A first grandchild's wedding is a wonderful thing.

Death

And then, after the wedding, news came of my older brother's death in Helsinki of a heart attack, at the age of 71. He had lived in northern Europe since 1921 and had only returned once to the States, in 1934, for a short visit. Both my sister and mother, however, had paid him long visits and he had kept up a long and most cheerful correspondence with my sister. Only two weeks before his death he had written me, telling of a fishing trip he had just enjoyed, of the political situation in Finland, and recommending ultra-short wave treatments, at least of twenty of them, as a treatment for my arthritis, saying that he had had them for painful joints in the knees and had not had a pain since. They cost him, he said, only fifty cents a treatment in Finnish money. Hospital care is seven dollars a day over there. Donald never wrote without asking God to bless us all. Though he tried to avoid controversy, because he disagreed with my religious and political attitudes, he found it hard not to allude to these differences and so he wrote more frequently to my sister. I enjoyed all his letters and most especially his discussion of the concerts he attended. When my sister visited him it seemed to me that she went to opera, ballet and concert every night in the week. Aside from mother and father, this is the first death among us and we feel it keenly. Family ties are strong.

All Souls

November is the month when we should most especially remember the dead. November first commemorates All Saints, canonized or uncanonized, and there are undoubtedly more of the latter than the former, since, as St. Paul says, we are all *called* to be saints, that is, to be holy—that is, to be whole men, in whom the life of the spirit has progressively become stronger so that in putting off the "old man," we become "new men." There is a great deal of talk in both Russian and Chinese Communist circles about the necessity of becoming "new men," and I hope and pray that Catholics will realize this necessity too. Christ took on our humanity so that we could put on His divinity. He showed us the way and we are a lifetime learning it.

The philosopher Unamuno writes in *The Tragic Sense of Life* that all men are haunted by the thought of death, no matter how hard they try to push it out of their consciousness. During this very season of October and November we see all things dying around us; there is a chill in the air and a sadness in the wind in the trees outside the window. Just to see the sudden rain of leaves in a gust of wind, to hear the sound of their dry rustle along the pavement, is a part of sadness. But the season is also crowned with glory, with promise, with a flaming assertion of God's promise. St. Paul expresses this faith, this mystery;

> "This corruptible body must put on incorruption, and this mortal body must put on immortality. But when this mortal body puts on immortality, then shall come to pass the word that is written, 'Death is swallowed up in victory! O death, where is your victory? O death, where is your sting?' "

When I think of all those in our house of hospitality in New York and on our farms, who lived and died with us, through all the long years, whose names are written down in

286

a little prayer book of mine containing the Office of the Dead, strange juxtapositions, such as Josephine and Father Pacifique Roy, Bebo Chandler and Solange Falgouste, Bill Duffy and Otto Spaeth—I think only of the mercy of God and how "He wills that all men be saved."

And of course through all my life I have prayed in our so persistent war times for those involved in war, directly or indirectly. God have mercy on us all, and may we say with Job,

"I know that my Redeemer lives, and that on that last day I shall rise out of the earth and be clothed again with my skin, and in my flesh I shall see God. It will not be some other being, but I myself shall see him. My own eyes shall look upon Him. This my hope lies deep in my heart."

1967

January 1967

□ It is not just Vietnam, it is South Africa, it is Nigeria, the Congo, Indonesia, all of Latin America. It is not just the pictures of all the women and children who have been burnt alive in Vietnam, or the men who have been tortured, and died. It is not just the headless victims of the war in Colombia. It is not just the words of Cardinal Spellman and Archbishop Hannan. It is the fact that whether we like it or not, we are Americans. It is indeed our country, right or wrong, as the Cardinal said in another context. We are warm and fed and secure (aside from occasional muggings and murders amongst us). We are the nation the most powerful, the most armed and we are supplying arms and money to the rest of the world where we are not ourselves fighting. We are eating while there is famine in the world.

Scripture tells us that the picture of judgment presented to us by Jesus is of Dives sitting and feasting with his friends while Lazarus sat hungry at the gate, the dogs, the scavengers of the East, licking his sores. We are Dives. Woe to the rich! *We* are the rich. The works of mercy are the opposite of the works of war, feeding the hungry, sheltering the homeless, nursing the sick, visiting the prisoner. But we are destroying crops, setting fire to entire villages and to the people in them. We are not performing the works of mercy but the works of war. We cannot repeat this enough.

When the apostles wanted to call down fire from heaven on the inhospitable Samaritans, the "enemies" of the Jews,

Jesus said to them, "You know not of what Spirit you are." When Peter told our Lord not to accept the way of the Cross and His own death, He said, "Get behind me, Satan. For you are not on the side of God but of men." But He also had said "Thou are Peter and upon this rock I will build my church." Peter denied Jesus three times at that time in history, but after the death on the cross, and the Resurrection and the Descent of the Holy Spirit, Peter faced up to Church and State alike and said, "We must obey God rather than men." Deliver us, O Lord, from the fear of our enemies, which makes cowards of us all.

I can sit in the presence of the Blessed Sacrament and wrestle for that peace in the bitterness of my soul, a bitterness which many Catholics throughout the world feel, and I can find many things in Scripture to console me, to change my heart from hatred to love of enemy. "Our worst enemies are those of our own household," Jesus said. Picking up the Scriptures at random (as St. Francis used to do) I read about Peter, James and John who went up on the Mount of Transfiguration and saw Jesus talking with Moses and Elias, transfigured before their eyes. (A hint of the life to come, Maritain said.) Jesus transfigured! He who was the despised of men, no beauty in him, spat upon, beaten, dragged to his cruel death on the way to the cross! A man so much like other men that it took the kiss of a Judas to single him out from the others when the soldiers, so closely allied to the priests, came to take him. Reading this story of the Transfiguration, the words stood out, words foolishly babbled, about the first building project of the Church, proposed by Peter. "Lord shall we make here three shelters, one for you, one for Moses and one for Elias?" And the account continues, "for he did not know what to say, he was so terrified."

Maybe they are terrified, these princes of the church, as we are often terrified at the sight of violence, which is present every now and then in our houses of hospitality, and which is always a threat in the streets of the slums. I have often thought it is a brave thing to do, these Christmas visits of Cardinal Spellman to the American troops all over the world, Europe, Korea, Vietnam. But oh, God what are all these Americans, so called Christians doing all over the world so far from our own shores?

But what words are those he spoke—going against even the Pope, calling for victory, total victory? Words are as strong and powerful as bombs, as napalm. How much the government counts on those words, pays for those words to exalt our own way of life, to build up fear of the enemy. Deliver us, Lord, from the fear of the enemy. That is one of the lines in the psalms, and we are not asking God to deliver us from enemies but from the fear of them. Love casts out fear, but we have to get over the fear in order to get close enough to love them.

There is plenty to do, for each one of us, working on our own hearts, changing our own attitudes, in our own neighborhoods. If the just man falls seven times daily, we each one of us fall more than that in thought, word and deed. Prayer and fasting, taking up our own cross daily and following Him, doing penance, these are the hard words of the Gospel.

As to the Church, where else shall we go, except to the Bride of Christ, one flesh with Christ? Though she is a harlot at times, she is our Mother. We should read the book of Hosea, which is a picture of God's steadfast love not only for the Jews, His chosen people, but for His Church, of which we are every one of us members or potential members. Since there is no time with God, we are all one, all one body, Chinese, Russians, Vietnamese, and He has *commanded us to love another*.

"A new commandment I give, that you love others *as I have loved you*," not to the defending of your life, but to the laying down of your life.

A hard saying.

"Love is indeed a harsh and dreadful thing" to ask of us, of each one of us, but it is the only answer.

February 1967

The Rev. A. J. Muste, known to all of us in the peace movement as A.J., is dead. The name Abraham means Father of a multitude, and he was that. If the peace movement in the United States had one outstanding figure it was A.J., and God gave him length of days to work. He was eighty-two years old when he died and many of us had seen him that last week of his life. Tuesday, the day of the blizzard, A.J. and sixty-one others were due to appear in court at Centre Street, to answer to a number of charges, beginning with "breach of the peace" and "conspiring to commit breach of the peace." In addition, there was a warrant out for A.J.'s arrest for failing to show up for one of the previous hearings on this charge. He had been in Hanoi at the time talking to Ho Chi Minh, together with an Anglican Archbishop Reeves, Martin Niemoeller and Rabbi Feinberg. The offense had been committed on December 15th and it was now February 7th and he had been around the world in that time, traveling to the ends of the earth, one might say, in search of peace.

The morning of the storm we awoke to find the city blanketed. No cars were running as we looked out of our windows at Kenmare Street, no trucks, and there was a most delightful silence and a most beautiful whiteness over the usually blackened city. Tom Cornell, of the Catholic Peace Fellowship, called up to tell us he would be over in his little Volkswagen to get us through, somehow, to the court, which is only about a mile away. And when he had delivered us, he went to Robert Gilmore's apartment on Eleventh Street, where A.J. was staying, to pick him up. It had been a bitter cold day on December 15th, when the group of sixty-two, led by A.J., stood on the steps of the recruiting station at Whitehall Street down at the foot of the canyon which was Broadway not far from the bitter gales of the harbor, sang Christmas carols, and called for peace. I was reminded of one of the antiphons in the breviary "*Through all the earth their voice resounds, and to the ends of the world their message.*"

The courtroom scene ended that day with suspended sentences for some and a continuation of the case for others, and Tom Cornell drove A.J. back home. Saturday morning saw him stricken with a heart attack. He was taken to St. Luke's hospital where he died in the early evening. Sunday he was to have met with Archbishop Helder Camara of Recife, Brazil.

On Monday, February 13th, he was to have spoken at Community Church with David Dellinger, and Barbara Deming about their recent visits to Hanoi and the meeting turned into a memorial meeting instead.

A.J. was founder and director of Brookwood Labor College at Katonah, New York. (The Reuther Brothers were alumni.) He had not only opposed war since 1918 but also had served the cause of labor, becoming involved in textile strikes in New England and in New Jersey and was arrested for picketing both in Lawrence, Massachusetts and Paterson, New Jersey.

Peter Maurin and I first met him when he took over the directorship of the old Presbyterian Labor Temple where he served from 1937 to 1940. As I remember it, the Labor Temple on the corner of Fourteenth Street and Second Avenue, functioned then as Community Church does now, and Peter Maurin felt that here was a beginning of what he called a new synthesis, an attempt to apply the teachings of the Gospel to the world today, the world around us. Above all, A.J. felt that war could not be reconciled with the spirit of Christ. "War does not bring peace, it merely breeds more wars," he said.

The thing that marked him especially was his relationship to the young. He listened to them and they listened to him, well "over thirty" though he was. He never judged the young, nor criticized them. He criticized the social order and by his writing as well as by his actions, tried to bring about a change in that social order. He walked on picket lines, he trespassed on missile bases, he was to be found in courtrooms and in jails as well as in the lecture hall and behind the editorial desk. He truly worked to make that kind of a world where it is easier to be good.

Mass Protest

Who are they, these 23 young people who went into the Cathedral on Fifth Avenue, while a score or so others picketed outside, at the ten o'clock Sunday Mass late in January, all with signs folded up underneath their coats? At the offertory, right after the sermon, they got up from their aisle seats where they had been following the ritual of the Mass, and displaying their signs, started to walk down the center aisle. The signs read, THOU SHALT NOT KILL.

At the same time twice twenty-three detectives tore the signs from their hands and hurried the protestors out of the Cathedral. The story made the front pages of the New York *Times* and also was repeated again and again on radio (we do not have a television so I do not know whether there was such covering then or later.) Aside from the tearing up of the signs there was no disorder, but all was accomplished with such dispatch that those who took part did not think that any of the congregation saw either signs or those who carried them. Announcement had just been made from the altar or pulpit however, that the congregation should remain calm, and later the charge was made that the parishioners experienced "emotional upset."

"We would have torn them apart," one old Italian woman in our neighborhood said, "if that had happened at old St. Patrick's," which I for one doubt. There is a strong anarchistic streak in all Italians. This neighborhood is their village, not to be confounded with Greenwich or East Village, and they have their own government of streets and neighborhood associations. In a way they are used to us, we have lived in Little Italy so long (fifteen years on Mott Street) and right now, the ten apartments the *Catholic Worker*'s family live in are just off Mott or Mulberry Streets. Once eight years ago when I had been arrested for protesting compulsory air raid drills and was about to be sentenced together with a dozen others, the pastor at old St. Patrick's asked me to speak at a Mother's Day communion breakfast, and when I told him I might be in jail at the time, he told me the invitation stood, and I was able to give the talk.

There would have been no occasion for such a demonstration at Mott Street's old St. Patrick's because it was the nationalist attitude of Cardinal Spellman which the young people were protesting. "My country, right or wrong," he had said, And "Nothing less than total victory . . . This is a war for civilization."

According to the *Village Voice*, one of the defendants, Richard Lourie, said that each of the detectives had a typewritten slip of paper with offenses listed: unlawful assembly, disturbing a religious meeting, creating a public nuisance, conspiracy and disorderly conduct. "But after we were there several hours a more serious charge was added, unlawful entry. The police were very polite but we didn't have anything to eat until seven o'clock when they fed us bread with marmalade and a cup of cocoa."

Could this be possible? In all the jail experiences around the *Catholic Worker* and a number of the editors have been jailed, we never had more than tea and two slices of bread with a slice of bologna between that tasted like rubber bands. Could it have been that the chancery office provided this little treat, marmalade and cocoa,—perhaps suffering from misgivings at their harshness?

I had not been at all shocked myself at the action of this group, all of whom knew each other, and who were part of larger groups protesting against the war in Vietnam. Catholics themselves, in stories of the lives of the saints, have been guilty of much more violent behavior. His own monks tried to poison St. Benedict and there was scandalous behaviour within the monastery itself, as a protest then against the so-called rigor of the saint. There must have been an awful fuss made too when St. Francis insisted on offering up the holy Sacrifice at Christmas in a stable.

One might say the chancery office behaved too harshly, and the judge later in the day did nothing to increase the respect of the protestors for law and order, with his innuendos. At least ten of those arrested taught at New York University, New York and Brooklyn Community colleges, New School, and Fairleigh Dickinson, and it was a first arrest for all but two, and they had been arrested in previous demonstrations.

I have always been struck by the unconscious esteem in which the Church is held, and the shock people feel when churchmen and Christians in general do not live up to their professions of faith. I can remember thinking, over forty years ago, before I was a Catholic, "What is this Church that people can say of those who profess membership in it, 'And he is a Catholic!' in tones of condemnation because they were not living up to their professions of belief?" It was so, I felt, that Cardinal Spellman was being judged. It was one thing for him to be visiting the soldiers, so far from home and family at Christmas time, but for him to *not love his enemy*, the so-called enemy,—not to follow the peace-directives of the Holy Father, Pope Paul V . . .

It is heartbreaking to think how often we all dishonor God the Father of us all, by not acting as though we believed that God was Father of all, that all men are brothers. As St. Paul wrote, "Because of you, the name of God is dishonored among the Gentiles."

I would not have participated in this demonstration—could it not be that these young people felt a sense of God's presence there, a sense of worship, of awe too, as I have always felt in church, a place set apart for worship? No, I would not myself have chosen such a place for a demonstration, but I have permitted my name to be used by the group in their effort to raise funds to defend themselves.

Vietnam

One of the visitors to Hanoi in January was Msgr. Georg Hussler, secretary general of a West German Catholic Welfare organization which is part of Caritas International and has for some time been making a financial contribution to the North Vietnam Red Cross and to the South Vietnamese National Liberation Front's Red Cross Organization and to the Red Cross in South Vietnam. Msgr. Hussler is the first Catholic high-ranking functionary, according to Harrison Salisbury of the New York *Times*, to visit North Vietnam since the establishment of the Communist regime, the first contact between Rome and Hanoi since 1954 when the Communists took over.

Here are the statistics about Catholics in North Vietnam, according to Msgr. Hussler. There are about 700,000 Catholics in the north. The generally accepted figure for the south is a million.

In Hanoi itself, which is not as heavily Catholic as the countryside, there are twelve churches with ten priests and about 20,000 worshippers. There are from 300 to 400 priests serving in North Vietnam but no Catholic schools. Children are taught at church and especially during two regular vacation periods each year. There are still a number of nuns and "many convents operating," the churchmen said, but conceded that many nuns had gone south. They said the official position was non-interference in religious matters.

The Vatican itself expressed gratitude to the New York *Times* for the Hanoi dispatches of Harrison Salisbury who was the first American newsman to report from North Vietnam, though many European newsmen had been sending similar reports.

Our dear friend A. J. Muste visited both Saigon and Hanoi these last months and met with hostility only in Saigon. A group of women, including the valiant Barbara Deming, also visited Hanoi and spoke for the women in the peace movement. Three times I have been invited to go to Vietnam and three times I have refused, not seeing any possible good served by my leaving my work at home. But for once, I regret my age, and wish that I were younger, and then indeed I would want to go as nurse or in some such service capacity, and so work for peace. I have been in too many demonstrations, have spent my short sentences in jail, and once again I long to witness as the Little Brothers and Little Sisters of Brother Charles de Foucauld are witnessing today, in North and South Vietnam. Little St. Therese Martin was almost sent to Hanoi Carmel but could not on account of her failing health. There are two Carmels in Vietnam, one in Saigon and one in Hanoi, and they are praying, we know, not for victory but for peace. Not just for peace in Vietnam, but for peace in the world. But we can only "hope against hope." If peace were declared in Vietnam tomorrow, there would still be world suffering, famine, injustice on a giant scale and the war between the rich and the destitute would go on. It was good to read this profession of faith of Habacuc in the Old Testament in the Lenten Lauds for Friday:

Though the fig tree blossom not
    nor fruit be on the vines,
Though the yield of the olive fail
    and the terraces produce no
        nourishment.
Though the flocks disappear from the fold
    and there be no herd in the stalls,
Yet, will I rejoice in the Lord
    and exult in my saving God.
God, my Lord, is my strength.

May 1967

Here is a gem I found in C. S. Lewis' *Letters* (Harcourt, Brace and World):

"The advantage of a fixed form of service is that we know what is coming. Extempore public prayer has this difficulty: we don't know whether we can join in it until we've heard it —it might be phony or heretical. We are therefore called upon to carry on a critical and devotional activity at the same moment, two things hardly compatible. In a fixed form we ought to have gone through the motions before in our private prayer; the rigid form really sets our devotions free. I also find that the more rigid it is, the easier to keep our thoughts from straying. Also it prevents getting too completely eaten up by whatever happens to be the preoccupation of the moment, war, and election or whatnot. The permanent shape of Christianity shows through. I don't see how the extempore method can help but become provincial and I think it has a great tendency to direct attention to the minister rather than to God."

C. S. Lewis "speaks to my condition," as the Quakers say.

The New Liturgy

Which leads me into reflections on the new Masses, the intimate Masses, the colloquial Masses, the folk-song Masses, and so on. By the intimate I mean those where everyone gathers close around the altar inside the sanctuary, as close to the priest as possible. Even the young ones have a hard time standing, shifting from one leg to the other, the girls with high heels ("If I'd known it was to be like this I would have worn my sneakers," one said), the older rheumatic ones with ever-increasing pain. By the intimate I also mean those offered in small apartments before a small group. I understand that permission for this has been granted in Harlem for some time now, and priests are offering the Mass in the poorest of homes block by block in their parishes, during the week— bringing Christ most literally to the people. This is wonderful.

But there is also the attempt made by some young priests to reach the young, to make the Mass meaningful to the young (the bourgeois, educated, middle-class young) where novelty is supposed to attract the attention but which, as far as I can see, has led to drawing these same young ones completely away from the "people of God," "the masses" and worship in the parish church. There is the suggestion of contempt here, for the people, and for the faith of the inarticulate ones of the earth, "the ancient lowly" as they have been called. Their perseverance in worship, week after week, holyday after holyday, has always impressed me and filled my heart with a sense of love for all my fellow Catholics, even Birchites, bigots, racists, priests and lay people alike, whom I could term "my enemies" whom I am bidden to love. Our worst enemies are of our own household, Scripture says. We are united, however, as people in marriage are united, by the deepest spiritual bond, participation in the sacraments, so that we have become "one flesh" in the Mystical Body.

I do love the guitar Masses, and the Masses where the recorder and the flute are played, and sometimes the glorious and triumphant trumpet. But I do not want them every day, any more than we ever wanted solemn Gregorian Requiem Masses every day. They are for the occasion. The guitar Masses I have heard from one end of the country to the other are all different and have a special beauty of their own. I have been a participant (it is not that I have just *heard* them) in such Masses with the Franciscan Brothers in Santa Barbara, with the students at St. Louis University, at the McGill Newman Club in Montreal and many other Newman meetings, and in Barrytown, New York, where the Christian Brothers, our neighbors, have a folk Mass every Saturday at eleven-fifteen. They are joyful and happy Masses indeed and supposed to attract the young. But the beginning of faith is something different. The "*fear* of the Lord is the beginning of wisdom." Fear in the sense of *awe*.

Here is another quotation from C. S. Lewis, in *Miracles* (Fontana Books; paperback):

Men are reluctant to pass over from the nation of an abstract and negative deity to the living God... .. An "impersonal God"—well and good. A subjective God of beauty, truth and goodness, inside our own heads—better still. A formless life force surging through us, a vast power which we can tap—best of all.

But God himself, alive, pulling at the other end of the cord, perhaps approaching at an infinite speed, the hunter, king, husband—that is quite another matter. There comes a moment when the children who have been playing burglars hush suddenly: was that a real footstep in the hall? There comes the moment when people who have been dabbling in religion (Man's search for God!) suddenly draw back. Suppose we really found Him? We never meant it to come to that! Worse still, supposing He had found us?

STRIKE LEADER COMES EAST

Last year we published at least eight stories on the progress of the "grape strike" which has been going on in California since September of 1965. During these two years of struggle and suffering there have been victories against what would seem to be overwhelming odds. Contracts have been signed with powerful growers, such as the DiGiorgio Ranches in Delano, Borrego Springs and Arvin, and on July 18th a representation election will be held at Marysville, the last DiGiorgio ranch not under contract. Contracts have been signed which the workers themselves negotiated with DiGiorgio, which have brought them higher wages, free health insurance and a grievance procedure to settle complaints.

Contracts have also been signed with Schenley. "Now we got rest rooms," one worker said, "and a place to wash our hands and paper to dry them. They put in some ice water in the summertime. Before we had no rest rooms. We had to walk out into the fields, and far too, because men and women work together."

One of the ranches of the Christian Brothers has signed a contract and three others will follow after an election.

We have been getting our news from two of our correspondents in California, and from the organ of the farm worker, *El Malcriado,* which is published both in Spanish and in English and has been edited from the beginning by Bill Esher, who was a member of the Oakland Catholic Worker group.

This last month we received a visit from the leader of the strikers, Cesar Chavez, himself. He and a few members of the Association of Catholic Trade Unionists spent a Sunday morning with us at the CW house at Chrystie Street and later on Monday night we saw him again at Union Theological Seminary, where those interested gathered to see what they could do to help on the East Coast. So far there has been no organizing among the people who pick apples and grapes in New York State, and potatoes in Jersey and Long Island. (New York is the third largest apple-growing state in the country.)

From 1934 on we have been concerned with this problem of destitution among farm workers, and we are particularly interested in Chavez because of his emphasis on nonviolence. He has a true recognition of the overall problems of agriculture, the problems of the small farmer and the large grower, what the factory system of farming has done to the morale of the employer, and the steady growth of class-war attitudes on the part of both grower and worker. But he has recognized that the problem is insoluble without tapping the deep religious instincts of the people he is leading for patience and perseverance. The banners of Our Lady of Guadalupe have been prominent in the strike and in the march on Sacramento, which took place during Lent this year, just as they were present during the violent wars for independence in Mexico in the past. When Cesar Chavez saw the picture of Our Lady of Guadalupe which has been hanging on our walls for so long that it is dark with age, he immediately left his seat at the table and stood before it a few moments before we began to talk.

He looks just like his pictures, perhaps even younger, straight black hair, face browned by the sun, and brown as an Indian's is brown. I remembered Archbishop Miranda, himself a Mexican, telling me proudly some years ago, "The Mexicans are a new race, a new people, neither Indian nor Spanish."

Chavez does not talk much in such conversations as these,

299

perhaps because there are so many more articulate people around him. The Rev. Jim Drake, member of the migrant ministry and active in the strike from the beginning, recently arrested for praying in front of the Capitol in Texas where the fight to organize has spread (so far without success) did a great deal of the explaining at the CW and at the Union meeting. I would like very much to hear Chavez speaking to the members of the Farm Workers Organizing Committee; or I would like to have a record of his talk at the close of the pilgrimage into Sacramento. When I do hear him, I believe that I will have heard three of the most vital leaders of our time, the other two being Martin Luther King and Fidel Castro. The first two are proponents of nonviolent revolution in our social order and Castro the first successful leader of a violent revolution in our hemisphere in recent times.

Chavez mentioned that the Catholic Workers from the Bay area had helped greatly with truckloads of food and clothing for the strikers. I was interested to learn that the housing where the strike occurred was the same that I visited during the Roosevelt period when the government put up such migrant camps as those portrayed in the movie, *The Grapes of Wrath*. They are still being used today, but now they are owned by the growers and rented to the workers.

The Housing Authority will build new units, a hundred in each camp, but the camps in Tulare County will be torn down by July 1st. The strikers are paying eighteen dollars a month, and the Housing Authority director says that the new units are sixty dollars a month. Actually, farm workers were paying eighteen a month for one shack and an additional eight dollars for a second in order to have bedroom space. A rent strike started when the rent was raised to twenty-two dollars a month for the first shack and eight for the second.

Chavez was in the East to receive an award from the League for Industrial Democracy in New York City and to visit Ithaca, where a group of Cornell students and others are interested in organizing the migrants in New York state.

He left the office of the Catholic Worker while the Sunday "line" was in full swing, and set out for a late Mass before driving up state to Ithaca. On Monday, in the driving rain and snow, he came back to New York to the larger meeting at Knox Hall, Union Theological Seminary.

The matter of a boycott of Vermouth Industries and all bottled goods bearing the name of Tribuno was taken up.

The aim is to force a contract with Perelli-Minetti and Sons, a Delano area grower where an unauthorized contract with the Teamster's union was signed while the farm workers were on strike. Actually, what the Farm Workers Organizing Committee is urging, and in this case by means of a boycott, is that a fair and impartial election be held.

Assumption Abbey, a Benedictine Foundation in North Dakota, gains a royalty on all bottles of Assumption Abbey liquor sold, in return for the use of its name. We urge the monks not to renew their agreement with the Perelli-Minetti people for the use of the name "Assumption Abbey." And if a settlement is not made we ask our friends to write to the abbot, asking him to take this up with the Perelli-Minetti people.

The head of Vermouth Industries is John Tribuno, whose office is in New York City. Forty per cent of his vermouth comes from what *El Malcriado* calls the Perelli-Minetti Octopus, which is made up of 26 interlocking family corporations.

Again we advise our readers to subscribe to the farm workers' paper, *El Malcriado* (Box 1060, Delano, California, subscription price $2.50 per year). The last issue contains stories of: the struggle of the farm workers in Texas, and Arizona; congressional hearings to bring the farm workers under the National Labor Relations Act; asparagus pickers' jobs in the Stockton area being taken by imported workers from Mexico while local Mexicans, Anglos and Filipino workers are left unemployed; stories too of a retired San Francisco longshoreman who is teaching the Mexican children of Delano how to play the recorder and giving them "a sound background in musical notation." There are art classes too for children and adults, and writing classes under one of the men from El Teatro Campesino, which brought a play about the strike up and down the West Coast to union audiences. There are also stories about the credit union, the co-op, the Farm Workers Service Center, and a co-op gasoline station which opened a month ago and which, as we sat there talking at the seminary on April 25, was damaged by two cartridge bombs which shattered the windows.

Cesar Chavez told us of the piece of land which the union had bought, seceding as it were from the town of Delano, and setting up some of their own services, which included a blood bank and a child-care center for strikers and workers.

These are all small beginnings and they are accompanied

by the suffering, the misunderstandings, the discouragements of all beginnings. But already great victories have been won when one considers the Schenley and DiGiorgio and Christian Brothers contracts.

When finally farm workers are organized in one small town after another and all together begin to feel their strength in this largest of all the United States' industries, which is agriculture, they may begin to have a vision of the kind of society where the workers will also be owners, of their own homes, a few acres, and eventually of large holdings in the form of cooperatives. Perhaps the growers have much to learn from them, and they from the growers, though it is hard to imagine these successful businessmen and owners of factories in the fields becoming willing to teach their workers how to run such large holdings. But such conversions towards a life on the land have taken place, by force, through revolution, or peaceably by a people persecuted and oppressed, as in the foundation of the kibbutzim of Israel, described in Martin Buber's *Paths in Utopia*.

June 1967

MICHAEL GOLD
(APRIL 12, 1894-MAY 14, 1967)

I last saw Mike Gold two years ago when I visited Oakland, where he was living with Elizabeth, his wife. She and I had gathered shells and rocks together on the beaches of Staten Island ten years ago, just as Mike and I had explored the beaches forty years before, picnicking with artists Maurice Becker and Hugo Gellert, sometimes on a Staten Island beach and sometimes at Palisades Park. It was the year the old *Masses* was suppressed, and during the last months of its existence there was a general feeling of irresponsibility, stemming from our incapacity to do anything in the face of the war into which we had just been dragged, after a Presidential election won with the slogan "He kept us out of the war." We were marking time.

When I first met Mike I had been working on the *New York Call*, a socialist paper that had a few anarchists and members of the Industrial Workers of the World on the staff. One editor was an A.F.L. man and another supported the Amalgamated Clothing Workers, which was out of the A.F.L. at the time, just as some unions are out of the A.F.L.-C.I.O. now. When it came to all the conflicts after the Russian revolution, we were young enough not to pay much attention to the old guard, but instead to rejoice in a victorious revolt of the proletariat and the peasants of Russia. We all went to meetings, to picnics, to dances at Webster Hall, stayed up all night and walked the streets, and sat on the piers and sang. Great things were happening in the world, along with the senseless capitalistic war, which to us represented the suffering and death that came before the victorious resurrection. I thought in those terms then. "Unless the seed fall into the ground and die, it remaineth alone. But if it die it bears much fruit." The suffering and the death that accompanied war and revolution seemed to make the keenness of our joy the more poignant. The revolution was world-shaking, it liberated the people, the ancient lowly, the burden bearers, the poor, the destitute, and opened up to them a new life. We longed ourselves to be able to take part in that suffering.

We were far away from it all, of course. We were young, we had found ourselves, in that we had a cause, and we served it in our writing. It was through his writing that I came to know Mike. In the summer of 1917 I had been left alone in the office of the *Masses* as an editor's assistant while Floyd Dell was on vacation and Max Eastman away on a money-raising and speaking expedition. I opened the office and answered the mail and sent back the work of some eminent poets with rejection slips and one written word, "Sorry." In my haste to get through with office duty and go out into the streets, to meetings, and to the beaches, the work of the *Masses* did not seem of vital importance.

I walked the streets of the East Side, which I had come to love (I had been living there for a year and a half), down on Cherry Street, on East Broadway, on Madison Street. I knew the Jews and their life there, I bathed with the women in those little bath houses (there were no baths or hot water in the tenements). I visited Mike's home on Chrystie Street, down the street from the present location of the Catholic Worker, and his mother, a stern and beautiful woman who wore the wig and observed the dietary laws, offered me food, even though I was a shiksa, but she did not speak to me.

My suffering at that time was brief, but Mike's was profound. I went to jail in Washington, upholding the rights of political prisoners. An anarchist then as I am now, I have never used the vote that the women won by their demonstrations before the White House during that period. But Mike was suffering because of the threat of the draft, which hung over all young men then, as it does today. It was a physical, as well as a mental and spiritual anguish and it undermined his health so that Max Eastman helped him to get away to Mexico, where the "draft dodgers," as they are always contemptuously termed, were taking refuge. (I would like to call attention here to the fact that one of the saints of the Catholic Church, the Cure of Ars, St. John Marie Vianney, a Frenchman who is still famous as a patron of parish priests, was a draft dodger and hid out in barns to escape the draft during the Napoleonic wars.)

In those days conscientious objectors had no rights. There was no alternative service. There were no discussions as to whether you were opposed to all wars or only the present one, whether your conviction was a religious one or not. Mike was certainly not opposed to war as such. He thought that the revolution had to be a violent one, and that although the workers did not want violence or advocate it, it would be forced upon them, and then they would be exercising their right to defend themselves and their dear ones. His faith in the class struggle and violent revolution never wavered over the years.

Mike came back from Mexico not long after the war was over, and it was at this time that he took the name Mike Gold, rather than Irwin Granich, which was his family name. It will always be as Mike Gold that he will be remembered.

I saw Mike some years later in Chicago, where I worked briefly for Bob Minor on the *Liberator*. Then I returned to New York and, thanks to the sale of my first novel to Hollywood, I was able to buy a beach bungalow on a section of Staten Island that is almost as undeveloped today as it was then. I was living a married life, spending a good deal of time reading and going through a painful and tortured, yet joyful process of conversion to a public acknowledgment of a faith. It was painful because I had to give up a common-law husband with whom I was very much in love and with whom I still feel a most loving friendship. I write of these personal matters because Mike was very much around at that time;

two of his brothers had bought a beach bungalow three doors down the road from mine, and we all swam and dug clams and fished together and spent long hours on the beach. One of his brothers was married and had two little children who played with my two-year-old daughter. Mike, who loved kids and did not yet have any of his own, came down often to be with us all.

Never for a moment did Mike try to argue me out of the step I was about to take. My small daughter was already baptized and I tried to get to Mass every Sunday in the little village church, although I was not yet a baptized Catholic. Mike was editor of the *New Masses* at the time, and I wrote a few things for him. He seemed to understand my misery and to sense that there had to be a price to pay, sometimes a heartbreaking price, in following one's vocation. Neither revolutions nor faith are won without keen suffering. For me Christ was not to be bought for thirty pieces of silver but with my heart's blood. We buy not cheap in this market. Because I was so unhappy I clung to my old friends. I did not know a single Catholic and I suppose I considered Mike my oldest friend.

Mike was indirectly involved with the beginning of the Catholic Worker. In 1932, I was doing some free-lance writing and Mike's brother George was one of the leaders of the hunger march that was to converge on Washington in December. George and Mike used to drop in to see me where I was living with my brother and his wife on the East Side, and I became so enthusiastic about the march that I went down to cover it for the *Commonweal,* along with the late Mary Heaton Vorse, who was covering it for, I think, the *Atlantic Monthly*. It was the march and the devout prayers I said at the shrine of the Immaculate Conception at Catholic University, that brought the French peasant and teacher, Peter Maurin, to my doorstep to start me editing the *Catholic Worker*.

Peter Maurin was a philosophical anarchist in the tradition of Kropotkin and never missed an opportunity to express his distrust of the State. He agreed with Jefferson that the less government there is, the better. He wanted to stay out of the N.R.A. (National Recovery Administration) and all the other initialed projects and he endorsed the union movement only as long as it kept the State out of its bargaining with the bosses. And of course *bargaining* was a bad word; labor was not a commodity to be bought and sold and bargained for. Man by his labor was creative, working for the common good, creating order out of chaos. Peter wanted to rebuild society within the shell of the old society, which meant patience, suffering and endurance, the kind of non-violence that characterizes the work of Cesar Chavez in Delano, California and the Rio Grande Valley of Texas.

One day, in the fifties, after Peter Maurin was dead, Mike, his wife Elizabeth and their two sons Carl and Nicholas visited us on Peter Maurin Farm on Staten Island. They had brought me a gift, an old print with a painted representation of a pilgrimage to the shrine of St. Anne of Brittany. They had brought it from France, carefully rolled in a newspaper. We framed it and hung it in the dining room of the farm. St. Anne is the patron saint of grandmothers, since she was the mother of the Blessed Virgin and the grandmother of Jesus of Nazareth. We still talked of how man's freedom could be protected, how man's basic needs could be provided for through collectives, or cooperatives, or farming communes, as Peter Maurin always called them, and how the State could progressively wither away. But we always came back to the problem of the use of force in bringing about the common good. For example, Mike pointed out that the *kibbutzim* were well-armed and part of a powerful state they had helped to build up.

I remembered the one time Mike had turned bitter against me and the *Catholic Worker*. "The brotherly love the *Catholic Worker* preaches would be more understandable if it were not that they were pro-Franco during the Spanish civil war," he wrote in his column "Change the World." We were not, of course, pro-Franco but pacifists, followers of Gandhi in our struggle to build a spirit of non-violence. But in those days we got it from both sides; it was a holy war to most Catholics, just as world revolution is holy war to Communists. I call attention to these fundamental differences about religion and the attitude to force to show how there can be strong personal friendship between a Catholic and a Communist and constant seeking of concordances and agreements.

It was indeed more than a personal friendship; it was a friendship between families. Mike was best man at my sister's wedding forty years ago and last week, when her son wrote to her of Mike's death, he recalled his gentle and loving spirit. He indeed had a gentle and loving spirit but some of his writing was strong stuff, because of the bitterness that the sight of poverty and human distress always inspired in him.

We lament his passing and send our sympathetic love to Elizabeth, thanking God that Mike left her sons and grandchildren to comfort her.

September 1967

If I don't wake up early enough to have a spiritual reading before rising to face the day, I feel cheated of a sustenance I badly need, considering the crowded days of conferences and visitors all summer in both country and city. This morning my reading was again from Father Ernesto Balducci's book, "John—the Transitional Pope" published by McGraw-Hill in 1964 and a real treasure. I have quoted from him before, and I have a special esteem for Father Balducci because he is a conscientious objector to war, and has suffered for it as the late Father Lorenzo Milani did. The quotation from Pope John he cites on page 127 is this:

"The love of truth. On the day of my episcopal consecration the Church gave me a particular mandate concerning it: 'Let him (the bishop) choose humility and truth and never forsake them for any flattery or threats. Let him not consider light to be darkness or darkness light; let him not call evil good, or good evil. Let him learn from wise men and fools, so that he may profit from all.'"

These powerful words are used in the consecration of bishops, and I think of them now as I rejoice in the fact that six or seven Catholic bishops have come out against the Vietnam war. That the lastest one to do so is Archbishop James Davis, of Santa Fe, New Mexico, reminds me of that great book of Willa Cather, "Death Comes for the Archbishop" which is about the first Bishop of Santa Fe and a most beautiful story of the period and surroundings.

September 8th, birthday of the Blessed Virgin. Twenty-two years ago today a dozen or so of us made a pilgrimage of penance to the shrine of Mother Cabrini, walking from 115 Mott St., where the Catholic Worker House of Hospitality was then located. We walked from Canal Street along Broadway to 208th Street. The Second World War had just ended. The bomb had been dropped in August on Hiroshima and Nagasaki (any means to an end!) and we have been living in fear and in "brush fire wars" ever since. The war goes on in

307

Vietnam. If it ceased tomorrow, it would be going on in some other quarter of the globe and we, as the richest nation, making so much money out of our armanents, would be very much involved still. The causes of war are still with us: fear, hatred, greed, and "each man seeking his own."

One of the early Fathers of the Church once wrote that if we could stand on a mountain top and see all the misery and tragedy of the world, we could not survive the horror of it. Now we have television and can indeed see what is happening, can witness the murder of Lee Harvey Oswald, the torture of prisoners in Vietnam, the death of our own soldiers—horror upon horror, until the mind and soul are blunted, sated with blood, blood which cries out to heaven. Indeed Jesus is in agony until the end of the world.

Juliana of Norwich said, and it is for our comfort, "the worst has already happened and been remedied." The worst being the Fall, and the remedy is still with us, "the same yesterday and today and forever." Even today, there are samplings of heaven, in love expressed, in peace maintained. "All the way to heaven is heaven, because He said, 'I am the Way.' " (All the way to hell can be hell too.)

Work is the good healer, the great remedy for many ills. Right now as I write, in the midst of the Friday hubbub of trucks with horns blaring, gears shifting at each light, the grinding up of the refuse of the city in sanitation trucks, the shriek of sirens, there is a labor of love going on. Two young men and two young women are engaged in thoroughly cleaning and "de-bugging" one of the apartments of this house of hospitality on Kenmare Street, where we will continue to live for two or three months more, until the house on First Street is renovated. There are three apartments on the second floor, one on the third, one on the fourth, and one on the fifth,—two apartments for men and four for women. A constant check is needed to keep them livable, and young men do not like to be checked, nor are they orderly. There are 25 apartments altogether in the house. The tenants are mostly Chinese or Italians and some of the apartments are visions of comfort, because these are the kind of tenants who have lived here, in what I call our Italian village for thirty years or more. The house is well built but slanting, a bit sunk or settled since the subways were built underneath. The ceilings are high and it looks out on two streets, so we have plenty of light and air—and plenty of fumes too.

Huge trucks go by loaded with steel drums of all colors,

with steel casings of mysterious and fantastic shapes, and huge round bodied trucks, which carry sugar, syrup, molasses and wine. I thought as I watched them this morning that if there were a depression—if peace should break out—these trucks would cease and there would be quiet on Kenmare Street. Once in my life time, as I travelled up and down the East Coast in the Thirties, I saw dead factories; wheels had stopped turning, no smoke, no fumes came from stacks and chimneys, the air was clear and quiet, and birds sang and weeds, including my favorite sweet clover, grew all around the factories.

But I must quit dreaming and go on with this writing. The trouble is, so much is happening day after day that it is hard to recall what happened during these past weeks that I must report on.

Last month, my friends, the Don Browns of Corning, New York, gave me hospitality on one of my "rural rides", to use Cobbett's title. Corning is in Steuben County, west of Binghamton and south of the migrant country. Negroes work on the potatoes, Puerto Ricans in the muck lands where they were then harvesting lettuce, and later the whites will harvest grapes. Don, who is a chemist in the Corning Glass Works, has long been concerned with the plight of the migrant. A hundred and twenty-five bills aimed at improving their condition have been introduced in Congress, but they have never got past committee. Whether or not the National Labor Relations Act will be broadened to include the farm worker is now being debated in Washington. It seems to me that this debate has been going on for a long time. The right of the farm worker to organize is under discussion, and some church groups are in favor of it, but with no right for the workers to strike for better wages and conditions.

They are not using the word *migrant* on the West Coast. Many have settled on the land, and though they travel to harvest the crops, it is within the limits of the Long Valley that they work. Some of the Negroes working in Steuben County have travelled all the way from Florida, and many go as far as Maine. But some of them settle in New York State, and Don Brown told me something about the unspeakable hardship they suffer in the cold of the winter in the packing sheds, where they sort the potatoes but often it is only a few days work a week.

I saw two of the great packing sheds, Schuler's and Mc-

Gunnicle's, great modern plants. But down an old railroad track nearby there were ten shacks where single men lived. We visited two camps near Avoka in which the houses were made of cement block with screened windows. In addition to a long dormitory with double-decker beds (bare mattresses and blankets) there was a kitchen where the workers could prepare their food.

It was a hot day, and in spite of the screened windows the flies came in through the door where the screen had broken through and hung about the bare light bulbs in the center of the dormitory. This was one of the best of the camps and was run by a Negro farm couple. Since he and his wife were both out in the fields, they obviously could not keep the place clean, and the entire place looked incredibly dreary to me. But then our own houses of hospitality present this same aspect, over and over again. The volunteer workers who come to us have to be ready for the most thankless labor, which they know, while they are doing it, will have to be done over and over again, week after week, day after day. It is hard to do a good job when you know that when you leave things will relapse into the same dirty clutter and confusion. One can only endure it by living with it permanently and continuing to cleanse the Augean stables. A grim thought, but this is both voluntary poverty and respect for manual labor. The first thing St. Francis after his conversion did was to repair a church, thinking the voice of God which he heard say to him "Francis, repair my Church" meant literally just that.

There are 120 camps within forty miles of Corning. Some are barracks-like houses and others are just truck bodies, very close together, so if one shack catches fire, everything is in danger. We asked one Negro who lived next to a shack where two men had been burned to death how his house had been spared and he said, "The Lord Jesus just put his arms around my house and saved it for me." Was this mischievous humor, or did he mean it? It is hard to think of Christianity as being alive when you see our fellow humans living under such conditions.

It is hard to call our brothers blacks, somehow (and should it be capitalized?) but today that is what they wish to be called. First it was Negro, then colored, and now blacks, and certainly the majority are not black any more than we are all "pink" as Bernard Shaw called us. But maybe the men I saw are not as sophisticated as the city Negro. Perhaps I should say Afro-Americans. Anyway, they have their own church and their own minister who preaches good long sermons, so the migrant ministry spent four hundred dollars on playground equipment so that the children could go out to play during the services, which take place Wednesdays and Sundays. The church is the center of the county and folk come from as far as thirty-five miles. It is so far away that they can shout praise and jubilation to the Lord as loud and long as they want, just as I have heard them do in Florida and even in Rome, where Langston Hughes' *Black Nativity* was put on, to the joy and delight of the Roman audience.

I saw the broken-down houses where not one but a number of families lived. In one such house there were twenty-four people living—men, women and children. I saw a corn crib which a young couple had lined with broken-up cartons to insulate it and where they had burned sticks of wood in an open pail to warm themselves while a child was born to them in the dead of winter. I saw the debris of another camp where one man raving with the fever of pneumonia had staggered out and fallen into an old pit which had once been covered by an old outhouse long since used for kindling wood. He was unable to get out and was found frozen to death the next day.

Father Paul Hanley Furfey once said to me in a conference that it is obvious from the 25th chapter of St. Matthew that God does not forgive ignorance. "When did we see you naked and not cover you, a stranger and never made you welcome? And the Lord will answer, 'I tell you solemnly, in so far as you neglected to do this to one of the least of these, you neglected to do it to me.'"

I remember how long we lived on Maryfarm at Newburgh, in the midst of apple orchards, and yet never knew who picked the crops, or realized how many of the workers were hidden away on the back roads in shacks never seen by those who drive by on the highways. It was only when we picked up an old sick Negro on the highway that we began to see the immediacy of the problem. It is all around us, just as every city is filled with ghettoes and slums.

If we keep harping on these things, it is in order to arouse the conscience. Because here in this Hudson River valley, when these black brothers and sisters of ours wish to settle, they are not made welcome. They may find jobs, the hard jobs, but how to find housing? That is the problem.

So this year, beginning next week in fact, a day-care center is being opened at the Catholic Worker Farm at Tivoli, to care for the pre-school schildren of the migrant families who have come north to harvest the apples. There will be children ranging from eight months old to six years. The center will be under the auspices of New York State, and workers, equipment and transportation are being provided by the State. Mrs. Ann George of Albany represents the New York State Migrant Child Care Committee, and is ably assisted by Mrs. Pearl Johnson, and Mr. Gus Rhodes and Mr. John Murray of the Dutchess County Office of Economic Opportunity.

I will be away while this activity takes place, so perhaps Deane will give an account of it in her October column. We are merely providing the space, the former casino and grounds, which are ample for the children, but planning the program has involved many telephone calls and consultations and our own education in the process. A migrant grandmother and an eighteen-year-old girl farm worker as well as our neighbor Mrs. Lorraine Freeman, and others will be working with the program, and there is a daily visiting of camps and mothers and children to prepare for it. Yesterday two men from Syracuse showed up from the State Day Care Training Center to bring cots, cribs, playpens, tables and chairs and a beautiful assortment of well built children's toys.

We've been having adults use the facilities of this farm in discussion all summer and many young swimmers in the pool, but these will be the youngest children we have yet accommodated, and at the sweetest age.

And as for me, I am setting out for Rome again.

From the eleventh to the eighteenth of October there will be an International Congress of the Laity, a gathering of twenty-five hundred Catholic lay people from all over the world, and, as I understand it, the talks and discussions will be in every language and simultaneously translated, just as at the United Nations, so that one will be able to don earphones and understand representatives from Africa, Asia and Europe. Our dear friend Marguerite Tjader Harris is taking care of my expenses and I shall try to repay her by giving a good account of the trip and the conferences for our ninety thousand readers.

Do we have so many? Who knows. We send out the papers, and they go to libraries and schools as well as to individuals. On the other hand, I once caught Mrs. Rubino, an old friend on East Fifteenth Street, lining her garbage can with a copy of the CW. But of course we get letters beginning, "I found your paper in a dentist's office"; or "I found your paper in a coal mine six miles out under the Atlantic Ocean," or "I found your paper under a mattress in a cheap hotel in Tampico." These last two testimonials as to how far the *Catholic Worker* travels are literally true, though we received them years ago.

More recently, on board ship in 1965 on my way home from the fast in Rome at which I participated, during the last session of the Second Vatican Council, I received at my table, tourist class, a bottle of wine, sent to me with the compliments of the purser of that ship of the American Export line. When he came to see me later, he said that he had received the *Catholic Worker* from one of the seamen who maintained a little circulating library on board ship and passed the paper around.

What need do we have for a circulation manager? Smokey Joe can just sit beside his desk and take the subscriptions which come in, and Gordon McCarthy will attend to the stencils.

HUGH MADDEN—R.I.P.

Hugh Madden is dead, struck down by a car as he was cycling his way to the shrine of Our Lady of Guadalupe in Mexico City, starting out early to be there on her feast day December 12. He had gotten as far as Glade Springs, Virginia and was killed instantly. We had his body brought back to Tivoli, where the Catholic Worker Farm has a cemetery plot, thanks to Monsignor Kane, and his funeral was last Friday, a requiem Mass at which Monsignor Kane delivered a eulogy. He was buried with all his fellow workers at the farm standing by, with Msgr. Kane and Father Markey from the Blessed Sacrament Fathers saying prayers at the grave.

Even before his death, Hugh had become a legendary figure on East and West coast in Catholic Worker circles.

The first time I met him was when Ammon Hennacy was picketing the tax offices. He was conducting his usual fast on one of the anniversaries of the dropping of the atom bomb on Hiroshima. Hugh had come east from California to join him in his picketing. He showed up on the line, dressed in rags, literally, a peculiarly patched together costume with a poncho which in some way was like a priest's chasuble. His old sweat-stained felt hat was studded with medals and buttons. Later he made a giant size CNVA symbol which was attached to the back of the seat of his bicycle. (This was not returned with his other belongings when his body was shipped back.) If the weather was hot he wore old army pants cut off at the knee, and being hipless he often had to hitch them up in the interests of modesty. Often his shirt did not meet the trousers in the rear, an added coolness but an added distraction to the beholder. There were assorted patches, also. His legs were thin and bare, and his feet were sandalled. He was in a way like a St. Benedict Joseph Labre in appearance, except that he kept himself clean. In all he was a clean, spare, gaunt figure of a man, with a little goatee on an otherwise cleanshaven face which brought out his resemblance to pictures of Uncle Sam, which the men at the farm at once dubbed him.

Following after Ammon on that picket line he made a strange figure. There was a beautiful young woman picketing with Ammon at the time, a forerunner of the hippies cult, scantily clad and barefooted, but of truly radiant beauty. The Paphnutius figure and the Thais figure ignored each other. It never occurred to Ammon that those who accompanied him on his picketings might bring contempt or ridicule on his cause.

One might be astounded at the picture of Hugh at first, but somehow the aspect of a man doing penance shone through. That very first day at twelve noon, he got down on his knees at the stroke of twelve, and there on that populous street, jostled by the crowd on their way to lunch, he bowed to the ground and prayed the Angelus, and since he had no bells to ring and there were no bells from neighborhood church to call to prayer, he pounded with his bare knuckles on the harsh pavement, to accent the three versicles and the three "Hail Mary's." "The angel of the Lord appeared unto Mary; she conceived by the Holy Spirit, Behold the handmaid of the Lord: be it done unto me according to Thy word. The word was made flesh; and dwelt among us."

He lived with us for a time at Spring Street, spreading a mat on the floor, and after prayers on his knees before a statue of the Blessed Mother he would sleep. He came to the farm at Staten Island and visited the beach houses. At the farm we had a ship's bell and he rang it each morning at six, again for the Angelus, again at noon and supper time. One time there was a sick priest with us, who slept late after sleepless nights, but that did not deter Hugh. He was stern with himself and though he said little he presented a stern visage to us.

For a time he ran the house of hospitality on the west coast. The house in Oakland was efficiently run, even harshly run, and many of the group protested his rule and Hugh came back East to us.

By this time I had heard a little more of the legend. He had been a seaman most of his life, and one story had it that he was washed ashore after being long adrift at sea (the ship had been torpedoed) and then had spent six years at Gethsemani, as a Trappist brother. He left there to work on the ranch he owned in California, where he had cows to milk and where the church was thirty miles away. The story is that he milked the cows Saturday night, set out for Mass, arriving in the morning and after attending Mass and receiving Holy Communion, walked the thirty miles back again. This was repeated winter and summer every Sunday. It was in front of that church too that he distributed *Catholic Workers* each Sunday. (In his belongings which were returned to us with his body there was a bundle of *Catholic Workers* which he had intended to distribute along the way to Mexico.

He lived with us at the Catholic Worker Farm these last years, between pilgrimages. In the summer he also cycled to Canada to visit the shrines of Our Lady and of Ste. Anne de Beaupre. He had a ten speed bicycle and it had carried him from Oakland to the east coast as well as to the Quebec shrine and the one in Mexico City. These wanderings of his reminded me of those of the Russian pilgrims, who travelled vast distances, from Archangel to Irkutsk.

At the farm there was no telling where he slept. There is a tunnel, a mysterious affair extending from the old de Peyster mansion in two directions, out front toward the high bank above the railroad tracks next to the river, and to the rear from the basement of the house under the driveway to the ravine which was originally the bed of a brook. On the other side the hillside ascends steeply through the woods up to the fields above where we have our vegetable garden. Hugh slept in this damp tunnel for a time until it crippled him and then one day I caught him digging a cave into the

315

patch of sunny hillside and bade him stop. It was liable to fall in on him, I said, and I deemed this childish nonsense.

Some boys were doing just such a thing, I told him, in Great Kills on Staten Island when a sandslide covered them and they were smothered.

He looked at me with a stubborn glint in his eye. Then he pointed to the chapel in the old school house and said, "I'm going to pray about this, and if the Holy Spirit as well as you, tells me to stop I will, but if He doesn't I'll hit the road."

Finally he settled in a cabin which had been put up by Domensky in the woods at the end of the property. It was well built but terribly cluttered. There were three windows and a little stove, and Joe had lived in it winter and summer until he decided to take to the desert outside of Albuquerque. I asked Hugh to take over the cabin and hold it in case of Joe's return but I am sure he never considered it his home.

Hugh had a small check from the government which he used to ask Walter Kerell to hold for him until he set out, and when he died he had ten dollars in cash and something over a hundred in travellers checks on his person. He earned his way with us by most conscientiously doing all the pot washing and he demanded Fels Naphtha soap for his dish washing. He baked the most peculiar concoctions of bread, mixing every kind of flour and cereal we had in the house. I liked his cornmeal loaf best myself. When there was a crowd living at the Roger La Porte farm before Peter Lumsden went back to England and sold the place, Hugh used to bring huge batches of his baking up there. His cooking was not up to either Hans's or John Filliger's standards, both of whom had cooked on ships. Hugh's seamen's papers showed many initials after his name but not that of a cook.

I cannot close without speaking of Hugh's behaviour in church which I am afraid was a grave distraction to our Tivoli population at first. Hugh liked to kneel in the aisle when he attended Mass. Someone explained to him that it was forbidden by canon law to take up money at the door for the pews, so he refused to use them. Also he always approached the altar rail on his knees and received communion kneeling.

When Monsignor Kane preached the funeral sermon (he had already offered one Mass the morning he heard of Hugh's death) he said he only spoke at this requiem, which was contrary to his custom, because he felt he owed so much to Hugh. The latter had stimulated his devotion to the Blessed Sacrament and to our Blessed Mother.

He said nothing in his sermon about Hugh's penitential practices, but later in the day he asked me if Hugh's pliers or his monkey wrench had been put in the coffin with him. He knelt on these, Monsignor Kane explained, adding hastily, "He didn't tell me, I caught him at it one day."

Hugh had told me once that he did penance. I had asked him why he had stayed so long in Mexico City, and he said he had been in the hospital with an infection. "A little too much penance," he added grimly, and from the way he put his hand against his side, I took it to mean he had been using an instrument of penance, such as I had heard or read of. Sure enough, when his "effects" as they are termed came back with his "remains," and Ron and I went over his clothes to see what could be given away on the Bowery, we found there a circlet, a belt, twisted at the end to form a hook and eye, which was, very simply, a piece of barbed wire.

Why penance? For the napalm, the bombings in Vietnam perhaps. Because we are all guilty. God help us.

November 1967

Via della Conciliazione is a long street stretching from St. Peter's to the Tiber and at the beginning of that street there is the Palazzo Pio with its great auditorium where the plenary sessions of the Third World Congress for the Lay Apostolate are being held. The last Congress was held ten years ago and many of the 3,000 people here were present at that Congress and speak of what a difference now. One man said, though he may have been exaggerating: "Last time there were twenty cardinals sitting on the platform and the speeches were each an hour long. This time the red hats are in the audience and only one now and then at the conference table." It was truly a meeting of the laity. And how hard it is to give an impression of such a meeting of folk from all over the world, from all the continents. I spoke to Alexy Boulevsky, from Moscow, who represented the Moscow Patriarchate.

There are so many pilgrimages to St. Peter's of peoples from all over Europe who come in their national costume that one could not tell which were attending the Congress and which were on a pilgrimage. On Sunday morning last there were four busloads of peasants from Yugoslavia in most beautiful costumes, men with their pure undyed wool suits set off with darker wool from black sheep and their perfectly round bowl-like hats; the women with long pantaloons and gayly embroidered aprons, looking like harem beauties. Eileen Egan, who has traveled the world over with Catholic Relief Services, went to them and with the aid of an interpreter found that most of them were Albanians. Mother Teresa, famed for her Calcutta work for the dying (she once spoke at the Catholic Worker) is an Albanian and Eileen found three of her cousins among the pilgrims.

The great square of St. Peter's, encircled by the Bernini colonnades, harbors many a picnic and all around the vast square, there in the shade of the pillars, families were eating their lunches, which included spaghetti, roast chicken and, of course, bottles of wine. It would be nice to see the same at St. Patrick's in New York.

I suppose I should have begun this account with the high honor paid me and the *Catholic Worker* at the Congress. On the feast of St. Teresa of Avila, whom I have so often quoted, I received Holy Communion from the hands of Pope Paul himself—truly an overwhelming honor. Only one hundred and fifty of the three thousand delegates, auditors, consulters and experts were so chosen. Of those one hundred and fifty, only one other was an American, an astronaut, Colonel James McDivitt, who presented the cone of his space capsule to the Holy Father.

A journalist came to me afterwards and wanted to know what my emotions were on this occasion, and I could only say that I had been concentrating so much on the proper procedure of walking up the carpeted stairs, and turning away and walking back along the priceless carpets, past the red upholstered armchairs where the cardinals and members of the Synod sat and getting back to my place, that I could think nothing, feel nothing, but only say most heartfelt prayer for Pope Paul, who has been ill, and who looked that morning as though he were under great strain. He seemed, however, as the Mass went on, to draw strength from the numbers of the people.

I was told of this honor the afternoon before, while I was in the great auditorium of the Palazzo Pio. I was listening with such intense interest to the words of Rev. Valdo Galland, general secretary of the World Student Christian Federation, who was talking about the situation in Latin America, referring particularly to the guerrilla warfare going on there, and the tragic death of Che Guevara, that I did not realize that Donna Myers was trying to tell me something important. So many people come up to greet you or tell you they heard you speak five, ten or fifteen years ago, that I kept saying to her, "Wait, I must hear this. I'll see you later." But she had another message to deliver and went on, telling me to pick up my special ticket right away.

Of course I was happy at that Mass, feeling as I did that I was representing the men from our soupline, the pickets from Delano, and all Cesar Chavez's fellow workers in California and Texas, and the little babies and small children of the agricultural workers who are at present at our farm in Tivoli in the day-care center.

I prayed, too, for all our readers and writers, all those who break bread with us, all those we encounter each day. I prayed for the dead, including Che Guevara, who figured so prominently in the minds of men this past week. And for Lolita LeBrun, one of the Puerto Ricans in prison for the violent assault on the House of Representatives some years ago, who had just written me, and for all those nonviolent ones who are in prison today, for their conscientious objection to the terrible Vietnam war in which we are now engaged.

When we 150 privileged ones were herded behind the wooden fences that are constantly being shifted around in St. Peter's, there were three ushers who kept track of us most carefully. We were their charges and they kept counting us. At first to see that no one else crept in, under the barriers, and later, I suppose, to see that there would be sufficient hosts consecrated for us in Pope Paul's ciborium. Anyway, it made me think of prisoners being counted over and over. Then too, they were watchful of our dress. One African woman in gorgeous native costume let her scarf slide down around her waist, exposing neck and shoulders and bare arms. An usher pushed in to redrape her. Another young woman did not have a veil and a piece of white chiffon was provided. It seemed to me that it was long before communion time that we were ushered out two by two, to form two columns on one side of the great central altar. We were pushed forward and then backward, so that we would be evenly distributed. It was then that I noticed how the carpets were attached to the marble floors by very wide pieces of scotch tape, a thoughtful piece of housekeeping to keep the cardinals from stumbling. I may say that I was very preoccupied with whether I was going to stumble, or whether one knee would give way under me as I ascended or descended the steps. And all during these distractions the Sistine choir sang a great Gregorian Mass, with the Magnificat at the end.

The Work of the Word

Acutally, the important part of the Congress was the workshops. At the big general meeting there were only a few speakers and most of the meetings were to listen to reports on the workshop. Since reports were in any of four languages, we were happy to use the very good earphones and transistor sets, which helped us to understand not only the French and Spanish speakers, but those who spoke indistinctly in English.

The workshops were groups of 15-60 people, English-Spanish, English-French, English-German, etc., with different chairmen who led discussion on man's spiritual attitudes, the family, tensions between generations, cooperation between men and women, social communications, economic development and access to culture, peace and world community and migration. There was another series of eight workshops later and after each series there was a general report. When our workshop on peace got through with nine hours of discussion, there was a summing up. There were six sections on peace and world community and each of the six had a report, and they all had to be combined into one report to be delivered at the plenary session. Then later, after more meetings with members of the various national delegations, resolutions were formulated and voted upon. It will be seen that it was amazing to find as much amity and order as there was. It was all beautifully planned and worked out and everyone felt that large segments of the articulate laity certainly had been heard.

But at the close of it all, it was inevitable that there should be some dissatisfaction, and the conviction that nothing had really been settled, especially in the fields of birth control and war. (Racism was condemned unanimously.)

Priests were of course in evidence accompanying their delegations. I heard one priest say that it was surprising how many of the delegates, far more than had been expected, were against birth control. Another priest said rather coldly that it was evident that the Congress was packed with conservatives. Practically all the priests I spoke to said that the decision was to be made by the married couples themselves, according to their conscience.

No one of course was really satisfied with the resolutions but most felt that they were beginnings of discussion, and that a great deal of work was necessary on the part of lay people to work and study and develop a strong conscience about the problems of the day.

Towards the close of the conference, four or five young people were invited to speak. (All the speeches at the Congress were truly brief.) One complained that youth was poorly represented and that no provision for them to come had been made. Another that the rural populations of the world were not represented. Another that the Congress was not ecumenical enough, that other religions of the East, for instance, were not represented. Also that the Third World be more represented at these congresses, and that they be held at centers other than Rome. One young man was cut short, rather rudely, I felt, when he said that young people had not much relationship with the Establishment, that little opportunity or time had been given them to get together or to express themselves, and that other people of middle age were speaking for them.

On the whole the young people spoke well and clearly at this small opportunity given them in the final meeting, which took place with the Synod of Bishops present and so many cardinals that a special place had to be reserved for them.

I spoke on the ship coming over to a class of sixty seminarians on their way to the American College at Rome, and here in Rome I spoke to all the post-graduate students of the American College, who were already ordained. I spoke also, with Tom Cornell, at a meeting of Italian peace workers at the YMCA in Rome, many of the members of the Fellowship of Reconciliation. I also was delighted to meet Fabrizio Fabbrini, former professor at the university here, who had been imprisoned for six months for his conscientious objection to military service. Those months he spent in an underground cell, with nine other prisoners who were there on other charges. They ate and slept and lived without work or without exercise. I consider him a modern martyr, and hope to interview him later.

I am sending back a mass of material—resolutions and speeches—to Marty Corbin for him to go over and cull from it things he thinks best. But probably the diocesan papers have carried far more complete stories than the daily press.

But I do want to share with our readers some of the delightful and more leisurely aspects of this journey.

The ship Marguerite Harris and I were travelling on was making an excursion trip and was packed to the full. Many Italian-Americans who have prospered in the States return to their country for visits and choose a long trip which will stop at many ports where they can shop and bring their purchases back to their staterooms. They do not have to pack and repack as they go from city to city and hotel to hotel, but remain on shipboard as if in a hotel for a month or more.

The *Raffaello* stopped at Madeira, then the Canaries, and after a few hours at Gibraltar we proceeded to Mallorca. Buses met us at each port and transported us up high mountains, through savage valleys, up more mountains, even on one occasion bringing us to the very tip of a volcano supposed to be extinct. Thinking of Martinique, I wondered how any householder could bear to build a dwelling down on the flat floor in the cone. Perched as we were on what seemed to be a wave of petrified lava, surrounded too by wave after wave of barren soil, we shuddered at the sight.

Madeira and Mallorca alone seemed fertile. I was delighted in Mallorca to visit the Carthusian monastery, which after its confiscation by the state back in the eighteen-thirties, rented an apartment there to Chopin and George Sand. The three-room apartments each looked out on a fragrant herb and flower garden, always with a little fountain, and surrounded by a wall. A place to sit and read the psalms as well as to cultivate a garden—fruits and vegetables, bees perhaps for honey, and why not a chicken or rabbit or two?

Chopin's piano was there and not only the manuscript of his music, but that of George Sand's book, *Winter in Mallorca*, a piece of writing that reminded me in its bitter humor of Mary McCarthy's. George Sand had her two children with her, Maurice and Solange, fifteen and twelve years old respectively. She scandalized the islanders and they were frightened to death of Chopin's illness. Also the island was overcrowded. There was a civil war going on in Spain, and Belver Castle, built in the thirteenth century for the Mallorcan kings, was crowded with prisoners. M. Laurent, the artist, visited it and said that he saw fifty naked Carlist prisoners, some only children, "boisterous as they filled their tins with coarse boiled macaroni while the guards sat smoking cigars and knitting stockings." The story was that there were 20,000 war refugees from the mainland on the island.

No wonder George Sand wrote: "Why travel unless you must? It is not so much a question of travelling as of getting away; which of us has not some pain to lull or some yoke to cast off? . . .

"I should like to envisage the human race as happier, hence calmer and more enlightened, and leading two complementary lives: a sedentary life of devotion to a happy home, work in the city, study and philosophical meditation; and an active life, of devotion not only to the honest exchange which will one day replace the shameful traffic we call commerce, but to inspirations of art, to scientific research and above all to the broadcasting of ideas.

"In a world I see the natural end of travel as a satisfaction of a need for contact, communication and the congenial exchange of ideas—pleasure should coincide with duty."

George Sand regarded the religion of the peasants as ugly superstition. She tells of a peasant awakened by his complaining pigs and reciting his rosary "in a dismal voice which, according as drowsiness came and went, died away or rose again like the distant murmur of the waves. From time to time the hogs still let loose a wild cry, whereupon the peasant would raise his voice without interrupting his prayer; and the gentle beasts, calmed by an *ora pro nobis* or an *Ave Maria*, grew calm at once."

Chopin, however, was deeply affected by the religion in the life of the people around him, and his religious attitude as well as his ill health caused him to break off their relationship.

1968

January 1968

A MEETING WITH IGNAZIO SILONE

☐ In wrestling with the problem of how to present the teachings of nonviolence in an age of mass violence, it seems to me that the writings of Ignazio Silone are of immense importance. When I first read *Bread and Wine* in the forties, I was deeply impressed, not only with the story of the revolutionary returning secretly from his exile in Switzerland, but with the call to a personalist approach which must precede any communitarian effort.

I had heard from Father Jack English, a former CW editor, of Silone's visit to the Trappist monastery of the Holy Spirit at Conyers, Georgia. Silone spent the day at the Abbey within the enclosure, and it was left to Father English to be guest master and converse with his wife, a beautiful Irishwoman whom he met during his exile in Switzerland. They had come to Atlanta to discuss the problems of the South and had been brought to the monastery by the editor of the *Atlanta Constitution* because there was an international meeting of the Trappist order going on there.

On another occasion Silone and his wife had visited New York and New England and had called the office of *The Catholic Worker*, but I did not receive the message until they were well on their way back to Italy.

So I was delighted when I was invited to dine with them

in Rome in late October. We went to a restaurant on the Piazza Carlo Goldoni that was usually very quiet, they said. There was a large area outside for dining; but it was a cool night, so we went into one of the small rooms, which, unfortunately, was very crowded and noisy that night. There were two tables full of noisy young Americans, one large party of uproarious Italians and still another family with small babies. So I did not get as complete an interview as I would have liked.

Silone wanted to learn more about Peter Maurin (our founder) and his peasant background. He knew of Marc Sangnier's movement and his journal, *Le Sillon*, which was suppressed in France at the time that Peter Maurin lived there. He also wanted to know whether I was a practicing Catholic, and expressed surprise at the opposition *The Catholic Worker* met with from some of the hierarchy. He spoke of Danilo Dolci, whom I was to meet later, and of whom I wrote in the last issue of *The Catholic Worker*. I knew from others that he had provided Dolci with generous financial help and had appeared in court during his many trials. He did not particularly like his campaign against the Mafia, though he said that it showed great courage. Perhaps he felt that the time consumed was time lost from his work of regional alleviation of destitution, through study groups, building up of cooperatives and the work toward irrigation and reforestation.

Silone himself was born in Pescina, an ancient town on the slopes of the Mariella mountains, in the Abruzzi. His father died when he was ten years old. There were three sons, and the oldest was injured when he fell from a roof where he was playing and broke his back. He was terribly crippled, but his mind was keener than ever. He died at fourteen. The other brother was tortured to death by the Fascists. His mother lost her life in a terrible earthquake when he was fifteen. He went to school first in the village and then later in a seminary, where he received a classical eduation. Don Orlione was a priest who had the greatest influence on his life and I imagine the wonderful priest portrayed in *Bread and Wine* was like him. He continued his education under the Jesuits in Rome. On one occasion he left school and wandered around Rome for three days; that and his Socialist leanings led to his expulsion. Later on, in the Mussolini era, he became a Communist and had to flee Italy and take refuge in Switzerland.

Fontamara was written in 1930 when Silone was in exile, and he said that writing was his only defense against despair. He was ill with tuberculosis. "Since it did not appear that I had long to live," he writes in the introduction, "I wrote with unspeakable affliction and anxiety, to set up as best I could that village into which I put the quintessence of myself and my native heath, so that I could at least die among my own people."

But he recovered his health and writing became the "secret dwelling place for the rest of a long exile." He writes that there is no definite break between the stories of Solitary Stranger in *Fontamara*, Pietro Spina in *Bread and Wine*, Rocco in *A Handful of Blackberries*, and Andrea in *The Secret of Luca*. The hero in *The Seed Beneath the Snow* is still Pietro Spina.

"If it were in my power to change the mercantile laws of literary society," he writes, "I could easily spin out my existence writing and rewriting the same story in the hope that I might end up understanding it and making it clear to others, just as in the middle ages there were monks whose entire lives were devoted to painting the face of Christ over and over again."

When he returned after his exile and reread the text of those first two books for Italian publication, he began rewriting them both, because of the continued development in himself "during all those years in which I had continued to live in them."

For one thing, the emphasis was no longer on urging peasant uprising—he had long since lost his faith in Communism or in any other revolution directed by a bunch of bureaucrats. The emphasis is now on the individual, who conveys the message, one man to another, of man's dignity and capacity for greatness. And greatness means the overcoming of temptation and the laying down of one's life for one's fellows, in other words, the victory of love over hatred and mistrust.

Fontamara is the name of a south Italian village where the villagers are constantly being deceived by the Trader, who came like an ordinary travelling salesman and began by buying up the apples on the trees when the peasants needed cash, and went on to buy up everything: onions, beans, lentils, pigs, hens, rabbits, bees, animal skins, road construction, land, and so on. The story begins with his diverting a small stream which takes all the water from the peasants' small fields. He gains control of the old-time landowners and works with a bank, which gives him all the money he needs. He finally becomes mayor of the nearby town. With the priest on the side of the Trader, the peasant in despair, each one looks to his own welfare at the expense of the others, each tries to get the best of what little water is left. The bits of land the peasants had are tied up in mortagages and debts, so they have to hire themselves out as day laborers. Each day they have to walk ten miles to their work and, in the evening when they return home they feel as "exhausted and degraded as beasts."

Berardo Viola has lost his land because of the treachery of the local lawyer and at the end goes away to Rome to search for work in order to marry Elvira, who has accepted him, penniless and landless though he is. So far he has been the one in the village to preach revolt, but now he thinks only of himself, and refuses to join the other peasants in any of their plans, which they had begun to make under his inspiration. He has converted them all and now he himself had changed. He has to take care of his own affairs, he says, and will not stay with the others or work with them any longer. Elvira pledges herself to go on a pilgrimage to save his soul. She has fallen in love with him as he was before, a landless peasant and a leader of the others who had kept some spark of hope and faith in themselves alive.

It is in Rome that after hunger and thirst in his attempt to cut through the bureaucracy and find work, he meets the Solitary Stranger. When they are arrested for vagrancy and share a cell together, he is brought back to his former way of thinking. He has gone through what can only be called a conversion. Elvira has on her pilgrimage begged the Virgin for his salvation, offering God her own life for him, and her offering had been accepted. During his absence she returns home to die of fever. Inspired by the Solitary Stranger, Berardo himself offers his life for the others and is killed by the Fascists.

The entire story, told by one or another of the peasants themselves, is not primarily a story of incipient violent revolution, though the peasants do plan to burn up the Trader's holdings. It is rather the story of failure, the story of redemption, the folly of the Cross which leads to the Resurrection. The same theme runs through Silone's work, *The Seed Beneath the Snow.* "Unless the grain of wheat fall into the ground and dies, itself remaineth alone. But if it dies it brings forth much fruit." . . . "Anyone who would save his life must lose it."

In one of his critical essays in *Politics and the Novel*, Irving Howe says that in the novels of Malraux and Silone, the true hero is the author himself. I felt privileged indeed in meeting Silone, a moral hero of our time, committed to the poor and the landless, the agricultural worker whom we have encountered in our own country in the novels of Steinbeck, *Grapes of Wrath* and *In Dubious Battle*. Certainly the poorest people in our own country are not the industrial workers, who have won their battle for the eight-hour day and the five-day week, and for some share in the prosperity of our urban civilization, only through bloody defeats during half a century and more of struggle. The struggle on the land goes on for the right to organize agricultural work, to bargain collectively, to build up community by way of cooperatives and social-service centers where Masses are offered up for the workers, and *campesino* players can put on their acts and their songs.

I am grateful indeed for the writings of Ignazio Silone. In a meeting in Switzerland for long after the Second World War, he said that those writers who sold their words to governments in the prosecution of a war were as guilty of profiting by war as the men who remained at home to work on the instruments of death—the bombers and the Bomb, the napalm and the anti-personnel bombs (and the personnel in those cases are mostly women and children, the old and the feeble).

When I first mentioned the book *Bread and Wine* in my column years ago, one of our Bishops, a good friend, wrote to me that he was sorry to see me praising a writer who spoke of the Holy Father (Pius XI) as Pope Pontius Pilate. *Bread and Wine* is the story of the return of an exile, who hides out in the mountains of the Abruzzi, disguised as a priest. When war is declared against Ethiopia he goes out in the night and chalks up his opposition on the public buildings of the village in which he is staying in the form of a large and repeated "NO!" When he is asked what good such a puny dissent does, and why he is risking his life, which is so precious to others, by such a futile gesture, he replies that as long as one man says "NO!" the unanimity of consent is broken. At that time it certainly seemed that the hierarchy and the clergy (all but Don Luigi Sturzo, that great Christian sociologist) were blessing that war.

As far as I know, Silone is not what is generally called a

328

practicing Catholic. I certainly did not presume to question him on the subject. But I do know that his writings bring to us the Christian message and my heart is warm with gratitude. I know too that he is interested in and follows all that is happening in the Church, not only in the ancient order of the Trappists, the monks of the desert, but also in "The Seeds of the Desert" (not the book of Father Rene Voillaume by that name, though it is a great one), but the seed scattered by the solitary, Charles de Foucauld, which bloomed in a new order, the Little Brothers of Jesus, who go out into all the poverty-stricken places in the world and work for their daily bread and live the life of the contemplative in the world. Let us all pray for each other, that we may learn this profound truth, the way of the Cross which leads to joy and fulfillment and eventually to victory.

February 1968

My sister and I used to call them the January doldrums. I'm having them now, faced as I am with a lot of work on the typewriter that I do not want to do. There are piles of mail to answer on each desk up here at Tivoli. Marge Hughes has a heap of letters. Stanley has a heap, I have a heap. Marge's Johnny has had flu and I've had a recurring cold. But do not think we are depressed. Interesting visitors arrive, there is interesting news in newspapers or magazines to be discussed, some good books come in from the publishers, and we are filled with vim. When we return to our desks, we are in the doldrums again.

Was it Dr. Abraham Low or Father John J. Higgins, S.J. (may they both rest in peace) who gave such simple and good advice in the group-therapy sessions known as Recovery meetings? To the woman who complained that she could not face the huge basket of laundry to be ironed—men's shirts and children's school clothes—the answer was: "Put the basket behind you, reach back and take out one shirt and iron it. Go on from there." It sounds idiotic, but I start my On Pilgrimage article in this spirit. Just to sit down and put one word after another. I write this for your comfort. We are all alike, in that we are in the doldrums or the deserts or in a state of *acedia* at one time or another.

329

I am at Tivoli as I begin to write this. My room faces the river and I get up every now and then to see a ship pass by—freighters from Finland, tankers, cement barges, tugs, Coast Guard boats breaking through the ice. The freight train that just passed distracted me. As I used to do as a child, I counted the cars, ninety-seven of them, many of them marked Pacific Fruit. They made me think of our friends, Julian Balidoy, Fernando Garcia, Severino Manglio, Juan Berbo, Nickolas Valenzuelo, and others who stayed with us last year, in a cold three-room apartment on Kenmare Street. They would rise at dawn or earlier to set out on their daily job of approaching wholesalers and retailers, asking them not to handle the grapes coming from California, where so many of the workers in the vineyards are on strike. They are trying to build up a union of agricultural workers, and have succeeded in winning contracts with the growers, each success won after the daily work of setting out on such visits as these and conducting continuing picket lines, which are in a way "supplicatory processions," prayers, to the good God that He will keep them from bitterness and hopelessness and class war. The world is full enough of war as it is and daily there are the threats of more wars. There are realignments of allies, a strange shuffling of forces. Weren't Russia and China our allies in the Second World War? And weren't Germany and Japan our enemies?

The alternative is to educate for nonviolence, love of brother (and all men are brothers) while being always on the side of the poor, a predilection shared by Almighty God and his son Jesus Christ, Who, in Matthew 25, told us to feed the hungry, clothe the naked, shelter the harborless, visit the prisoner (or even better, ransom him), visit the sick, and bury the dead—decently, with respect for that silenced body which has served for this all too brief life on earth.

God is on the side even of the unworthy poor, as we know from the story Jesus told of His father and the prodigal son. Charles Peguy, in *God Speaks*, has explained it perfectly. Readers may object that the prodigal son returned penitent to his father's house. But who knows, he might have gone out and squandered money on the next Saturday night, he might have refused to help with the farm work, and asked to be sent to finish his education instead, thereby further incurring his brother's righteous wrath, and the war between the worker and the intellectual, or the conservative and the radical, would be on. Jesus has another answer to that one: to forgive one's brother seventy times seven. There are always answers, although they are not always calculated to soothe.

I can sympathize with the instinct of righteous wrath which leads people to take to arms in a revolution, when I see the forgotten aged in mental hospitals, and men sleeping in doorways on the Bowery, or fishing in garbage cans for food, and families in the slums, often with no heat in such weather as we have been having, and migrants in their shanty towns. We have heated the apartments at Kenmare St. with the gas oven day and night while the temperature was down to five below zero. We were more comfortable than the people in the better apartments across the street, where the boiler burst or froze up. Our cold-water pipes were frozen in half of our house but we were able to fetch water from one another's apartments. There are two toilets to a floor and one on each floor was frozen and had to be padlocked.

The pickets from Delano have arrived, forty-five of them. They came by rented bus. The heating system failed on the trip. Now they are being given hospitality by the Seafarers International Union at 675 Fourth Avenue, in Brooklyn. I have spoken at communion breakfasts in the dining room of their hall, so I know how comfortable and well fitted out it is, an indication of the gains the union movement has made over the past thirty years.

It is less than three months ago that I was visiting Danilo Dolci and travelling around western Sicily, which has since been stricken by earthquake and bitter rain and cold. Our most heartfelt sympathy goes out to Dolci and to his fellow workers, and we hope that some of our readers will send him checks that will help them in the additional work which such a disaster has forced upon them. No matter how much governments and the Red Cross do, there is always more to be done. And donations, however small, are a reminder of sympathy. "Love is an exchange of gifts," St. Ignatius once said. Two of Dolci's books, *A New World in the Making* and *Waste* can be obtained from the Monthly Review Press, 116 West 14th St., New York, for $7.50 and $6.75 respectively. We highly recommend the *Monthly Review*, to which we turn for information about Latin American affairs. Subscription: $6.00 a year.

I did not mention in my last account of my pilgrimage to Italy and England (December 1967) that, although I went by ship, I returned by air. In my many trips around the country over the years, I have usually gone by bus, partly on the grounds of economy and also because it was convenient from the standpoint of the visits I made to various houses of hospitality. I would use a visit to a Texas school, where I received perhaps two hundred and fifty dollars, plus expenses, as an excuse to make a tour of Catholic Worker groups. Usually, by the time I got to San Francisco I was exhausted. But I can no longer use economy as an excuse. A trip to Minneapolis, for instance, is about seventy dollars by non-stop flight, and you can arrive as fresh as when you started out. When one has reached three score and ten years, travelling can be exhausting. It was this exhaustion after my Italian trip that made me overcome my fear of flight, which I think most of the older generation shares. Certainly it is just as easy for a huge plane to stay in the air as it is for a ship the size of the Waldorf Astoria to remain afloat. I can only marvel at men's accomplishment in this technological era and meditate again on the lack of development of our spiritual resources. I like to think of St. Paul's words: "Though this outer man of ours may be falling into decay, the inner man is renewed day by day." In the modern world it seems just the opposite: the outer man's youth is renewed by science and comfort and the inner man is corrupted by materialism. Anyway, I am partaking with joy of the beauty and comfort of flying now, and will try to pay for it with harder work and better use of my time.

In Rome I had met a Father Galli, who runs a center for young boys. He entertained a group of us at dinner one night on a roof garden just above the center where movies are shown and lectures and instruction given. He regaled us with stories of his visits to Staten Island and, on the morning of my departure, met Eileen Egan and me at the airport with a huge bunch of roses, and a relic of St. Helena for Eileen and a relic of the Holy House of Loretto for me. "This also has flown," he said to me, referring to the fact that the Holy House was supposed to have been miraculously flown from Palestine to Italy. (Pope John XXIII once made a pilgrimage to the Holy House.) I am sure that many of our modern iconoclasts would like to bomb it out of existence.

But it was my rosary that I clutched in my hand as I made the plane a minute before we took off. Wedged between a priest and a brother on their way to London, I was reminded of the crowded buses of Mexico, where people (and sometimes sheep and chickens) were packed so close that I used to think that in the accident which always seemed imminent one would be well cushioned. The plane started off with an increasing roar of the engines, which, rising to a crescendo, made me think of a recurrent nightmare of my early childhood, a dream of a great roaring, beginning quietly and increasing to unbearable noise, which I somehow associated with my idea of God. What this noise conveyed to me now was a sense of enormous power, lifting us with a great thrust into the air. I didn't realize that my eyes had been closed until I opened them to notice that we were already above the clouds and our heavenly conveyance was quite smooth, that is, until we began to feel that we were driving over rough roads. One of my seat mates said, "bit of wind, probably," and none seemed concerned. It was a small, one-class plane and it took the stewardesses the two or three hours of the flight just to serve the luncheon. I ate heartily, although I don't remember what I ate.

Feeling that I was now an experienced air traveller, I left England on a Pan Am two-class plane a few weeks later. It cost 75 pounds to fly and 95 to take the ship, and that did not include tax or tips to the omnipresent stewards, two for each table, two for each cabin, one for library, one for deck, etc. When they have cafeteria style and dormitory on ships, I will revert to sea voyage, but until then, for the aforementioned reasons, I plan to take future long trips by plane.

We arrived at the airport in good time for our flight but had to wait about three hours—a slowdown, one of the other travellers said, after we heard that half a dozen other flights had been delayed. The waiting room was so commodious and it was so interesting to see all the families, whose children crawled happily about under foot, that I quite enjoyed the delay. And the flight itself was unbelievably beautiful, sailing as we were above the clouds, looking down over another world, of hills and mountains and deep valleys and even craters, all tinted rose and golden and deep purple, inspiring a great awe and thankfulness in the beholder, to the Creator of heaven and earth. "The world will be saved by beauty," Dostoevski says in *The Idiot*. And certainly beauty lifts the mind and heart to God. Coming down to refuel over Gander, in Newfoundland, the dark wild tundra laid out below us was broken up by sky-reflecting streams and lakes. All around the horizon were the remains of the sunset, a rainbow band as far as the eye could see, that faded quickly into the dark of night.

To get back to England—The first meeting in England was at a Friends Hall, and was the Pax annual meeting, where Archbishop Thomas J. Roberts, S.J. was to speak. He arrived late and left early, being on his way to a dinner meeting. He was full of energy when he arrived, having just left a peace vigil in front of St. Martin in the Fields, across from Hyde Park, where the peace groups, including a number from the Pax Society, had been standing in the rain a good part of the afternoon. Prayer goes with a vigil, and the Archbishop told us delightedly that the nuclear-armed submarine, the blessing of which was being protested by the group, had stuck in the mud after being launched and had to poise there in ignominy until the tide came in and floated it off. The tides had not obeyed King Canute!

The Archbishop told of a delightful assignment he had received: to act as chaplain on a former troop ship which used to carry thirty thousand men. Troops are now transported by air, he explained, and with the breakup of the British Empire, a new use has been found for the ships. They are turned into floating schools, with dormitories for school children. The trip he is taking will be along the west coast of Africa, with a chance to stop at all the country along the way. Amidships, in what used to be officers' quarters, instructors and their families can be accommodated.

It was on a bitterly cold Sunday afternoon that David Cohen came to the Gresham Hotel, near the British Museum, to pick up Eileen and me to take us to tea in the East End, where he lives. Here was an entirely contrasting section of London. We took the bus through the quiet Sunday afternoon streets, and during our subsequent walk David was most anxious that we see some of the ancient synagogues in the East End. David is a Jewish scholar, and in addition to working for a living, spends nights at meetings and searching scripture to find all the parts of the Old Testament that foretell the coming of the Messiah and the evolution of the rites of the Catholic Church from Jewish tradition. He brought out page after page of manuscript as we sat at the kitchen table in his little three-room flat on Thrawl Street, eating sandwiches and drinking hot tea to keep warm. There was not a bit of heat in this old housing, which had been considered most comfortable when it was put up by the Rothschilds perhaps a century ago. That afternoon we saw Petticoat Lane, where there are push carts and an open air market every Sunday morning. We passed Toynbee Hall, named after Arnold Toynbee, "who died in the prime of youth in 1883 while engaged in lecturing on political economy to the working men of London."

While on my way to Taena Community, my bus took me to Cheltenham, Gloucester, where I was invited to meet David Hoggett, a young man who was paralyzed from injuries received in a fall while he was working with the International Voluntary Service groups of students. He has been flat on his back ever since, and has the use of only one hand and arm, but he can type, and he runs a free rental library which is kept down to room size by being very selective. The books deal with non-violence, community, the common good, peacemaking and social change. You can get a catalogue by writing to the Commonweal Collection, 112 Winchcombe Street, Cheltenham, Glos., England. "Normally the library pays the cost of dispatch, and the borrower, that of returning the book . . . But no one should be hindered for financial reasons from borrowing, and if necessary stamps for return postage will be sent with the book." We have contributed a few books to his library and I have borrowed a few of Danilo Dolci's which I could not afford to buy here.

Such valiant service warms the heart.

April 1968

Just three weeks ago (we are going to press on April 25) Martin Luther King was shot as he stood on the balcony of a motel in Memphis, Tennessee. It was seven o'clock in the evening when the news was imparted on every television screen, and proclaimed on every radio. It was six midwest time and seven o'clock in New York. I was sitting in the kitchen of one of the women's apartments on Kenmare Street looking at a news cast when the flash came. *Martin Luther King shot in Memphis*. I sat there stunned, wondering if he was suffering a superficial wound as Meredith did on his Mississippi walk to overcome fear, that famous march at which Dr. King joined him, at which the cry "Black Power" was first shouted, about which Martin Luther King wrote in his last book *Where Do We Go From Here?* A book which all of us should read because it makes us understand what the words Black Power really mean. Dr. King was a man of the deepest and most profound spiritual insights.

These were the thoughts which flashed through my mind as I waited, scarcely knowing that I was waiting, for further news. The dreaded words were spoken almost at once. "Martin Luther King is dead." He was shot through the throat, the bullet pierced his spinal cord and he died at once. His blood poured out, shed for whites and blacks alike. The next day was Good Friday, the day commemorated by the entire Christian world as the day when Jesus Christ, true God and true man, shed His blood.

"Unless the grain of wheat fall into the ground and die, it remains alone. But if it die it produces much fruit." Martin Luther King died daily, as St. Paul said. He faced death daily, and said a number of times that he knew he would be killed for the faith that was in him. The faith that men could live together as brothers. The faith in the Gospel teaching of non-violence. The faith that man is capable of change, of growth, of growing in love. Dr. King died daily and already in his life there were men, his immense following capable of continuing his work in the same spirit, such as Ralph Abernathy.

Cynics may say that many used non-violence as a tactic. Many may scoff at the outcry raised at his death, saying that this is an election year and all candidates had to show honor to a fallen black hero. But love and grief were surely in the air those days of mourning and all that was best in the country—in the labor movement, and the civil rights movement and in the peace movement cast aside all their worldly cares and occupations to go to Memphis to march with the sanitation union men, on whose behalf, during whose strike, Martin Luther King had given himself; and to Atlanta where half a million people gathered from coast to coast to walk in the funeral procession, following the farm cart and the two mules which drew the coffin of the dead leader.

Always, I think, I will weep when I hear the song, "We Shall Overcome," and when I read the words, "Free at last, great God, Free at last."

But the healing of grief is in those words that I had been hearing sung every Sunday at the Church of the St. Thomas the Apostle, in the Mass composed by Mary Lou Williams, herself a black composer and jazz musician, herself internationally famous. "I am the resurrection and the life. He who believes in me shall never die but have life everlasting."

We should have had accounts this month of Bob Steed's

trip to Memphis to cover the march of the sanitation workers. Bob is from Memphis and used to help the House of Hospitality which we had there for some years, just off Beale Street. It was run by Helen Caldwell (Riley) for the children of the women who went out during the harvesting of cotton, who were picked up early in the morning by truck to go across the river into Arkansas, or some miles south into the Delta Region of Mississippi. I visited there, and slept in the store which was filled with little cribs and watched the mothers coming in before daylight to deposit their babies and small children with perhaps a can of evaporated milk and some bread. Helen and I slept on cots in the big store front. Later there was a house down an alley. Bayard Rustin came to see us there, from the, of course, segregated Y.M.C.A.

We should also have had a story of a 24-hour pilgrimage to Atlanta made by Paul Muller of California, who has been helping us these last months at Chrystie Street. He flew down to the funeral of Martin Luther King one night and back the next.

But it is a wonder the young people around the *Catholic Worker* got anything done this last month. Good weather has meant many visitors to the city, and many demonstrations in Central Park, and other places. Holy Week has always a holiday (holy day) atmosphere, and all through the month, the March issue of the *Catholic Worker* was being mailed out, slowly but surely. Our chief mailer, Tom Hoey, has been ill, and besides that there is a constant turnover of volunteers, what with this being war time. There is much preparing of defense before draft boards and courts, and much waiting. Our CW family is large, and everybody does what he or she can, but there is the soup line and many lame, halt and blind to be cared for, and the first work to neglect is the paper work, of course.

It made us happy this month to receive two letters, one from South America and the other from New Zealand, telling us that ship mail always meant a late arrival of the paper, but that the articles are timeless.

So we beg our readers' indulgence for being so late.

September 1968

We started out from Tivoli, New York, fifty miles south of Albany, at 9:30 this morning. Kay Lynch was my companion and driver. We arrived in Washington, D.C. just before dinner. The annual Liturgical conference was holding its opening meeting, and I had accepted an invitation to receive an award. I was to make a three-minute acceptance speech. I had accepted because our old friend Father Robert Hovda had asked me, and because I welcomed the great privilege of being with Rev. Martin Luther King, who was to give the opening address. What a tragedy had occurred since that invitation came! Dr. King had truly laid down his life for his brother. Rev. Andrew Young spoke instead, and his talk on nonviolent revolution, over an hour long, held a crowd of four or five thousand people intent and sympathetic. The close of the evening was a tremendous burst of sound from the magnificent choirs of the Ebenezer Baptist Church of Atlanta and a Baltimore choir, with two soloists of thrilling quality. There was also a symphony orchestra: four poems of Father Thomas Merton had been set to music, a tribute to Dr. Martin Luther King and an inspiring call to action. The music, composed and conducted by Alexander Peloquin, raised us all from our seats. I understand that the concert will be repeated at Lincoln Center later in the year. It was truly music which could bring the walls of Jericho down. The next day I heard the talk of Father Daniel O'Hanlon, S.J., an outstanding young theologian, whom I had met on ship going to Rome during the last session of the Council. As usual he was inspiring. Since I was anxious to get on to the South (in spite of the 97-degree heat) we left without hearing the other talks or attending the workshops.

We arrived at Conyers, Georgia, at five in the afternoon, in time for vespers. It had been terribly hot on the two-day trip from Washington, and the little guest house of the Trappist Abbey had welcome shade and an air conditioner in the kitchen, which was closed off from the rest of the house, where, fortunately, there were fans. Kay wanted to swim in the little lake near the house but was warned by one of the brothers against water moccasins. After supper, I was invited to speak to all the brothers (as both priest and brother are now called). Compline was late that night. It was a sympathetic audience and I'm sure we'll have many prayers in our present difficulties (which are many). We visited the bookshop, where Brother Hugh assured me that he was unable to sell any of my books. "People don't read the same stuff down here that they do up north," he said. Knowing how much of a rightist Brother Hugh is, I was sure he never gave a good sales talk, but probably advised people against what I wrote. But he loves us and gave me all the books of Father John McKenzie, the Biblical scholar, that I did not already have. Also a copy of Julian of Norwich and the *Cloud of Unknowing*. He is 76, blind in one eye, and is sure he is going to have a nervous breakdown. Can he really still be keeping that harsh rule? Up at 2 a.m., Matins and Lauds and Mass at four-thirty. And the long fasts, the hard labor and the gruelling heat! It is his vocation, and his happy face shows it.

We were up at five-thirty, Mass was at six-thirty, concelebrated by the Abbot and Father Peter, with Brother Dan assisting. Brother Dan is a black and a former S.N.C.C. worker. We had breakfast with Father Abbot Augustine, and he guided us to the right road. We went away laden with books, money, lunch and loving kindness. And I must not forget! Was it Br. Paul who said he would send me a cactus garden, which I was not able to carry along with me? "If you give the plants a soaking every six months it is enough," he said. "You can't neglect them enough." What with my frequent trips, it will be an ideal house garden for me.

We stopped at historic Selma for breakfast at 7 a.m. The more I think of it, the more I admire the tremendous demonstration which took place here. Priests, nuns and laity, the thousands and thousands who gathered for that historic march, that supplicatory procession, will never forget it—will look upon it as a peak experience. Now, a few years later, people are apt to denigrate it, to be a bit ashamed of their own ardor, to feel that little has been accomplished, that things remain the same. But it was a great awakening for thousands of people. They embraced hardship and fatigue, exhaustion and contempt. I blessed them in my heart as we drove on.

We drove on good roads through miles and miles of dense woods, and then rolling grazing lands. Few houses, few people were encountered. And I kept thinking of the COFO youngsters, who came from colleges in the north and east and midwest and lived in shacks, literally in a wilderness, and whose teaching furthered the growth of knowledge among the poorest, so that they could pass literacy tests and register, and go to the polls and vote. A few days later I was to see Fanny Lou Hamer on television at the Democratic convention in Chicago, addressing literally millions of people. She was one of a delegation half Negro and half white. I could only think of how she had suffered alone, was cruelly beaten in prison, following her inner voice, the voice of the Spirit. What struggles Charles Evers and Julian Bond have had to go through, overcoming the fear and discouragement which is common to us all. I thought too of Marge Baroni, whom I was going to visit in Natchez, her constancy, her daily work in the Poverty Program, fighting discouragement in others, keeping the vision alive of a country where men can live like men, holding their heads high in the knowledge that they are sons of God, and brothers.

In Natchez

When I woke up this morning and began to sort out my impressions of all I had seen and heard yesterday, the tears began and I could only keep on reading the Psalms, with their cries for help to a God who does not seem to hear. Because the suffering certainly goes on, down here and up North, in Vietnam, in Nigeria, in Biafra—and everywhere. It is a sure thing that the freedom God endowed us with is a terrible gift, and He has left us to do the job ourselves: the job of ploughing through the morass of sin and hatred and cruelty and contempt that is all around us, a morass that we ourselves have made.

"Our God is a consuming fire . . . It is a terrible thing to fall into the hands of the living God." These words come to mind when I think of the situation of my friends Louis and Marge Baroni. That fire has consumed the dross of any social life for them. They no longer have any. For the last three years they have been shunned by the other white people of Natchez, the city they both grew up in. At Sunday Mass people go up to the altar rail with them and then avert their heads. "With the host in their mouths, the Bread," Marge says, "they keep their bitter looks."

It is of course because of the integration work that they have been doing. It is hard for me to write about it. Their two boys, aged eight and ten, "don't know about the shot fired a few weeks ago," Marge said. "They don't know about the threat to blow Louis up." The F.B.I. came to Louis and told him that men had been observed tinkering with his car. This was after a Negro at the tire factory where he works had met a violent death from a bomb planted in his car. Since then Marge has driven Louis to work every day. He works six full days a week. Efficiency experts and "industrial engineers" always find ways to increase the work of each man in the plant. There is a union, however, and his job is safe.

I went on to weep over all the things I had seen the day before. I forgot about those things I had been thankful for; that we had been able to drive around with Fred Greene, Jr. a senior at Tuskegee Institute, without being shot at, that we could sit in a restaurant on the highway and have sandwiches and milk and pecan pie together. And that I had visited the clean and well-equipped offices of the Adams-Jefferson Improvement Association, which has an integrated office staff.

No, I forgot about these things. I could only feel the impact of the problem itself, which struck me with full force all that day. Of course, some gains have been made in this war which is going on at home. We had first gone to Duncan Park, a former plantation which had been left to the city for recreational purposes, and in which no blacks had set foot until recently. Now they are there.

On the day I visited there was a picnic going for a hundred or so Negro children, accompanied by their mothers, older sisters and babes in arms. They were all having their lunch as we came, hot dogs, cokes, pastries and pies, and they sat on benches, on the grass in a pavilion, on the swings, and even on the porch of the mansion itself. However, when the white caretaker began to hose down the porch, the counsellor called the children away, fearing that they would make a mess with their lunches. After lunch, many of the children went over to the softball field and began to play. I was glad to see that they could go beyond the picnic grounds; at first, they had seemed to be hovering on the edge of the park. But no, they had the big field for softball, and later we saw some blacks playing tennis at one of the courts. It had taken demonstrations on the part of the Negroes to integrate this park, demonstrations which the police had met with a show of force: clubs, chains, baseball bats and dogs. (The clubs and bats had been used on the demonstrators but not the dogs.)

Fred Greene was in charge of the recreation program for the summer and had opened up ten centers so that groups from all around could take turns using the facilities of Duncan Park. (Except for the swimming pool, which has been closed to both blacks and whites for the past two summers.) Later we visited another recreation center (was it the poorest?), merely a large dirt back yard fenced in, with a few bits of playground equipment, crowded with little ones and teenagers. But it was at least a place where the children could get together without being tormented by the police or dispersed for loitering.

Before we left the neighborhood we visited the house of a Negro woman who had spent time in Parchman penitentiary for taking part in attempts to integrate the city auditorium. She was a large, stout woman who had made her living cooking in the homes of white people. She is a good cook and had always found work until she began demonstrating, and then she had to find another way to earn her bread. She started a little home industry by skinning and roasting peanuts and was harassed by the authorities until she was finally granted a permit. You got the feeling that she would persist in whatever she did.

I stayed one week with the Baronis, and on the last night I went to the Josephite church, where Father William Morrissey, S.S.J. has been working for years. There was a program given by the twenty-two teachers and their pupils in the tutorial program which all of them had enjoyed so much; and what a pure joy that love of learning is! There was singing and dancing and recitations. The hall was full and the windows all open and it was not too hot. But I could not help thinking as we came away that the Church, meaning in this case the white church, is not keeping step with the efforts of the state. They are not giving what they have, they are not supplementing the efforts of the young people.

And as for the state, "They expect us to make bricks without straw," Marge said, "cutting down on the whole poverty program as they have." Another friend told of how the food program in the school was limited—only one lunch to a family, the other children to do without. Only ten per cent of the poor are to be fed. The Church is leaving too much to the State.

During the depression, when we had a house of hospitality in St. Louis, parochial school children brought an extra sandwich, to be packed in cartons and brought to the house of hospitality to feed our breadlines. And in the churches in Washington, parishioners brought canned goods and staples to put in large offertory boxes in the back of the church for those who needed it. It is not only that these fundamental works of mercy are not being practiced enough, but there is

342

not enough sharing of equipment. Movies, screens, tape recorders, projectors, and other machinery.

We left Natchez today, driving north to Greenville. We were sad to part with the Baronis and with Eddie Reed, a seminarian on his way now to Louvain, who had headed the tutorial program.

Next month I will continue the story of my travels, and tell of a most interesting visit to Port Gibson, where Berry Morgan lives on an old plantation with her three children; and of our visit to Greenville, and Greenwood, and the boycott which is going on there, under the leadership of Father Nathaniel, Franciscan, and of the schools we visited, and the day we spent with Sister Peter Claver, Missionary Servant of the Most Holy Trinity, at Gadsden, Alabama, and of our visit to the Trappist monastery of the Holy Cross at Berryville, Virginia, our last stop before returning to Tivoli.

How strange it seems that I have had this peaceful trip through our usually violent south, while in Chicago 26,000 police and troops were mobilized to combat some thousands of young people, mostly students in ugly violence not only against an unarmed multitude of young crusaders, but within the convention hall itself.

October 1968

It is mid-October and the weather is still warm. There has been no wind and the leaves are still on the trees. The maples and the oaks and the sumac are brilliant, but in general the trees are still green. There is scarcely a hint of frost in the air; only at night a chill arises, a foretaste of the cold to come.

Aside from the pettiest of annoyances, which are part of life, there is generally calm and quiet in the morning, to do one's work. If only there were not the radio! The news of a North Vietnamese island half obliterated, bombarded by the guns of a reactivated warship. The bloody death and destruction of that land at the other end of the world, in the name of Defense. In the mail comes word from Ndubisi Egemenye, a Biafran student of journalism at Duke University, also a cry of anguish, recounting again the massacres which

343

have occurred, the last one in 1966 of 35,000 East Nigerians, the Biafrans, and telling too of the slow agony of death by starvation of the besieged, the non-combatants, the women and the children. We have already forgotten the mass extermination that went on in Indonesia two years ago, in the name of wiping out Communism.

How to be happy in this world where even nature itself, in sudden hurricane or typhoon or earthquake, suffers and groans? How to sing of the glory of God in this strange land? "By the waters of Babylon, there we sat and wept," living as exiles, as we are.

It is only in the light of this anguish that one can understand the attempt made by the Catonsville Nine and the Milwaukee Fourteen, amongst whom are so many of our friends, to *suffer with* these fellow human beings so devastated by war and famine. These men, priests and laymen, have offered themselves as a living sacrifice, as hostages. Next to life itself, man's freedom is his most precious possession, and they have offered that, as well as the prayer and fasting they have done behind bars, for these others.

In case there are those among our readers who do not know why these men have suffered trial and imprisonment, if radio or television or press has not reached them—it is because they have destroyed draft records in Maryland and Wisconsin, the 1-A files, which meant the next men to be called in our criminal drafting and enslavement of young men for our immoral wars. Where we have not sent men, we have sent weapons, planes, bombs to do the work in other countries' wars. There are many other actions—of refusal to work in any industry pertaining to war or to pay taxes for war—being undertaken that we cannot include here, that are too numerous to list.

We can only thank God and try to add our prayers and sacrifices.

Because newspaper coverage of the burning of the files has been so meagre, this issue of the *Catholic Worker* has stories by Michael Ketchum, of our New York staff, who went to the trial in Baltimore, which took place in mid-October. We print also the talk Barbara Deming made at one of the rallies which occurred every night from Sunday until Thursday, which drew more than a thousand young people from colleges all around, and many priests and seminarians. During the day the streets were filled with peaceful demonstrators, beginning with a march of almost thirty blocks to the main post office, where the trial was being held. St. Ignatius Church Hall was given over to the demonstrators. Meals were served there and hospitality was given by the Jesuits and the Christian Brothers throughout the city. At the close of the trial and before disbanding, there was a great clean up, not only of the hall and the washrooms, but even of the sidewalks up and down the street. I was present only for the Sunday and Monday night meetings, and sat in on the trial for the first day. It was a remarkably peaceful and intensely interesting week for all who participated.

We are going to press this month on October 25th and are finally reconciled, as I hope our readers are also, to the fact that, unlike almost every other periodical, we are not publishing on the fifteenth of the preceding month, nor will we ever. This means that we cannot warn our readers at the beginning of October about what is going to happen during the month, but only tell them what has happened. We are not really a newspaper, but a periodical coming out once a month, occasionally skipping an issue when we are broke or shorthanded, and there is many a great event which we miss commenting on. We are warmed and heartened by two letters received recently from readers who tell us that ship route to India or Africa will do very well, because the articles in the *CW* are timeless. They add that they cannot bear to miss a copy.

The rest of this month and the beginning of November will find me travelling to Rochester, New York, and Montreal, but otherwise I remain either in St. Joseph's house, 36 E. First St., New York or at the Catholic Worker Farm at Tivoli. How good it would be to be snowed in at Tivoli for a time!

To give a brief resume of the past month: we had two Friday meetings when all who came joined in work, helping mail out the *CW* and the appeal. Plenty of work to do there still. On the other Friday night meetings we had talks by Father James Megivern, chairman of the Theology Department of St. John's University, Ned O'Gorman, the poet, who told of his days in the Addie Mae Collins Center, at 2029 Madison Avenue in Harlem, where he and several assistants help all the little children on the block from dawn till dark; and Paulette Curran, who told us about the impromptu classes and the learning which are going on during the New York City teachers' strike, where the children stayed for three hours on one subject if their attention was held, or got up and walked out and found another more interesting teacher to listen to or work with.

I visited Ned O'Gorman's place during the month and saw the two cheerful store fronts in the appalling slum area of Harlem, where the vice and crime portrayed in Malcolm X's *Autobiography* flourishes. It was so beautiful a fall day that many of the children had been taken to the parks and museums and only the littlest remained. The place is painted and papered with pictures of all kinds, and the walls are lined with books. Visitors came and went, and on the wide sidewalks in front people met together to talk. Down on the East Side, in the Italian and Jewish neighborhoods, old people and mothers and babies are always hauling out chairs and sitting in the sun and I wished that Ned had benches or more chairs to decentralize the crowd and make, as it were, another room, an outdoor one. We always used to bring out chairs on Mott Street. Our neighbors would take advantage of them, and if they liked a chair they took it upstairs to their own apartment. But then they were always giving us furniture too.

There is a big church on the corner of Ned's street which is kept locked up all day so that there is no chance to "make a visit." I myself like a nice big parish church, where one can get a wonderful sense of space and privacy and quiet. Nativity Church, on Second Avenue and Second Street, is our present parish and was when we lived at 223 Chrystie Street. Many a man from the Muni (the Municipal Lodging House, on Third Street) went to morning Mass and dropped in during the day to sit in the sun of the Blessed Sacrament.

If I wrote to Archbishop Cooke and asked that Nativity Church be kept open during the day, I wonder if the pastor and curates would agree. Of course, things would get stolen. If there are curtains, heavy rich red plush ones, in front of the confessionals, they might be taken home to be used as covers in the cold tenements, where too often the furnace breaks down. Or the candlesticks might disappear from the altar, to supply the light when the welfare check was used for food and the gas and electric was shut off.

We ourselves were threatened that way at Tivoli by the Central Hudson Gas and Electric last month because we had missed paying our monthy bill. No leeway given, "Pay, or we come on Monday to shut off the electricity," which means that heat goes off and the pump that fills the reservoir stops functioning for the thirty-five people around the house at Tivoli, who now include two newly born infants and people who have passed three score and ten. Of course the bill was large, $128, but we got it paid by collecting it here and there from everyone we encountered. Some of our young residents who have been picking grapes chipped in a ten here and there, and one girl gave twenty dollars. We really have never been quite so broke as we are right now, but the appeal is going out and little by little the bills will get paid.

The only other time we bought a house in the city, back in 1950, it was the same, but the butcher, the baker and the grocer all waited for months and months. None of these co-operators are chain stores, needless to say.

But to return to how the church in Harlem could be used by the entire neighborhood: There is always a basement and a hall, and what does it matter if only a handful of people get to daily Mass? There could be a good literature rack, and perhaps an organ recital a few times a week, and a choir to practice and to put on some concerts. But of course what pastors worry about is desecration of the Blessed Sacrament of the Altar. As though the dear Lord could not take care of Himself.

But I promised to tell more about my three weeks' trip through Mississippi in August. It is not so far a cry from Harlem to Mississippi after all. What with declining farm equipment and the lack of educational and health facilities, more and more Negroes are moving north to the big cities.

According to *Fortune* magazine, 77 per cent of all Negroes lived in the South in 1940. Now just over half do. "Because migrating Negroes are subjected to less study than migrating birds, nobody knows how many have moved out of the South since 1960, when the last census was taken. But there is fragmentary evidence to suggest the migration is changing in direction." But they are returning not to the rural South, but to the cities. One half of the entire Negro population are in the cities, compared to one third in 1940.

There is more employment offered to the Negro now in Southern cities and when a Negro woman was elected Chancery Clerk in Port Gibson, Mississippi, a town half way between Natchez and Jackson, she found little cooperation in the county to help her begin her new job. So the local priest, a Missionary Servant of the Most Holy Trinity, went to Berry Morgan, a convert to the faith, asking her to help out with what aid she could give and her moral support. Berry promptly found herself being boycotted by her neighbors, but she was of such established position, and was so completely happy as a convert and a writer, that it did not bother her much.

Hearing about our visit to Natchez from her friend Marge Baroni, Berry drove down one day and took Kay Lynch and me home with her to spend the night. She lives on Albena Plantation, a six-hundred-acre tract in the northern, Delta section of the state. The house and lawn are surrounded by a picket fence and then there is what I can only describe as rain forest shutting them in. Trees, trees, everywhere, and when I asked her if there was no garden near the house she indicated that there was a clearing away in the back, where there was a clear field for a garden. Other such fields dotted the woods, connected by dirt roads so numerous that Berry herself has not explored all of them. Some fields comprise a few acres, others fifteen or twenty-five, and there are cattle grazing, and horses. It is a strange land there along the Mississippi, a country of loess soil that is like powder, or silt, and all but impossible to cultivate, and I guess it is the trees and the shrubbery that hold it down. But the roads have been worn down so that they are between steep high banks. There is a section of Mississippi near there, fifteen by twenty-five miles, which is uninhabited. I felt trapped in these woods and am sure I would never dare to set foot in this dense jungle because of the rattlesnakes.

Berry's three children were not afraid but most at home in that countryside, and hated to go back to school in New Orleans the following week. The house was furnished with massive beds with canopies, and wardrobes, and great dressers, and there was an air conditioner in the room with the bed canopy and a television set in an alcove off the hall. The Convention was going on, but we did not stay up to watch it. Our hostess announced that she always rose at four to write, so she was ready for bed at seven-thirty.

"I am really a plagiarist," she said, "listening to Bach while I work and translating it into prose." She gave me a copy of her *Pursuit*, the Houghton Mifflin Literary Fellowship Award Novel, which was highly praised by Walker Percy, a novelist whom I esteem. She is planning a book of her short stories, which appeared in the *New Yorker*, about the people of the South; the collection will be called *The Mystic Adventures of Roxie Stoner*. I'm looking forward to it.

So we went to bed early, and she passed on to me her copy of *One Dimensional Man* by Herbert Marcuse, which I in turn was to pass on to her sixteen-year-old son, who would be sitting up waiting for it. I had been hearing a lot about Marcuse recently, first at a conference in New England, and then from Brother Hugh, who asked me during my talk to the Trappist priests and brothers at Conyers, Georgia: "Isn't all the ferment among youth due to one M-a-r-c-u-s-e (he spelled it out) who is infecting them with Marxism?" And now here in this Southern planation in the midst of the woods.

Greenville and Greenwood

When we arrived at Greenville we were met by Father Messina, a native Mississippian, who took us to the five-thirty Mass which Father Thomas Reed was offering. (Eddie Reed, his brother, had been in charge of the tutorial program in Natchez for the summer, and left for Louvain last month.)

Greenville is in the very heart of the Delta region, where Cotton is King, as they say, where the land stretches out for miles, flat as a pancake. Next to Texas, Mississippi is the greatest cotton-producing state in the country and this in spite of the fact that seventy per cent of the state is forest, according to the latest *World Almanac*. The school run by the Sisters of Mercy in Greenville is extremely well integrated. Some of the sisters had us to supper, and afterwards we drove around to see the largest housing project in the South, which was going up building by building, with lots of space around the eighty buildings of four units each. Sister Ann from Chicago was living with one of the Negro families and was going to join some other Sisters in working with the inhabitants of the project.

It was the opinion of the blacks we met with that the best work in Mississippi, the most militant work, was being done by the Delta Ministry, which has a paid staff of 35 and annual budget of three hundred thousand dollars, so that they can afford to hire full-time workers in eight counties. They also have ties with individual and local groups in eleven other counties. Those who want to keep up with what is happening in this state ought to subscribe to this *News Letter*, Box 120, Tougaloo, Miss., 39174, which reports on the cooperatives in this and neighboring states.

The next morning, we travelled on to Greenwood to be in time for the Mass at the Franciscan Center, where our old friends Stanley Borowski and Larry Evers once worked for some months with Father Nathaniel. This was years ago, before the violence erupted over the Freedom Schools and voter registration. Father Nathaniel is responsible for starting a boycott, similar to the one in Natchez a year ago which I read about in a copy of the *Wall Street Journal* picked up in a subway. There was a front page, right hand column story of the boycott and its successful outcome in opening up more jobs to the Negro. (It is a shame we have to get our news from the subway because our fellow workers in Natchez are too busy working for the cause there to write us about it!)

Many of the Pax Christi women who come to work with Kate Jordan, who has been working with Fr. Nathaniel for many years, are getting degrees to teach in the Negro and white colleges in the South. I met our old friend Alma Taylor and a new friend, Shirley Foley, who is going to Boston University. There are many volunteers in this movement who come for the summer and stay for training for work in the South.

My only criticism of the working Greenwood is in regard to the dogs. There were a couple of fiercely barking police dogs which the women had to lock up on a porch every time we passed from one building to another of the large group which makes up the Center in Greenwood. When I suggested that I stay at the rectory, the priest assistant to Father Nathaniel said that I would not like the Doberman Pinschers which they had there either. Why the dogs? "They are dog lovers around here" one of the girls said. "To keep out those who steal" was another explanation.

But when you remember the police dogs used against children in Birmingham, and have seen the dogs which accompanied the police in Baltimore, on their short leashes as the officers patrolled the streets; and saw them being taken out of vans and hoisted up and over a fence around the little park opposite the post office where the trial of the Catonsville Nine was going on, you cannot help but think that the presence of dogs showed fear and distrust of the very folk one lived amongst. "If anyone takes your cloak, offer him your coat too," Jesus said.

I reproach myself, too, for my fear of dogs. St. Francis said, "Be subject to every living creature" quoting the words of St. Paul, and he added, "Even to the dog who is about to bite you." How far we are from living what we believe.

Aside from this reproach, I have nothing but admiration for the tremendous amount of work done by this group of dedicated women, and I'd recommend too their paper, *The Center*, so send for a copy (708 Avenue I, Greenwood, Mississippi).

December 1968

Readings and Ruminations: One of my bedside books, *The Days of the Lord*, is a compilation of the writings of the saints, past and present, published by Herder and Herder and edited by William G. Storey, an old friend of the *Catholic Worker*, teacher at Notre Dame, husband and father. Here you can find the best of theologians and scripture scholars of all periods. If that doesn't tempt you to buy this book, which comes in three parts (you can buy one at a time), let me illustrate how it works for me.

For December first, Blessed Edmund Campion is represented: a Jesuit, educated in Germany and Bohemia (now part Czechoslovakia) he was, back in England in 1580, a true underground priest (not a playboy), knowing that sooner or later he would be captured, tortured and killed. He begins: "I confess that I am a priest, though unworthy, of the Catholic Church, and through the great mercy of God vowed now these eight years into the religion of the Society of Jesus. Hereby I have taken upon me a special kind of warfare under the banner of obedience, and also resigned all my interests or possibilities of wealth, honor, pleasure and other worldly felicity." He goes on to tell how under obedience he journeyed from Prague to England (he would go anywhere as bidden) and "my charge is of free cost to preach the gospel, to instruct the simple, to reform sinners, to confute errors—in brief to crie alarm spiritual against proud vice and proud ignorance, wherewith many of my dear countrymen are abused."

And I began to think of Father Dan Berrigan, also a Jesuit, and his approaching martyrdom of three years in prison for destroying draft records and the debate which has gone on among the Catholic brethren as to whether or not this is an effective way of reaching the conscience of Catholics bred to a more conventional style of priesthood and apostolate. I will leave it to our readers, who I hope will get hold of this encyclopedic treasure of a book, to continue the reading which started in me a train of reflection. Most of our readers will begin by wondering why Father Berrigan does not fit the conventional image of a saint. Even those quotations from priests of the present day who have suffered martyrdom, imprisonment or suppression do not immediately help us understand him. I am thinking of the excerpts from Father Alfred Delp's prison letters, from the writings of Father Henri de Lubac, S.J. and Father Yves Congar, O.P. There were two other books that helped me greatly; by Robert L. Short, a theologian student at the Divinity School of the University of Chicago, who started working his way towards a degree by interpreting the theological significance of the famous cartoon, "Peanuts," drawn by Charles M. Schulz. The first book, *The Gospel According to Peanuts*, was published by the John Knox Press, of Richmond, Virginia, in 1964 and had gone into 17 printings by March, '67 (the edition I have.) The second, *The Parables of Peanuts*, is by the same author and published this Fall by Harper and Row (paper back, $1.95). Both books are delightful; but it is from the first that I would like to quote.

Why can't Father Berrigan be like Campion or other Jesuit heroes? I might have quoted Hugh of St. Victor, who brought most forcibly to my attention that each human being created by God is *unique* and that God has the special love for each one that such uniqueness requires, but more telling for today is Robert Short's explanation, in his essay "The Church and the Arts," which introduces his *Gospel*.

Mr. Short reminds us that: "How shall we sing the Lord's song in a foreign land?" is the question the Church, always finding itself *in* but not *of* the world, urgently needs to consider today. And illustrating the indirect approach of Fr. Dan Berrigan, one might quote with him from Kierkegaard's *Journals*; "If one is to lift up the whole age, one must truly know it. That is why those ministers of Christianity who begin at once with orthodoxy have so little effect and only on few. . . . One must begin with paganism." And St. Paul: "To the Jews I became as a Jew, in order to win Jews . . . to those outside the law I became as one outside the law . . . to the weak I became weak, that I might win the weak. I have become all things to all men, that I might by all means save some."

I'd like readers to send those *Peanuts* books to all our fellow workers who are in prison, beginning with our editors and special friends: Father Phil Berrigan, S.S.J., Dan Kelly and David Miller, at Federal Prison Camp, Allenwood, Pennsylvania; Thomas Lewis, Federal Penitentiary, Lewisburg, Pennsylvania; Robert Gilliam, Federal Correctional Institute, Sandstone, Minnesota; Mike Vogeler, Medical Center for Federal Prisoners, Springfield, Missouri; Suzanne Williams, Federal Penitentiary, Alderson, West Virginia. You can get a list of prisoners for peace from the War Resisters League, 5 Beekman St., New York, N. Y. 10038. Anyone sending books must send them directly from the publisher, and that means, of course, that such gifts will be arriving long after Christmas. However, the traditional Catholic season ends on February 2nd, so that there is plenty of time. It is to be hoped that the books will be passed on to other prisoners who have little contact with their friends outside.

One of the saddest things Jim Wilson told us on coming out of Allenwood after 22 months in prison, was that so many prisoners did not get even one Christmas card, while the conscientious objectors got thousands. And the saddest thing about Jim's and David Miller's imprisonment is that each became a father after he went to jail. Their only contacts with their little ones are the meager visits permitted. Jim did not watch the 22 months growing of his little son Nathan, and David is still being deprived of seeing those early years of his two little ones. Thank God Cathy and the children have moved fifteen miles from the prison and started a guest house for the relatives of prisoners who cannot afford the high cost of motels or hotels or tourist rooms in the area. "He who loves sons and daughters more than me is not worthy of me," said Jesus. It is because they love children, and learn about love through their own children; because they see Christ in the least ones, the littlest ones, that they can perhaps begin to love all children, neighbors' children, children near and far, loving them in practice as well as in dreams.

The December 6th issue of *Commonweal* has a long letter from Phil Berrigan to his brother Dan, telling, warning, perhaps, of the tedium of prison, the deserts to cross, the death in life, the lovelessness—in fact, the dark night of the senses and the dark night of the soul. It seems to me that they often intermingle. I pray that in writing it, in the very ability to articulate it, the dull grey of his situation was somewhat lightened. I was always much impressed, in reading prison memoirs of revolutionists, such as Lenin and Trotsky (not to speak of Father Walter Cizek, S.J.) by the amount of reading they did, the languages they studied, the range of their plans for a better social order. (Or rather, for a new social order.) In the Acts of the Apostles there are constant references to the *Way* and the New Man. So in spite of the fact that priests are not ordained in order to start farming communes and replace the banking system and installment-plan buying with the credit union and cooperative, their very preaching of voluntary poverty and, above all, their setting the example, will do much to further the revolution. And what greater and purer means are there than prayer and suffering?

These are great men, the Berrigan brothers, and they are both young, they already have a following among the young, in and out of the Church. . . .

1969

January 1969

STRIKE LEADER

☐ Dolores Huerta is one of the heroines of the by now famous grape strike which began in Delano, California, in September 1965 and which is still going on in the form of a boycott, from one crisis to another. There are many leaders of the farm workers all over the country, and I wish I could interview them all, in California, in Texas, in New Mexico, in the thirty cities of the United States where the weapon of the boycott is being used.

Cesar Chavez, head of the union, has been ill for some time and had to withdraw from active participation. He has been given worldwide recognition, and I would place him with the late Martin Luther King, and with Danilo Dolci and Vinoba Bhave, as an outstanding example of a nonviolent leader. We like to write about individuals in these movements for social justice, because, in a way, they are the word made flesh. We talk about what ought to be done, and here are the people doing it, putting flesh on the dry bones of principles and ideals. There must be the *idea*, the theory of the personalist and communitarian revolution, but the idea must be clothed with flesh and blood.

Dolores Huerta, who came from Delano, is a young, strong, and beautiful woman, mother of seven children, and the leader of the grape boycott in the Manhattan area. A big job. A year ago five or six pickets began the work, going from store to store, up and down the streets of Manhattan, to the big Hunts Point Market, to the chain stores, to the boats that were bringing grapes from the West Coast, telling of the injustices done the farm workers, the conditions under which they had to live, their struggles for better housing, wages and hours, and demanding that they be included with other workers under the National Labor Relations Act, from the benefits of which they have been excluded from the time the law first went into effect. Our friends, Filipino and Mexican picketers, who shared our poverty in a flat on Kenmare Street last year, went back to their families in Delano for Christmas in 1967 and returned with a score or more of other workers, driving in a donated unheated bus to begin their Northeastern campaign in earnest. It is this group that Dolores leads.

One of the great things accomplished by the Farm Workers Union was the awakening of conscience among other unionists. The United Automobile Workers had been helping them from the beginning. For a time they were in conflict with the Teamsters, who controlled the hiring of workers in the packing sheds, but this has been resolved. The taxi drivers union helped them valiantly, and other unions have contributed. But a most outstanding gift in the way of hospitality was from the Seafarers International Union, which gave them board and lodging at the union headquarters at 182 21st St., Brooklyn, where they have stayed for over a year.

The first contract won as a result of the strike was with the Di Giorgio Corporation, and the most recent setback is a result of the fact that Di Giorgio has sold his lands. Di Giorgio holdings had far exceeded the 160-acre limitation that was designed to help the small farmers irrigate their lands and limit the amount of free or government-subsidized water provided to large growers. Di Giorgio made an agreement with the Federal government under which he would receive unlimited water subsidies for a ten-year period, after which he would sell off his "excess lands."

Dolores is presently living at the Seafarers' headquarters with three of her seven children; a sixteen-year-old girl who is in high school and two boys, ten and eleven. The girl is helping her both on the picket line and in speaking to groups. She doesn't like the school, she says, because tickets are required for admission to the cafeteria and because Negroes are bullied. The boys dislike their school, complaining of the long hours, eight to three-thirty, and the lack of physical training. It must be hard indeed after southern California. And it must be hard on Dolores.

"But we have gotten eighteen chain stores to take grapes out of their markets, and only Gristede's in Manhattan is holding out. Two hundred and fifty A. and P. stores have responded to the boycott, and now we are going after the independent fruit stores. This is an even harder job."

"We have a lot of good help," she told me, "young people who have worked in Vista and are experienced in reaching people. One of them was present in Birmingham, Alabama when the explosion killed four children in the Baptist church. Another is a Provo who has worked in Holland."

They were planning, she said, to call a conference for all the workers from the thirty cities involved and I suggested that she telephone Father Jeremiah Kelliker, head of the Graymoor Fathers, who offered his facilities at Garrison, New York, to the Peacemakers when they visited him a year and a half ago. The Christian Brothers at Tarrytown, New York, gave us hospitality during our PAX conference last summer and were able to put up forty people. The Christian Brothers and the Jesuits in Baltimore gave hospitality to many of the young students who came from all over the country for the recent trial of the "Catonsville Nine" who had napalmed draft records.

The closing of many seminaries and high schools run by religious orders may be a matter of great concern to churchmen but it also may mean that doors must be opened for many other kinds of work. There is a great debate going on now as to the relevance of the parochial-school system. It is hard to reconcile oneself to the loss of priests, through lack or loss of vocations, but Cardinal Newman foretold much when he spoke of the development of doctrine and the consulting of the laity. We can go back to St. Peter himself, recalling the phrase "the priesthood of the laity." The old-fashioned doctrine of abandonment to divine providence should make one accept the changes which are taking place with peace of heart. "All things work for good to those who love God," and "Eye hath not seen nor ear heard what God hath prepared for those who love Him," may apply not just to a future life, but to this world in which we live. I do not feel that I am digressing when I bring this in, because hospitality is a theme dear to the hearts of the Catholic Workers. To us it means a development of love, and a casting out of fear—the stripping ourselves to share with others, walking as

357

new men, in a new way. It is also "hoping against hope." It is acting "as if" all men believed they were brothers. It is fundamental to any work we undertake in the social order with Mexicans, Filipinos, Indians and, above all, Negroes. How the church needs to *know* them, to love them and to serve them!

God help us all to grow in this knowledge and love and service, following Him who came not to be served but to serve.

February 1969

We certainly must have the long view into the future to see and realize the awakening of the masses of people throughout the world and the growth of a new vision among them of a world which is personalist and communitarian. The great problem is: *what means are to be used?*

Thank God we are not living in that time when Africa was divided between all the European powers, and England, France and Holland dominated the Far East, when nobody knew or cared that their comfort in the West was built on the blood, sweat, and tears of toilers of the world.

The battle at home now is to conquer the bitterness, the sense of futility and despair that grows among the young and turns them to violence, a violence which is magnified by the press, the radio and television. We lose sight of the poor people's cooperatives and boycotts, the conquest of bread, as Kropotkin called it, which goes on daily in Alabama, Mississippi, Louisiana, not to speak of California, Texas, and all the states where Mexicans have been imported for agricultural labor. They have come into our cities too, so that "workers and peasants" have united in the struggle and the story of the grape pickers' nonviolent long drawn out battle has reached Canada and the shores of Sweden and Finland, where dock workers have refused to unload the grapes picked by scab labor in California. Our own government, our enemy the State, has become the instrument of the growers in buying up the grapes and shipping them overseas to the troops in Vietnam.

The work of unionization, the formation of credit unions and cooperatives, especially cooperative housing, must go on, as must the work of building up hope and a sense in men of their own capacity for change, and for bringing about change.

The only thing that keeps hope alive is work, and study must go with it, to keep one's hope and vision alive.

Faith

I was talking to Mike Gold, my old Communist friend, when he returned from France with his wife and two sons years ago. Our Christian-Marxist dialogue went like this:

"My sons are named Karl and Nicholas," he reminded me as we spoke of his children and my grandchildren.

"My second grandson is called Nicholas too."

"But mine is named after a different person than yours. Mine is named after Lenin."

"Mine after the saint by that name and the Nicholases in Russia are too, though they may not know it."

So I stopped the argument, having had the last word, by inviting him over, and he brought me a present, a picture of St. Anne, from Brittany, carefully rolled in a newspaper, so that it was flat for framing. While we stood in the *Catholic Worker* kitchen and talked the dialogue continued:

I said: "How hard it is to have faith in men when we see their racist attitudes, their fears of each other fed by the daily press. There is a lot of racism around the *Catholic Worker* movement, made up as it is of men from the Bowery and skid rows, as well as from the colleges. Class war and race war go on daily and we are a school for nonviolence." His eyes alight with faith, Mike said, "But it is the poor and the wretched, the insulted and the injured, who bring about the changes in the world, the great changes that are taking place."

I could not help but think that just as we cannot love God whom we do not see unless we love our brother whom we do see, it followed that our faith in man (as he could be) should increase our faith in God and His ever-present aid. "I can do all things in Him who strengthens me." "Without Him I can do nothing." And this very small conversation made me pray the more.

But how can we show our love by war, by the extermination of our enemies? If we are followers of Christ, there is no room for speaking of the "just war." We have to remember that God loves all men, that God wills all men to be saved, that indeed all men are brothers. We must love the jailer as well as the one in prison. We must do that seemingly utterly impossible thing: love our enemy.

Penance

This last month I spoke to a convocation of youth, fifteen hundred of them, in Toronto; to fifty members of the Association of Urban Sisters, working in Roxbury, Massachusetts; at a meeting in the Methodist Church, of Red Hook, New York, attended by our friends and neighbors of towns surrounding Tivoli. There were also members of the Veterans of Foreign Wars there. It was a peaceful meeting, all in all.

The Boston meeting was held on Ash Wednesday, and I spoke of penance. I said that I could understand a Kateri Tekathwitha taking on the severest of penances to atone for the cruelty of her people to the Europeans and for the white cruelty to the Indians. (One must judge oneself first.) Or the penances of a St. Rose of Lima, in a time when the Indians were systematically being killed off, and African slave labor was being imported to supply the labor which the Indians could not stand up under.

Penance seems to be ruled out today. One hears the Mass described as Sacrament, not as Sacrifice. But how are we to keep our courage unless the Cross, that mighty failure, is kept in view? Is the follower greater than his master? What attracts one in a Che Guevara and Ho Chi Minh is the hardships and the suffering they endured in living their lives of faith and hope. It is not the violence, the killing of one's enemies. A man is a man, and to hear him crying out in pain and anguish, whether he is friend or enemy, is to have one's heart torn in unutterable sorrow. The impulse to stand out against the State and go to jail rather than serve is an instinct for penance, to take on some of the suffering of the world, to share in it.

Father Anthony Mullaney, O.S.B. who is one of the "Milwaukee Fourteen" priests and laymen who burned draft records with napalm—"burning property, not people"—told me, when I met him in Boston the other day, that over a hundred of the students of St. Anselm's in Manchester, New Hampshire, signed a petition to the court, which they are going to send when the Milwaukee 14 are sentenced, offering to divide up the months or years the fourteen have to serve, and take on the sentences for them. He will be speaking next month at Town Hall, and we will learn more about this. What is this but an offer to do penance, another example of trying to follow in the steps of Christ, who took on himself our sins and in so doing overcame both sin and death?

This is, in effect what Chuck Matthei, Chicago draft refuser, is doing, in not cooperating with the prison authorities when they seized him most brutally and literally dragged him, handcuffed, to West St. Federal prison in New York, where he is now fasting from food, and sometimes water, too.

To just read about these things or hear of them is not enough. One must meet Chuck and see the brightness of his face, feel the gentle and joyous and truly loving spirit, to get a glimpse of an understanding of what he is doing.

The thing is to recognize that not all are called, not all have the vocation, to demonstrate in this way, to fast, to endure the pain and long drawn out nerve-racking suffering of prison life. We do what we can, and the whole field of all the works of mercy is open to us. There is a saying, "Do what you are doing." If you are a student, study, prepare, in order to give to others, and keep alive in yourselves, the vision of a new social order. All work, whether building, increasing food production, running credit unions, working in factories which produce for true human needs, working in the smallest of industries, the handcrafts—all these things can come under the heading of the works of mercy, which are the opposite of the works of war.

It is a penance to work, to give oneself to others, to endure the pinpricks of community living. One would certainly say on many occasions, "give me a good thorough, frank outgoing war, rather than the sneak attacks, stabs in the back, sparring, detracting, defaming, hand to hand jockeying for position that goes on in offices and 'good works' of all kinds, another and miserably petty kind of war." St. Paul said that "he died daily." This too is penance, to be taken cheerfully, joyfully, with the hope that our own faith and joy in believing will strengthen Chuck and all the others in jail.

Let us remember too, those "mutineers," the soldiers who protested the killing of one of their number by a shot in the back in the Presidio on the West Coast, and their sixteen-year sentences at hard labor.

So let us rejoice in our own petty sufferings and thank God we have a little penance to offer, in this holy season. "An injury to one is an injury to all," the Industrial Workers of the World proclaimed. So an act of love, a voluntary taking on oneself of some of the pain of the world, increases the courage and love and hope of all.

"Is it wicked to take pleasure in spring and other seasonal changes? To put it more precisely, is it politically reprehensible while we are all groaning under the shackles of the capitalist system, to point out that life is frequently more worth living because of a blackbird's song, a yellow elm tree in October, or some other natural phenomenon which does not cost money and does not have what the editors of the left wing newspapers call a class angle?"

This is a quotation from George Orwell which comforts my heart. We are certainly all subject to guilt feelings when we contemplate the "military-industrial" complex and meditate on the fact that the United States is supplying arms for nine other countries, and when we see pictures of famine. Certainly sorrow and relief from sorrow make up our lives. Life and death go together. "As dying yet behold we live," St. Paul said. Pain is an inbuilt thing in life. Anguish and joy go together. Father Thomas Berry, C.P., who is teaching courses in Buddhism at Fordham University, was telling us these things at a recent Friday night meeting (the monthly PAX meeting).

I guess women know these things instinctively. A woman's anguish is turned into joy when a child is born into the world. Henri Daniel-Rops once asked, after the crucifixion when the apostles and disciples all hid in fear, what did the women do? "They went on about the business of living, pounding the spices and procuring the linen cloths in which to embalm the body." They went on about the business of living. There are the three meals to get, the family to care for, "the duty of delight" that Ruskin spoke of, for the sake of others around us who are on the verge of despair. Who can say there is no delight, even in city slum, especially in an Italian neighborhood where there is a pot of basil on the window sill and the smell of good cooking in the air, and pigeons wheeling over the roof tops and the tiny feathers found occasionally on the sidewalk, the fresh smell of the sea from the dock of the Staten Island ferry boat (five cents a ride).

Peter Maurin used to say, "Man is spirit, woman is matter," and I knew what he meant by this obscure Thomistic utterance. Woman is close to the material things of life, and accepts them, this integration of soul and body and its interaction. St. Teresa of Avila said once that if her nuns were melancholy, "feed them steak!" She reminded us too—"All things are passing."

Family Visit

It was not yet spring when I went to Vermont to pay a visit to my daughter and the five children who are still at home. Becky Hennessy Houghton is in Laconia, New Hampshire, Sue Hennessy Kell is in Sudbury, Ontario, Eric is in Vietnam and Nick, also married, is now on a construction job in the neighborhood of Springfield, Vermont. I missed seeing the two oldest girls and their husbands but I did see Nickie and his wife Brenda and their new baby Sheila Ann, born two months ago. Mary works after school (she is a senior in high school) but is always able to "cope," as far as one can see, and never seems tired. Marvellous youth. When asked how she feels, she always says "wonderful." I have decided that that is what we all should do instead of starting to exchange symptoms. Maggie is the one who always answers letters and is always ready to take on the ironing. Martha too is most responsible, and between the three of them there is a great work of sewing, washing, ironing and school work. They are all better at cooking than at dish washing, but I happen to like that simple job if I can get to it before my daughter Tamar, who swiftly disposes of disagreeable tasks before I can get at them. Katie and Hilaire are the youngest, nine and eleven, and are out-of-doors children, regardless of the snow on the ground. In fact, Katie was already fitting up a playhouse in the old chicken coop, even though she had to go through the deep snow to get to it. Hilaire was busy tapping trees for maple syrup and before I left there was a few gallons to his credit.

As to home crafts, in addition to her weaving Tamar has been making soap and I brought back some dozen cakes of it. Since the two towels I use are also handwoven and handspun by my daughter, I have those samples of beauty in the midst of a city slum. Peter Maurin used to say that men make their money by the machine and spend it on handmade products. Certainly I treasure those towels and enjoy using them.

During the winter the grade school in Perkinsville which Tamar's children attend has had a course in skiing, two afternoons a week, the school bus taking the children to and from Mt. Ascutney. A number of other schools took part in this program too. There is a great turnover and exchange in skis and ski equipment. Hilaire has his own, bought him by one of his older brothers, but Martha had a loan from a schoolmate. This was the last afternoon of the season, March 28th, and Tamar and I sat on the porch of the ski lodge and watched the children—except Hilaire, who was apt to ski on the more hazardous slopes on the other side of the lodge.

It was a lovely afternoon in the sun looking down over a long valley and up a great slope of mountain, where the figures of young people looked terribly small as they speeded down through the snow. Already it was melting and slushy, but I was so glad to be there. It was the first time I have watched skiers except on television. A few days later snow fell again.

Life and Death

This month has seen the death of two of our dear friends, Fred Lindsey and Marie Langlots, both of whom have been part of our family for many years. There is a picture of Marie in my book, *Loaves and Fishes*, as she sweeps out our dining room and meeting room at the end of a long day. But there are many more pictures of her in my mind and heart. She was my room mate for a time on Kenmare Street and when we moved to First Street she was already so ill that she needed the peace and quiet of an apartment of her own, and we settled her across the street so she could be close to us. She had to keep that fierce independence which had so long been her way of living. One could not give her an apple without her bringing you the next day half a dozen more. She used to get me a sandwich and a piece of fruit to take on my trips. "Lunch on the bus," she would say. She helped our Italian neighbors by bringing their littlest children to school, and she did a heroic job winter before last, helping our then landlady, Mrs. Vaccaro, clean the accumulated ice out of the gutters on the roof which melted into the top floor apartments. A dangerous job which made me shudder. But Marie and Mrs. Vaccaro were valiant women. Marie also kept us all supplied with newspapers and every Thursday she brought me a copy of the *Village Voice*. For a long time she refused to go to a clinic or to the hospital for her ulcerated legs, and kept telling us of home remedies which her mother always used. She loved her family and the farm land from which she came, but an adventurous spirit brought her to the city, which fascinated her. However, she was looking forward to getting a round-trip ticket back to Missouri to see her sister and other relatives in the fall.

She finally consented to go to Bellevue—every other nearby hospital was packed to the doors, and, although one could get clinic care at Beth Israel or St. Vincent's, there were waiting lists at both hospitals and they had to send on the patients who came to them to the city hospital, Bellevue.

"How good they have all been to me," Marie said to us, the last day of her life. "The doctors, not one, but many of them, come many times, and they answer all my questions. The nurses and attendants have all been so good to me. The meals are very good," and she proceeded to tell us just what she had for breakfast, lunch and supper.

She was tired that day, so Pat Rusk and I left about fifteen minutes before visiting hours were over. She was going to be operated on the next day and she wanted to rest. We kissed her goodbye. Tom Cornell had brought her a flowering plant and she had flowers from others. In a few days, she said, she would like some bananas, her favorite fruit. "Put the window up a little higher, the air is so sweet." An hour later, she breathed her last, most peaceably. Dear Marie.

Her sister in Missouri was notified and the body was sent back to the midwest to rest in that good farmland she so loved. She knew her scripture and quoted often from Old and New Testaments. "I am the resurrection and the life; he who believes in me even if he die, shall live; and whoever lives and believes in me shall never die."

Fred Lindsey

Fred, who had worked so long with us at the farm, doing everything from cooking, dish washing, painting, cleaning out cesspools and even nursing the sick—he is with us still in our hearts. But the picture of him which I love the most is that of his tender care of Agnes Sidney in her last days. Her hair had been long, done in a sparse knot at the back of her neck. She had a bright Irish eye and a jaunty way with her, even in her eighties. (She was the wife of a barge captain who had lived at sea for many years.) When it was impossible for her to manage her hair, Fred took over, not just with the combing of it. One day I came in to find that he had given her not only a haircut, but a shampoo. And it was either Fred or Mike Sullivan who brought in Agnes' coffee at the crack of dawn each day. When I shared this morning service with her she used to look over at me with a twinkle. "The life of Riley," she'd say.

Fred was a Mormon and had long lived away from his own family. We were his family, and when I recall all the little incidents of his stay with us over the years, I realize more fully how much like a family we are, with all its joys and troubles, the love and the stress of living together. That is what a house of hospitality should be. Fred rests in a little Protestant cemetery in New Jersey and we know, not only that "our Redeemer liveth, but that in our flesh we shall see God our saviour." Even the tragic Job felt these things.

How easy it is to have this faith in the Spring, with new life bursting through the ground and buds appearing on what to all appearances is dead wood.

June 1969

My shoes are covered with dust and I am down at the heels indeed, what with tramping through the dust of the Hutterite colonies in South Dakota and Montana, the Indian camps on the Nisqually River, southwest of Tacoma, Washington, and now the Forty Acres of the Farm Workers' Union, which is the pride and joy of Cesar Chavez's heart. Cesar Chavez is the head of the farm workers, more properly called the United Farm Workers Organizing Committee (U.F.W.O.C.-AFL-CIO) since the strike began in 1965. It is going on right now in the Coachella Valley in California, an organizing drive which has gone into Texas, Arizona, New Jersey, New York and many States in between.

When my bus arrived at Delano, which is about three hours northeast of Los Angeles, I was met by Father Ed Fronske, one of the young priests from Our Lady of Guadalupe Church. He drove me to the half dozen small houses rented by the union to house the offices of organizers, strikers, credit union, etc. These were not the homes of the organizers and union workers, which are scattered around Delano. The three-room building I was taken to has one bedroom, where Cesar spends many hours a day flat on his back. When visitors arrive he comes out into the main office, where a Chilean volunteer sits at a typewriter and a telephone. When I arrived, Cesar's wife Helen was preparing some supper in the kitchen, which was a large enough room to eat in. There was a lovely little flower garden and a picket fence around the house. The first picture I saw when I entered was a blown-up head of Gandhi. (We have one on the wall of St. Joseph's House in New York.) There were also picture of Emilio Zapata, the Mexican campesino who spent his life fighting for land for the people who worked, and of Our Lady of Guadalupe.

Cesar had visited us in New York at our old place on Chrystie Street and had prayed at our picture of Our Lady of Guadalupe as soon as he entered the room and saw it. I had met him also on another occasion when he was in New York again. He greeted me warmly from his prone position and told me that Ammon Hennacy had been to see him and had given him a copy of his book. "But I already had a copy and had read it," he said. We agreed that Ammon's articles, which we had entitled "Life at Hard Labor," were first rate. He also spoke appreciatively of Joe Geraci's long review in the May issue of Jerry Mangione's book about Danilo Dolci, *A Passion for Sicilians*.

The things we spoke of that first afternoon were Dolci's work in Sicily (we will have another review of a book by Dolci in a future issue of the *Catholic Worker*), of the Hutterite colonies that I had just visited and of Vinoba Bhave of India. It was our discussion of the *moshavim* of Israel, which Cesar said he preferred to the *kibbutzim*, that sparked our visit to the Forty Acres. It made me happy indeed to see that the dreams of the farm workers under his leadership would include the beginnings of another social order, planning for new institutions which could grow up within the shell of the old; cooperative farms, perhaps, which would be village communities surrounded by orchards, vineyards and ranches. Are there any growers with such vision?

There were evidences of harassment at the Forty Acres, which lie between the town dump and the road. Five hundred shade trees and quick-growing windbreak trees had been planted on the border near the dump and a fire had all but destroyed a score or more of the trees. There were indications, however, that the trees would revive. The long grove has greatly increased in height and thickness in the last two years, though the soil was desert all around us. "Alkaline," one of the drivers commented, kicking at the salt-like surface. "It needs to be washed."

Other trees had been planted, a well had been drilled, there was a water tank, beginnings had been made. Across the road was the great impersonal agency of the Voice of America, which could reach the Far East, Vietnam itself. Down the road there were some friendly neighbors, one of them a house mover. Here too there were new highways cutting through the streets of towns and eliminating the shabby homes of the poor. Two large unpainted buildings had been moved onto the Forty Acres by this same house mover. But the building to which Cesar pointed with pride was an adobe headquarters to which visitors in the future would come. This was one of two buildings that are ambitious indeed in size. Yet one can see that as a national headquarters they will be no more than sufficient to house the business of the union. Cesar mentioned that Jack Cook, who wrote articles about the Texas melon strike a few years ago, and about Delano's grape strike, had painted a good part of one of the buildings. Cesar appreciates a worker-scholar and certainly needs more of them to help with carpentry. Right now all work has ceased, because of the new strike in the Coachella Valley.

It was here at Forty Acres that Cesar conducted his twenty-five-day fast in much the same manner that Danilo Dolci or Gandhi went through their fasts. A man in such a position lives a public life; he must always be available to all who are working with him, a man who gives himself completely to a cause. Another room was used to offer up Masses during the fast. Certainly Chavez relies on the life of the spirit, a life of discipline, in carrying on this tremendous moral struggle with the growers of those rich valleys of California.

Next evening there was a memorial Mass at the Filipino Hall for Robert Kennedy. It was the first anniversary of his death, and Chavez will always remember that Kennedy came and broke bread with him as he ended his fast. He considered him a *companero* in a very deep sense. Both Catholics, both devout, it did not seem that the wealth of one made any difference between them.

The Filipinos can be proud of their large hall, where all the strike meetings are being held. Indeed, the strike was started by Larry Itliong, a Filipino, Pete Velasco, another Filipino, was heading the strike down in the Coachella Valley and Julian Balidoy headed the boycott team when they first arrived in New York, in the fall of 1967, and stayed with his four companions at our Kenmare Street apartment.

The Mass was offered by Father David Duran, of Corcoran, California, near a great cotton-growing area. Cesar had asked me to read the epistle which begins: "The life of the just are in the hands of God and the torment of malice shall not touch them. In the sight of the unwise they seemed to die but they are at peace."

The memorial eulogy was given by Paul Schrade, regional director of the United Auto Workers, who was the most seriously wounded of the five others who were shot with Robert Kennedy. It took three priests to distribute the communion bread while all sang. De Colores had begun the Mass, O Maria was the communion hymn, and Nosotros Venceremos concluded it.

Bread was distributed after Father Duran had blessed it after the Mass (he is a Mexican and it is a custom) and everyone broke off a piece and passed the bread on to his neighbor. After the Mass there were many introductions and many speeches, what with busloads of the thirty-two labor leaders from all over Canada bringing greetings.

"Taste and see how good the Lord is," and "I am the Bread of Life," were the words on the two long banners which hung on either side of the altar.

Larry Itliong and Cesar Chavez chaired the meeting and Juanita Brown, who, with her husband, heads the worldwide boycott of table grapes, was the interpreter. She is a beautiful young woman with a lively charm.

The best thing about my being called upon to speak at this meeting was that it gave me a view of the packed hall with the beautiful dark faces of the Filipinos and the Mexicans, men, women and children, the seats all filled, and the aisles and the three sides of the hall also packed in close ranks, no one restless, for four solid hours. They broke out now and then in a crescendo of applause which became faster and faster clapping of hands and a stamping of feet which died down then as suddenly as it had flared up. And of course there were the shouts of *Viva la Causa, Viva la Huelga,* over and over again.

Coachella Valley

The first table grapes ripen in the Coachella Valley, which lies below Indio and just north of the Salton sea. A desert has been made to bloom by irrigation, and I saw the wonders of the date center of the world with its thousands of palms

369

(one town is called Thousand Palms) not yet ready to be harvested. There are also cotton, asparagus and citrus fruits in this valley, but the harvest at the present time is grapes.

In the date forests, if one can call them that, the workers can be sheltered by shade from the boiling heat, which often goes above 110. The few days that I was there, the Lord seemed to be tempering the wind to the shorn lamb; I did not suffer from the dry heat, and by using a blue bandanna as a sunbonnet, I worked under the harsh glare of the sun.

The strike headquarters is a long parish hall, in back of a Seventh-day Adventist church. There were rooms for offices, for dining hall and kitchen, and other rooms had been given over for the men and women who were working in the strike. Dolores Huerta was there, with some of her children, and Amalia Uribe is a teen-age Dolores who was active every day in picketing of the ranches, as they call the vineyards here. But most of the pickets were men. Meals were served at the hall, and the Adventists had told the strikers that they could use the little church for religious services. There was a large tree-shaded area in front of the hall, and an outdoor dining area, where people sat around under a shelter. Meetings were held in the evenings out of doors, which made it a little hard to speak. I think that a City College student and I were the only New Yorkers there. But there are of course others in this great struggle who are neither Mexicans nor Filipinos. James Drake, always spoken of as a member of the migrant ministry, is an "Okie," as I was very glad to hear, because it made me realize that he had far more than a "man of the cloth's" realization of the problems involved. He was raised in the Valley and went to school in the small neighboring town of Thermo. His father had been a Methodist minister on a ten-acre farm in Oklahoma and taught school for forty dollars a month as well as serving the church. They managed to live on this salary and the food they raised.

From the beginning Jim Drake has been in the forefront of this strike of agricultural workers, the first in history that has had a grass-roots foundation.

There are two lawyers always on the scene, Jerry Cohen in Delano and David Averback, from Delano but now staying in Coachella. I had been put up at his house with other women when I arrived and enjoyed his hospitality. He has given not only himself to the strikers, but his house too, with its fine library, comfortable beds and a swimming pool in the back yard where Cesar Chavez comes to exercise. He is under

370

the care of a doctor the Kennedy family sent him who had taken care of John Kennedy, who also suffered from a back ailment. David is crippled and has to go about on crutches, a big, powerful-looking, handsome man.

I could not help but think as I spent these days in Delano and Coachella that the calmest, most peaceful person in this countrywide struggle is Chavez himself. One of the other leaders told me that he was all but developing ulcers with the tension they were under. But Chavez, though he shows the strain of the long hours of consultation and explanation to visitors of the history of the strike, the philosophy on nonviolence, the history of agriculture itself in the Long Valley, shows no sign of impatience or tension. On one occasion, when he was being questioned by two men of another small group brought from Canada by the growers, perhaps to counteract the great impression made by the formal Canadian delegation, he was asked "Now that you have ruined half the growers in the valley, how long do you think it will take you to ruin the others?" The statement (it could hardly be called a question) was accompanied by such a look of hatred and wrath that it made me realize that the few who took turns in guarding Chavez were indeed needed.

Cesar had already been talking for two hours and got up at this point, begging to be excused with perfect courtesy. "You are not asking honest questions," he said calmly. He has clearly overcome the fear that one almost feels instinctively when faced with such naked hate. Studying Gandhi no doubt helped, and I must remember to report that he expressed gratitude to Eileen Egan for sending him a copy of the Gandhi memorial calendar, put out by the War Resisters League, which I have praised so highly in previous columns.

A Working Day

But to get back to Coachella, I was given hospitality in the four-room house of the Uribe family and when the meeting was over at which I was again asked to speak, Jose Junior drove me to the outskirts of the town to the comfortable little house where I got acquainted with others in the family. Two of the seven brothers were married and had sons, and there were two daughters. The youngest son was going to college and had been exempt from the draft because he had been scarred by allergies to the poison sprays used in the grapes.

I soon learned more about the hard work that had held

371

such a family together. During the strike the pickets were rising at three in the morning so that they could go to the union hall, eat breakfast, and receive their assignments to various fields. Sometimes they had to drive ten miles to a vineyard. It was about five o'clock when I arrived with Doug Adair and Marshal Ganz, two other "Anglos," as we are called, and Julian Balidoy and others, part of a long caravan of cars. A sheriff was already at the strike hall to direct traffic and drove behind us. I don't know how many sheriffs there were, but I know there were two cars that stayed with us all morning.

Usually the workers are at the job as soon as it is light, pickers, foremen, superintendents, even some of the growers in an emergency such as this. But this morning the workers (scabs) were slow to arrive. Every evening the pickers' camps were visited by strikers who persuaded many to strike, then directed them to other jobs, such as melon picking, which were available at the time. Perhaps this delay in arrivals meant that the visits the night before had borne results.

It was probably near six when the first loads of workers came, a carload of six or seven women who slowed down at the entrance and listened to the strikers for a few moments until a foreman appeared in another car and, leaping out, urged them in. After that the cars came thick and fast, including a busload. Our cars were lined up along the road at various entrances along a half-mile strip, and the two sheriff's cars stayed at our gate because most of the workers seemed to be coming there. They were urged to stop work, to quit, pled with and beseeched, and Amalia's voice through the loudspeaker on one of the cars brought tears to the eyes, so persuasive and so plaintive did she sound. She is only eighteen, is a freshman at the College of the Desert and with her entire family is active in both the strike and boycott.

It was a beautiful morning, and until then the birds had been giving such a paean of praise to their Maker, that I kept thinking of Deane Mowrer and how she would have loved to hear this bird symphony. The sun was already hot and there was no breeze. There was such a dust haze, a heat haze, that one could not see the mountains, which on clear days are not too far away, near Palm Springs, San Gorgonia, still covered with snow, and San Jacinto.

We all carried signs and we did not have to keep moving but stood on either side of the entrance, close enough together so that cars would have to slow down to enter. There

372

was a moment of danger when an enraged foreman, or perhaps a grower, put on a sudden spurt of speed and swerved almost straight at Doug and me, so that we had to leap back.

Doug showed the mark of the tires to the sheriff who was taking down the name of one of the strikers who had trespassed into the rows of grapes to talk to a striker. The name of the picker was taken also. The sheriff was perfunctory about both complaints.

But there had been violence. A strike bulletin read: "Antonio Lopez kicked in the ribs and beaten by Irving Felstien, grower; Beatrice Sanchez, had her arm twisted behind her back by Bill Smith; Jose Irube, threatened with a rifle by a grower; Nicholas Buenrostro, cut in the face with grape scissors by unknown person; Armando Sanchez, kicked in the face and body and beaten by a foreman." (The above are only a few incidents of violence.)

"We have to sacrifice to deserve," the bulletin continued. "The Farm Workers' Union is built on sacrifice. Farm Workers such as Hope Lopez and Higinio Rangel have fasted for as long as ten days for success of the grape boycott in strange eastern cities.

"The strike and boycott of grapes is a peaceful, nonviolent yet direct action to remove oppression and social injustices committed against the farm worker. We call upon all of those working to heed this call for non-violence and leave the grape fields so this non-violent action will be successful."

One could see that the words, the actions of the strikers were having their effect. Those in the vineyard worked slowly, stood hesitating in the long alley lined with empty boxes. If all the other pickets were making the same impression, there was certainly a slowdown.

I went out one morning at three and the morning before that I had joined the picket line at ten o'clock. I thought of how each day these men and women strikers and non-strikers had to work from daylight until noon, and stopped work only to resume it later on when the heat was not so bad for the grape. I saw men squeezing a grape and testing the running juice for sugar content. The worker himself has to thin the leaves, pick out only perfect bunches, strip off any defective grape before putting it in the paper-lined box to be taken to load on the truck finally and carted to the warehouse. I saw children in the field, helping their parents. Stripping, thinning at $1.10 an hour,—that was what Jose Uribe's mother was paid, with a penny extra for each vine thinned.

One could only do fifty vines a day, he said, so that made fifty cents a day, and for a six-day week, three dollars extra. But the grower did not pay for the thinning and when Jose and his mother went to collect that extra three dollars, the grower threatened them with a rifle.

Remember these things, you whose mouth waters for table grapes; remember the boycott, and help the strikers.

How many things I am leaving out (but I will write more later). I have only now arrived from the West Coast, with this flood of impressions, a bit dazed from sitting up for three nights and two days on Santa Fe and Penn Central. Fare is $110 by train, and $158 by plane. We must contribute to the strike fund, and contribute small sacrifices of endurance too. Among us at the Catholic Worker, only Ammon knows such a life at hard labor as these brothers of ours endure.

So this story is written with an appeal to our readers to help these agricultural workers whose struggle has gone on for four years now, from one end of the country to the other. It is the first breakthrough to achieve some measure of justice for these poorest and most beloved of God's children. Send help to

United Farm Workers,
Post Office Box 695
Delano, California 93215

BULLETIN

Just as my news story about the new grape strike at Coachella was completed we learn from a June 13th UPI news release in the New York *Times* that ten major Coachella Valley grape growers have asked Federal officials to arrange an immediate meeting with the United Farm Workers' Organizing Committee. This is the first major breakthrough in a three-year labor stalemate and undoubtedly comes as a result of the grape boycott, which has been going on all over the country. The growers term the boycott illegal and immoral.

The next day the *Times* printed a slightly longer account. James Drake and Peter Velasco announced that the union's executive board in Delano had voted unanimously to begin the talks. The union said that it was joining the ten growers in asking the Federal Mediation and Conciliation service for a joint meeting. Mr. Drake called for twenty-four-hour negotiations and said that the boycott activity would continue until a settlement was reached.

One union spokesman in Los Angeles said that there was no need of Federal intervention, that with good faith on both sides there could be progress towards a settlement. Nevertheless, the union joined the growers in seeking intervention. A still later dispatch stated that the other growers in the state would *not* negotiate.

The following list of benefits which have been obtained from the nine or ten growers who have already signed contracts with the union was printed on a strike bulletin and passed out to those workers in the fields who had not yet joined the strike. These sad pages show the modesty of demands of these field workers who have been for so many years denied the right to organize into a union. At least thirty strikes in the past forty years have been short-lived failures.

Following are some of the benefits enjoyed by Union members working at those ranches where the UFWOC AFL-CIO has contracts:

1. WAGES:

General labor	$1.90
Maintenance men	2.20
Irrigator	2.10
Truck Driver	2.30
Crew leader	2.15
Tractor Driver	2.30
Forklift Driver	2.30
Working Foreman	2.40
Shop Mechanic	2.55

The above rates will be increased in the amount of 10c. per hour effective August 1, 1969. Harvest workers will be paid an average hourly rate of $3.25. (Thus, in the 1969 harvest, a worker will average $3.25 per hour. At no given time will he make less than $2.00 per hour.)

2. SPECIAL BENEFITS: The grower pays 10c. per hour into a special fund which pays for health insurance for the worker and each member of his family.

3. HOLIDAYS: All employees shall receive eight hours' pay at their straight time hourly rate for Labor Day, Independence Day, Christmas Day.

4. VACATIONS: Workers with 1,600 hours in the last 12 months are granted one week vacation with pay, computed on the basis of 2 percent of the gross earnings in that 12 months. After 3 years' work, the employee receives two weeks' paid vacation at 3 percent of the gross earnings.

5. **PENALTY PAY:** Employees required to work more than 9 hours a day will be paid 25c. per hour in addition to their regular pay. Employees told to show up for work who are not given work will be paid for four hours at their regular rate of pay.

6. **RELIEF PERIODS:** Shall be fifteen minutes for each four hours worked.

7. **SENIORITY:** When filling vacancies the employer will give preference to workers with greatest seniority provided they have the qualifications to perform the work under normal supervision. There will be no discrimination according to race or religion in hiring and determining seniority.

8. **HIRING HALL:** Employers request workers through the Union hiring hall. The Union shall provide the needed workers within 72 hours. Workers not provided through the hiring hall can be hired directly by the employer.

9. **HEALTH AND SAFETY:** Adequate toilet facilities, drinking water, first-aid equipment and protective garments are provided. A safety committee made up of union members and management is the watchdog.

10. **GRIEVANCE PROCEDURES:** No worker can be fired without just cause. If a worker believes he has been fired without cause there are procedures to guarantee his rights.

11. **LIFE INSURANCE:** If a member whose dues are paid dies, his family receives $1,000. If any member of the family should die, the family receives $500.

12. **CREDIT UNION:** Any member of the Union can borrow up to $300 from the Union's Credit Union at 1 percent interest.

13. **SERVICE CENTER:** The union provides services for all members who are in need of help with income tax, naturalization, welfare or workman's compensation cases, etc.

December 1969

Sometimes our hearts are heavy with the tragedy of the world, the horrible news from Vietnam, Brazil, Biafra, the Israeli-Arab war. And here it is Advent and Christmas time again, and with it the juxtaposition of joy and sorrow, the blackness of night, brightness of dawn. What saves us from despair is a phrase we read in "The Life of Jesus" by Daniel-Rops, "getting on with the business of living." What did the women do after the crucifixion? The men were in the upper room mourning and praying and the women, by their very nature, "had to go on with the business of living." They prepared the spices, purchased the linen cloths for the burial, kept the Sabbath and hastened to the tomb on Sunday morning. There very work gave them insights as to *time*, and doubtless there was a hint of the peace and joy of the resurrection to temper their grief.

"The past year has been difficult," one of our friends writes, "particularly in dealing with the problems of relevancy. To many in the peace-resistance movement, feeding and sheltering the poor is looked upon as non-revolutionary and a mere band-aid applied to a cancerous world. To many, only when the American giant is confronted at its jugular vein is it worth-while. So our involvement and work has really been put into question. Perhaps we attempted to justify ourselves too much or spent too much time attempting to answer the question. But it seems clearer (now), and it can never be completely clear: we must continue with our work and look upon it as a practical response to a revolutionary gospel. The fact remains that while slaying the giant, the wounded have to be cared for. Perhaps those who come by can see the necessity of caring for one another and recognizing the importance of community."

We have heard this same word, "a band-aid to a cancer," from Boston and Milwaukee and even from the Australian bush within the last year. Perhaps it is only those words of the gospel about the corporal works of mercy, which in a way include the spiritual works of mercy, that has kept us going all these years. We are commanded over and over again by Jesus Christ himself to do these things. What we do for the least of these, we do for Him. We are judged by this. It is the picture of the last judgment in the 25th chapter of Matthew. Actually, we here at the Catholic Worker did not start these soup lines ourselves. Years ago, John Griffin, one of the men from the Bowery who moved in with us was giving out clothes, and when they ran out he began sitting down the petitioners to a hot cup of coffee, or a bowl of soup—whatever we had. By word of mouth the news spread, and one after another they came, forming lines (during the Depression) which stretched around the block. The loaves and fishes had to be multiplied to take care of it, and everyone contributed food, money and space. All volunteers who come, priests and people, nuns and college students, have worked on that line

377

and felt the satisfaction of manual labor, beginning to do without themselves to share with others, and a more intense desire to change the social order that left men hungry and homeless. The work is as basic as bread. To sit down several times a day together is community and growth in the knowledge of Christ. "They knew Him in the breaking of bread."

We have said these things many times in the pages of *The Catholic Worker*, but is to reassure these dear friends that I write this again. Perhaps it is easier for a woman to understand than a man. Because no matter what catastrophe has occurred or hangs overhead, she has to go on with the business of living. She does the physical things and so keeps a balance. No longer does the man sit as a judge at the gate as in the Old Testament where the valiant woman is portrayed. Now when women are putting their hand to the machine gun and joining in the violence which is racking us, the men join in the healing and the nourishing, the building and the spinning and the weaving, the cultivation and the preservation of the good earth. Now there is neither bond nor free, Greek or Hebrew, male or female—we are a little nearer to the heavenly kingdom when men are feeding the hungry. It is real action as well as symbolic action. It is walking in the steps of Jesus when he fed the multitude on the hills, and when he prepared the fire and the fish on the shore. He told us to do it. He did it Himself. . . .

Tom Sullivan called and told me our friend Fr. Kohli was having a prayer and scripture meeting every Friday night at St. Patrick's Church at Glen Cove, Long Island. Tom is not far from Glen Cove and attends these meetings. He spent nine months with the Trappists in Conyers and has the habit of prayer. Now he is a counsellor at Roosevelt School on Long Island, which is 90 percent Black. Tom keeps me up on news from the Trappists in Georgia where he goes to make a visit and a retreat each year. I get interesting letters from another Trappist monastery, Nuestra Senora de Solentiname on Lake Nicaragua, from Ernesto Cardenal, poet friend of Thomas Merton who made his novitiate at Gethsemane under Fr. Merton. He expressed much interest in the book I had mentioned to him on Catholic Pentecostals which emphasizes a return to prayer. "We try," he writes, "to give this message with our life here in Solentiname and the reason for the existence of our little community is prayer. We have two young married men in this community, and it is not, properly speaking, a monastery in the traditional sense of the word. We do not pretend to follow any preconceived model. *La Primera regla es que no hay reglas.* This sounds very much like our rule, 'Love God and do as you will,' which St. Augustine wrote so many years ago. In other words, if you love God your will is His will!"

This Tuesday morning I set out by bus for Loretto, Pennsylvania where John Butler, who helped us most of last summer, is in the seminary. I was to speak at St. Francis College and at the Seminary. From Harrisburg on we had climbed steadily all afternoon and arrived at Ebensburg after dark where I was met by John and another seminarian. Seminarians are radical, but the audience at the college was a bit belligerent over some of the points I made about interracial justice. They could overlook my pacifism, they expect that of a woman, but my assertions that there was hostility when a Black moved into a white neighborhood, and that white people were harassed and intimidated if there was any possibility of their selling to a Black buyer, met with vehement denials. There was no discrimination and the Blacks could buy into any neighborhood they wanted, several members of the audience asserted, and with hostility.

John and his friends do a good deal of work in Altoona and Johnstown among youth groups, so they know the problems. Next day we visited a very modern coal mine (though I didn't go down), and I was instructed in detail by the manager about the very complicated and up-to-date safety devices, and about how much it cost to start an operation and how long it would take to get any return on the investment of some ten millions of dollars. Which led me to ruminate aloud on the whole structure of our society and the idea of money being fruitful and producing more investments and interest and dividends, and under all this superstructure, man's labor, his work in pitch darkness, aside from the light of his miner's lamp, his long journey to his work underground, disputes about portal to portal pay, etc. Miners put in an eight-hour day, and have a half hour for lunch and six hours of work, they are such distances under ground. Orwell's *Road to Wigan Pier*, which is a study of unemployment in Britain, has a long section on the work of a miner which is a must for those interested in man's *work*. I asked if the men could stand upright, and the manager admitted that in some places the men had to work bent over all day. "They get used to it."

We were high in the Alleghenies and the trees were already stripped bare, but the scene was beautiful. When I think of man's work, and what men are capable of, the great knowledge they have in so many fields, it hurts to realize that so much genius and hard labor are put forth in the interests of profit for the idle few, for the haves of our society, who have the money to invest, who know how to play around with money, make it increase, under our system. In the middle ages money lending at interest was considered a sin and classed with sodomy. How far we are from thinking of work in this light.

In Cleveland I spoke to the First Friday Club, and had a good visit with Iola Ellis and Joseph Newman. Afterwards I went to Our Lady of the Wayside Farm where Bill and Dorothy Gauchat have their hospice for crippled and retarded children. I have always been so impressed with the loving kindness and the beauty of the surroundings where these children are being cared for. There are ten or eleven of them now, some of them blind and deaf, some of them epileptic, twisted and distorted in body, some of them little crib cases, some of them able to sit up in a chair, some of them able to crawl a little, and all of them with an expression almost of listening on their pale and suffering little faces. I saw how much music could do to lighten their sorrowful waiting. One little blind one with two earphones lifted her hand and beat time to the music which was being played, and another tapped with his feet on the floor. A little black baby in a high crib who has just about everything wrong with him likes to be taken out of his crib and rocked for a while each night by Dorothy, and one can see a sweet little smile stir over his face as she holds him. And he, too, responds to music, classical or rock.

The hospice is on Colorado Avenue between the towns of Avon and Lorain. It is a beautiful old building with many large rooms on the first floor where all the children must sleep. Upstairs there are playrooms and a kind of gymnasium where the older ones can exercise. Because her house space is so limited and the children who survive need larger beds and therefore more space, Dorothy has been carrying on a campaign for funds. It has been impossible to get money from state or foundation, but by personal appeal over the last few years, the Gauchats have been able to raise $75,000 of the

$150,000 which are needed to put up a large wing for the children. Never a day passes when there are not more requests for care for these little ones. If she can raise another $25,000, a bank will loan them an additional $50,000 so that building can begin in the spring. We hope our readers will help in this good work. So many of these little ones are left to die in mental hospitals, the only other place where they can be put. As Jean Vanier, son of the former Governor General of Canada wrote in the Jesus Caritas Bulletin, "These little ones are good for two things, they can *be* loved, and they can love. These innocents! Sinless and suffering, a mystery, not 'vegetables' but little human beings, capable of loving, and evoking love!"

It was my great joy to be present when a bishop of the Cleveland diocese came to this home. There at Our Lady of the Wayside Farm he confirmed these little ones, together with one child of Dorothy and Bill, Colette. Later at the church in Avon, an adopted son of the family received the sacrament from a wheel chair. At the church service there was organ music and a choir and three or four boys playing on trombones and other horns and the congregation sang and the sounds of triumph rose to heaven. Ever since hearing the horn in the Gelineau Psalms, I have loved horns in the church. At the Christian Brothers at Barrytown they once had organ and trumpets at one of their celebrations. The more instruments, the more music, the merrier. Rejoice, even in tribulation. We must remember the Dailiness of Grace, as one of the Village Voice writers titled her interview with me a few weeks ago.

I visited the thrift shop which Iola Ellis operates to help support a settlement house for Blacks in Cleveland. I visited a community of married folk who live in four adjoining houses. The families have moved back in from the suburbs to the heart of the city and aside from the schools not being so good, they are well pleased with the move. They are closer to the poor, to the urban problems. They are near each other, near a church, and a few blocks away there is a house with eleven rooms where two priests live with the single members of the community. Because I had to go to Detroit I had too short a visit with them, but I feel close to this effort, this beginning.

Detroit

In Detroit, I stayed with Louis Murphy and Justine (and now only two of the children are home, Bridget and Christine, but with Maureen, Sheila and Kevin dropping in from their work). Sheila shares an apartment with another girl and works at the *Ad Hoc Committee*, the name blazoned over a large bank-like building downtown where other radical groups are centered. She is interested right now in working on the problem of police brutality, and sending observers to demonstrations. Kevin is doing his alternative service in a large mental hospital on the other side of Detroit. We had dinner with friends at the Martha House, teachers from Monteith, men in the labor movement, and Fr. Kern, a parish priest most written about for his hospitality and interest in all the affairs and problems of this hemisphere. Martha House and St. Francis House have been Catholic Worker Houses of Hospitality for thirty years.

Lou drove me to see Mother Brennan who helped us this summer at Tivoli during the Pax conference and for a week afterward, and whom all of us will always think of with love and gratitude. We drove also to see the new house of hospitality at Saginaw which Jim Hanink and his wife started last June and which is beginning a precarious existence. Repairs have been made, rooms painted, equipment brought in, and now there is a request for rent payments to be made. The group needs help, and we sent the Michigan mailing list to them so that they can send out an appeal. It was good to meet with them briefly and talk to the men who were there, who were already starting the work of the kitchen and the upkeep of the place. There was one family man and wife and baby, the man an invalid and the mother working nights as a waitress. Paulette Curran who was with us at Tivoli all summer, is contributing her services and only today a letter came from another girl who wished to be assigned to some work and I thought of Paulette's need for an assistant.

In Ann Arbor I went to a Pentecostal meeting at the Newman center. I have never heard more beautiful singing. Prayer ran like a murmur through the hall, and I thought of the breath of the Spirit passing over the waters. There was one speaking with tongues, brief and clear, though I do not know what language it could have been, and there was an interpretation. There was a scattering of older people in the group of worshippers, but mostly they were all young. The mood of waiting, of expectancy, was strong. Here was faith. If you ask your father for a loaf will he give you a stone? If you ask for a fish, will you be given a serpent? If your earthly father knows how to give you good gifts, how much more will your Heavenly Father hear the prayers of His children?

Ask and you shall receive, seek and you shall find, knock and it shall be opened to you. And I felt a blaze of joy that this is so, and that here, and all over the country there are these groups growing, in prayer, in glorying, in thanksgiving, and in asking.

The need for prayer! All those at that meeting were going out to a hostile world, a world of such horrors just this last week that it is hard to see how happiness can ever come to us again. I accuse the government itself, and all of us, because we are Americans, too, of these mass murders, this destruction of villages, this wiping out of peoples, the kidnapping, torture, rape and killing that have been disclosed to us so vividly this past month. Reparation is needed. We must do penance for what we have done to our brothers. We are our brother's keeper.

But meanwhile in this hushed room there was prayer, for strength to know and to love and to find out what to do and set our hands to useful work that will contribute to peace, not to war.

Love is the measure by which we will be judged.

CURTIS BOOKS IS PROUD TO BE
THE PUBLISHERS OF

☐ THE LONG LONELINESS by Dorothy Day   (01034 $1.25)
The Long Loneliness is Dorothy Day's own story of growing up free, of participating in the prime social and artistic movements of our time, of living with a man and raising a child out of wedlock, and of helping to found **The Catholic Worker**, which combines day-to-day religious faith with direct action to better the human condition on earth. A work of total candor and sublime beauty, it offers an indelible encounter with human greatness.

☐ LOAVES AND FISHES by Dorothy Day   (01035 $1.25)
Loaves and Fishes is Dorothy Day's own story of the **Catholic Worker** and the indomitable men and women who made it work. She writes with glowing eloquence, warm humor, honest pride and profound humility, in a book that gives bright new meaning to the age-old phrase—Hope, Faith and Love.